Asian Americans

Association for Asian American Studies Series
  Reflections on Shattered Windows (1988)
  Frontiers of Asian American Studies (1989)
  Asian Americans: Comparative and Global Perspectives (1991)

Asian Americans
Comparative and Global Perspectives

Edited by
Shirley Hune
Hyung-chan Kim
Stephen S. Fugita
Amy Ling

Washington State University Press
Pullman, Washington

Washington State University Press, Pullman, Washington 99164-5910

©1991 by the Board of Regents of Washington State University
All rights reserved
First printing 1991

Printed and bound in the United States of America on pH neutral, acid-free paper. No part of this book may be reproduced or transmitted in any form or by any means, electronic or mechanical, including recording, photocopying, or by any information storage and retrieval system, without permission in writing from the publisher.

Library of Congress Cataloging-in-Publication Data
Asian Americans: comparative and global perspectives/
edited by Shirley Hune ...[et al.].
p. cm.
"Papers presented at the sixth meeting of the Association for Asian American Studies (AAAS) held June 1-3, 1989 at Hunter College of the City University of New York"—Pref. Includes bibliographical references.
ISBN 0-87422-071-8 (pbk.: alk. paper)
1. Asian Americans—Congresses. I. Hune, Shirley. II. Association for Asian American Studies. Meeting (6th:1989:Hunter College)
E184.06A843   1991
973'.0495—dc20   91-56 CIP

Cover graphics by Annette Chin.
Background mural ©City Arts, Inc.
Nineteenth century Japanese railroad workers in foreground.

Contents

Preface   vii
Acknowledgments   xi

Part One: Comparing Old and New Area Studies
  Area Studies and Asian American Studies: Comparing Origins, Missions, and Frameworks   *1*
    Shirley Hune

  From Area Studies to Ethnic Studies: The Study of the Chinese Diaspora in Latin America   *5*
    Evelyn Hu-DeHart

  African and Asian American Studies: A Comparative Analysis and Commentary   *17*
    Gary Y. Okihiro

  Asian American Studies and Asian Studies: Rethinking Roots   *29*
    Sucheta Mazumdar

Part Two: Historical Aspects
  Memories Compared, Lives Globalized   *45*
    Hyung-chan Kim

  To Merge with the Mass: Left-Wing Chinese Students and Chinese Hand Laundry Workers in New York City in the 1930s   *49*
    Renqiu Yu

  The Founding and Development of the Palolo Chinese Home, 1917-1988: A Case Study of Chinese Integration in Hawaii   *57*
    Xin Liu

  Unbinding the Feet, Unbinding Their Lives: Chinese Immigrant Women in San Francisco, 1902-1931   *69*
    Judy Yung

  Racial Order and Contestation: Asian American Internees and Soldiers at Camp McCoy, Wisconsin, 1942-1943   *87*
    Peggy Choy

  The Collective Memories of Communities   *103*
    Wendy L. Ng

  Coroners' Reports as a Historical Source for Asian American History   *113*
    Lee S. Hayakawa

Part Three: Contemporary Asian American Issues
  Demographics, Economics, and Politics   *119*
    Stephen S. Fugita

  Contemporary Anti-Asian Activities: A Global Perspective   *123*
    Tomoji Ishi

  Political Participation among Chicago Asian Americans   *137*
    Yvonne M. Lau

  Indochinese Refugees' Responses to Resettlement Via the Social Welfare System   *153*
    Jeremy Hein

  New Urban Crisis: Intra-Third World Conflict   *169*
    Edward T. Chang

  Conception of Ethnicities by Koreans: Workplace Encounters   *179*
    Kyeyoung Park

Part Four: Literature and Art in Comparative and Global Perspectives
  "Emerging Canons" of Asian American Literature and Art   *191*
    Amy Ling

  Subversion or Affirmation: The Text and Subtext of *America Is in the Heart*   *199*
    Marilyn Alquizola

  The Formation of Frank Chin and Formations of Chinese American Literature   *211*
    David Leiwei Li

  Mother/Daughter Writing and the Politics of Race and Sex in Maxine Hong Kingston's *The Woman Warrior*   *225*
    Wendy Ho

  Asian American Daughters Rewriting Asian Maternal Texts   *239*
    Shirley Geok-lin Lim

  Mirrors of the Self: Autobiography and the Japanese American Writer   *249*
    David Mura

  Children of the Chinese Diaspora: A Comparison of Lee Kok Liang's *Flowers in the Sky* and Maxine Hong Kingston's *China Men*   *265*
    Woon Ping Chin

  Comparing the Contemporary Experiences of Asian American, South Korean, and Cuban Artists   *277*
    Yong Soon Min

Notes on Contributors   *289*

Preface

As the field of Asian American Studies enters its third decade much progress has been made—in retrieving and recovering contributions of Asian American history and literary works, writing national histories of the various Asian Pacific American groupings, conceiving theories to explain specific Asian American institutions and social formations, producing original Asian American expressions and other works, and critiquing existing interpretations, concepts, methodologies, and creative presentations. Most importantly, much progress has also been made in rooting Asian American studies as an integral part of United States history and civilization.

The essays in this volume were drawn largely from papers presented at the sixth national conference of the Association for Asian American Studies (AAAS) held June 1-3, 1989, at Hunter College of the City University of New York. The theme of the conference, "Comparative and Global Perspectives of the Asian Diaspora," was selected to draw attention to a fundamental condition of the Asian American experience—its international dimension. It was to help us to move Asian American Studies beyond ourselves; to locate our local history and our personal condition within the context of national and global history; to find our common ground with others in the United States and abroad, Asian Pacific American and non Asian Pacific American alike; and to generate the kind of research, scholarship, teaching, and community activities that will create a more just world.

Panels and other conference events were organized to facilitate discussion on aspects of both the global and national dimension within a comparative framework. The comparative perspective was encouraged as a means to better discern similarities and differences as well as to examine continuity and change in Asian American history and culture in the United States and elsewhere; across time (i.e., historical periods) and space (i.e., regions); and between Asian Pacific groupings and with other subordinate or dominant groups. In addition, variables such as gender, class, generation, age, and political interests can be utilized. Comparative studies can also help clarify influences of culture, historical forces and timing, social structure, demographics, and public and private policies as opportunities and constraints in determining how Asian communities in the diaspora develop and transform themselves and their societies at large in countries of origin and settlement.

The 1989 conference at Hunter College was the largest gathering of the Association for Asian American Studies to date, with over fifty panels, workshops, and cultural events. It was an honor for me as President of the Association for Asian American Studies to host the first AAAS conference to be held on the East Coast. Panelists represented all Asian and Pacific national groupings and came from various regions of the United States; the number attending from the Midwest and East Coast, as well as from Canada and Asia, increased significantly. Most encouraging was the participation of large numbers of undergraduate and graduate students who will become our next generation of teachers, scholars, writers, artists, and educators.

The AAAS anthology series seeks to support research, theoretical developments, and creative efforts of those in the field of Asian American Studies in all its disciplines and expressions. This is the third volume in the series, and like the previous ones it aspires to encourage emergent students of the field and to provide established scholars and writers with an opportunity to expand the boundaries of knowledge and inquiry and to experiment with innovative interpretations, approaches, and methodologies.

The editorship of AAAS anthologies is a *collective* one, reflective of the spirit of the Asian American Studies movement. It was not an easy task to select from amongst the many excellent papers submitted for our consideration. All the submissions underwent a review by the entire editorial committee with assistance from additional referees from the association membership who hold special expertise. Along with meeting scholarly criteria, principles for acceptance in this volume included addressing the theme of the conference, contributing to our understanding of underrepresented Asian Pacific groups and regions in the nation, or providing fresh insights with new data, sources, and imaginative approaches. Additional consideration was given to enabling the voices of students and those coming into the field to be heard. After the final selection was made, each editor was responsible for a particular part of the volume and brought to the undertaking distinct specializations, interests, backgrounds, and skills.

This volume is divided into four parts organized around different aspects of the theme of comparative and global perspectives. "Part One: Comparing Old and New Area Studies" offers a unique discussion on similarities and differences between established international area studies and the newer domestically focused ethnic studies programs, especially Asian American Studies. "Part Two: Historical Aspects" contains articles illuminating past events in Asian American history, many with new interpretations or resource bases. The articles in "Part Three: Contemporary Asian American Issues" examine current events affecting Asian American communities comparatively and globally, some with potentially explosive political dimensions. "Part Four: Literature and Art in Comparative and Global Perspectives" largely features new contributors and novel approaches.

The editors hope that you share our enthusiasm for this venture. This collection of essays is meant to provide a vision and to stimulate existing research agendas while pointing the way to new possibilities for Asian American Studies that include comparative and international aspects. Finally, I would like to thank the other editors of this volume for their willingness to volunteer time and energy from other activities and for sharing its responsibilities with me.

    Shirley Hune
    Hunter College of the City University of New York
    1990

Acknowledgments

The sixth national conference of the Association for Asian American Studies from which these papers are drawn was held at Hunter College, June 1-3, 1989, with the support of the Office of the President at Hunter College of the City University of New York. We would especially like to thank President Paul LeClerc for the generous funding which provided the staff and other support services essential for the planning and conduct of a national conference. Former President Donna Shalala, now Chancellor of the University of Wisconsin-Madison, also contributed an initial seed grant. In addition, we gratefully recognize Margaret M. Chin, who coordinated the conference activities with Lily Li; the staff of the Asian/American Center at Queens College, CUNY, especially Lori Kitazono; and the Simon H. Rifkind Center for the Humanities, City College, CUNY, for their support.

The editors acknowledge the work of the Conference Committee: Shirley Hune (chair), Gail M. Nomura, Gary Y. Okihiro, Meena Alexander, Amy Ling, and John Kuo Wei Tchen; along with Association for Asian American Studies Executive Council members Russell Endo, Evelyn Nakano Glenn, Lane R. Hirabayashi, Chalsa Loo, Gregory Yee Mark, and Stephen H. Sumida for the program that generated the articles for this volume. Thanks also go to Philip Tajitsu Nash and Betty Lee Sung for their assistance on specific conference arrangements. A special thanks to the Asian American students at Hunter College who assisted in so many ways. The final preparation of the manuscript was completed at Hunter College and we give our deepest appreciation to Margaret M. Chin and July Tay for their assistance. We also thank Annette Chin for the cover design.

As always the Association for Asian American Studies would like to thank the Washington State University Press for their continued support and commitment to this series.

Part One
Comparing Old and New Area Studies

Area Studies and Asian American Studies: Comparing Origins, Missions, and Frameworks

Shirley Hune

The educational reform efforts that emerged out of the social movements of the late 1960s in the United States brought us such curricular innovations as ethnic studies and Women's Studies. In two decades, they have become new area studies on American college campuses.

For Asian Americans, the struggle for educational change in that period was for greater access to and participation in the educational process. They especially sought to have their history and culture reflected in the curriculum. The result was the demand for and adoption of Asian American Studies courses and programs at a number of colleges and universities across the nation. University structures initially viewed ethnic studies, including Asian American Studies, primarily as a form of *compensatory* education that would add to but not substantially alter the institution. But as I have discussed elsewhere in much greater detail, Asian American Studies has, in fact, been *transformatory*. In its efforts to restructure such broad areas as academic disciplines, research methodology, pedagogy, ethics, hiring practices, fellowship awards, and more, it has been engaged in *changing* higher education in all its facets (Hune 1989). In short, the new area studies have been part of an effort to democratize higher education.

By the end of the 1980s, Asian American Studies and other ethnic studies units had become permanent features in higher education as distinct programs. Some would say they were ghettoized or at best marginalized. Moreover, in response to the new demographics and other political considerations, college campuses which had previously ignored student demands for Asian American courses had begun to compete with one another to hire Asian American specialists.

The 1980s were also a time for reflection on the quality of American education and its ability to keep the nation economically competitive, particularly in the face of the success stories of West Germany and Japan, followed by a number of smaller Asian states. While the business sector has worried about the capacity of America's public schools to produce the next generation of literate workers, many educators have begun to reconsider the question of what constitutes an educated person today. What must one know to be a citizen of the twenty-first century?

Conservative educators, the most notable being Allan Bloom (1987), have deplored the decline of academic standards and the weakening of the curriculum through too much choice and special interest group courses. For them, diversity is a weakness and a potential threat to national security. A strong nation requires a common knowledge base: a core curriculum. Given the reality of a multicultural population and the political need to educate the plurality, these educators can be found calling for a common core of knowledge that all students must know to be truly educated as the new foundation of the state. However, upon closer examination, that common core is based largely on Western civilization studies. Hence, one must ask in supporting the notion of a core curriculum, whose core is this?

Conservatives who do pay lip service to the concept of a multicultural American society shroud their acceptance of pluralism behind a thick veil of Euro-Americancentrism. The most vocal is Diane Ravitch (1990) who praises multiculturalism for the American public school curriculum when it is framed within Euro-American values, but excoriates ethnic studies approaches as particularistic and promoters of race hatred when they offer alternative perceptions of American history and its development (Cox 1990). It is not surprising that conservative counterparts in American universities are most comfortable with curriculum revisions that, while more comprehensive of the world's cultures domestically and internationally, continue to preserve a Eurocentric view of American history and a Euro-American interpretation of global history.

Liberal educators, on the other hand, have recognized the necessity of multicultural education programs and practices in the contemporary world when the majority of the world's population and major sectors of the United States are predominantly African, Asian, and Caribbean and Latin American in origin. Such educators have called for educational revisions that are akin to a "curriculum of inclusion" where the curriculum is "balanced" or "mainstreamed" with courses or readings representative of women and of the Third World within or the Third World without. At its best, the new curricula will embody the viewpoints of the "people without history" as Eric Wolf (1982) has so aptly phrased; that is, the experiences of those who have been excluded, disenfranchised, and rendered less powerful. Currently, on many university campuses, reformist educators are calling for new education requirements that will have all students taking courses on some aspect of ethnic studies, global studies, and Women's Studies in order to graduate. In some instances, institutions are developing entirely new courses integrating the new history and social sciences. In other cases, students are to select from a list of designated courses, many of which have not been restructured to incorporate ethnic studies or Third World perspectives.

It is timely in this debate over general education requirements and core curricula to consider the kind of ethnic studies and international studies courses the next generation of students will enroll in and to examine the relationship of the new area studies of ethnic studies to old area studies, specifically Asian Studies, African Studies, and Latin American and Caribbean Studies. Fortunately, the Association for Asian American Studies has within its active membership scholars who are knowledgeable in both areas.

Evelyn Hu-DeHart, Gary Y. Okihiro, and Sucheta Mazumdar, the authors of the following three essays, were asked to reflect on their experiences specifically for the Hunter College AAAS conference. All three have done research and published extensively in their respective area whether it be Latin America and the Caribbean, Africa, or Asia. At the same time, each has sought and found a home in Asian American Studies. The authors were asked what they had learned from being trained in one of the old area studies and if there were similarities and differences with ethnic studies, especially Asian American Studies.

It is clear that the three area studies discussed here— Latin American and Caribbean Studies, African Studies, and Asian Studies—share much in common with each other in their origins and development in the United States, a commonality that differs quite distinctly with their ethnic studies counterparts. The old and new area studies clearly differ in origins, missions, and frameworks. The old area studies were created from the top down by the elite structure with the support of the U.S. government, while ethnic studies programs originated from the bottom up as part of a protest against the existing educational structure that excluded them. Those trained in the area studies tend to receive major financial support from public and private foundation sources, while those in ethnic studies receive very little support. Area studies have high status on campus; ethnic studies may be viewed as politically necessary, but many still question their academic legitimacy.

Area studies see as their mission the provision of experts on specific regions of the world, particularly the "Third World." As these experts attempt to better inform the United States about Asia, Africa, and Latin America, improving its ability to influence change in these areas, they become agents of social control. The majority of these experts, our authors tell us, are white males of European heritage—outsiders and rarely representative of their regions. Ethnic studies specialists, on the other hand, tend to be insiders. They are members of the communities they study whose histories and cultures they seek to authenticate and present without distortions and omissions. They become agents of resistance against the social order, seeking to use knowledge and information to empower their communities, to provide them with better services, and to limit further exploitation.

One's mission affects the way research and scholarship are framed. Evelyn Hu-DeHart, Gary Okihiro, and Sucheta Mazumdar provide many insights as to why some topics are studied. Whose interests are served? They also suggest some areas that need greater attention. What are the lessons to be learned? These essays provide a unique contribution to Asian American Studies and force us to ask questions about how we approach the field. As ethnic studies programs become part of the established curricula, it is important that we not lose sight of Asian American Studies' origins and mission, and that the questions and problems we choose to examine contribute not only to scholarship but to the liberation of our communities and the creation of a more egalitarian world.

References

Bloom, Allan. 1987. *The Closing of the American Mind.* New York: Simon and Schuster.

Cox, Clinton. 1990. "Diane Ravitch. Who Is This Woman and Why Is She Smiling?" *The City Sun* (New York), March 14-20, 9, 34.

Hune, Shirley. 1989. "Opening the American Mind and Body: The Role of Asian American Studies." *Change* (November/December):56-63.

Ravitch, Diane. 1990. "Diversity and Democracy: Multicultural Education in America." *American Educator* 14:16-20, 46-48.

Wolf, Eric R. 1982. *Europe and the People without History.* Berkeley: University of California Press

From Area Studies to Ethnic Studies: The Study of the Chinese Diaspora in Latin America

Evelyn Hu-DeHart

Latin American and Caribbean Studies (LACS, or simply "Latin American Studies") as a field of area study in United States universities emerged in the post-war period, and was given special impetus by the National Defense Education Act (NDEA) of the 1960s and early 1970s. The NDEA funded critical language and area studies in response to perceived Soviet incursion into the Third World, beginning, for Latin America, with the Cuban revolution of 1959. My own graduate studies were funded entirely by NDEA. Just as the NDEA was winding down, Asian American Studies as a field of ethnic study was being established in the aftermath of the student upheavals of the late 1960s in California, following the examples of Black and Chicano studies.

Latin American Studies has grown into a major academic program with considerable prestige on American campuses. The field encompasses a large territory—all of the Americas that were once colonies of Spain and Portugal— and spans some 600 years of time from the pre-Colombian civilizations to the present day. Although originally conceived as an interdisciplinary field of inquiry and analysis, most Latin Americanists are in fact trained in traditional disciplines and publish in their respective fields (history, literature, political science, anthropology, sociology, economics, etc.).

Early attempts at promoting a doctoral degree in Latin American Studies, e.g., at the University of Texas at Austin, were not successful when it was discovered that the graduates had difficulty being hired by universities still organized along traditional disciplinary departments. I also know of no effort anywhere to make Latin American Studies into a discipline and a department of its own.

Today, Latin American Studies programs proliferate in American colleges and universities, granting interdisciplinary undergraduate certificates and degrees as well as the master's degree in some large state and private institutions. Their faculties are composed of scholars drawn from traditional disciplines, in which they are hired, rostered, and tenured. Because of this continuous link with established disciplines, Latin American Studies is still dominated by white male scholars; although, to be fair, women have gained some ascendance. A small, but prominent, group of scholars trained in European (especially British) and Latin American universities are also active in the field and are represented on Latin American faculties of American institutions. Latin American Studies has trained very few American ethnic minorities, including Latinos. In fact, LACS programs have reached out more successfully to Europeans, Latin Americans, and even, recently, Asian nationals, than to Spanish-speaking Americans.

The leading professional association, the Latin American Studies Association (LASA), which meets once every eighteen months, has been instrumental in linking Latin American Studies scholars worldwide, including those in the People's Republic of China and the Soviet Union, as well as those in Latin America and the Caribbean. Most meetings have been held in the United States, but one recent meeting was held in Mexico, and the 1989 meeting was in Puerto Rico.

This successful outreach, particularly to Latin America itself, is important because, after all, the field of study deals with Latin America. Nevertheless, given the United States's immensely greater resources and larger number of professional academics, Latin Americanists from this country have literally invaded Latin America, mining their archives and harvesting their research fields for data, and have produced a prodigious amount of scholarship published and disseminated by university presses. This scholarship has in turn defined much of the nature of the field and has set the terms of the debate on many facets of Latin American culture, politics, and society.

Most general histories of Latin America that came out of LACS make no mention, or at best refer only in passing, to Asians. Usually, when this does occur, it is in the context of the Manila galleon trade of the sixteenth to eighteenth centuries between the twin Spanish colonies of Mexico in the New World and the Philippines in the Far East. Sometimes, these histories briefly mention the large Chinese coolie trade to Peru and Cuba in the nineteenth century. In a general history of Mexico, some reference may be made to the massacre of Chinese during the Mexican revolution, but not to the expulsion and subsequent expropriation of Chinese property in northern Mexico. In a general history of modern Brazil, one might encounter some discussion of Japanese immigrants. A few dissertations have been written exclusively about Asians, but none I know of have been published as monographs

(Jacques 1974; Meagher 1976). There is an occasional article that deals with the Chinese in the context of a larger social issue; such is the case with historian Charles Cumberland's study of the "The Sonoran Chinese and the Mexican Revolution," published in the leading historical journal of the field, the *Hispanic American Historical Review,* in 1960. Overall, Asians have been omitted from LACS, their presence and contribution to Latin American/Caribbean history and society generally ignored.

Compared to Latin American Studies, Asian American Studies has a shorter academic history and much smaller corpus of academic practitioners, and has experienced an ongoing struggle to be established and gain recognition on American campuses. With its origins in American universities, Asian American Studies has focused on the migration and subsequent settlement experiences of various Asian groups to the United States, starting with the early history of the Chinese and Japanese, and broadening into Filipinos, Koreans, Asian Indians, and Southeast Asians. Only recently has the field made a move toward recognizing the importance of the Asian diaspora throughout the Americas and the world.

Unlike LACS, Asian American Studies is dominated by Asian American scholars, many of whom are self-taught, retooled from other professions or disciplines, who come from a background of community activism. Also unlike LACS, Asian American Studies, in agreement with its counterparts in African American and Chicano/Latino studies, sees itself as possibly methodologically distinct from traditional disciplines, and not just filling gaps in our knowledge about culture and society. Furthermore, also along with the other ethnic studies fields, Asian American Studies has not abandoned its interdisciplinary commitment—which is part of its methodological distinction—even as it recognizes the constraints posed by the rigid academic organizational structure of universities still committed to the same traditional disciplines. Thus I see that some Asian American scholars, along with many in African American and Chicano/Latino studies, will continue to fight for real departmental status, i.e., the right to hire and tenure scholars in their fields, and validate their own scholarship. Some, of course, such as the University of California at Berkeley, and San Francisco State, already have that status.

Let me make explicit the profound differences implied by these brief descriptions of "area studies" versus "ethnic studies." LACS when conceived was fundamentally reactionary—that is, it was in reaction to America's perceived loss of its empire in the western hemisphere. The United States government's support of LACS (and other area studies) was to train university scholars who could presumably inform the government on how to stop this erosion of United States hegemony. Besides academia, trained Latin Americanists have worked for various United States agencies, including the State Department, the Defense Department, the Agency for International Development, and the

Central Intelligence Agency. Historically, and still today, much research funding in LACS comes directly from government sources, beginning with the NDEA discussed above, and including the Fulbright program, AID, the Inter-American Foundation, and many others. In the 1960s, the Defense Department's financial sponsorship of social science research in Latin America led to the Project Camelot scandal, amid charges of the United States government using scholars to control social change (i. e., prevent revolutions unfavorable to United States interests) (Horowitz 1967).

The Camelot scandal did serve the purpose of prompting many Latin Americanists to assert their independence from the government. The critique of the Vietnam War and of United States imperialism in general in the 1960s and 1970s, as well as extensive travel to Latin America itself and mentoring by Latin American intellectuals, have also influenced a new generation of Latin Americanists who have begun to examine Latin American history and issues from a Latin American perspective and in the interest of authentic Latin American development. In the past ten years, some Latin Americanists have produced an exciting new scholarship that breaks away from liberal assumptions and is informed by Marxism, neo-Marxism such as "dependency theory," or other critical perspectives.

Asian American and other ethnic studies have enjoyed no history of cozy relationships with the United States government, and for good reason. Ethnic studies began with minority students demanding changes in the college curricula, at first simply because they wanted inclusion and representation. By this demand alone, ethnic studies students and faculty challenged the prevailing Eurocentric worldview of America, and its dominant self-image as white and democratic. From its inception, ethnic studies scholarship has been revisionist, and its goal is a re-visioning of America. Understandably, ethnic studies programs enjoy no priority with government funding agencies, have received modest support from certain private foundations, and have to fight perennially for a miniscule piece of university budgets. These facts, plus their almost exclusively minority faculties, have resulted in their low status on campuses. In the immediate future, Asian American Studies (and to some extent Chicano Studies) can gain some ground by playing the theme of what might be termed the "demographic imperative" of the year 2000, when California will lead the country in becoming heavily populated by Asians and Latinos. Some Asian American scholars might also see growth opportunities in the new economic and geopolitical realignment called the Pacific Rim. Finally, the new ethnic studies requirements on a growing number of campuses will boost enrollment.

With few exceptions, Latin Americanists and Asian Americanists, admittedly two very distinct groups of scholars, have been largely unmindful of each other's existence and uninterested in each other's scholarship. They have not interacted with each other, exchanged research ideas and results, or learned from each other's methodological approaches. (I should note, however, that women scholars in both fields have been influenced by feminist scholarship, and have made significant contributions to the field of Women's Studies as well as gaining some representation on Women's Studies faculties.)

The study of the Asian diaspora is a natural bridge to bring these two fields closer together. For LACS, the study of Asians in Latin America will focus on their legitimate place in history and their contributions to the formation of certain Latin American societies. For Asian American Studies, the examination of the Asian experience in Latin America and the Caribbean will broaden the scope of the field, complete our understanding of Asian immigration to the western hemisphere, and complement our considerable knowledge of the Asian experience in the United States.

The rest of this essay surveys some of the key literature produced to date on Asians in Latin America, focusing on studies of the Chinese, which I know best through my own work. The purpose is not to provide a comprehensive bibliographical essay, but to illustrate what has been done. As with Asians who have immigrated to the United States, Asians who have immigrated to Latin America and the Caribbean share the common experiences of being immigrants, cheap labor, and newcomers to an already multiracial society that was nevertheless dominated by a European ethnicity and white power structure. Within these broad similarities, however, because of great variations over time and space—the specific demographic, social, political, and economic characteristics of the host societies at the time of immigration, the conditions in Asia itself, and the size, age, gender, and occupational makeup of the immigrant groups themselves—the experiences differ considerably in detail and consequences.

Historically, countries that send and receive immigrants are societies in flux and undergoing profound changes. These forces condition and determine the immigrant experience at both ends. In the case of Chinese immigrants, the reasons why millions of people from South China were induced to leave their homes in the nineteenth and twentieth centuries have been quite thoroughly discussed, fairly well documented, and generally agreed upon by scholars. Their research cites the Taiping rebellion, the Chinese revolution, European colonialism, and population pressures on limited land as "push factors," and the growing demand for cheap labor in the western hemisphere, especially the dynamic economy of the United States, as among the "pull" factors.

While earlier studies of Chinese movement overseas usually included some discussion of Latin America and the Caribbean, the first serious study of Asian migration specifically to Latin America was published in 1942 by the Institute of Pacific Relations. Anita Bradley's *Trans-Pacific Relations of Latin America* provides some statistical information and a general sketch of Chinese and

Japanese immigration to Mexico, Central and South America, and the Caribbean.

A meticulously researched and thoroughly documented study of Chinese immigration to Latin America and the Caribbean in the nineteenth century is the 1976 dissertation by Arnold Meagher entitled "The Introduction of Chinese Laborers to Latin America: the 'Coolie Trade,' 1847-1874." This fine dissertation was never published and Mr. Meagher's professional whereabouts are not known. Anyone interested in the beginnings of Chinese immigration to Latin America should begin with these works.

In 1971, a small college press in Kentucky published Duvon C. Corbitt's *A Study of the Chinese in Cuba, 1847-1947,* which also focused on the coolie trade, with some attention to the post-coolie period. Since then, only one U. S.-trained Latin Americanist, the historian Rebecca Scott, has treated the Chinese coolie issue in Cuba in a serious, analytical way. In her 1985 work entitled *Slave Emancipation in Cuba: The Transition to Free Labor, 1860-1899,* she examines the question of whether Chinese coolies, working alongside African slaves, constituted an extension of slavery or a transition to free labor.

The most thorough study of the Chinese in Cuba is by French Canadian ethnohistorian Denise Helly. Her 1979 book, *Idéologie et Ethnicité: Les Chinois Macao à Cuba,* focuses on the trade itself at both the sending (Macao) and the receiving end, as well as on the coolies' plantation life and their interactions with black slaves and white masters. Perhaps because it is published in French and the author is not a known Latin Americanist, the work is not generally recognized in LACS circles. In Cuba itself, historians Juan Pérez de la Riva (1978) and Juan Jimenez Pastrana (1983) have published excellent pieces on the Chinese coolies and Chinese contributions to Cuban history. Because they are notable Cuban scholars, their works have gained greater recognition among Latin Americanists.

In 1951, before the advent of LACS programs, Duke University Press published Watt Stewart's *Chinese Bondage in Peru,* a well documented study of the Chinese coolie trade to Peru and the political-diplomatic maneuverings around this issue in Peru, China, and internationally. Although long out of print in the United States, the Spanish translation of this work is still in print and widely recognized in Peru.

Stewart in turn has stimulated Peruvian scholars, foremost among them the historian Humberto Rodríguez Pastor, to pursue the study of the Chinese in their country. After years of writing and publishing small pieces, in 1989 Rodríguez Pastor compiled one comprehensive volume entitled *Hijos del Celeste Imperio en el Perú (1850-1900): Migración, Agricultura, Mentalidad y Explotación.*

Thirty years after Stewart, and working with some of the same documents as Rodríguez Pastor, U.S.-trained Latin American historian Michael Gonzales integrated imported Asian laborers into his study of Peru's plantation system in the nineteenth century. In his monograph *Plantation Agriculture and Social Control in Northern Peru, 1875-1933* (1985), Gonzales explores at length the critical importance of first Chinese, then Japanese, imported contract labor in Peruvian plantations immediately after the termination of the coolie trade and before the Peruvian planters finally turned to native wage laborers from the highlands.

As the above titles illustrate, the few existent studies of the Chinese in Latin America tend to revolve around the question of the Asians as cheap labor. This is entirely logical, of course, as Asian migration to Latin America and the Caribbean during the nineteenth century cannot be separated from both the larger context of international labor migration as well as the internal demands for cheap foreign labor in the receiving countries. Thus immigration and labor studies come together under one topic. Asian American Studies scholars have fully recognized the significance of this close connection between immigration and labor (Cheng and Bonacich 1984).

Another theme that Latin American Studies and Asian American Studies share is race and ethnicity, and out of that, acculturation and assimilation, and race relations and racial conflicts. In exploring this broad theme, Latin Americanists have traditionally focused on American Indians and blacks: the first as victims of the conquest and of the conquistadores, both secular and religious; the second in the context of slavery and plantation economy; and both as part of the region's experience with race mixture and cultural syncretism. The literature is too vast to begin to enumerate here, but a good example of race and ethnic studies is Magnus Mörner's little book *Race Mixture in the History of Latin America* (1967). This brief history of miscegenation among white, Indians, and blacks is a good introduction into the way Latin Americanists deal with issues of race and ethnicity, the relationship between miscegenation, acculturation and assimilation, and the intersection between race and class. Unfortunately, Mörner mentions the presence of "Asiatics," but does not factor them into his analysis.

Colonial society was a *sociedad de castas*, a self-consciously multiethnic population of whites, Indians, and blacks, and all possible mixtures of the three. Each racial mixture, or *casta*, had its distinctive socioracial terminology, with corresponding social status that clearly favored lighter skinned mixtures. From the familiar mestizo and mulatto, there were at least fourteen other categories, including one curiously named *chino* to designate the dark complexioned, hence socially undesirable, offspring of a mulatto and Indian (Mörner 1967:59). If Asian Americanists unfamiliar with colonial Latin American terminology encounter the term *chino*, they may be tempted to assume that it means Chinese. Indeed, such was the case with Stan Steiner in *Fusang: The Chinese Who Built America* (1979), who thought a Chinese–

the *chino* Antonio Rodríguez—helped found the early California settlement of Ciudad de Los Angeles in the eighteenth century. He was in fact a member of a motley crew of marginalized, mostly mixed-race individuals—eight Indians, three mulattos, two blacks, one mestizo, and two Spaniards—seeking their fortune on New Spain's far northern frontier. To designate a Chinese or an individual of Asian origin, colonial records used the term *chino de Manila*.

In 1973, Peruvian anthropologist Luis Millones edited a volume on *Minorías Etnicas en el Perú*. The title suggests that Millones was influenced by research in the United States; "ethnic minorities" is not a term or concept characteristically employed in the study of non-white groups in Latin America. Millones's chapter on the Chinese in Peru is a superficial sketch with only a tentative analysis of their acculturation and assimilation into a racially mixed society.

While Millones attempted no theoretical innovation in analyzing Chinese ethnicity in a Latin American context, Denise Helly, whose work on the Chinese coolies in Cuba was cited above, considered the introduction of the Chinese, and their separate racial and ethnic identity, a phenomenon of major importance; it helped dismantle the slave ideology that upheld Cuban society in the nineteenth century and created a new social and economic order based on "ethnic minorities." The slave ideology was erected on the basis of the separation and hierarchical ordering of two races, white and black, master and slave. This racist ideology could not be maintained, however, in the face of the Chinese, who were neither white nor black, master nor slave, but who occupied an intermediary position with the possibility of being free when their contracts expired. The Chinese made it possible for the blacks to contemplate their collective liberation from slavery. They mediated the polar opposition between white and black, freedom and bondage. Ironically, while facilitating the maintenance of slavery in a period of gradual abolition, the Chinese coolies at the same time posed a potential threat to the structure of social domination and its attendant political stability. By their very presence—and indeed by their active participation in movements for the abolition of slavery and in occasional outbursts of violence against the planters' exploitation—they helped bring an end to slavery in Cuba. At the same time, the Chinese were perceived as a separate ethnic group and constituted a separate social segment excluded by both whites and blacks. Helly argues that the formation of a Chinese ethnicity in Cuba presages the emergence of ethnic minorities in modern industrial societies, characterized by a new imperialism based on international corporations and the massive transfer of labor from poorer to richer parts of the world.

Orlando Patterson, noted scholar of the British Caribbean, also explores the question of Chinese ethnicity in the Caribbean in an essay that compares Chinese immigrants in Jamaica with those in Guyana (Patterson 1975). He argues that based on the economic opportunities available to them, the Chinese in these two Afro-Caribbean societies made conscious, rational choices regarding whether or not to maintain their ethnicity and cultural distinctiveness. In Jamaica, because the Chinese seized the opportunity to enter the retail trade and thus fill a void, "success in this venture allowed for, and reinforced, a choice of ethnic consolidation." By contrast, the Chinese in Guyana had to enter a range of occupations in order to survive, and in pursuing these occupations, the choices "of synthetic creolization and the abandonment of Chinese culture were the most rational courses of action." Both Helly and Patterson's analyses, although very different kinds of work, suggest that far from maintaining their ethnicity at all costs, as is generally perceived of Chinese overseas, external forces were instrumental in determining whether a separate Chinese ethnicity was formed and maintained. These useful insights into race and ethnicity emerged when two scholars, who incidentally are not generally identified with Latin American or Asian American studies, incorporated the Asian factor into their analysis.

Immigration and nationalism are other themes explored by both Latin Americanists and Asian Americanists. In the American West, nativist responses to immigrants, including Chinese and other Asians, played a prominent role in shaping national and regional identity and culture. Mexico's nationalism in the post-revolutionary period, as I have attempted to show in my studies of the Chinese in Mexico (Hu-DeHart 1980, 1985), was also shaped in part by xenophobia and nativism. Chinese immigrant entrepreneurs, for example, in the northwestern state of Sonora (south of Arizona), became too prominent in local retail commerce in the post-revolutionary period. Their expulsion from the state in the early 1930s and the subsequent expropriation of their commercial properties marked the culmination of decades of antiforeignism in a border state. Furthermore, in justifying the persecution and expulsion of a basically law-abiding immigrant community, the Sonorans had to devise a racially based ideology—a kind of racism that eventually dissipated once the goal of eliminating the Chinese presence from their midst was accomplished (Hu-DeHart 1982).

If the Chinese as coolies have been insufficiently studied, post-coolie Chinese immigration to Latin America is an even less-explored topic. An early and sketchy ethnographic study by Alice Jo Kwong on "The Chinese in Peru" (1958) was not followed up until the 1970s, when Asian American anthropologist Bernard Wong conducted field work in Peru and published the first comparative studies of Chinese Americans and Chinese Peruvians (1978, 1985). French Peruvianist Isabelle Lausent completed a fine study of a small but important Chinese community in a highland (sierra) town, and a pioneer study on the Chinese in the frontier region of the Peruvian Amazon (1983, 1986). Studies of the Chinese shopkeepers in Jamaica by Howard Johnson and Jacqueline Levy continue this direction of research (Johnson 1983; Levy 1986).

My own publications have also focused on the successful incursion of the Chinese into the local commerce in Mexico and Peru, placing the investigation both within the larger environment in which these Chinese operate and the internal skills and resources that they bring with them as immigrants (Hu-DeHart 1980, 1985, 1988). Chinese participation in the opening of large-scale commercial agriculture in Baja California, Mexico, in the early twentieth century has also been significant (Hu-DeHart 1985-1986). In conducting this research, I have found little help within LACS scholarship, because not only have Latin Americanists not paid much attention to Asian and other immigrant communities (except as labor), they have not paid much attention to the petite bourgeoisie in general, which happens to be dominated by immigrants.

Fortunately, when I looked to Asian American Studies for models, I found an abundance of good research on Asian immigrant communities. For example, theories of "middleman minorities" (Bonacich 1973) are useful as a conceptual framework, and studies of Asian immigrant entrepreneurs in the United States (Bonacich and Light 1988) are helpful as comparative models. Sucheng Chan's acclaimed work on the Chinese in California agriculture (1986) provides me with another comparative model as I continue my investigation of Chinese agricultural activities in Mexico and Peru.

I am convinced from my own research to date that early Chinese immigrants in parts of Mexico, Peru, Cuba, and Jamaica were instrumental in developing agriculture in frontier areas and virgin land, and most importantly, in creating modern commercial infrastructures where none, or only very rudimentary forms, had existed. This particular role that the Chinese carved out for themselves throughout Latin America and the Caribbean cast them in the role of "middleman minorities," whereby they occupy a middle stratum between an elite (local or foreign) and the native masses. As outsiders, immigrants, and recent arrivals, they were quick to recognize and exploit new economic opportunities created by land and natural resource development, the transformation of peasants into wage laborers, and the subsequent expansion of the local consumer market. As ubiquitous shopkeepers—in Mexico and Peru the term *chino* has become synonymous with the corner grocer—they became a highly visible and indispensable part of the working person's daily struggle for survival; yet they were closely identified with the oligarchy, and with colonialism and imperialism, even though they were seldom the key players or major beneficiaries of the social order. Not surprisingly, at the point of colonial or neo-colonial breakdown, Chinese merchants and native popular classes have clashed. This conflict is not unique to the western hemisphere, of course, but has been documented in many parts of Asia and Africa as well.

Research into the Asian diaspora in the Americas constitutes a natural bridge between Latin American/Caribbean Studies and Asian American Studies. As a Latin Americanist studying the diaspora, I have benefited immeasurably by borrowing some analytical tools and comparative models from Asian American scholars. As Asian Americanists in turn incorporate Latin American Studies scholarship, they will enrich their understanding of the global Asian immigrant experience.

References

Bonacich, Edna. 1973. "A Theory of Middleman Minorities." *American Sociological Review* 38:583-598.
Bonacich, Edna, and Ivan Light. 1988. *Immigrant Entrepreneurs: Koreans in Los Angeles*. Berkeley: University of California Press.
Bradley, Anita. 1942. *Trans-Pacific Relations of Latin America*. New York: Institute of Pacific Relations.
Chan, Sucheng. 1986. *This Bittersweet Soil: The Chinese in California Agriculture, 1860-1910*. Berkeley: University of California Press.
Cheng, Lucie, and Edna Bonacich, eds. 1984. *Labor Immigration under Capitalism: Asian Workers in the United States before World War II*. Berkeley: University of California Press.
Corbitt, Duvon C. 1971. *A Study of the Chinese in Cuba, 1847-1947*. Wilmore, Kentucky: Asbury College Press.
Cumberland, Charles. 1960. "The Sonoran Chinese and the Mexican Revolution." *Hispanic American Historical Review* 40:191-211.
Gonzales, Michael J. 1985. *Plantation Agriculture and Social Control in Northern Peru, 1875-1933*. Austin: University of Texas Press.
Helly, Denise. 1979. *Idéologie et Ethnicité: Les Chinois Macao à Cuba*. Montreal: University of Montreal Press.
Horowitz, Irving Louis. 1967. *The Rise and Fall of Project Camelot: Studies in the Relationship Between Social Science and Practical Politics*. Cambridge: MIT Press.
Hu-DeHart, Evelyn. 1980. "Immigrants to a Developing Society: The Chinese in Northern Mexico, 1875-1932." *Journal of Arizona History* 21:49-86.
_____. 1981. *Missionaries, Miners and Indians: Spanish Contact with the Yaqui Nation of Northwestern New Spain, 1533-1820*. Tucson: University of Arizona Press.
_____. 1982. "Racism and Anti-Chinese Persecution in Sonora, Mexico, 1876-1932." *Amerasia Journal* 9:1-28.
_____. 1984. *Yaqui Resistance and Survival: The Struggle for Land and Autonomy, 1821-1910*. Madison: University of Wisconsin Press.
_____. 1985. "La comunidad china en el desarrollo de Sonora." In *Historia General de Sonora. IV. Sonora Moderno: 1880-1929*. Hermosillo: Gobierno del Estado de Sonora.
_____. 1985-1986. "The Chinese in Baja California Norte, 1910-1934." In *Proceedings of the Pacific Coast Council on Latin American Studies*. San Diego: San Diego State University Press.
_____. 1988. "Chinos comerciantes en el Perú. Breve y preliminar bosquejo histórico, 1869-1924." *Primer Seminario Sobre Poblaciones Inmigrantes*. Lima: Consejo Nacional de Ciencias y Techología.
Jacques, Leo, M. D. 1974. "The Anti-Chinese Campaign in Sonora, Mexico, 1900-1931." Ph.D. dissertation, University of Arizona.
Jiménez Pastrana, Juan. 1983. *Los Chinos el la Historia de Cuba, 1847-1930*. Havana: Ciencias Sociales.

Johnson, Howard. 1983. "The Anti-Chinese Riots of 1918 in Jamaica." *Immigrants and Minorities* 2:50-63.
Kwong, Alice Jo. 1958. "The Chinese in Peru." In *Colloquium on Overseas Chinese*, edited by Morton Fried. New York: Institute of Pacific Relations.
Lausent, Isab. 1983. *Pequeña propriedad, poder y economía de mercado: Acos, Valle de Chancay*. Lima: Instituto de Estudios Peruanos.
_____. 1986. "Los inmigrantes chinos en la Amazonía Peruana." *Bulletin Institut Français d'Etudes Andines* 5:49-60.
Levy, Jacqueline. 1986. "The Economic Role of the Chinese in Jamaica: The Grocery Retail Trade." *The Jamaican Historical Review* 15:31-49.
Meagher, Arnold J. 1976. "The Introduction of Chinese Laborers to Latin America: The 'Coolie Trade,' 1847- 1874." Ph.D. dissertation, University of California, Davis.
Millones, Luis. 1973. *Minorías Etnicas en el Perú*. Lima: Universidad Católica.
Mörner, Magnus. 1967. *Race Mixture in the History of Latin America*. Boston: Little, Brown.
Patterson, Orlando. 1975. "Context and Choice in Ethnic Allegiance: A Theoretical Framework and Caribbean Case Study." In *Ethnicity: Theory and Experience*, edited by Nathan Glazer and Daniel P. Moynihan. Cambridge: Harvard University Press.
Pérez de la Riva, Juan. 1978. *El Barracón: Esclavitud y Capitalismo en Cuba*. Barcelona: Ed. Crítica.
Rodríguez Pastor, Humberto. 1989. *Hijos del Celeste Imperio en el Perú (1850-1900): Migración, Agricultura, Mentalidad y Explotación*. Lima: Instituto de Apoyo Agrario.
Scott, Rebecca. 1985. *Slave Emancipation in Cuba: The Transition to Free Labor, 1860-1899*. Princeton: Princeton University Press.
Steiner, Stan. 1979. *Fusang: The Chinese Who Built America*. New York: Harper and Row.
Stewart, Watt. 1951. *Chinese Bondage in Peru: A History of the Chinese Coolie in Peru, 1849-1874*. Durham: Duke University Press.
_____. 1976. *La servidumbre china en el Perú*. Lima: Mosca Azul. Wong, Bernard. 1978. "A Comparative Study of the Assimilation of the Chinese in New York City and Lima, Peru." Comparative Studies in Society and History 20:335-358.
_____. 1985. "Family, Kinship and Ethnic Identity of the Chinese in New York City, with Comparative Remarks on the Chinese in Lima, Peru, and Manila, Philippines." *Journal of Comparative Family Studies* 17:349-370.

African and Asian American Studies: A Comparative Analysis and Commentary

Gary Y. Okihiro

My graduate education, I must confess, was very much a product of the times. I entered the history program at the University of California at Los Angeles in 1967 without a designated area of interest, and settled on African Studies largely because it was one of the least developed areas of specialization and because it was the 1960s—peace, flower children, Black power. Also, that was before San Francisco State, before ethnic studies, before Asian American Studies. My growing interest in Africa took me away to that continent from 1968 to 1971—the formative years for ethnic studies—and, though not a founding participant, I benefited from the struggle for ethnic studies when upon my return I joined John M. Liu and Ron Hirano as the first cohort of graduate students at UCLA's Asian American Studies Center.

Despite the apparent unrelatedness of African and Asian American studies, I was impressed with their intersections and early on viewed my work in both areas as complementary; in fact, I now see that this comparative approach is essential to my understanding of both African and Asian American history. At the same time that I wrote about African resistance to European encroachment, I offered an interpretation of Japanese resistance in America's concentration camps, and, while using oral tradition to reconstruct Africa's precolonial past, I conceptualized oral history as method and theory in ethnic studies. Good comparative studies, nonetheless, do not simply transpose methodological and theoretical constructs from one time and place to another; they also explore differences, as well as commonalities, that cast new light on both fields of study.

What I propose to undertake in this essay is to compare the scholarly literature in African and Asian American studies, their evolution, and their similarities and contrasts. The study of Africa predates African Studies as we know it today, beginning in written form in early Egypt, Islamic North Africa and the Sudan, and along the Swahili coast, and in oral form among all of Africa's people. I will limit this discussion of African Studies to the more recent, much smaller body of knowledge about the peoples of Africa written in the tradition of European scholarship, and will examine schools of thought in African and Asian American studies and not the thematic coverage of Asians in Africa and the United States. Finally, at the risk of oversimplification, I survey the broad and complex areas with an eye toward connections and separations between the two fields of study.

Convergences

The articulation between Europeans and people of color is the fulcrum upon which African and Asian American studies turn. African history, for instance, is periodized as before, during, and after colonialism (precolonial, colonial, and independent Africa), while Asian American history is similarly divided into the periods of immigration and of contact and interaction. When, how, and to what effect are the principal questions asked about the European presence that pivots and drives both fields.

African Studies owes its beginnings to European expansionism and colonialism in Africa during the late nineteenth century. Foremost among the disciplines that sought a systematic ordering of African society was anthropology as practiced, on the whole, by scholars, missionaries, and administrators of the colonial powers. The predominance of anthropology reflected the racist intellectual division of labor of the day: historians, political scientists, economists, and sociologists studied Europe and European-settler states, "Orientalists" studied non-European, literate societies and states, while anthropologists studied "primitive" peoples and societies frequently referred to as "tribes."

Eurocentrism permeated some of the major assumptions of anthropology. Primitive societies were assumed to be static and the scientist's task was to recapture tribal tradition or custom in the now familiar "ethnographic present." European contact and political, economic, and cultural change was a major theme of those works and one that followed from the first assumption that dynamic cultures shattered and assimilated stagnant ones (Wallerstein 1983:155).

Anthropological studies were commonly commissioned by colonial governments, enabling a more informed version of colonial rule. Isaac Schapera, writing in the preface to the first edition of his landmark work, *A Handbook of Tswana Law and Custom,* noted that colonial administrators asked him to undertake the project and that the primary object of the book was "to place on record, for the information and guidance of Government officials and of the Tswana themselves, the traditional and modern laws and related customs of the Tswana tribes of the Bechuanaland Protectorate" (1970:vii, xxv).

Historians explained their lack of interest in Africa in terms of the Eurocentric assumptions they shared with anthropologists. Africans, they maintained, had no history because they were bound by tradition and were thus changeless. Africa, advanced Hegel in his 1930 Berlin lectures, "is no historical part of the World; it has no movement or development to exhibit," and Oxford historian Hugh Trevor-Roper observed that the African past contained "only the unrewarding gyrations of barbarous tribes in picturesque but irrelevant corners of the globe" (Wilks 1970:7).

According to that view, African history began with the advent of Europeans on the continent, and thus the history of Africa was the history of Europeans in Africa and not of the indigenous peoples. The historiography of South Africa illustrates that Eurocentrism. Although divided along the competing white ethnic lines, both Afrikaner and British traditions sharply articulated the deeds and institutions of whites upon inert, undifferentiated blacks (Thompson 1966:212-236).

The dominant paradigm in Asian American Studies derives from the "nation of immigrants" ideology of U.S. origins and identity. More specifically, the study of Asians in America was framed as problematic—the "Oriental question." Asians posed a problem for whites who saw America as a "melting pot" that fused diverse peoples into a homogeneous whole; groups like Asians, however, who were physically and culturally distinct from whites, could not blend into the mainstream, and thereby comprised a problem for both the American identity and for the "unmeltables" (Strong 1934).

Subject to exclusion and discrimination, Asians constituted a social problem that merited scholarly attention. Liberals argued that Asians, like Europeans, were immigrants to these shores, and like nineteenth-century European immigrants who were the objects of WASPish nativism, Asians faced animosity and prejudice. However, unlike Europeans, went the argument, Asians came with the sojourner mentality, persisted in keeping their culture, and, accordingly, must shoulder some of the blame for anti-Asian sentiment.

A book that perhaps best exemplifies that Eurocentric liberal tradition is Gunther Barth's *Bitter Strength: A History of the Chinese in the United States, 1850-1870* (1964). Chinese were like other immigrants to America, in Barth's account, but they were unlike Europeans in that they came as sojourners without a desire to become Americans. Chinese, thus, remaining uninvolved in the life around them, were easily exploited and became targets for anti-Asian sentiment. It was only after humanitarians and American ideals converted them from sojourners to immigrants did the Chinese enjoy and participate in the promises of democracy.

The Oriental question extended beyond America's definition of self to the international arena of politics and commerce. America's anti-Chinese movement, for example, revealed domestic fractures, but it also held implications for the nation's role in the Pacific. Mary Roberts Coolidge's *Chinese Immigration* (1909) and Bruno Lasker's *Filipino Immigration to Continental United States and to Hawaii* (1931) were written as contributions to the debate on an American public policy problem—exclusionary immigration laws, race relations, and international politics. Romanzo Adams's slim monograph, *The Japanese in Hawaii* (1924), considered the merits of the widespread fear of Japan's takeover of Hawaii, and Yamato Ichihashi's *Japanese in the United States* (1932) began as immigration research and appeared in print as an answer to charges made by anti-Japanese partisans.

Although Asian American Studies has since its inception been pulled in the Asian Studies direction, the dominant force in its development has been European American ideology. The intellectual implications of viewing Asian American Studies as Asian diaspora studies have been alluded to elsewhere (Hung 1984; "Chinese Americans, Who Defines Us?" 1988: vii-ix), although deserving of far greater explication and analysis.[1] I simply point to the hold that European American ethnic studies exercises over Asian American Studies and to the well-known though little appreciated fact that Marcus Hansen, Robert Park, Oscar Handlin, and Milton Gordon have exerted a greater influence over Asian American Studies than have W. E. B. Du Bois, Carter G. Woodson, and E. Franklin Frazier.

A convergence in the development of African and Asian American studies is in their beginnings, rooted in an examination of "the other" and steeped in Eurocentric assumptions of stasis and tradition on the one hand and change and innovation on the other. Research functioned to facilitate colonial rule in Africa and to inform public policy in the United States, and Eurocentrism defined both fields of study—African Studies as the study of Europeans among Africans and Asian American Studies as the study of Asian migrants in a nation of European immigrants.

African Studies was profoundly affected by the anti-colonial struggles of the post-World War II period in Africa. Reclaiming the past and decolonizing the culture of the oppressed antedated and accompanied the drive for political liberation. From among the many, I refer to Cheikh Anta Diop's studies on the African origin of civilization in Egypt as representative of this genre of scholarship.

Diop's *Nations Nègres et Culture*, originally published in 1954 and reprinted as *The African Origin of Civilization* (1974), argued that Egyptians were black Africans, and, as such, mathematics, science, religion, agriculture, and medicine were invented by Blacks who thus founded civilization. Diop described the conditions surrounding the book's writing: "I began my research in September

1946; because of our colonial situation at that time, the political problem dominated all others." While a student in Paris, Diop was elected secretary general from 1950 to 1953 of the Rassemblement Démocratique Africain (RDA), a nationalist movement in French West Africa.

Diop and his fellow RDA students saw culture as a vehicle for creating an anti-colonialist mentality among students who were being trained for privileged positions in the French colonial bureaucracy. French colonialism, unlike the British version, directed an elite group from among the colonized toward assimilation or conformity to the dominant culture. Diop wrote *Nations Nègres et Culture* as an antidote to that poison of self-erasure: "The cultural concept especially will claim our attention here; the problem was posed in terms of restoring the collective national African personality" (Diop 1974:xii-xiii).

During the 1950s and 1960s, independence from colonial powers influenced the rise of nationalist literature in African Studies, primarily, but not exclusively, from universities in Africa. At the International Congress of African Historians in 1965 held significantly at University College, Dar es Salaam, Tanzanian President Julius K. Nyerere acknowledged that the developing countries of Africa benefited from scholarship about Africa from outside the continent. "At the same time," he asserted, "it is natural and right that Africa's new Universities and institutions should from now on take a leading part in this work. The primary sources are here, in Africa, and the primary interest is not really other people's desire to understand us, but our own desire to understand ourselves and our societies, so that we can build the future on firm foundations" (Nyerere 1968:3).

The nationalist school developed a key concept that would influence a generation of Africanists; arising out of the "Dar es Salaam school," the idea was of African agency, formulated as resistance. In a two-part article published in the *Journal of African History* (1968), Terence O. Ranger showed the connections between African resistance and modern mass nationalism in East and Central Africa. African politics, he argued, was not only shaped by European initiatives, but also by African resistance to colonialism, which was not only efficacious in altering the pattern of domination, but also shaped the environment out of which came modern nationalism.[2]

The anti-colonial struggles waged by peoples of the Third World had a direct influence on the struggle for ethnic studies in U.S. universities. The students at San Francisco State in the fall of 1968 formed a coalition called the Third World Liberation Front and the demand at the University of California, Berkeley, in January 1969 was for a Third World College. "The Third World movement," they wrote, "was and continues to be a demand of colonized peoples for freedom and self-determination—for the right to control and develop their own economic, political, and social institutions" (Murase

1976:208). Historian Vincent Harding (1987:40) wrote of that period: "this is not an unexpected relationship between political and social struggle on the one hand, and the search for history on the other hand. Indeed, this tie between the struggle for history and the struggle for a new future has been typical of almost all the post-World War II anti-colonial struggles of the non-white world."

The institutionalization of Asian American Studies was an outcome of the Third World student movement that repudiated "brainwashing" and advocated relevance in education. The research and curriculum of the university, the strikers claimed, should respond to the needs of America's minority communities and help create a just society. That social movement gave rise to ethnic studies programs and nurtured a new generation of Asian American scholars who studied and applied works from the African anti-colonial struggles, such as the writings of Frantz Fanon (1963) and Albert Memmi (1965). Social self-determination meant intellectual self-definition, and Asian American Studies sought to control the terms of the discourse and depict the colonized not as mere victims, but as active participants in the shaping of history.

The anti-colonial struggles in Africa and the fight for ethnic studies in the United States advocated the common goals of reclaiming the past, decolonizing and reconstituting the identity and culture of the oppressed, and seeking self-determination and liberation. Both bodies of scholarship have generally evolved toward what St. Clair Drake (1987) has called the "vindicationist tradition," and both have induced a similar response.

Nyerere's nationalist formula did not sit well outside the continent with African Studies scholars who were establishing the academic legitimacy of their field of study. Was not scholarship universal, they asked, and why should Africans have proprietary rights over an area of human knowledge? Moreover, they held, nationalist writings aimed specifically at economic development, political consensus, and national identity were anti-intellectual and biased. Finally, who can say what is authentically African or determine a truly African epistemology?

Despite those objections, the intellectual implications of African nationalism could not be easily dismissed, and the persistent questions of scholarship for whom and for what purpose remained among the thorniest for students of Africa. So-called value-free research and scholarship devoid of social conscience remained a target for the left. "Africa has been a laboratory for too many American careers; too many papers and books are simply status symbols in the social system, the social struggle, of the domestic academy, shaped by that system and couched in its limited and evasive language," charged a political scientist. "There have been too many grants and too few demands" (Diamond 1966:5). Furthermore, writings that purported to be value-free, pointed out the critics, actually favored conservatism and the status quo (Lemarchand 1973).

Most recently, persistent voices raised in the spirit of completing the unfinished business of Africa's decolonization have called attention to the need to overthrow the "tyranny of received paradigms" to the ethics of cross-cultural research, and to the scholar's social responsibility to Africa's oppressed masses (Neale 1985; Jewsiewicki and Newbury 1986; Ake 1979; Said 1982). Those contentions, however, are brushed aside as rhetorically attractive, but unclear as to what they might mean in practice. Scholarship unfettered by social context or meaning—termed scientific—remains the norm in African Studies, because scrupulous adherence to that standard has earned legitimacy for a field once shunned as the futile study of "the unrewarding gyrations of barbarous tribes in...irrelevant corners of the globe."

Like the African anti-nationalists, European American ethnic studies proponents saw the American experience as governed by universal principles and as a human laboratory for the study of interactions among diverse peoples. Park (1950:150) formulated his race relations cycle idea as a generalization: "In the relations of races there is a cycle of events which tends everywhere to repeat itself...the race relations cycle takes the form...of contact, competition, accommodation and eventual assimilation." Gordon (1969:vii) asserted: "The United States of America, as the classic example of a highly industrialized nation made up of people of diverse ethnic origins, constitutes, both in its history and its current situation, a huge living laboratory for the serious study of various underlying patterns of ethnic interaction."

Despite the radical origins of the field, very few Asian American Studies scholars have truly challenged the "tyranny of received paradigms." Sucheng Chan (1978) observed that even the anthology compiled as a counterpoint to conventional wisdom lacked an analytic framework that could both integrate the experiences of diverse Asian American groups and provide a radical explanation for the international and domestic contexts of Asian American history. Chan proceeded to outline those contexts in terms of international capitalism, migration, and development and dependency. Other critical assessments of Asian American Studies scholarship reveal a preponderance of descriptive as opposed to analytical studies, and cultural rather than structural explanations (Hirata 1976:20-26).

There are exceptions to that norm, comprising the beginnings of what might eventuate into a school or tradition. Some of the more influential ideas that could serve as foundation include the theories, and their modifications, of migrant labor (Cheng and Bonacich 1984), world-system (Liu 1985), internal colonialism and cultural hegemony (Takaki 1979), and resistance. Prominent variables—gender, race, and class—of themselves comprise entire systems of analyses such as theories of gender relations, racial formation, and labor market segmentation (Glenn 1986; Omi and Winant 1986).

Scholars and activists are measuring anew progress in Asian American Studies against the standard of transformative scholarship or research designed to promote social change. Pedagogy and the curriculum have been subjected to similar scrutiny (Loo and Mar 1985-1986; Miller 1985-1986; Morales 1986-1987; Okihiro et al. 1988). Speaking before the National Asian American Studies Conference, Penny Nakatsu predicted: "If Asian American Studies is not rooted within the life-experience of each of our communities and does not illuminate the forces which bear upon our communities' destiny and foster the development of significant social change, the attainment of institutional credibility would be an empty prize" (Nakatsu 1974:5-9). Fifteen years later, Asian American Studies programs continue to exist in universities and apparently are undergoing a revival and expansion of sorts, but radicals point to the depoliticization of the field, its apparent aimlessness, and its lack of a conceptual framework.

African Studies has progressed from scholarship for the governance of "primitive" peoples to nationalism and Afrocentrism, while Asian American Studies has moved from an integrationist ethic to a demand for democratic inclusion in American society. At the same time in both fields, Eurocentrism remains the rule, and self-definition and politically committed scholarship are circumscribed by gatekeepers—old and new—through faculty appointments, tenure and promotion decisions, and publication outlets and research grant awards.

Divergences and Commentary

African Studies, nonetheless, clearly enjoys a greater degree of academic legitimacy than does Asian American Studies. Members of the former are among the luminaries of traditional disciplines and are regularly consulted by government agencies, foundations, and the private sector. In contrast, Asian American Studies and ethnic studies broadly, almost by definition, are placed in a defensive posture, having repeatedly to justify their existence. Members are commonly marginal to traditional disciplines and are less frequently consulted even in their areas of expertise.

Although African Studies predates Asian American Studies, the African Studies Association in the United States was founded in 1957, only about a decade before ethnic studies became institutionalized, and I can recall how the appointment of Terence O. Ranger as chair of Manchester University's Department of History during the mid-1970s was hailed by Africanists as a major vindication of the field. (Ranger is now Rhodes Professor of Race Relations at Oxford.) Longevity alone thus fails to explain the acceptance enjoyed by African Studies as compared with Asian American Studies. Rather, I believe that the essential difference rests in the degree of detachment from an explicit political agenda.

Works like Bernard Magubane's *The Political Economy of Race and Class in South Africa* (1979:xii), for instance, penned "to chart a clear ideological and analytical direction . . . based on the belief that the [anti-apartheid] movement's strategy must be based on a correct historical understanding," rubs against the scholarly grain, while the liberal *White Supremacy* (1981), a comparative history of white supremacy in the United States and South Africa by Americanist George Fredrickson, is bestowed landmark status.[3] In general, Africanists have not been keen about having the objects of their research determine priorities or needs, nor have they been taken by the idea of an engaged scholarship wherein scholar and community participate in critical discourse.

Another fundamental difference between African Studies and Asian American Studies derives from their respective audiences and perceived roles. American and European Africanists are for the most part outsiders looking across cultures and serving as interpreters of Africa for the West. Curiously, despite the saliency of European colonialism in their analyses, race is minimized even in revisionist studies of South Africa which stress class and relegate race to the dustbin of an archaic liberalism. Asian Americanists, on the other hand, are largely insiders who also see themselves as interpreters, but for their communities vis-à-vis the dominant group. Whether as race relations experts, cultural brokers, or advocates, accordingly, the principal nexus in Asian American Studies is race.

The contrasts, I believe, underscore the need in African Studies for a politically committed, accountable, and liberatory scholarship, and for a greater appreciation of the centrality of race and racial dynamics. Asian American Studies, reflectively, could benefit from the African Studies ideas of social formation and articulation, and, in a negative way, from the direction charted by African Studies in distancing itself from the vibrant and impoverished communities that nurtured it and gave it substance. Instead, unfortunately, the hard lesson learned by Asian Americanists who survive and thrive in the institution is the same one recognized by Africanists early on, that science (legitimacy) mandates value-free research in a language virtually unintelligible to the communities it purportedly speaks for.

That latter lesson bears restating. We, in Asian American Studies, carry a special responsibility to those who have given us this opportunity to study, write, and teach, but we could be speaking merely among ourselves and our collegiality might become a narcissistic exercise. We are challenged to shape the present and future for our children and our communities, but we could easily blunt our initiative for the sake of avoiding polemics and rhetoric. We understand the need for social change, but we could soften as we join the club and get fatter. African Studies, Asian American Studies; for whom and for what purpose?

A committed and engaged scholarship, it seems to me, is the ultimate source of our animation and test of our authenticity.

Notes

1. I am not alluding to reciprocal relations between Asians in America and in Asia or to the impact of return migration; rather, I refer to the study of Asians in America as overseas Asian communities—as an extension of Asian Studies.
2. For a review of trends in political science and African Studies, see James S. Coleman and Halisi, "American Political Science and Tropical Africa: Universalism vs. Relativism," *African Studies Review* 26 (3/4):25-62.
3. I do not question Fredrickson's political commitment, nor do I mean to undervalue a work I consider to have exceptional merit. I simply contrast the reception accorded those books.

References

Adams, Romanzo. 1924. *The Japanese in Hawaii: A Statistical Study Bearing on the Future Number and Voting Strength and on the Economic and Social Character of the Hawaiian Japanese.* New York: National Committee on American Japanese Relations.
Ake, Claude. 1979. *Social Science as Imperialism: The Theory of Political Development.* Lagos: University of Ibadan.
Barth, Gunther. 1964. *Bitter Strength: A History of the Chinese in the United States, 1850-1870.* Cambridge: Harvard University.
Chan, Sucheng. 1978. "Contextual Frameworks for Reading Counterpoint." *Amerasia Journal* 5 (1):115-129.
Cheng, Lucie, and Edna Bonacich, eds. 1984. *Labor Immigration under Capitalism: Asian Workers in the United States before World War II.* Berkeley: University of California.
"Chinese Americans, Who Defines Us?" *Amerasia Journal* 14 (1988):vii-ix.
Coolidge, Mary Roberts. 1909. *Chinese Immigration.* New York: Henry Holt.
Diamond, Stanley. 1966. "The End of the First Republic." *Africa Today* 13:5-9.
Diop, Cheikh Anta. 1974. *The African Origin of Civilization: Myth or Reality.* Westport: Lawrence Hill.
Drake, St. Clair. 1987. *Black Folk Here and There: An Essay in History and Anthropology,* vol. 1. Los Angeles: University of California Center for Afro-American Studies.
Fanon, Frantz. 1963. *The Wretched of the Earth.* New York: Grove.
Fredrickson, George M. 1981. *White Supremacy: A Comparative Study in American and South African History.* New York: Oxford University.
Gee, Emma, Bruce Iwasaki, Mike Murase, Megumi Dick Osumi, and Jesse Quinsaat, eds. 1976. *Counterpoint: Perspectives on Asian America.* Los Angeles: University of California Asian American Studies Center.
Glenn, Evelyn Nakano. 1986. *Issei, Nisei, War Bride: Three Generations of Japanese American Women in Domestic Service.* Philadelphia: Temple University.
Gordon, Milton M. 1969. Foreword to *Japanese Americans: The Evolution of a Subculture,* edited by Harry H. L. Kitano. Englewood Cliffs: Prentice-Hall.
Harding, Vincent. 1987. "Power from Our People: The Sources of the Modern Revival of Black History." *Black Scholar* 18.
Hirata, Lucie Cheng. 1976. "The Chinese American in Sociology." In *Counterpoint: Perspectives on Asian America,* edited by Emma Gee et al. Los Angeles: University of California Asian American Studies Center.

Hung, Nguyen Manh. 1984. "Refugee Scholars and Vietnamese Studies in the United States, 1975-1982." *Amerasia Journal* 11 (1):89-99.
Ichihashi, Yamato. 1932. *Japanese in the United States: A Critical Study of the Problems of the Japanese Immigrants and Their Children.* Stanford: Stanford University.
Jewsiewicki, Bogumil, and David Newbury, eds. 1986. *African Historiographies: What History for Which Africa?* London: Sage.
Lasker, Bruno. 1931. *Filipino Immigration to Continental United States and to Hawaii.* Chicago: University of Chicago.
Lemarchand, Rene. 1973. "African Power through the Looking Glass." *Journal of Modern African Studies* 11:305-314.
Liu, John Mei. 1985. "Cultivating Cane: Asian Labor and the Hawaiian Sugar Plantation System within the Capitalist World Economy, 1835-1920." Ph.D. dissertation, University of California, Los Angeles.
Loo, Chalsa, and Don Mar. 1985-1986. "Research and Asian Americans: Social Change or Empty Prize?" *Amerasia Journal* 12:85-93.
Magubane, Bernard Makhosezwe. 1979. *The Political Economy of Race and Class in South Africa.* New York: Monthly Review.
Memmi, Albert. 1965. *The Colonizer and the Colonized.* New York: Orion.
Miller, Maurice Lim. 1985-1986. "Whom Should Academic Researchers Serve?" *Amerasia Journal* 12:95-99.
Morales, Royal F. 1986-1987. "Pilipino American Studies: A Promise and an Unfinished Agenda." *Amerasia Journal* 13:119-124.
Murase, Mike. 1976. "Ethnic Studies and Higher Education for Asian Americans." In *Counterpoint: Perspectives on Asian America,* edited by Emma Gee et al. Los Angeles: University of California Asian American Studies Center.
Nakatsu, Penny. 1974. Keynote Address to *Proceedings of National Asian American Studies Conference II,* edited by George Kagiwada et al. Davis: University of California.
Neale, Caroline. 1985. *Writing "Independent" History: African Historiography, 1960-1980.* Westport, Connecticut: Greenwood.
Nyerere, Julius. 1968. "Speech by the President of Tanzania, Mwalimu Julius Nyerere." In *Emerging Themes of African History,* edited by T. O. Ranger. Nairobi: East African Publishing House.
Okihiro, Gary Y., Shirley Hune, Arthur A. Hansen, John M. Liu, eds. 1988. *Reflections on Shattered Windows: Promises and Prospects for Asian American Studies.* Pullman: Washington State University Press.
Omi, Michael, and Howard Winant. 1986. *Racial Formation in the United States: From the 1960s to the 1980s.* New York: Routledge and Kegan Paul.
Park, Robert Ezra. 1950. *Race and Culture.* New York: Free Press.
Ranger, Terence O. 1968. "Connexions between 'Primary Resistance' and Modern Mass Nationalism in East and Central Africa." Parts 1, 2. *Journal of African History* 9 (3,4):440, 443-448, 452-453, 631-639, 641.
Said, Edward. 1982. *Covering Islam: How the Media and the Experts Determine How We See the Rest of the World.* New York: Pantheon.
Schapera, Isaac. 1970. *A Handbook of Tswana Law and Custom.* Second Edition. London: Frank Cass.
Strong, Edward K., Jr. 1934. *The Second-Generation Japanese Problem.* Stanford: Stanford University.
Takaki, Ronald T. 1979. *Iron Cages: Race and Culture in Nineteenth-Century America.* New York: Knopf.

Thompson, Leonard M. 1966. "South Africa." In *The Historiography of the British Empire-Commonwealth,* edited by Robin Winks. Durham, North Carolina: Duke University.
Wallerstein, Immanuel. 1983. "The Evolving Role of the Africa Scholar in African Studies." *African Studies Review* 26:155-161.
Wilks, Ivor. 1970. "African Historiographical Traditions, Old and New." In *Africa Discovers Her Past,* edited by J. D. Fage. London: Oxford.

Asian American Studies and Asian Studies: Rethinking Roots

Sucheta Mazumdar

> Too often, the plight of the Asian-American is one of forced rejection of his own culture in favor of the dominant one in order to survive. This process of accommodation, which often appears under the guise of acculturation, has produced considerable psychological damage. An awareness of this predicament is essential, not only in understanding the self, but also in evolving a new value system so that the Asian-American can carve out a cultural existence as well as an economic existence in this country.
> Therefore, the study program of Asian Studies is to include the following areas of scholarship: community commitment, awareness of the Asian-American identity, Asian and Asian-American culture, and the dynamics of racism (Asian American Political Alliance 1971:265).

So reads part of the manifesto of one of the groups intimately involved with the establishment of a formal Asian American Studies program at Berkeley in 1969. The projected overlap between Asian and Asian American studies in the formal academic arena while maintaining distinctive arenas of cultural practice and community involvement, as proposed by the Asian American Political Alliance, has proved impossible to implement in practice.

Let me begin with what has happened in the past twenty-year history of Asian American Studies, though as a subfield of immigration history it has existed much longer. At present on most campuses, with a few rare exceptions, Asian American Studies functions at best in an uneasy alliance with scholars of American history and civilization. Robert E. Park's assimilationist model has so permeated intellectual discourse on immigration studies, that, though challenged and shown to be inadequate in explaining the experience of immigrants of color, it continues to mold research agendas (Hune 1977:24-32). The implicit acceptance of this model has meant that Asian

American Studies has been located within the context of American Studies and stripped of its international links. This nationalist interpretation of immigration history has also been a more comfortable discourse for second- and third-generation Americans of Asian ancestry. Tired of being thought of as foreigners, these scholars have been particularly reluctant to identify with Asian Studies and its pronouncements on the distinctiveness of Asian cultures in counterpoint to Euro-American culture. As Asian American Studies programs have become more a part of formal academia, the links with the community have been weakened rather than strengthened. This has also led to a further distancing between the university and newly arrived immigrants from Asia and their cultural milieu (Endo and Wei 1988:8-9).

The "identity crisis" which so engaged the minds and hearts of the 1960s generation of Asian American activists also remains unresolved (Tachiki et al. 1971). As one essay in the collection *Roots: An Asian American Reader* asked, how can Japanese Americans resolve their identity crisis when they are faced with a two-part dilemma: experiencing a national pride at the achievements of Japan and a simultaneous awareness that this national identity implies a disengagement of Japanese Americans from Third World peoples and from the working class exploited by Japan (Odo 1971:243- 244). To some extent the response of many in Asian American Studies to this dilemma has been to distance themselves from the Asian heritage altogether. As the index of *Amerasia* for the years 1971-1987 shows, questions of ethnic identity have shifted firmly to these shores, to questions of psychological adjustment and economic assimilation (Espiritu 1988). Like the middle classes among other minorities, like the black bourgeoisie who seek to distance themselves from Africa and often talk condescendingly of African culture (Frazier 1971:297), second- and third-generation Asian Americans are ambivalent about Asia.

As the following narrative details, Asian Studies also entered a period of soul searching in the late 1960s. But this turmoil, much of it linked to the anti-war movement, did not bring the field closer to Asian American Studies. Though some scholars of Asian Studies do, on a personal level, have some interaction with faculty and curricula in Asian American Studies, by and large most ignore Asian American Studies. Asian American Studies, with its politics of protest and challenge to existing curricula of higher education in America, has been seen as "too political" by a field used to thinking of politics only in distant lands. The centrality of race and issues of racism in scholarship on Asian American Studies have also been uncomfortable topics for Asianists who have tended to leave such issues unexamined.

But as we enter the 1990s, the socioeconomic realities of the world beyond campus perimeters and campus politics are setting up new challenges to both Asian Studies and Asian American Studies. The post-World War II internationalization of capital and labor, and the restructuring of the global economy with increased momentum since 1970, has had a particularly profound impact on the relations of the United States with Asia and on the composition of the Asian American community. United States trade with Asian countries across the Pacific has soared. For example, by the early 1980s two-thirds of California's total trade volume of $71,000,000,000 was with Asian countries of the "Pacific Rim" (Kim 1986:75). It is no longer adequate to study, as much of Asian Studies did, "the impact of the West on Asia" or focus on "tradition versus modernity," where modernity was equated with the West and industrialization (Cohen 1979). With the so-called "Four Tigers" of South Korea, Taiwan, Hong Kong, and Singapore, in addition to Japan, challenging the economic hegemony of the United States, the time has come to study "the impact of Asia on the West." Pacific Rim programs on many campuses, with an explicitly interdisciplinary and interregional approach, are already challenging the validity of "area studies" programs which formed the organizational principle for the various subfields within Asian Studies.

The "new immigration" of the post-1965 period has had equally fundamental implications for Asian American Studies. Because immigration from countries other than Japan has been continuing, Japanese Americans who had formed the largest community among the Asian Americans, and had been the focus of much research, will be the smallest of the six major Asian American groups by 2010 (Bouvier and Agresta 1985:31-38). The 1980 census found that over sixty-one percent of the Asian American community was foreign-born; the 1990 census will definitely report an even higher percentage. And since the immigrants are entering the country as adults, their use of languages other than English is likely to continue. New York's Chinatown, for example, the largest Chinese American community in the nation today, has nine Chinese-language daily newspapers and most of its residents are literate only in Chinese. Without language training in the various languages of Asia and some understanding of the cultures and history of Asia, second- and third-generation Asian American scholars and other American scholars are unable to communicate with the very community whose voices and experiences they hope to represent.

The voice of the community has also changed. As Asian Americans vote two-to-one in Flushing, New York, for George Bush over Michael Dukakis and vote en masse for the Republican candidate Giuliani over the black Democratic candidate Dinkins in the recent mayoral elections *(India West*, January 5, 1990, 51), the progressive politics once identified with Asian American Studies is open to challenge by the middle-class "model minority."

With the "new immigrant" groups such as Korean Americans, Filipino Americans, Vietnamese Americans, and Asian Indians gaining political and economic clout through the demographics of immigration, Asian American Studies programs have had to meet the demands of their changing constituency.

Increasingly under pressure for neglecting the history of recent immigrants, Asian American Studies programs have frequently turned to first-generation immigrant scholars from these communities to carry out the research and teaching. But these scholars, while providing the necessary language skills and access to the community, often have no background in American history and are only marginally interested in the history of race relations in this country or in ethnic groups other than their own. Consequently, these scholars have very little interest in comparative research. Furthermore, as they are often middle-class and upper-class immigrants from countries which have recently experienced communist revolutions, these immigrant scholars' political perspective is inherently conservative. Thus, Asian American Studies finds itself replicating the framework of area studies borrowed from Asian Studies, with individuals working on their own racial and ethnic subgroups.

Both Asian Studies and Asian American Studies are therefore confronted with the need to restructure programs and rethink the frameworks within which curricula were designed in the late 1960s and early 1970s. The question then arises as to the potential for supportive and mutually collaborative efforts between Asian Studies and Asian American Studies. This essay will address that question in the conclusion, and begin here with an overview of the history of both fields; for, to a great extent, the potential for collaboration lies in how that history is read and understood.

The Nineteenth Century: Asian Studies and the Colonial Project

Very broadly, the history of Asian Studies can be demarcated into three distinct periods: the "Orientalist"[1] phase, which started in the late eighteenth century and can be said to have continued until the 1920s; the period 1926 to 1968, which was marked by a tremendous increase in the level of professional training, but which left unchallenged many of the basic Orientalist assumptions of the field; and the post-1968 period, when many of the premises of inquiry of both the earlier periods came under scrutiny and question.

American universities first approached Asian Studies from the perspective of Europeans. As Martin Bernal points out in his *Black Athena: The Afro-Asiatic Roots of Greek Civilization*, an interest in China and India developed in the "surge of European self-confidence" that accompanied the Enlightenment when several intellectuals felt freer to show a preference for non-European cultures (Bernal 1988:172). Others, in their reaction to feudalism and traditional Christianity, turned to investigate other societies that appeared far more secular. At the end of the seventeenth century, both Egypt and China drew admirers. Reflecting this adulatory aura surrounding Chinese civilization, Benjamin Franklin wrote in 1768:

Could we be so fortunate as to introduce the industry of the Chinese, their arts of living and improvements in husbandry...America might become in time as populous as China (Isaacs 1972:95).

As the French and British colonial penetration of the Indian subcontinent proceeded apace in the late eighteenth century, there was also a growing interest in ancient Indian culture. This interest gathered momentum in Germany from the works of Orientalists like William Jones, who discovered the linguistic links between Sanskrit, the classical language of India, and Latin and Greek. The first chair of Sanskrit was established in Berlin in 1818, and the model of German Sanskritic Studies was followed by Oxford and Harvard. The American Oriental Society, based on the European model and established in 1843, focused on the languages, philology, and philosophy of the ancients. This interest in Indic Studies, however, had very little to do with the land and people of India. Very early in its career, Indian and South Asian Studies became relegated to the realm of philosophical and philological studies, one from which it was not to emerge until the 1960s.

Chinese Studies, though also focused on the reading of classical texts and philosophy, began under slightly different auspices. One of the first American merchants to make a fortune in China was D. W. C. Olyphant. A particularly pious New Englander, he provided the funds in 1830 to establish the first American missionaries in Canton (Isaacs 1972:126). Missionaries began to serve as interpreters and translators for the Western governments and their gunboat diplomacy which imposed treaties on China in rapid succession after the Opium War of 1839-1842. This link between business, government, and missionaries was to shape Chinese Studies for well over a hundred years. Formal teaching of Chinese began when Boston traders raised money for a "Chinese teachership" at Harvard in the late 1870s (McCunn 1988:20).

Unlike Chinese and Indic studies, the introduction of Japanese Studies came from pragmatic concerns stemming from the growth of Japanese military and political influence. Though numerous missionaries, businessmen, and American teachers had been travelling to Japan since the 1850s, the notion that Japanese culture was entirely derivative of the Chinese slowed the development of Japanese Studies. The University of California, Berkeley, started a position in Japanese in 1896, the year after Japan's victory over Qing China. In the following decade, particularly after the Russo-Japanese War, both Stanford and the University of Washington established positions in Far Eastern History and Oriental Languages (Jansen 1988a:10-11).

The extraordinary increase in racism and racist ideologies in Europe and America during the late eighteenth century had of course begun to include pejorative racial classifications of "the yellow races" (Gobineau 1971:238). Benjamin Franklin, for all his adulation of the Chinese, did not want them here: "Why increase the Sons of Africa, by Planting them in America, where we have so fair an opportunity, by excluding all Blacks and Tawneys [as he identified most of Asia], of increasing the lovely White?' (Takaki 1989:16).

These ideologies began to find intellectual support in theories of a "stagnant" East whose "civilization had long appeared stationary" (Bernal 1988:240), and notions of a "passive and degenerate East" crumbling under Western impact. The "Age of Respect" had given way to the "Age of Contempt" as Harold Isaacs points out in his detailed analysis of American images of Chinese and Indians. The Chinese immigrants, as the first of the immigrants from Asia, were also the first to be subjected to domestic versions of this racism, including its particular equation of blacks and Chinese (Takaki 1989:100-101). In the nineteenth and twentieth centuries, racism at home and imperialism abroad were to acquire a grotesque symbiosis. Apostles of British imperialism turned avidly to cheer on the Americans; Kipling wrote the "The White Man's Burden" to celebrate American colonization of the Philippines.

Asian Studies did not begin to confront issues of imperialism or racism till the emergence of radical politics in the 1960s. But this linked history of racism and imperialism, and the project of decolonization, provide a common ground for collaborative inquiry between scholars in Asian Studies and those in Asian American Studies. As Robert Blauner points out, and I quote at length from him here, race relations within America cannot be understood in isolation from the colonial project.

> The insistence on viewing American race relations from an international perspective is an important corrective to the parochial and ahistorical outlook of our national consciousness. The economic, social and political subordination of third world groups in America is a microcosm of the position of all peoples of color in the world order of stratification. This is neither an accident nor the result of some essential racial genius. Racial domination in the United States is part of a world historical drama in which the culture, economic system, and the political power of the white West has spread virtually throughout the entire globe. The expansion of the West, particularly Europe's domination over non-Western people of color, was the major theme in the almost five hundred years that followed the onset of "The Age of Discovery." The European conquest of Native American peoples, leading to the white settlement of the Western hemisphere and the African slave trade was one of the leading historical events that ushered in the age of colonialism. Colonial subjugation and racial domination began much earlier and have lasted much longer in North America than in Asia and Africa, the continents usually thought of as colonial prototypes. The oppression of racial colonies within our national borders cannot be understood without considering worldwide patterns of white European hegemony (Blauner 1982:517-518).

The Professionalizing of Asian Studies

By the beginning of the twentieth century, as the actual contact of America with Asia increased, the need to develop a more structured approach to training and research on Asia became evident to all interested parties. The memoirs and travelogues of missionaries and businessmen on the one hand, and the extremely specialized training of philologists and classicists on the other, had left vast arenas of Asian culture and history untouched and uncomprehended. The level of general knowledge about Asia was apparent from comments such as those by President McKinley, who, when appointing a certain Professor Oscar Williams to the position of consul at Manila, declared it was "somewhere away on the other side of the world," but he "did not exactly know where" since he 'had not had time to look it up" (Karnow 1989:87).

By the 1920s, several universities, such as those on the West coast and the Ivy League campuses, had started offering some courses on Chinese and Japanese history. A major new impetus to develop these fields was to come from the American Council of Learned Societies in the late 1920s. For a variety of historical reasons, ranging from the fact that China was the single largest theater of American missionary enterprise in the world and the perception that the market of millions held out hope for American business as the promised land, Chinese studies was to emerge and remain the premier focus of Asian Studies. To this end a first "Conference for the Promotion of Chinese Studies" met at the Harvard Club in New York in 1928. Minutes of the meeting show that the gathering deplored the concentration on Indic and Semitic fields in academia, discussed the American apathy toward Chinese Studies, and strongly recommended the need to nurture scholars who would go to Europe and then to China to develop expertise on the subject of China (Jansen 1988b:142). One young scholar who thought of doing just that in 1929 was John King Fairbank. He was to become one of the most influential figures in Chinese Studies in the post-World War II period.

The world of Asian America was far removed from the consciousness of elite institutions. That there were almost 75,000 Chinese and 140,000 Japanese in the continental United States with language schools, newspapers, scholars, and writers was not considered to be an avenue for learning about China or Japan. Going to Europe was deemed the only avenue of learning. Fairbank went to Balliol College, Oxford, to find that no instruction in Chinese language or history was available. His memoirs reflect an unintended irony: "It kept me out of any sinological rut and let me approach Modern China as the West had done in the nineteenth century largely through British eyes" (Fairbank 1982:26).

The Second World War and the decade of the 1940s saw, not unsurprisingly, a major expansion in Chinese and Japanese studies. In the summer of 1941, the office of Coordinator of Information with a Research and Analysis Branch had been set up and its staff recruited mainly from the universities (Fairbank 1982:173). This group of "specialists" was an odd mixture in terms of training and temperament as well as politics. Several, it would seem, would fit Fairbank's description of one: "His forte was a mix of legality and moralism, well suited to the traditional American flatulence about the Open Door" (Fairbank 1982:177). Numerous Asian Americans as well as Asian scholars were also recruited during the war effort.

But if the war opened up some degree of communication between white and Asian American and Asian scholars on Asia, the integral connection set up between United States foreign policy interests, U.S. intelligence, and American academia during the war shaped the politics of Asian Studies in the post-war period. First of course came Cold War politics, the hysteria over the "loss of China," and McCarthyism. In addition to affecting the careers of many scholars in both Chinese and Japanese studies, and dismantling research centers which had done pioneering work (the Institute of Pacific Relations, for example), the political heritage of the Cold War was to reinforce conservative tendencies. Ideological caution, whereby it "became second nature to indicate at the beginning of an article, by some word or phrase that one was safely anti-communist" (Fairbank 1982:338), became the established norm. A corresponding preoccupation with elite class politics and ideologies developed among researchers in the field, to the exclusion of attempts at understanding peasant society and culture, working-class politics, or the histories of racial and ethnic minorities in Asia. In working on China, for example, scholars focused almost exclusively on the Han Chinese and the Confucian tradition. Hindu caste hierarchies became the focus of those seeking to explain Indian culture and society, while for those working on Japan the myriad manifestations of the samurai ethic became the key to understanding Japanese history. The National Defense Education Act (NDEA) of 1958, providing the economic underpinnings of growth in the field, cemented the tie-in with academia and government. Carving up the world according to United States and Soviet "spheres of influence" was combined with considerations of naval and military strategy to determine levels of funding for various fields of study. The study of Southeast Asia has been particularly affected by this approach, with funding for Vietnamese Studies, Indonesian Studies, or Thai Studies ebbing and flowing according to United States involvement in the internal politics of those countries and the politics of petroleum companies.[2]

The Radical Challenge and Modern Asian Studies

The Vietnam War and the events of 1968 served to challenge the cozy relationship that existed between government and major scholars within academia. The role of the intellectual as social critic and conscience of a generation, stilled by McCarthyism and a pattern of resistance to critical self-analysis, was to some extent revived (Cohen 1979:104). Many scholars of China in particular felt extremely pained and responsible for the total ignorance that surrounded

United States foreign policy decision-making on the subject of Vietnam. The widespread sense of disillusion and dissent among many of the younger generation of scholars found some vent in the formation of an alternative organization, the Committee of Concerned Asian Scholars (CCAS). A new publication, the *Bulletin of CCAS*, sought to bring into critical inquiry the politics of the earlier generation of Asia (particularly China) specialists. A bold article in the October 1969 issue of the *Bulletin*, James Peck's "The Roots of Rhetoric: the Professional Ideology of America's China Watchers," seemed to send shock waves through the field. Issues such as imperialism and anti-communism were suddenly placed on the table. This radical politics, in permitting a new discourse, did not lead to a transformation of the field as such, but certainly broadened it. Marxist theories, "dependency theories," peasant studies, and Women's Studies were all accommodated within the field by the 1980s. However, the legacy of the area studies approach, based on the colonial history of the areas, has continued, though there is now some effort to sponsor comparative research.

The national organization, the Association of Asian Studies, has close to 7,000 members and around 3,000 attend the national meetings. This not only makes the AAS one of the largest professional organizations in the country, it is the largest society of its kind in the world. Over thirty-five percent of the membership is concentrated in the China and Inner Asia field by area of specialization. The annual conference draws participants from Asia as well as from Europe, and even attracts an occasional scholar from Mexico. Both Asian Americans and non-resident Asians form a significant portion of the membership, though there are very few other minorities—such as black and Hispanic Americans—represented in the field. (Information based on inquiry to the Office of the Association of Asian Studies, and the *Asian Studies Newsletter*, 1989, 34 (4).)

Asian Studies and Asian American Studies: Some Shared Research Agendas

Numerous scholars in Asian Studies have long been interested in studying migration and diasporas. Chinese diaspora studies have probably attracted more researchers than some of the other fields. Victor Purcell, a noted Asianist, has written very extensively on the Chinese in Southeast Asia, and since the 1950s numerous monographs have appeared: W. Skinner's *Chinese Society in Thailand;* the two volumes by W. E. Willmott, *The Chinese in Cambodia* and *The Chinese of Semarang: A Changing Minority Community in Indonesia;* E. Wickberg's *The Chinese in Philippine Life, 1850-1898;* H. Con et al., eds., *From China to Canada;* C. Coppel's *Indonesian Chinese in Crisis;* and J. Watson's *Emigration and the Chinese Lineage: The Mans in Hong Kong and London.* There are also several studies on the Chinese in Malaysia, in Singapore, and in Sarawak, and a few on the Chinese in New Zealand, Australia, and India. A very large number of scholars writing on the Asian American experience are also trained as scholars of China, Japan, Korea, India, and Southeast Asia. If one were to tabulate research done by scholars of Asian Studies on topics such as overseas communities and national political movements, themes of diplomatic history and immigration policies, and add related issues such as remittances and economic development, in addition to diaspora studies, a computer search would yield a hefty bibliography.

The need for Asian American scholars to be somewhat familiar with this research done by Asianists is two-fold. In terms of historical research, if any conclusions are to be reached regarding the specificity of the American experience, an understanding of immigration and settlement patterns as well as discrimination elsewhere would provide some comparative perspective. Is the racial discrimination experienced by Chinese Americans, for example, comparable to the discrimination faced by ethnic Chinese in Malaysia? The other impetus for greater attention to this research on the Asian diaspora arises from the present trends in immigration. "Second-phase immigration" among both Chinese Americans and Asian Indians is increasing (that is, immigration to the United States via prior residence in Southeast Asia, Africa, the Caribbean, or England). As of 1983, the Current Population Survey Ancestry Supplement indicated that only sixty-five percent of those with Asian Indian ancestry were immigrating directly from India; the remaining thirty-five percent were born in Trinidad, Guyana, Tobago, and the United Kingdom (Bachu 1984:10). Ignoring studies of the Asian diaspora, many of which deal with the history of Asians who were taken as indentured laborers to work on colonial plantations and mines, also raises questions about the class politics of Asian American Studies. Is the field so wrapped up in the myth of the model minority that it wants to distance itself from the history of those Asian Americans who do not migrate as professionals?

Scholars of Asian Studies, on the other hand, could benefit from dialogue with Asian American scholars working on race and ethnicity. Research in Asian Studies on subjects such as race, ethnicity, and identity is increasing in response to the powerful role these ideas are playing in political movements within Asia. Ethnic minorities within China such as Muslims and Tibetans, the Naga and Mizo people in India, and many other groups are questioning the cultural and political hegemony of various governments. The Dalit or "Downtrodden," as the Indian Untouchables prefer to be called, the Burakumi, and Koreans in Japan are actively involved in social and political struggles that draw on the literature and experience of similar struggles against racism elsewhere. The Dalit movement, for example, has consciously drawn on the Civil Rights Movement, the struggle of the African National Congress, and the Black

Panthers for inspiration (Joshi 1987:68). Struggles with a vision of social change are perhaps less hampered by national boundaries than academics who study these movements.

The International History of Asian American Studies: Remembering 1968

The 1968-1969 Third World strikes at San Francisco State and the University of California at Berkeley, which brought Asian American Studies programs to university campuses, are now part of the blurred history of the radical 1960s. For many, if not all, of the Asian American activists involved in the Third World student strikes in San Francisco and elsewhere, the international dimensions of what they were involved with were amply clear. Several of the articles in the collection *Roots: An Asian American Reader,* published in 1971 but consisting of various items dating from 1969 onward, clearly indicate this (see, for example, Odo et al. 1971:223-246).

Recent discussions of the origins of the Asian American Studies movement, however, have tended to focus only on the domestic context of the student protests and the establishment of Asian American Studies (for example, Lou 1988:157; Chan 1978:115; Endo and Wei 1988:6). At most there is some reference to the "wider movement for social change in American society" (Chan 1978:115). But surely that was not all there was to it? A movement for social change limited to these shores?

As all of us who lived through 1968 remember, the year marked the crest of a worldwide struggle against racism, against capitalism, against bureaucratic socialism, struggles which exploded with the escalation of the Vietnam War. Not only in San Francisco and Chicago and New York, but from London to Paris, from Prague to Berlin, from Warsaw to Rome, from Mexico City to Calcutta to Tokyo, students everywhere confronted governments and university administrators, and struggled for social reform. In Paris, student and worker protests erupted into street fighting and triggered the largest general strike in history. For two months, France was paralyzed and the government brought to its knees as almost 10,000,000 workers seized control of their workplaces (Stolze 1988:11).

It was no accident that everywhere these protests were led by students. The post-war economic boom (which was fizzling out in the late 1960s) had been associated with the baby boom. Compared to the pre-war period, the number of students in universities between 1950 and 1964 had tripled in France, doubled in West Germany, increased by sixty percent in Britain and fifty percent in Italy, and more than doubled in the United States (Stolze 1988:10). These students were no longer children from privileged ruling-class backgrounds. They came from lower middle-class and working-class families.

Many experienced intense alienation and intellectual turmoil as they were confronted with the sterile contents of a liberal arts curricula that followed prewar models of education and had been designed as an entry into ruling positions for privileged males (Anderson 1987:228).

Asian American Studies was very much a part of this movement for revision of curricula and a broader demand for educational reform. Drawing on the support of groups such as the Inter-collegiate Chinese for Social Action (ICSA) which sought to combine education with community activism in San Francisco Chinatown, the Asian-American Political Alliance, and other similar groups, the first courses on Japanese Americans and Chinese Americans were put together as part of the ethnic studies program at San Francisco State College (Lyman 1977:177-199). So the very genesis of Asian American Studies was international.

As the 1970s and 1980s progressed, Asian and Asian American histories became inexorably linked by the expansion of the "global assembly line" into Asia. When the first major symptoms of the post-war economic crisis became apparent in the 1960s and profits at home began to decline, many American manufacturers moved to the Third World in an attempt to increase profits by hiring cheap labor and setting up "export trade zones." Multinationals spread to Hong Kong and Taiwan first, then to South Korea and Mexico, and then to the Philippines, Singapore, and Malaysia, and now to Indonesia, India, Bangladesh, and Sri Lanka.

When workers in one area begin to organize for health and union benefits and a minimum wage, the multinationals can always move to another location where Third World governments are only too willing to accommodate them: "The manual dexterity of the Oriental female is famous the world over. Her hands are small, and she works fast with extreme care . . . Who, therefore could be better qualified by nature and inheritance, to contribute to the efficiency of a bench-assembly production line than the Oriental girl" coos a Malaysian government investment brochure (Fuentes and Ehrenreich 1984:16).

When the factories move in search of higher profits elsewhere, leaving thousands of workers without employment in economies which already have rampant inflation and unemployment, such as that of the Philippines, immigration offers the only hope of survival. The waiting list for immigration visas from the Philippines to the United States is now forty-two years long (Karnow 1989:13). Remittances from overseas relatives have become the sole means of survival for many families. There are over 1,000,000 Filipinos in the United States, over 400,000 in Saudi Arabia, Bahrain, and Kuwait, in addition to thousands of others in Hong Kong and Singapore. Together they send home an estimated $1,000,000,000 — an amount equal to one quarter of the earnings of the Philippines from exports (Karnow 1989:21).

The other legacy of the internationalization of the economic crisis has been the debt crisis of the Third World. As profits began to decline in the late 1960s, banks in the United States began to try and turn profits by providing loans to Third World countries under a variety of guises of promoting development. But, given the generally sluggish economy and faced with growing worker-peasant dissatisfaction in many of these Third World countries, the loans often went to buy arms for repression and strengthened the position of the ruling-class elites. The loans did not bring development; instead they brought inflation rates of over one hundred percent a month in many areas and enormous burdens of debt. Such circumstances eat up the revenues of governments and leave even less for social programs. The servicing of these debts in the Philippines, for example, consumes $28,000,000,000 annually, or forty percent of its earnings from exports (Karnow 1989:425). Political repression and impoverishment linked to the role of U. S. capitalism and militarism in the Third World have reshaped the direction of immigration to the United States—not only from Asia, but also from the Caribbean, Central America, and Latin America.

The existing textbook paradigm of American immigration history, which would have us believe that the first phase of mass immigration to the United States (1880-1920) was a matter of the huddled masses seeking "change and choice," who then lived happily ever after as newcomer and nation were transformed by assimilation (e. g., Kraut 1982), is clearly inadequate. But the need is not for a simple revision of American history that would accommodate those who were excluded in the first writing of this history, such as Asian Americans. The need is to define a new paradigm which contextualizes the history of Asian Americans within the twentieth-century global history of imperialism, of colonialism, and of capitalism. To isolate Asian American history from its international underpinnings, to abstract it from the global context of capital and labor migration, is to distort this history.

In conclusion, as one sees national barriers crumbling in Europe in the fall of 1989, with the common European currency and common European passport to be a reality in two years, one has to question the logic of turning to nationalist interpretations of history. Drawing boundaries and arbitrarily isolating the immigrants' history and culture of the homeland under the rubric of Asian Studies, and focusing only on his or her existence after arrival in the United States as shaped by the American context, assumes "America" could be understood independently of "Asia" or vice versa. This does not appear to be innovative methodology given international realities. As Eric Wolf writes:

> The habit of treating named entities such as Iroquois, Greece, Persia, or the United States as fixed entities opposed to one another by stable internal architecture and external boundaries interferes with our ability to understand their mutual encounter and confrontation... It is thus likely that we are dealing

with some conceptual shortcomings in our ways of looking at social and political phenomena, and not just a temporary aberration. We seem to have taken a wrong turn in understanding at some critical point in the past, a false choice that bedevils our thinking in the present" (Wolf 1982:7).

A more collaborative enterprise between Asian Studies and Asian American Studies, an attempt to forge new paradigms, would certainly go a long way in remedying this "false choice."

Notes

1. "Orient," literally the place in the heavens where the sun rises, became, as Edward Said has commented, part of the vocabulary of colonialism; the vast supine colonized world of Asia contrasted constantly with the virile and vigorous "Occident." See Said (1979) for further elaboration. Until fairly recently, the phrase "Oriental" Studies was used in American academia to designate what is now termed Asian Studies.
2. Many have forgotten the U. S. petroleum companies' scramble to Indonesia in 1965 where we "exported democracy" once more, funded a coup by pro-American generals which killed half a million Indonesians, and opened Indonesia to foreign investment. The continental shelf of Southeast Asia, the largest shelf with shallow waters, is also the world's largest deposit of petroleum.

References

Anderson, Margaret. 1987. "Changing the Curriculum in Higher Education." *Signs* 12 (2):222-254.
Asian American Political Alliance. 1971. "Asian Studies: The Concept of Asian Studies." In *Roots: An Asian American Reader,* edited by Amy Tachiki et al. Los Angeles: University of California Asian American Studies Center.
Asian Studies Newsletter. 1989. 34 (4).
Bachu, Amara. 1984. "South Asian Immigrant Women in the United States: A Statistical Overview." In *South Asian Women at Home and Abroad: A Guide to Resources,* edited by Jyotsna Vaid et al. Committee on Women in Asian Studies, Monograph Series No. 2. Maxwell Center, Syracuse University.
Bernal, Martin. 1988. *Black Athena: The Afro-Asiatic Roots of Greek Civilization.* New Jersey: Rutgers University Press.
Blauner, Robert. 1982. "Colonized and Immigrant Minorities." In *Classes, Power and Conflict,* edited by Anthony Giddens and David Held. Berkeley: University of California Press.
Bouvier, Leon F., and Anthony J. Agresta. 1985. "The Fastest Growing Minority." *American Demographics* (May):31-46.
Chan, Sucheng. 1978. "Contextual Frameworks for Reading Counterpoint." *Amerasia Journal* 5 (1):115-129.
Cohen, Paul A. 1979. *Discovering History in China.* New York: Columbia University Press.
Endo, Russell, and William Wei. 1988. "On the Development of Asian American Studies Programs." In *Reflections on Shattered Windows: Promises and Prospects for Asian American Studies,* edited by Gary Y. Okihiro et al. Pullman: Washington State University Press.

Espiritu, Yen Le, comp. 1988. *Amerasia Journal Index of Volumes 1-13, 1971-1987.* Los Angeles: University of California Asian American Studies Center.
Fairbank, John King. 1982. *Chinabound.* New York: Harper and Row.
Frazier, E. Franklin. 1971. "Behind the Masks." In *Race Awareness,* edited by Ruth Miller and Paul Dolan. New York: Oxford University Press.
Fuentes, Annette, and Barbara Ehrenreich. 1984. *Women in the Global Factory.* Boston: South End Press.
Gobineau, Arthur, comte de. 1971. "Races." In *Race Awareness,* edited by Ruth Miller and Paul Dolan. New York: Oxford University Press.
Hune, Shirley. 1977. *Pacific Migration to the United States.* Washington: Smithsonian Institution.
India West. Report on Survey of Asian American Legal Defence and Education Fund. January 5, 1990, 51.
Isaacs, Harold. 1972. *Images of Asia.* New York: Torchbook. Originally published as *Scratches on Our Minds: American Views of China and India.* New York: Harper and Row.
Jansen, Marius, ed. 1988a. *Japanese Studies in the United States.* Ann Arbor: Association of Asian Studies.
———. 1988b. "Japanese and Chinese Students Compared." In *Japanese Studies in the United States,* edited by Marius Jansen. Ann Arbor: Association of Asian Studies.
Joshi, Barbara, ed. 1987. "Perspectives on Dalit Political and Cultural Movements." *South Asia Bulletin* 7 (1/2):68-96.
Karnow, Stanley. 1989. *In Our Image: America's Empire in the Philippines.* New York: Random House.
Kim, Illsoo. 1986. "Asian Americans and the Economic Order." In *Dictionary of Asian American History,* edited by Hyung-chan Kim. Westport: Greenwood Press.
Kraut, Alan M. 1982. *The Huddled Masses.* Arlington Heights: Harlan Davidson.
Lou, Ray. 1988. "Virgin Land: Nineteenth Century Chinese American Social History." Review of *Chinese Gold: The Chinese in the Monterey Bay Region* by Sandy Lydon. *Amerasia Journal* 14 (2):157-161.
Lyman, Stanford. 1977. *The Asian in North America.* Santa Barbara: ABC Clio.
McCunn, Ruthann Lum. 1988. *Chinese Portraits.* San Francisco: Chronicle Books.
Melendy, H. Brett. 1981. *Asians in America.* New York: Hippocrene Books.
Miller, Ruth, and Paul Dolan, eds. 1971. *Race Awareness.* New York: Oxford University Press.
Odo, Franklin, Mary Uyematsu, Ken Hanada, Peggy Li, and Marie Chung. 1971. "The U. S. in Asia and Asians in America." In *Roots: An Asian American Reader,* edited by Amy Tachiki et al. Los Angeles: University of California Asian American Studies Center.
Okihiro, Gary Y., Shirley Hune, Arthur A. Hansen, John M. Liu, eds. 1988. *Reflections on Shattered Windows: Promises and Prospects for Asian American Studies.* Pullman: Washington State University Press.
Said, Edward. 1979. *Orientalism.* New York: Vintage Books.
Stolze, Ted. 1988. "1968 and Democracy from Below." *Against the Current,* n. s. 3 (4):9-13.
Tachiki, Amy, Eddie Wong, Franklin Odo, and Buck Wong, eds. 1971. *Roots: An Asian American Reader.* Los Angeles: University of California Asian American Studies Center.

Takaki, Ronald. 1989. *Strangers from a Different Shore.* Boston: Little, Brown and Company.
Wolf, Eric R. 1982. *Europe and the People without History.* Berkeley: University of California Press.

Part Two
Historical Aspects

Memories Compared, Lives Globalized

Hyung-chan Kim

The historical section of this anthology includes six essays. At first glance, the titles of these studies give the impression that they are not related to each other and that they deal with rather disparate historical topics. In some respects they are different from each other simply because they were written by six scholars whose academic interests vary widely. They are also different due to the fact that each of the various national or ethnic groups known collectively as the "Asian American minority" has accumulated varying experiences on the basis of its unique intraethnic community, social, and political dynamics as well as its historical relations with the larger white society. Nevertheless, two major themes run through these seemingly different essays.

The first centers around the idea that each ethnic community has its unique experiences accumulated through time and acted out in space by individuals whose lives have been irrevocably affected by them. One of the essential aspects of historical research, if it is to be meaningful, is to demonstrate how individual experience is intertwined with community collective experience, and how the individual derives life-meaning from the community. No man is an island, and therefore one's effort to draw life-meaning is inseparably related to how a person becomes part of a community either by means of assimilation or accommodation.

The second theme centers around the idea that much of the life-meaning the individual draws has been encoded in the collective experiences, either in the form of unwritten or indescribable memories of people or in the form of physical documents. It is the historian's task to decode and disrobe history of its disguised appearance for its true message.

The study by Renqiu Yu describes how certain members of the Chinese Anti-Imperialist Alliance of America developed their own definitions for terms such as "working class," "petty bourgeoisie," and "class struggle" and how these Marxist terms were understood by members of the Chinese Hand Laundry Alliance. Yu argues that the disparity which existed between the two groups in terms of their understanding of these concepts prevented them from working together for common goals. Before they could collaborate to accomplish their purposes in the New York Chinese community, they first had to develop a common ground in regard to concepts and language use. What Yu's historical analyses show us is that a vision for a better world could be shared by different groups with varying social and political background only if they could be integrated to understand concepts and language. Common understanding of their different worlds, therefore, paved the way for common struggle.

The study by Xin Liu deals with a different kind of integration. While Yu's study examined the integration of two Chinese groups with varying social backgrounds and interests within the New York Chinese community, Liu's research analyzes the integration of the Chinese immigrants into the polyethnic society of Hawaii. Liu argues against the commonly accepted concept of assimilation which, the author claims, does not apply to the Chinese immigrants in Hawaii because their experience is uniquely different. Chinese immigrants' adaptation to the polyethnic society of Hawaii has historically gone through three different patterns of orientation: intraethnic, extraethnic, and interethnic. These three hypothetical patterns are examined in the author's study on the founding and evolutionary development of the Palolo Chinese Home for the elderly. During the early period of the Home's development, Chinese immigrants showed a closer integration into the Chinese community's values, mainly consisting of filial piety and respect for the elderly. This close identity with Chinese traditional values may be considered as part of intraethnic adaptation. At a later stage of development, the Chinese immigrants in Hawaii evidenced their "Americanization," in that their value system showed a major change from the Confucian to the Christian orientation, thus suggesting extraethnic adaptation. However, the contemporary trend, influenced by the ethnic diversity of the residents of the Home, their native-born status, a relatively secure economic base supported by residents' social security payments, and their stable family life, points to an interethnic adaptation. Such an orientation shows that the Chinese immigrants have been truly integrated into the polyethnic society of Hawaii.

The study by Judy Yung goes beyond the physical and conceptual confines of local communities, the central focus of the previous two studies, although it also deals with social change and individual adaptation or integration resulting from being caught either voluntarily or involuntarily in its vortex. Individual adaptation to the rapid social change both in China and America from the 1900s to 1930s is the focus of this study. It shows how three Chinese immigrant women deeply touched by Western liberal ideas then sweeping through China came to America and transformed their own lives. In the process of "unbinding their feet," to adopt a metaphoric expression used by the author, they unbound not only their own lives, but also the lives of many other Chinese women and men who had been bound by their old traditional values of unequal status. Yung's study shows that social change in one corner of the world could have a revolutionary impact on another part of the globe, thereby suggesting the global nature of social change and its unique local characteristics as evidenced in the lives of these three women.

The next three essays are based on the individual and collective experiences of yet another ethnic group within the Asian American community, namely, the Japanese Americans. Peggy Choy focuses her attention on how the rhetoric used by both local newspapers in the community where Camp McCoy was located and by camp officials as reported by researchers, distorted the real intent behind the racial category that separated the Japanese American internees from the Japanese American soldiers serving in the 100th Battalion. While the internees were portrayed as "dangerous enemy aliens," or "Japs," the soldiers of the 100th Battalion were described as "Hawaiians" or "good Americans regardless of color." These two separate ways of categorizing the same racial group demonstrate that racial characterization is not rigidly fixed, but subject to change, particularly if the people being categorized put up a resolute struggle to redefine themselves.

Wendy Ng's study attempts to uncover the hidden meaning behind the collective memories of the Japanese Americans in the community of Hood River, Oregon, who were interned during World War II. Memory is another way of encoding messages based on the lived experiences of people, and therefore their real life-meaning can be unravelled only if historians know how to decode them through rigorous research. Because Issei people want to push unpleasant memories of incarceration out of their consciousness, their grandchildren, the Sansei, receive only filtered memories which tend to deflect the true meaning of what was actually experienced during those difficult times. Collective memory cements a community's past with its present and future, but, in this case, the filtered and therefore incomplete collective memory's process of cementing Sansei tends to develop a less-than-certain and stable identity.

A rather unique way of decoding the hidden life-meaning of Japanese Americans is suggested in Lee Hayakawa's study. His archival research demonstrates how important sources of information such as coroners' reports can be in studying problems associated with crimes of passions and anti-Anglo violence in the Japanese American community, as well as in studying the quality of their lives.

When the six essays are examined in light of the two themes identified and discussed above, the reader is provided with a perspective that enables one to understand Asian American experiences in comparative and global contexts. Whether or not the Chinese Americans' struggle to put down their roots in their new homeland can be compared with Japanese American efforts to survive in this hostile environment is not the issue. What is important for our own development both as members of the Asian American community and as scholars is the realization that although we have come from different places and have diverse backgrounds, we have all become part of this ethnic community. Even more importantly, our community of Asian Americans exists as part of a much larger and inclusive community of humankind—the global society. This sense of inclusiveness should be our ultimate realization.

To Merge with the Mass: Left-wing Chinese Students and Chinese Hand Laundry Workers in New York City in the 1930s

Renqiu Yu

From the 1860s to the 1940s, China sent tens of thousands of students to study in the United States. Some works have examined aspects of these students' experiences in the United States as well as the role of the returned students in modern China (La Fargue 1942; Wang 1966), but there are relatively few studies on the relationship between the Chinese students and working class Chinese Americans. This paper, based on the available Chinese materials, attempts to present a preliminary exploration of the meaning of the relationship between left-wing Chinese students and a group of Chinese hand laundry workers in New York City in the 1930s and 1940s. This paper argues that the students' efforts to merge with working-class Chinese Americans helped the latter group shift from a "sojourner" mentality to an identification with the settled society.

The left-wing Chinese students in the New York Chinese community of the 1930s discussed here were all born and grew up in China. They came to the United States to study in graduate school after finishing their college education at home. One of the leading members, Xu Yongying (Hsu Yungying), was a graduate of the class of 1924 of Qinghua School, a special school preparing Chinese students for study in the United States. While studying at Qinghua, Xu became an activist in the May Fourth student movement of 1919, and joined a political society, Weizhenghui, which advocated "sav[ing] China through political reform" *(Qinghua Daxue Shigao* 1981:78). Before coming to the United States in 1924, Xu and his friends went to Guangzhou to see Sun Yat-sen for his advice. Sun, the founder of the Republic of China, encouraged the young students to take part in the struggle to reform China (Shiji 1983:74).

These Chinese students joined the Kuomintang (KMT; the Nationalist Party) either in China or after coming to the United States, and they constituted the left wing within the KMT in the United States. In 1927, these left-wing Chinese students in the United States were shocked by the Kuomintang-Chinese Communist Party split and the reorientation of the KMT. They denounced the leader of the KMT right wing, Chiang Kai-shek, as a "traitor of the revolutionary cause," and renounced their KMT membership.

This small group of Chinese students founded a left-wing organization, the Chinese Anti-Imperialist Alliance of America (CAIA) in 1928, and soon published a radical biweekly Chinese language newspaper, *Xianfeng Bao* (the Chinese Vanguard), aimed at launching a movement among "overseas Chinese workers and peasants" to oppose the "reactionary policies" of the KMT (Lai 1976:67). However, they had little success in mobilizing and organizing Chinese Americans. The majority of the Chinese community was apathetic to their revolutionary preaching.

So, beginning in 1933, five years after the founding of the CAIA, these left-wing Chinese engaged in a serious and painful examination of the reasons for their failure. According to Xu Yongying, the students' basic problem was the "separation between the left and the overseas Chinese mass"; the left-wing Chinese engaged in abstract discussions on how to overthrow the capitalist system, but "became insensible to the daily sufferings that the mass was enduring." Therefore, they could not sense what the "mass" sensed, and thus became indifferent to the mass's demands for solutions to their everyday hardships.

In addition, Xu pointed out, the left-wing Chinese had a contemptuous attitude toward those to be "awakened" to revolutionary ideas. They condemned the "unawakened" as "stupid" and "anti-revolutionar[y]," and even labelled some of the poorest in the Chinese community as "capitalists" or "imperialists" because these people refused to accept their political views. "Then, of course," Xu concluded, "the mass condemned us as 'crazy' and 'mad' " (the Chinese Vanguard [New York], hereafter cited as CV, February 15, 1933, 4).

Why did the left-wing Chinese have such contempt for the mass? Xu pointed to their backgrounds as one of the reasons. Before they joined the CAIA, they were graduate students in universities and were actually part of the elite within the KMT. Xu Yongying himself was the editor of the *Guomin Ribao,* a KMT newspaper in San Francisco. His colleagues working for the Chinese Vanguard were also former KMT cadres (for example, Liu Kemian, member of the standing committee of the KMT Philadelphia branch; Zhao Yue, member of the executive committee of the same branch; Chen Huijian, chairperson of a trade union in San Francisco; and He Zhifeng, member of the standing committee of the KMT Chicago branch).

When they were in the KMT, Xu reflected, these students had separated themselves from ordinary Chinese Americans and "were rarely aware of the mass's painful struggle in everyday life. After they resigned from the KMT, they tried to merge with the mass. However, it [was] not easy for them to shake off the influences they were subject to within the KMT for so many years." Xu urged his fellow students to correct their mistake, to "overcome various difficulties, and merge with the mass [*zhoudao qunzhong zhong qu;* literally, "go into the mass"]" (CV, March 1, 1933, 4).

This kind of serious self-criticism led the left-wing Chinese students to pay more attention to the issues of the Chinese American communities. In the 1920s, these students had focused almost exclusively on China's domestic issues. Now the issues of the Chinese American community also became their concern. While attempting to approach working-class Chinese Americans, the Chinese students accepted the Marxist theory of class struggle and attempted to apply it to the reality of Chinatown. Here they encountered a problem: this theory simply did not seem to work.

From an orthodox Marxist point of view, the left-wing Chinese stressed that they should approach those of the working class employed in heavy industries. Then they found that the majority of the Chinese in the U.S. were "small craftsmen and small businessmen," such as hand laundrymen or store owners, who were considered "petty bourgeoisie." Before getting to know these "petty bourgeois" well, the left-wing Chinese students jumped to the conclusion that "although we should not overlook their revolutionary tendency, as a whole, the petty bourgeois often oscillate and lack determination in a struggle" (CV, October 1, 1933, 1).

This approach to classifying the Chinese American community reflected the Chinese left's dogmatic application of the Marxist theories. They seemed to have a permanent dilemma: how to approach and organize the Chinese proletariat. Since there were few Chinese industrial workers, as some of the Chinese left themselves recognized, they were never able to organize a proletarian organization which met their exacting sense of what a genuine proletarian organization should be. Frustrated, these students repeatedly discussed the same issue again and again in the pages of the Chinese Vanguard. From February 1933 to May 1934, there were at least a dozen articles discussing how to "work among the proletariat"; basically, these students wanted to approach the Chinese American proletariat, but could not find it.

Busy with their debate on the "overseas Chinese proletariat," and considering the Chinese hand laundry workers as "petty bourgeoisie" who lacked "revolutionary spirit," the left-wing Chinese were surprised by the emergence of the Chinese Hand Laundry Alliance (CHLA) in 1933, the first workers' organization founded by several hundred Chinese hand laundry workers on the East Coast.

The founding of the CHLA was described by a contemporary Chinese American as "a revolution in New York's overseas Chinese community" (Lei 1981). It marked an important development of the progressive, grass-roots forces in the Chinese community in the 1930s. Emerging in the following years as the largest occupational organization in the New York Chinese community, the CHLA became an influential force which challenged and weakened the dominance of the merchant elite establishment in Chinatown, and put much effort into improving the hand laundry workers' conditions.

However, when the Chinese hand laundry workers organized themselves to fight a discriminatory ordinance proposed by the city government—a yearly $25 licensing fee for all public laundries, plus a security bond of $1,000 *(Yilian Wuzhounian Tekan* 1938:44)—the left-wing Chinese basically ignored the organization. Even after the CHLA successfully won the case against the discriminatory ordinance, the Chinese left still did not think much of it (cf., CV, October 1, 1933, 1).

Interestingly, many hand laundry workers were actually inspired by the ideas of the left-wing through reading the Chinese Vanguard. As a radical Marxist publication boycotted in Chinatown by the KMT and established forces, its staff members had to distribute the paper by themselves. Sometimes they just gave free copies to the Chinese hand laundries or restaurants. One Chinese who later became a left-wing activist recalled how he was "enlightened" by the paper:

> There were several Chinese-language newspapers in New York City in the 1930's, such as *Shang Bao, Guomin Ribao,* and there was a left-wing paper too—*Xianfeng Bao* (the *Chinese Vanguard),* a bi-weekly. I hadn't found a job yet, so a lot of time I stayed home reading newspapers, and I found that *Xianfeng Bao* suited me fine. Through reading the newspaper, I began to understand some hows and whys, my mind became progressive, and gradually, I approached the people of *Xianfeng Bao* (Zhang 1981:327).

In dogmatically following the orthodox Marxist class analysis theory, however, the Chinese left failed to see the effect of their newspaper's influence among the hand laundry workers. One editor of the Chinese Vanguard even regarded distributing the paper to the small hand laundries as "choosing the easy way," and "working in the least difficult places." He believed that the left missed "the most important and at the same time the most difficult work" of distributing the paper to the Chinese proletariat in large factories, ships, and big restaurants (although he did not seem to know whether such a Chinese proletariat existed) (CV, October 1, 1933, 1).

Having no conception of service economy or immigrant economy ("ethnic economy"; cf., Tchen 1987:xxxi), concepts helpful in understanding class relations in American society, the Chinese left failed to understand that entrenched clan and family relationships distorted and complicated class relations in the

Chinese community. Furthermore, they did not pay much attention to the hand laundry workers' own ideas of their class status.

The basic difference between the Chinese left and the CHLA was that the majority of CHLA members, as hand laundry workers, never shared the Chinese left's vision of a proletarian revolution in the United States in which the Chinese Americans' fight against racial discrimination and class oppression constituted an integral part. The left was never successful in persuading CHLA members to accept their idea of class struggle. The Chinese hand laundry workers did not see themselves as part of the American "proletariat" or "working class," probably because of their painful memory of the anti-Chinese agitation of that class in the past, and their experience of being forced into the hand laundry business as a result of the Chinese exclusion acts and white workers' competition.

Nor did the hand laundry workers perceive themselves as "petty bourgeoisie" as the Chinese leftists saw them. Within the American context, if an immigrant regarded himself as a "petty bourgeois," he might think of himself as a would-be bourgeois. To a Chinese hand laundry worker under the severe restrictions of the Chinese exclusion acts and racial discrimination, the prospect was so bleak that he might never dream of becoming a would-be bourgeois in American society. The Chinese hand laundry workers saw themselves as a "poor laboring class" suffering from racial discrimination and economic exploitation, and they stood up to fight the city government to maintain their basic human dignity and a minimum living standard.

One year after the founding of the CHLA, the Chinese left found that they could no longer ignore its existence as the largest grass-roots occupational organization (with a membership of 3,000) in the Chinese community. They came to accept the hand laundry workers' self-definition as "poor laborers," and began to regard them as "the ally of the proletariat" (CV, April 15, 1934, 1). In the following years, the Chinese left extended help to the CHLA in its struggles against racial discrimination and economic oppression, and they became close allies in the Chinese salvation movement (cf., Kwong 1979:72-76).

With different political outlooks, the Chinese left and the CHLA were able to become allies because they communicated through the medium of a shared political language that was entirely Chinese in origin. The language that the Chinese left used in their dialogue with the CHLA was a language that both sides shared. In its columns, the Chinese Vanguard used such terms as "proletarian revolution" and "massive class struggle" to discuss the situation in Chinatown. However, in the left's exchanges with the CHLA, the terms were very different. Not "capitalist class," but "CCBA evil gentry and local despots [*Zhonghua Gongsuo Tuhaoliesheng*]." Not "proletariat," but "the poor laboring class [*Qiongcu laogong jieji*]," and "relying on the strength of the mass [*Yikao Qunzhong Liliang*]." These three terms, with distinct Chinese color, were widely used in China, especially in Guangdong Province, after the May Fourth student movement of 1919.

As immigrants from the radicalized Guangdong Province, the Chinese hand laundry workers were familiar with the revolutionary vocabulary used at that time. Even within the context of the Chinese American community, the term "evil gentry and local despots" seemed adequate to define the Chinatown elite, whose behavior, in the eyes of the hand laundry workers, was similar to that of landlords and local government officials in China. The term "poor laboring class," then, as ambiguous as it was in Chinese (including all lower class laborers) nevertheless helped the hand laundry workers find a name for their place in American society.

Although it was through the Chinese revolutionary vocabulary that the Chinese left was able to "merge with" and influence the Chinese hand laundry workers, the left nonetheless wanted to integrate the CHLA's struggle into the broad American working class movement. From such a point of view, they found the "sojourner mentality" of first-generation Chinese Americans a substantial obstacle. As Xu Yongying pointed out:

> Due to the restriction of the U.S. immigration laws, few overseas Chinese can obtain the [U.S.] citizenship, [most of them] do not have a normal family life. [Therefore,] most of them have no intention to settle [in this country] permanently; the majority are with the idea "to earn [a] few cents and return to China." The overseas Chinese feudal-capitalist class exploits this idea, and promoted and strengthens this idea through various clan and family organizations ... As a result, the starting point to arouse the [political] consciousness among overseas Chinese is the China issues, rather than the class struggle within the overseas Chinese community (CV, February 15, 1933, 3).

Xu emphasized that the Chinese left must start establishing a base among the "settled" overseas Chinese, i.e., those Chinese who were to settle in the United States permanently.

As part of its efforts to help the first-generation Chinese get rid of the "sojourner mentality," the Chinese left actively promoted a close relationship between the CHLA and some progressive American organizations. An opportunity came in October 1934, when the CHLA became engaged in a legal fight against a city government discriminatory ruling. When applying to obtain or renew their operating licenses, all Chinese hand laundry operators were required to submit their passport or other legal documents to prove their "legal entry" into the U.S. Since it was a public secret within the Chinese community that many Chinese hand laundry workers did not have such "legal papers," the ruling was interpreted by the community as another attempt to destroy the "community lifeline" – the hand laundry business. The Chinese left came to the aid of the CHLA and encouraged it to "coalesce with all mass organizations of Chinese and Americans, such as the CAIA and the International Labor Defense," to abolish the discriminatory ruling (cf., CV, October 14, 1934, 3, and October 20, 1934, 3).

It was through the help of the Chinese left that the CHLA established its contacts with some progressive organizations outside of Chinatown, such as the American Friends of the Chinese People and the International Labor Defense. This was a significant development. Relations with American organizations were one of the positive factors that facilitated the Chinese community's shift from "sojourners" to "settlers."

Later, in the Chinese American salvation movement during the 1930s and 1940s, the left-wing Chinese abandoned their militant class-struggle stand and merged with ordinary Chinese Americans. Xu Yongying and He Zhifeng became editors of the *China Daily News,* a New York-based Chinese language newspaper funded mainly by the CHLA. They helped shape a "Chinese American consciousness" for the first-generation Chinese, one that maintained Chinese culture and concerned itself with the fate of China, while simultaneously identifying the United States as "home."

In the process of "merging with the mass," it is worth noting that left-wing Chinese students gradually developed an emotional tie with ordinary Chinese Americans. Let me end by quoting from Mr. C., an acquaintance of Xu Yongying and a veteran CHLA member, whom I interviewed in February 1988:

> Mr. Xu Yongying was a very nice guy. I respected him a lot. He was from Shanghai, a *liuxuesheng* [overseas Chinese student]. How did we communicate with each other? Well, he learned Cantonese. He managed to talk in broken Cantonese. He was very honest and hard-working. He always had trouble making a living. He once worked as a waiter in Chinatown but soon lost that job. Then he went to 125th Street to polish shoes for people to make a few dollars. He never had any money. Sometimes he would ask me, "Hey, Old Horse (my nickname)," give me a quarter. I have no money to go home." I would give him a quarter. Life was tough for him. But he always worked hard. He was a sincere man. He . . . had an emotional identity with the Cantonese community. He later went back to China and became the Head of the Bureau for Foreign Affairs in Shanghai People's Government. Then he had cancer. He said, I would die soon. Before I die, I would like to go to Taishan to live for a while. I have so many friends from Taishan, how could I die without living in their hometown for some time? So he went to Taishan and lived there for two or three months. Soon after he returned to Shanghai, he died. He died in the 60's.

Note

The author wishes to express gratitude to Mr. Him Mark Lai for providing valuable materials and for his critical comments.

References

[Chinese Vanguard] *Xianfeng Bao*. Biweekly newspaper, New York.
Huaqiao Shi Lunwen Ji [Essays on Overseas Chinese History, vol. 2]. 1981. Guangzhou: Ji'nan University.
Kwong, Peter. 1979. *Chinatown New York, Labor and Politics, 1930-1950.* New York: Monthly Review Press.
La Fargue, Thomas E. 1942. *China's First Hundred.* Pullman: State College of Washington Press. (Reprinted in 1987 by Washington State University Press, as *China's First Hundred: Educational Mission Students in the United States, 1872-1881.*)
Lai, Him Mark. 1976. "A Historical Survey of the Chinese Left in America." In *Counterpoint: Perspectives on Asian America,* edited by Emma Gee et al. Los Angeles: University of California Asian American Studies Center.
Lei, Zhuofeng. 1981. "1933-nian Niu Yue Huaren Xiyiguan Lianhehui chengli qianhou [Before and after the establishment of the Chinese Hand Laundry Alliance of New York in 1933]." Oral history interview. In *Huaqiao Shi Lunwen Ji*, vol. 2, 333-339.
Qinghua Daxue Shigao [A History of Qinghua University]. 1981. Beijing: Zhonghua Shuju.
Shiji. 1983. "Shihuang." In *Qinghua Xiaoshi Congshu (Renwuzhi I).* Beijing: Qinghua University Press.
Tchen, John K. W. 1987. Introduction to *The Chinese Laundryman: A Study of Social Isolation,* by Paul Siu. New York: New York University Press.
Wang, Y. C. 1966. *Chinese Intellectuals and the West.* Chapel Hill: University of North Carolina Press.
Yilian Wuzhounian Tekan [The Chinese Hand Laundry Alliance Fifth Anniversary Special Bulletin]. 1938. New York: Chinese Hand Laundry Alliance.
Zhang, Manli. 1981. "Lu Mei guiqiao, qian Meizhou Huaqiao Ribao she yewuzhuren Zhang Manli Xiansheng fangwen lu [Record of an interview of a Chinese returned from America: Mr. Zhang Manli, former business manager of the *China Daily News* of New York]." In *Huaqiao Shi Lunwen Ji,* vol. 2, 322-332.

The Founding and Development of the Palolo Chinese Home, 1917-1988: A Case Study of Chinese Integration in Hawaii

Xin Liu

Introduction

Deep in the Palolo Valley in Honolulu, there is an adult residential care home called the Palolo Chinese Home. The history of the home can be traced back to 1917. At the turn of the twentieth century, many aged and indigent Chinese laborers, fending for themselves, lived in Honolulu's poor tenement districts. In an effort to help these men, secular leaders joined forces with Christian ministers, the United Chinese Society, the Associated Charities of Hawaii, and the Territorial Legislature; and the Palolo Chinese Home was opened in 1920. Licensed by the State of Hawaii Department of Health as an adult residential care home, the Palolo Chinese Home is now open to all regardless of race, religion, or sex. This paper examines Chinese immigrant integration into the polyethnic society of Hawaii through a case study of the historical and contemporary Palolo Chinese Home.

Immigrant integration has been studied by many scholars, and one of the key related concepts is assimilation. Reflecting national trends until the 1960s, assimilation theory was favored by most scholars of Hawaii's race relations (Wittermans 1980-1981:156). During the 1960s and 1970s, however, several views of ethnic pluralism began to appear in the literature. One scholar who challenged the conception of assimilation was Lucie Cheng Hirata.

> Given a polyethnic society, the adaptation of immigrants takes on a different pattern. Since there is a lack of an ethnically homogeneous core to serve as the point of reference for immigrants, the concept of assimilation is less applicable than in a situation where a predominant core exists. The assimilation continuum is here reconceptualized as a set of three patterns of integration: intraethnic, interethnic and extraethnic, all of which are stable modes of

adaptation. The intraethnic pattern refers to the complete absorption of the immigrant by his ethnic community; the extraethnic pattern refers to complete absorption by a community or communities other than one's own ethnic community; and the interethnic pattern refers to the situation where the immigrant is simultaneously integrated into his own ethnic community and the community or communities of other ethnic groups (Hirata 1971:3).

Based on five years' living experience in Hawaii, I believe that cultural pluralism is the more realistic interpretation of various immigrants' cultural and social lives. Therefore, this study will utilize Lucie Cheng Hirata's three patterns of integration as guidelines in interpreting the historical and contemporary Palolo Chinese Home and, in so doing, test the validity of her theory in this instance.

The Founding of the Palolo Chinese Home

Filial piety and respect for the elderly are among the pillars of traditional Chinese society. According to these social norms, older people should be respected and indigent ones sheltered. This cultural heritage played an important role in generating the turn-of-the-century Chinese community's response to the needs of poor elderly Chinese men; it was the motivation for early Chinese immigrants societies (such as district associations, surname societies, and secret societies) as they developed welfare programs to help the elderly. In fact, some societies were founded partially to address the needs of the indigent elderly. Many societies provided shelter and subsistence for their aged, indigent members. The See Dai Doo Society, for example, a district association organized in 1901 in Honolulu, maintained an apartment house for its poor and aged members.

Practically speaking, it was an economical and wise investment for an aged bachelor to have joined an organization when he was in his youth. New members of the See Dai Doo, for example, paid a one-time fee of three dollars. This money could be regarded as a kind of old-age insurance policy; when the See Dai Doo member became old, incapacitated, and unemployed, he could ask to live on the society's premises without worrying about his rent. The society would apply to one of the local welfare agencies for financial aid on his behalf. If he wanted to return to China, the members would help him do so. If he died in Hawaii, the society would take care of some of his funeral and burial expenses if none of his relatives claimed the body. His remains could be subsequently exhumed and sent back for reburial in his ancestral village. Hence, the society functioned as a surrogate family for an elderly bachelor (Lee 1941:19).

The opening of the Wai Wah Yee Yuen, or Chinese Hospital, in Honolulu in 1897 is another example of concern for the elderly among local Chinese immigrants who cherished the tradition of filial piety. In 1896, a petition signed by 327 of the leading Chinese inhabitants was submitted to the legislature. It asked for a grant of land "in or near Honolulu" upon which the United Chinese Society could build "a hospital for the care of the sick and also in connection therewith a home for the aged, infirm and helpless Chinese." Land in the Palama section of Honolulu was given and a fund-raising campaign was initiated. With $1,950 donated by the China Engine Company, and other money contributed by the United Chinese Society and some other Chinese and Caucasian residents, the hospital opened in 1897 (Glick 1980:243).

Despite the efforts by Chinese societies to take care of their indigent elderly, there were actually far more needy members than most could afford to support. The *Annual Report of the Associated Charities of Hawaii* of 1917 shows that 220 resident single men applied for relief that year. Among more than a score of nationalities, 108 (or 49 percent) were Chinese *(Annual Report of the Associated Charities of Hawaii* 1971:5). The growing number of elderly Chinese men in desperate need of help thus prompted the Associated Charities to seek to alleviate this problem. The first steps taken were the appointment of a special committee in 1917 headed by the Chinese consul and the addition to the Associated Charities staff of a Chinese worker, Mrs. E. E. Goo, who later became the first administrator of the Palolo Chinese Home. By 1920, the Associated Charities, with the support of prominent members of the local Chinese community, had raised $10,000 to purchase the former Gospel Mission Home—fifteen acres and six buildings—in Palolo Valley. This property was remodelled and opened in 1920 as the Palolo Chinese Home (Catton 1959:45-46). The close linkage between the association and the home can be seen in the annual reports of the Associated Charities. The first eight men moved into the home in November 1920, and, almost every year thereafter, updated information about the home, along with its financial statement, was included in these reports. The link between the home and the Associated Charities of Hawaii (later the Social Service Bureau) accounts for its success in avoiding serious financial troubles. Included among the major welfare institutions of Honolulu, it has grown and developed with the larger society.

The Home from the 1920s to the 1970s

Since its foundation, the host country's culture, the oversight of charitable organizations, and particularly the role of the United States government, have had a significant impact upon the development of what has been since its foundation a mainstream social welfare institution. Structurally speaking, the home has become increasingly Americanized, and this tends to prove the validity of the assimilation theory. Nevertheless, focusing on the lives of the residents at the home, a different picture emerges: the persistence of the Chinese immigrants' culture as it has mingled with cultures of other ethnic groups. Thus, as a one-dimensional assimilation theory is inapplicable in this case, Hirata's three patterns of integration appear to have more validity.

Charitable Organizations and the Palolo Chinese Home

Honolulu was one of the pioneers in establishing a general financial campaign to support the city's welfare institutions. The first United Welfare Campaign was conducted in 1919, the year the Associated Charities became a charter member of the United Welfare Fund. Since then a campaign to support welfare institutions has been a yearly undertaking *(Teacher's Manual of the United Welfare Fund* 1926:5-6).

The Palolo Chinese Home was administered by the Associated Charities of Hawaii, or its successors, until 1941, when it became an autonomous agency under its own board of directors, the majority of whom were of Chinese ancestry (Catton 1959:45-46). One distinctive impact of the Associated Charities of Hawaii upon the home was the practice of social casework. At the Palolo Chinese Home, records of more than 300 closed cases have been preserved. A representative case covers in great detail the time when the subject came to Hawaii, his plantation work experience, his link with Chinese societies, the first time he asked for assistance from the Associated Charities, his changing attitudes toward entering the Palolo Chinese Home, and his later life there. It also shows the level of care at the home and certain aspects of life there. The description of each man's life is the most important part of the record because each of the more than 300 closed cases found at the home is unique in its own way. This not only makes the study of the history of the home most fascinating, but also displays the application of the techniques of modern social case work—treating each resident as a separate entity, and, consistent with Western cultural values, underscoring a focus on the individual.

Impact of the U. S. Government Policy toward Aging

Until comparatively recent times, support for the aged has been a private concern, shouldered by families, ethnic and religious groups, and other voluntary and charitable organizations. The late nineteenth century represented a major turning point, however, as the problems of the aged became increasingly a public concern. The U. S. Congress finally passed the Social Security Act in 1935 (Ward 1984:309). Old-age assistance had a direct impact upon the home's admission policy. When the home was basically a charitable institution financed by private donations, its policy was oriented simply toward admitting homeless and penniless old Chinese men. However, as it came to depend more and more upon the government for financial support, it gave preference to those applicants who could qualify for financial aid from the various governmental agencies (Tan 1967:39). Moreover, as the major financial supporter of the home, the United States government also assumed increasing regulatory and administrative control.

The home was also strongly influenced by Christian values, practices, and organizations. In its files we find that Easter and Christmas were celebrated and that "the pastors of the Chinese Christian Churches came in to offer voluntary worship services and pastoral guidance" (Feng n.d.:5). Nevertheless, compared with the larger trend of Christianization outside, the home in the 1930s remained less "conquered" by Christianity. Among more than 300 closed cases, we find that only two residents were Christians at the time they entered the home and only one was converted to Christianity after he was admitted. This reality had much to do with the strong emphasis on things Chinese, which was and has remained a unique feature of the home.

Preservation of Things Chinese at the Palolo Chinese Home

The local Chinese have always been proud of the fact that they were the first in the United States to help found a care-home for indigent Chinese immigrants. They have tried everything within their means to support the home, both financially and morally, including fund drives for new buildings. Money, food, clothes, cigarettes, and Chinese magazines have been regularly donated as well. The link between the local Chinese community and the home tells us at least two things. First, the home was considered part of the community and its residents were members of the larger Chinese "family." Neglecting the old members of the "family" was a disgrace to the whole community, which felt obliged to support the home and take care of its residents. Secondly, the home was an embodiment of Chinese culture where traditional values and customs were observed. It was a place with which the local Chinese could identify and thereby perpetuate their cultural values and customs. Consequently, the link itself enhanced the persistence of the immigrants' culture in the home.

Deeper insight into this issue of cultural persistence can be gained by examining the values and beliefs, as well as aspects of the daily lives, of the home's residents. Among the early residents, there was a strong sense of Chinese patriotism. During the Sino-Japanese War, the records of the Honolulu police department in 1939 indicate that the only fight about the war was not between a Chinese and a Japanese, but between two inmates of the Chinese old men's home. One radical among them ventured the opinion that China's management of the war was not all it might have been. Another resented this as sacrilege, and resented it so furiously that the police had to be called in (Burrows 1970:50-51).

One day in August 1945, when the old men at the home heard that the Allies had won the war and Japan had surrendered, they were so excited that they could not sleep. Collecting $154, they intended to buy firecrackers to celebrate the victory. However, because these were illegal, they instead gave the money to the Chinese Relief Association for children in Guangdong Province, from which most of the immigrants in Hawaii had come *(New China Daily Press,* August 16, 1945, 4).

Many cases found in the home files show that the early residents did not believe in Western medicine—in seeing a doctor, going to the hospital, or, especially, in having an operation on any part of one's body. All they believed in was Chinese medicine.

In addition, the majority of the early Chinese immigrants to Hawaii were men without families. When they became old, as we have seen, many turned to their societies for help. These societies functioned as their extended families. As ashamed as they already were because they were childless, they rejected the idea of going to a culturally unfamiliar institutional care home. That was why it was very hard to persuade any of them to enter the home when it was first founded. Only the most destitute or the weakest ones ended up in Palolo.

Most early residents were first-generation immigrants. They did not understand English, never went to an American school, and were always segregated from the host society either on the plantations or later in Chinatown. Only familiar with Chinese language, music, medicine, and food, they led their lives in a Chinese way, even when they were in an Americanized institution. However, as Chinese as they were, they were by no means entirely cut off from other ethnic groups, with whom in a very limited way they did intermingle. Only when the island-born Chinese entered the home, however, did the picture begin to change significantly.

The Contemporary Home

Statistics compiled by the writer in December 1987 (see Table One) suggest four major changes in the home since those early days. The first and most important is the diversity of the present home. There are women as well as men, and residents of varying ethnic backgrounds. They speak different languages and belong to different religions. Secondly, more than 60 percent of the residents were born in the United States, making them very different from the first-generation immigrants. Thirdly, the majority of the residents were or are married and have families or children. They made their own choice to enter the home rather than to stay with their children. Finally, as most residents receive Social Security payments from the government, a charitable organization (the Aloha United Way) now plays a very small role (less than 4 percent of the home's budget) in financial support.

According to 1987 statistics, 17 percent of the home's residents are married, and many of them are parents. Women constitute 45.7 percent of residents. The fact that many of them chose to leave their own children and stay at the Palolo Chinese Home reflects the changed attitudes among island-born Chinese toward the concept of family and institutional care facilities like the Palolo Chinese Home.

In traditional Chinese society, great emphasis was placed by Confucius and his disciples on the importance of the family. As a result, respect for family and parents has become the central feature of Chinese civilization (Lang 1946:9). By contrast, in America, the family as an institution exists mainly to provide an environment in which the individual can be brought up and trained to go out into the world as a full member of society. When the children reach adulthood, there is usually, in many respects, a breakup of the family (Baker 1979:26). Children with their own goals put their interests above those of their families.

Island-born Chinese have been influenced by the American conception of the family. "I chose to enter the home, because I don't want to be a burden to my children who have their own careers and lives," one resident insisted. It is apparent that later residents enter the home with attitudes quite different from those of early residents, who felt great shame at ending up in a care home. For the island-born Chinese, living in a care home in one's advanced years has become a culturally sanctioned practice.

Of the contemporary residents, over fifty percent are Christians. Although their parents might not have been practicing Christians, their early education, often in Catholic or Protestant schools, had a strong and lasting impact upon their religious beliefs. Like food, water, and other daily necessities, religion has become an essential need for them. The home, supported by community religious groups, provides them with many opportunities to fill this need.

Unlike early residents, who had a strong belief in Chinese medicine, very few residents now go to see traditional Chinese doctors or take Chinese herbs. Many residents say that they once used *zhong yao* (Chinese for "herbs") when they were young because their parents asked them to do so. "I wouldn't mind taking herbs now when I get sick," one resident maintains. "They work on me." While Chinese medicine is quite familiar to most residents and while they still believe in its effectiveness, it is no longer used. The attitude toward surgery has also changed. Since it was not acceptable to sever any part from one's body, surgery was never developed in ancient China, and some early residents of the home resisted undergoing any surgery. Now, residents have no hesitation in accepting needed surgery. They have totally accepted the host country's methods of medical treatment.

As Westernized as they might be, island-born Chinese still exhibit many Chinese traits. About fifty-one percent of the residents are bilingual. Most island-born Chinese residents can speak both Cantonese and English because their parents sent them to Chinese language schools when they were young. For some residents, Chinese filial piety remains a meaningful concept. One male resident keeps a list of the names of his relatives in China. Before each Chinese New Year, he mails ten dollars to each of his relatives, although he has never seen many of them who live in China. "This is filial piety. Right here," he says. When the writer was about to go back to China for a visit, he insisted on giving her a red packet with money in it. It was once a Chinese custom to give friends or relatives money when they were going on a trip. He maintains the custom today although it is not now commonly practiced in many parts of China.

Many local Chinese organizations and individuals still donate money or gifts to the Palolo Chinese Home and regard their annual visits to it as their major charitable service each year. They associate the home with their Chinese cultural heritage and their ethnic group identity. Even the architecture at the home reinforces the impression that it is still a place solely for Chinese. Arriving by car, one first sees some Chinese characters meaning "CARE HOME FOR OVERSEAS CHINESE" on the wall of the dining room. Above the roof of the women's building, there is a symbol of the Chinese character *shou*, meaning "longevity." The home has curved roofs that follow the lines of a pagoda (so that the bad spirits will slide down and then up again, to be blown away). Throughout the home, the colors green, red, and yellow are used generously because among the Chinese green stands for growth, red for good luck, and yellow for long life.

In the 1970s, the first Japanese male was admitted to the home and the first Filipino secretary was hired. Gradually, the home changed from a culturally homogeneous place to a multiethnic care home facility. As one of the staff commented: "There is a little bit of everything."

Demographically, there are now not only Chinese, but also Japanese, Vietnamese, Caucasians, Hawaiians, and Filipinos. The food is more cosmopolitan than it once was. It varies from Chinese jook and Hawaiian poi with fish, to Italian spaghetti and Japanese sushi. Holidays of different ethnic groups are celebrated at the home: Chinese New Year, the Moon Festival, Christmas, Thanksgiving Day, Halloween, Valentine, and Japanese Lantern Day, for example. Outside recreational groups visiting the home no longer come only from the local Chinese community. "We have not only the Chinese 'Longevity' dance, but also the Hawaiian 'hula', Mexican folk dances, and traditional Japanese dances," says the activity program director. "When residents go out, they go to all kinds of activities, not limited to things of Chinese style." In short, the current milieu of the home, both inside and outside, is much broader than it was before. It is more open and more cosmopolitan. When people of different ethnic backgrounds live together, it is very difficult to draw a clear-cut line between American and Oriental cultures. More often than not, what one sees is the blending of different cultural traits. Due to the nature of the blending, it is not easy to generalize about the residents.

Conclusion

During the 1880s and 1890s, Chinatown life (in Honolulu) "was dominated by activities and organizations meeting the needs and wishes of sojourner immigrant men" (Glick 1980:136). Unlike other Chinese organizations, the Palolo Chinese Home is a product of the combined efforts of both the Chinese and the host community in Hawaii. Located far from Chinatown, the home's history reveals a different perspective on early Chinese immigrants' integration. On one hand, the home's founding was an early effort by Chinese immigrants to adapt to, and thus to integrate in some measure into the larger American society when the aged Chinese became a problem beyond the ability of Chinese societies to solve. It reflects a shift in the immigrants' reliance upon welfare programs provided only by local Chinese organizations to more dependable ones supported by institutions of the host country. Thus the home, from its very beginning, has been part of the mainstream of welfare institutions.

The lifestyles of the residents in this little 'Chinatown," however, showed a strong emphasis on things Chinese. Most early residents were first-generation immigrants and theirs was a Chinese way of life even though they were in an "Americanized" institution. Regarding the home as part of the community and a symbol of their cultural tradition, the local Chinese not only tried hard to support it financially, but identified it with their culture and the preservation of things Chinese. This linkage enhanced the persistence of the immigrants' culture.

In the current home, things Chinese are still quite visible. The architecture, the use of Cantonese, a belief in "Chinese manners," celebration of the Chinese Moon Festival and New Year, and most importantly, many new residents and nurses' aids from China, all make one aware of its strong ethnic flavor. In terms of its population, languages, religions, values, and food, however, the home is much more diversified and cosmopolitan. Even among the island-born Chinese, we see "Chinese" ethnic traits manifested in an inconsistent way. In contrast to the first-generation residents, the island-born Chinese have been strongly affected by the tug of war between Chinese and Western cultural values. Thus, a blending of cultures would be a better way to describe the home.

That the integration of the Palolo Chinese Home has involved extraethnic, intraethnic, and interethnic directions does not validate assimilation theory;

it suggests rather that in the case of the home, Hirata's three patterns of integration are more applicable.

Table One
Population of the Palolo Chinese Home,
December 1987

Number of Residents			
Male	38		54.3%
Female	32		45.7%
Total	70		100.0%
Ethnicity			
Chinese	53	(24m, 29f)	75.7%
Japanese	10	(9m, 1f)	14.3%
Vietnamese	2	(1m, 1f)	2.9%
Caucasian	2	(1m, 1f)	2.9%
Hawaiian	2	(2m)	2.9%
Filipino	1	(1m)	1.4%
Language			
Chinese (only)	17	(3m, 14f)	24.3%
English (only)	14	(8m, 6f)	20.0%
Vietnamese	2	(1m, 1f)	2.9%
Japanese (only)	1	(1f)	1.4%
Bilingual	36	(26m, 10f)	51.4%
Birthplace			
U.S.A.	43	(27m, 16f)	61.4%
Foreign	26	(9m, 17f)	37.1%
Unknown	1	(1m)	1.4%
Religion			
Protestants	29	(14m, 15f)	41.4%
Buddhists	12	(3m, 9f)	17.1%
Catholics	7	(5m, 2f)	10.0%
Mormons	1	(1m)	1.4%
None	11	(8m, 3f)	15.7%
Unknown	10	(7m, 3f)	14.3%
Marital Status			
Married	12	(10m, 2f)	17.1%
Widowed	32	(9m, 23f)	45.7%
Divorced	5	(3m, 2f)	7.1%
Separated	1	(1m)	1.4%
Single	20	(15m, 5f)	28.6%
Source of Income			
Soc. Security	57	(35m, 22f)	81.4%
Private	10	(2m, 8f)	14.3%
Both	3	(1m, 2f)	4.3%

References

Annual Report of the Associated Charities of Hawaii. 1971.
Baker, Hugh D. R. 1979. *Chinese Family and Kinship.* New York: Columbia University Press.
Burrows, Edwin G. 1970. *Hawaiian Americans: An Account of the Mingling of Japanese, Chinese, Polynesian, and American Cultures.* Hamden, Connecticut: Archon Books.
Catton, Margaret M. L. 1959. *Social Service in Hawaii.* California: Pacific Books.
Feng, Lillian W. M. n.d. "Palolo Chinese Home: An Institution for the Aging in Hawaii." Unpublished manuscript.
Glick, Clarence E. 1980. *Sojourners and Settlers: Chinese Migrants in Hawaii.* Honolulu: Hawaii Chinese History Center and The University Press of Hawaii.
Hirata, Lucie Cheng. 1971. "Immigrant Integration in a Polyethnic Society." Ph.D. dissertation, UCLA.
Lang, Olga. 1946. *Chinese Family and Society.* New Haven: Yale University Press.
Lee, Evelyn. 1941. n.d. "The Role of Chinese Organizations in Relation to Social Work." Unpublished manuscript.
New China Daily Press. August 16, 1945.
Tan, Binky. 1967. *Role-Taking and Role-Making.* M.A. thesis (sociology), University of Hawaii.
Teacher's Manual of the United Welfare Fund. 1926. School Committee of the United Welfare Fund of Honolulu.
Ward, Russell A. 1984. *The Aging Experience: An Introduction to Social Gerontology.* New York: Harper and Row.
Wittermans, Elizabeth. 1980-1981. "Inter-Ethnic Relations in Hawaii." *Social Process in Hawaii* 28:165.

Unbinding the Feet, Unbinding Their Lives: Chinese Immigrant Women in San Francisco, 1902-1931

Judy Yung

Women's emancipation was heralded in San Francisco's Chinatown on the afternoon of November 2, 1902, when Sieh King King (Xue Jinqin), an 18-year-old foreign student and ardent reformer, stood before a theater full of men and women and gave one of the eloquent orations for which she was renowned.

Sieh King King had grown up and attended missionary school in the treaty port of Shanghai, where she and other reformers were heavily influenced by Western contact. In 1901, she had delivered a stirring speech before 500 people in Shanghai in which she protested the Chinese government's intention to grant Russia special rights in Manchuria after the Boxer Rebellion failed. But in San Francisco, according to newspaper accounts, she "boldly condemned the slave girl system, raged at the horrors of foot-binding and, with all the vehemence of aroused youth, declared that men and women were equal and should enjoy the privileges of equals" *(San Francisco Chronicle,* November 3, 1902). Her talk and her views on women's rights were inextricably linked with the 1898 Reform movement in China, which advocated that China emulate the West and modernize in order to throw off the yoke of foreign domination. Elevating women's status to the extent that they could become educated mothers and productive citizens was part of the larger reform effort to modernize, strengthen, and defend China against further imperialist encroachment (for a fuller account of the Reform movement and women's emancipation in China, see Chesneux, Bastid, and Bergere 1976; Beahan 1976).

Sieh King King's speech evidently made an impact upon her audience; one newspaper reported that women listened "like zealots" and men "with every sign of approval." And later that evening, in a banquet held in her honor, women were allowed for the first time to sit in the main banquet hall and enjoy the same food as the men. A year later, Sieh King King again "expounded her views on the role of Chinese women and the need to abolish outdated Chinese customs and emulate the West," this time to an exclusively female audience of 200 *(San Francisco Chronicle,* November 3, 1902; *San Francisco Examiner,* November 2, 1902; *Chung Sai Yat Po,* October 12, 1903).

After that, she was not mentioned again in the local English- or Chinese-language newspapers. But her views remained alive in the *Chung Sai Yat Po* (Chinese American Daily Paper), a Chinese newspaper widely read by the Chinese in America. Started by Presbyterian minister Ng Poon Chew in 1900, *Chung Sai Yat Po* was heavily influenced by nationalism and Christianity. The newspaper favored reform in China and advocated equal rights for all Chinese Americans (Lai 1987:31; Hoexter 1976: chapter 12).

What Sieh King King advocated on behalf of Chinese women—unbound feet, equal rights, education, and public participation—remained for the next three decades at the heart of social change for Chinese women. This was due largely to the continuous influence of nationalism and women's emancipation in China, the work of Protestant missionary women in Chinatown, and outside-the-home socioeconomic opportunities that opened up to immigrant women. By 1931, immigrant women had made considerable progress toward freeing themselves of social restrictions and moving into the public light. Footbinding was no longer practiced, prostitution had been eradicated, and a substantial number of women were working outside the home, educating themselves and their daughters and playing a more visible role in community affairs. This discussion of the lives of Chinese immigrant women from 1902, when Sieh King King introduced her feminist views in San Francisco, to 1931, the beginnings of the Great Depression in the United States and of Japanese aggression in Manchuria, will illustrate how socioeconomic developments in China and the United States facilitated the unbinding of their feet and of their lives.

From Guangdong to San Francisco

At the time of Sieh King King's speech, China was still suffering under the stranglehold of Western imperialism and the inept rule of the Manchus. Life for most Chinese was disrupted and survival precarious. Consequently, despite the exclusion laws and anti-Chinese hostilities in America, able-bodied peasants in Southeast China continued to migrate overseas. And as increased numbers of Chinese sojourners here became settlers, some found the means by which to send for their wives or to establish families in America. Approximately twelve percent of Chinese immigration during the exclusion period consisted of women (mostly wives of merchants or United States citizens) as compared to three percent prior to the Chinese Exclusion Act of 1882 (these percentages were computed from immigration statistics in Chen 1980:201; Coolidge

1909:502; and Kung 1973:101). By the early 1910s, Western influence and manufacturing in China had taken hold in the treaty ports and had to a large extent transformed the lives of women employed there, but most women immigrating to America were coming directly from the villages of Guangdong Province where traditional roles of Chinese women still prevailed.

Among these women were Law Shee Low and Wong Ah So, who both emigrated as obedient daughters to escape poverty at home. In Law's case, her family succumbed to poverty after repeated visits of roving bandits in the Chungshan District of Guangdong Province. Speaking of her arranged marriage to a Gold Mountain man, she said, "I had no choice; we were so poor. We had no food to go with rice, not even soy sauce or black bean paste. Some of our neighbors even had to go begging or sell their daughters, times were so bad. So my parents thought I would have a better future in Gold Mountain." Her fiance was a salesman in San Francisco and a Christian. He had a minister from Canton preside over the first "modern" wedding in his village. She was eighteen and he, thirty-four. In 1922, nine months after their wedding, they sailed for America (information about Law Shee Low is drawn from her interview with Sandy Lee, May 2, 1982, and with the author, October 20, 1988).

In contrast, Wong Ah So, who was a year older than Law Shee Low, came from the port of Hong Kong. According to her story,

> My father was sometimes a sailor and sometimes he worked on the docks, for we were very poor. I was 19 when this man came to my mother and said that in America there was a great deal of gold. Even if I just peeled potatoes there, he told my mother I would earn seven or eight dollars a day, and if I was willing to do any work at all I would earn lots of money. He was a laundryman, but said he earned plenty of money. He was very nice to me, and my mother liked him, so my mother was glad to have me go with him as his wife ("Story of Wong Ah So" 1946:31).

Out of obedience to her mother and with the intention of earning money to support her parents and family, Ah So sailed to America with Huey Yow in 1922. He had a marriage certificate prepared and told her to claim him as her husband to the immigration officials upon landing in San Francisco, but, unlike Law's case, no marriage ceremony was conducted. Upon landing, Ah So did as she was told, but as she admitted later, "in truth [I] had not at any time lived with him as his wife [prior to landing]" ("Story of Wong Ah So" 1946; Cameron 1925:170).

Some women, like Jane Kwong Lee, were from middle-class backgrounds and came for educational reasons. Born in 1902 to wealthy parents of the Toishan District, Guangdong Province (her family owned land and her father and uncle were successful businessmen in Australia), Jane was able to acquire a Western education in the treaty port of Canton. There she was first exposed to American ideas of democracy and women's emancipation. During her last year in school, she became involved in the May Fourth student movement, in which students across China agitated for political and cultural reforms. At the time of her graduation from middle school, she observed that classmates were either entering technical institutions or getting married. "I thought otherwise," she said. "I enjoyed studying and I wanted to be economically independent. In that sense, it was clear in my mind that I had to have as much formal education as possible" (Lee n.d.:152).

Although she wanted to become a doctor, medical school was out of the question, as her father's remittances from Australia were no longer sufficient to support both her and her younger brother's education. Aware that graduates trained in American universities were drawing higher salaries in China than local graduates, she convinced her mother to sell some of their land in order to pay her passage to America. In 1922, she obtained a student's visa and sailed for America, determined to earn a doctorate and return home to a prestigious academic post (the life history of Jane Kwong Lee is drawn from her unpublished manuscript, "A Chinese American," and from interviews with the author on October 22 and November 2, 1988). Jane's educational background and earlier exposure to Western ideas would lead her to a different life experience in America as compared to Law and Ah So, who came as Gold Mountain wives from a more sheltered and impoverished environment.

The San Francisco Chinatown that greeted Law, Ah So, and Jane in 1922 was a far cry from the slum of "filth and depravity" of bygone days; after it was totally destroyed in the 1906 earthquake and fire, Chinese community leaders and merchants seized the opportunity to create a new "Oriental City" on the original site. The new Chinatown, in stark contrast to the old, was in appearance cleaner, healthier, and more modern with its wider paved streets, brick buildings, glass-plated storefronts, and pseudo-Chinese architecture (Light 1974; Choy 1990; Whitfield 1947). The Chinese hospital and a significant number of Chinese schools, churches, newspapers, and civic and political organizations were newly established in the wake of the earthquake. In an effort to improve their livelihood and image, as well as China's, whose low international status was seen as the cause for the racial oppression and humiliation they suffered, Chinese immigrants invested in large-scale business enterprises and contributed to nationalist causes while community leaders worked with outside law enforcement agents to eliminate gambling, prostitution, drugs, and other vices (see Wang, n.d.). As in China, women's emancipation was an integral part of this reform effort. Since the 1911 revolution in that country, queues and footbinding had been eliminated and more of Chinatown's residents were dressing in American clothing and adopting democratic ideas. Arriving in San Francisco's Chinatown at this juncture in time gave immigrant women such as Law Shee Low, Wong Ah So, and Jane Kwong Lee unprecedented opportunities for social change in their lives. Of the three, Ah So became the greatest beneficiary.

Escaping "A Fate Worse Than Death"

Upon landing in America, Wong Ah So's dreams of wealth and happiness vanished after she found that her husband Huey Yow had been paid $500 by a madam to procure her as a slave girl.

> When we first landed in San Francisco we lived in a hotel in Chinatown, a nice place, but one day, after I had been there for about two weeks, a woman came to see me. She was young, very pretty, and all dressed in silk. She told me that I was not really Huey Yow's wife, but that she had asked him to buy her a slave, that I belonged to her, and must go with her, but she would treat me well, and I could buy back my freedom, if I was willing to please, and be agreeable, and she would let me off in two years, instead of four if I did not make a fuss ("Story of Wong Ah So" 1946:31).

For the next year, Ah So worked as a prostitute for the madam in various small towns and was forced to borrow $1,000 to satisfy Huey Yow, who was harassing her and threatening her life. Soon after, she was sold to another owner in Fresno for $2,500. Even as her debts piled up and she became ill, she managed to fulfill her filial duty by sending $300 home to her mother enclosed with a letter which in part read:

> Everyday I have to be treated by the doctor. My private parts pain me so that I cannot have intercourse with men. It is very hard . . . Next year I certainly will be able to pay off all the debts. Your daughter is even more anxious than her mother to do this. As long as your daughter's life lasts she will pay up all the debts. Your daughter will do her part so that the world will not look down upon us ("Story of Wong Ah So" 1946:34).

Then one evening at a banquet she was recognized by a friend of her father's who sought help from the Presbyterian Mission Home on her behalf. Ten days later, she was rescued and placed in the care of Donaldina Cameron, the director of the home. As she wrote, "I don't know just how it happened because it was all very sudden. I just know that it happened. I am learning English and to weave, and I am going to send money to my mother when I can. I can't help but cry, but it is going to be better. I will do what Miss Cameron says" ("Story of Wong Ah So" 1946:32-33). A year later, after learning how to read Chinese and speak English and becoming a Christian, Ah So was married to Louie Kwong, a merchant in Boise, Idaho (cf., Pascoe 1989).

Wong Ah So's story recalls the plight of the many Chinese girls brought to the United States as indentured servants to work as prostitutes in the latter part of the nineteenth century (see Hirata 1979a). But by the time Ah So was sold into prostitution, the traffic had gone underground and was on the decline due to the Chinese exclusion laws, anti-prostitution legislation, and the efforts of Protestant missionaries. In 1870, seventy-one percent of Chinese women in San Francisco were listed as prostitutes; by 1910, the percentage had dropped to seven percent (Hirata 1979a:24; the 1910 percentage is based on my own computation from United States Census of Population manuscript schedules, San Francisco, California, 1910). The turning point came in 1913 with the passage of the Red-light Abatement Act, which authorized local officials to raid and effectively close almost all brothels in the city, including those in Chinatown (Asbury 1933, chapter 12; Issel and Cherny 1986:106-109; Shumsky and Springer 1981). What remained of the trade was left for Cameron and Police Sergeant Jack Manion of the Chinatown Detail to finish off.

Most well-known for her rescue work in Chinatown, Donaldina Cameron was a product of the Social Gospel and Progressive movements, which sought to uplift the "uncivilized" throughout the world and eradicate political corruption and social vices in the nation's cities. Unable to work effectively among Chinatown bachelors and spurned by white prostitutes, she found her calling among "the most helpless and oppressed group of women and children who live within the borders of these United States of America"— Chinese prostitutes and slave girls (attributed to Donaldina Cameron in Pascoe 1989:634). Chinese prostitutes were singled out for rescue because of their helpless, indentured status, and because white prostitutes would have rebuffed any attempts to rescue them (cf., Dobie 1936:234; Dillon 1972:156). Cameron made it her crusade to free them from "a fate worse than death" by first rescuing them, and then inculcating them with Christian moral values. Numerous accounts in newspapers and religious publications describe in vivid detail the dangerous rescue raids led by Cameron, credited with rescuing 3,000 Chinese women during her forty years of service at the Presbyterian Mission Home.

Once rescued, girls were brought back to the mission home to be educated, trained in the domestic arts and industrial skills, and, most importantly, Christianized. Regroomed to lead a productive and upstanding life, some were returned to China under the guard of Christians while others were encouraged to enter companionate marriages with Chinese Christians or to pursue higher education and help with missionary work (for a study of the views and work of Protestant women, including Donaldina Cameron, see Pascoe 1986). Wong Ah So was the direct beneficiary of these rescue missions and was among the last to be so rescued, Christianized, and married off to a Chinese Christian.

Homemaker, Worker, and Partner

Immigrant wives like Law Shee Low also found their lives transformed by the socioeconomic conditions in Chinatown. Life in America was as hardworking as in China but more rewarding. Having survived the ordeal of detention at Angel Island (Lai, Lim, and Yung 1980; Yung 1977), Law moved into a one-room tenement apartment in Chinatown with her husband and assumed the dual roles of homemaker and worker. While her husband worked in a restaurant on the outskirts of Chinatown, she stayed home and sewed baby clothes for a manufacturer for a dollar a dozen. Her husband was only bringing home $35 a month, barely enough to cover rent and food. As she had one child after another (eleven in all; eight survived), she found it easier to stay home and sew even though other women were beginning to work in the Chinatown sewing factories. Besides, she had been inculcated with the idea that the proper place for a woman was at home. As she recalls those days, "There was no time to feel imprisoned; there was so much to do. We worked like crazy. We had to cook, wash the clothes and diapers by hand, the floors, and sew whenever we had a chance to sit still." Given that she had no ice box, modern stove, or hot water, and did not use canned foods, these were all time-consuming tasks. "That's what happens when you are poor. It was the same for all my neighbors. We were all good, obedient, and diligent wives. All sewed; all had six or seven children. Who had time to go out?" (Law Shee Low interview with Sandy Lee, May 2, 1982)

Fortunately for Law, her husband turned out to be cooperative, supportive, and devoted. Until his illness in the 1950s, he was the chief breadwinner: first cooking at a restaurant, then picking fruit in nearby Suisun, sewing at home during the depression years, and finally working in the shipyards during World War II. Although he refused to help with housecleaning, he did all the shopping, helped cook the rice, and hung out the wash on the rooftop or in the hallways. In his own way, he showed concern for his wife. "When he was afraid I wasn't eating, he would tell me to eat more. Even though it was an arranged marriage, we got along well. I didn't complain that he went out every day. We hardly talked. Good or bad, we just struggled along as we had work to do."

As far as children were concerned Law, like her neighbors, had not known how to interfere with nature. "We didn't know about birth control. We would become pregnant every year without realizing it. Even if we didn't want it, we didn't have the money to go see the doctor." All of Law's children were born at home, with the help of neighbors or the local midwife. She was not even aware that she had been pregnant when she had the first of three miscarriages at home. Fortunately, her husband wanted children and was more than willing to provide for them whether they were boys or girls. "Other men would scold their kids and beat them. One woman who had four kids told me her husband would drag her out of bed and beat her because she didn't want to have any more kids. We heard all kinds of sad stories like that. But my husband never picked on me like that" (Law Shee Low interview with Sandy Lee, October 20, 1988).

It was not until her children were older that Law went out to work in the sewing factories. After her husband became ill, she did the shopping and began going to the Chinese movies on Saturdays, but she still did not leave the confines of Chinatown. Prior to that, she basically stayed home. So seldom did she go out that one pair of shoes lasted her ten years. When she first arrived, a "Jesus woman" came to teach her English. But after she became busy with her first baby, she told her not to come anymore. Because they were poor, she was frugal. She gave most of her earnings to her husband (since he did the shopping), made her own clothes and those of her children, and managed to send remittances home to her family periodically. The neighbors in her building were all from Lung Do, the same area of Guangdong Province, and they became lifelong friends. They often visited and chatted, and occasionally—three or four times a year—they would go out to visit friends in the evening or go shopping together.

Since their first responsibility was to their families, many immigrant wives like Law found themselves housebound, with no time to learn English or to participate in social activities outside the home. Their husbands continued to be the chief breadwinner, to hold the purse strings, and to be their liaison to the outside world. But in the absence of the mother-in-law, immigrant wives usually ruled the household and assumed the responsibility of disciplinarian, culture-bearer, and of maintaining the integrity of their families. With few exceptions, they were hardworking, frugal, and tolerant, faithful and respectful to their husbands, and self-sacrificing toward their children. As such, they were indispensable partners to their husbands in their efforts to establish and sustain family life in America. And although they presented a submissive image in public, many immigrant women were known to "wear the pants" at home.

Overall, as compared to their predecessors, immigrant women in the early twentieth century were less tolerant of abuses to their persons and more resourceful in upgrading their status, thanks to the influence of the press, the support of Protestant organizations in the community, and a legal system that was sympathetic toward abused women. The *Chung Sai Yat Po*, from the vantage points of both the nationalist reformer and the Protestant missionary, was particularly outspoken in its support of women's emancipation. Numerous editorials and articles spoke out against footbinding, polygamy, slavery, and arranged marriages, and advocated women's education and equal rights (see Yung 1988). Although most immigrant wives like Law Shee Low could not read the Chinese newspapers (according to my computation from the 1910 manuscript census for San Francisco, California, thirty-two percent of foreign-born Chinese women were literate in 1910), they were affected by the expressed public opinion filtered through their husbands, neighbors, and social reformers looking after their interests. As Law noted, after the 1911 revolution, it was no longer considered "fashionable" to have bound feet, concubines, or slave girls. And as housebound as Law was, she was aware of the mission homes that rescued prostitutes, helped abused women, and offered classes for children and immigrant women. According to newspaper accounts and the records of the Presbyterian and Methodist mission homes in Chinatown, a number of women were also successful in seeking retribution through the American courts, winning divorce and settlements on grounds of desertion, adultery, or physical abuse (such cases are described in Pascoe 1986, 1989; and documented in the *San Francisco Chronicle, San Francisco Call,* and *Chung Sai Yat Po).*

In 1916, with the establishment of the Chinese YWCA (Young Women's Christian Association), another important community resource became available to immigrant women. The YWCA offered classes in English, advice on household sanitation and baby care, personal interpretation services on medical visits and on trips to other public agencies, and help with employment, immigration, and domestic problems. Statistics and community support speak to the organization's effectiveness in serving women in Chinatown. During the 1920s, the YWCA's membership reached 800 and an average of 15,000 persons a year benefited by its services. Even in the midst of the Great Depression, women who were earning only $1.25 a day on a 10- or 12-hour schedule did not fail to give $1 to renew their membership, nor did the community fail to come through with $25,000 to help build the new facility at its present site on Clay Street. Most importantly, the Chinese YWCA changed the attitudes of immigrant women toward American institutions and drew them out of their homes to seek self-improvement and social interaction.

Chinese Women in the Labor Market

Compared to Wong Ah So and Law Shee Low, Jane Kwong Lee had an easier time acclimating to life in America. Not only was she educated, Westernized, and English-speaking, but she also had the help of affluent relatives who provided room and board, financial support, and important contacts that enabled her to eventually strike out on her own. Arriving in the middle of a school semester and therefore unable to enroll in a college, she decided to look for gainful employment. In spite of her educational background and qualifications, she found only menial jobs and domestic service opened to her. "At heart I was sorry for myself," she said. "I wished I was a boy. If I were a boy, I could have gone out into the community, finding a job somewhere as many newcomers from China had done" (Lee n.d.:10).

But as a Chinese woman, she had to bide her time and look for work appropriate to her race and sex. Thus, until she could be admitted to college, and during the summers after she enrolled at Mills College, she tried a number of jobs where mostly Chinese women were employed, including embroidery work at Joe Shoong's factory, sorting vegetables in the wholesale district, working as a live-in domestic for a white family, picking shrimp, sorting fruit at a local cannery, and sewing flannel nightgowns at home. Finding all of these jobs taxing and low-paying, she did not stay long at any of them, but she came away with a better appreciation of the diligence and hard work that immigrant women applied to the limited jobs open to them. As she observed, "They were very capable of doing hard labor in order to earn money to help their families. Most of their husbands worked as waiters and didn't make enough to support the family. There wasn't much work for the women, mostly sewing or picking shrimp at home" so they could "take care of the children while they worked for a living, or else outside in the canneries in the summer."

As it was for other immigrant women, the patterns of work for Chinese women were shaped by the intersection of the local economy, ethnic traditions, and family and childcare needs; race, however, was an additional influential factor. From the turn of the century until the 1929 Depression, San Francisco experienced growth and prosperity. Ranked the eighth-largest city in the country, it was the major port of trade for the Pacific Coast and was touted as the financial and corporate capital of the West. Jobs were plentiful in the city's three largest economic sectors—domestic and personal service, trade and transportation, and manufacturing and mechanical industries—but they were filled according to a labor-market segmentation based on race and sex, with Chinese men occupying the lowest tier as laborers, servants, factory workers, laundrymen, and small merchants while Chinese women, further handicapped by prescribed gender roles, worked primarily as seamstresses at home or in the garment factories for low piece-rate wages (Issel and Cherny 1986:76-77; Yamato 1986, chapter 4). Investigations by the Industrial Welfare Commission and the Chinese YWCA in the 1920s indicate that Chinese women were employed by the growing garment industry and food processing factories because they were "cheaper" labor. Although most did not work under sweatshop conditions, they were clearly at a disadvantage because of cultural and language differences as well as race and sex discrimination (Lissner n.d.).

Under these circumstances, Jane's being Chinese and a woman proved liabilities in the job market, but, because she was educated and had good contacts among Chinese Christians, she was better off than most other immigrant women. She eventually got a scholarship at Mills College, and part-time work teaching Chinese school and tutoring Chinese adults in English at the Chinese Episcopal Church in Oakland. After earning her bachelor's degree in sociology, she married, had two children, and returned to Mills College, where she received a master's degree in sociology and economics in 1933. She later spent many years working for the Chinese YWCA and for a number of Chinatown newspapers as a journalist and translator.

For most other immigrant women, who worked in factories, it was not an easy task juggling the double burden of homemaker and wage earner. But as long as there were jobs for them, and working outside paid more than home work, women were compelled to leave their children at home and enter factory work. Garment shops were particularly attractive workplaces for mothers because they could bring their children there and employers permitted the women flexible work schedules, which worked to the advantage of all parties concerned. Employers profited by paying the women at piecerates and employees worked whatever hours they could depending on when family duties called. However, since most of the seamstresses did not speak English, they were easily exploited. Without union protection, they worked long hours for little pay and often under unsanitary conditions (Lissner, n.d.; "Miscellaneous Accounts"; Lan 1976:352).

Although most Chinese women worked out of economic necessity and were exploited in the process, there was a side benefit to be gained. Working outside the home gave them a new sense of freedom, accomplishment, and camaraderie. They were no longer confined to the home, they were earning money to contribute to the family income or for themselves, and they were making new acquaintances and becoming exposed to new ideas. Some used their earnings to send remittances back to their families in China or to invest wisely in jewelry and property. As Jane observed, having money to spend made the women feel more liberated here than in China: "They can buy things for themselves, go out to department stores to choose their own clothes instead of sewing them. I remember when I came to America, I felt so cold. The first thing I thought was to buy a coat and shoes. So I had to work in the factories to make money and I used my money to buy clothes for myself. I felt so free" (Jane Kwong Lee interview with author, October 22, 1988).

The Beginnings of Social Activism

For working-class women like Law Shee Low, family and work responsibilities consumed all their time and energy, leaving little left over for self-improvement and even less for community involvement. But this was not the case for a growing number of educated, middle-class women like Jane Kwong Lee, who, inspired by Christianity and nationalism, took the first steps toward becoming socially active in the community. Prior to the 1911 revolution in their homeland, Chinese women in America followed the tradition of remaining publicly invisible. They seldom ventured out of their homes except perhaps to shop or go to the Chinese opera, where they sat in a segregated section apart from the men. The Protestant churches were the first to offer them an opportunity to become involved in an organized activity outside the home. In the early 1900s, a small but visible number of Chinese women attended

Sunday services, English classes, meetings, outings, and Christmas programs sponsored by churches. Some of the churches also organized Chinese women's societies to stimulate Christian activity at home and in China. Members of the [Congregational] Mothers and Daughters Society, for example, collected dues which were sent to the villages to support the work of Bible women there (Woo 1983:231, 264; author's interviews with Florence Chinn Kwan, October 7, 12, and 14, 1988). Chinese women committed to the Christian cause were among the earliest female leaders in the community to organize events on behalf of women, the church, and national salvation. For example, Mrs. Ng Poon Chew, who was brought up and educated at the Presbyterian Mission Home, was indispensable to her husband in his role as minister, newspaper editor, and champion for civil rights and nationalist reform. She was actively involved in the establishment of the Chinese YWCA in 1916 and led many fund-raising drives on behalf of China and the Chinatown community (data on Mrs. Ng courtesy of Peggy Pascoe; see also Hoexter 1976:153, 155-158, 170).

Aside from Christianity, the intense nationalist spirit that took hold in the early 1900s also affected Chinese women in far-reaching ways. Not only did the reformist call for modernization include improving conditions for Chinese women, but it also called for their active participation in national salvation work. Fundraising for disaster relief and revolution in China opened up opportunities for women here to become involved in the community, develop leadership abilities, and move further into the public light. The Tongmenghui, founded by Dr. Sun Yat-sen in 1905 to overthrow the Qing dynasty and establish a republic in China, was the first political organization to accept women into its ranks. Several tens of women were known to have joined the San Francisco branch in 1910 (Zeng 1986:141-142). While women in China participated in benefit performances, enlisted in the army, and engaged in dangerous undercover work, women in San Francisco also did their share for the revolutionary effort—making speeches on behalf of the revolution, donating money and jewelry, and helping with Red Cross work—sometimes under the auspices of Protestant churches, other times under the banner of the Women's Young China Society *(Chung Sai Yat Po,* May 25 and November 21 and 27, 1911, and January 12, 1912; *San Francisco Call,* October 29, 1911).

Although the success of the revolution and the establishment of a republic in China failed to bring peace and prosperity to their native land, it did have a lasting impact on the lives of Chinese American women, marking the beginnings of social activism for them. According to the *San Francisco Examiner,* May 10, 1914, Mrs. Ow Yang and Mrs. Chu-Chin Shung, wives of the outgoing and incoming Chinese consuls, caused a stir when they attended a Chinese banquet with their husbands. "The fact that women were present was taken as an indication of the democracy in the new China," wrote the reporter. A year later, on July 26, 1915, the same paper found it newsworthy to report that Chinese women not only marched in a parade through Chinatown for the first time, but were present at a banquet hosted by the Chinese Nationalist League of America: "the tiny footed women were...seated alternately with the men, just like Americans." Even more extraordinary, according to the article, "after the banquet these women arose, one at a time, and standing upon those tiny feet they made speeches just as the men did."

Jane, arriving as a liberated woman at the time when she did, did not hesitate to join other women in becoming socially active in the Chinatown community. Unencumbered by traditional gender roles, she soon became known as both a public speaker and woman leader. "The community accepted me as one of their leaders, not only because of my ability to speak fluently, but also because I was a college student," she said (Lee n.d.:55). Jane was known for her loud-voiced and forceful-mannered speeches—in Chinese at churches, before public gatherings on street corners in support of Christianity, and before the Chinese Six Companies and other Chinatown organizations on behalf of the Chinese YWCA or for one nationalist cause or another. She also made presentations in English to Caucasian groups interested in learning more about Chinese culture, and travelled as a Chinese delegate to YWCA functions outside of Chinatown. On one of these occasions, she was so moved by an ongoing discussion on racial discrimination that she surprised herself and African Americans at a YWCA meeting by speaking up for them. "I said, you are all equal. Nobody is inferior to another" (Jane Kwong Lee interview with author, November 2, 1988).

Like many other immigrant women, Jane felt strongly about her homeland and always took the leadership in supporting nationalist causes in the community. She wrote, directed, and acted in a number of plays to raise funds for flood relief, for a new school building for her alma mater in Canton, and for the war effort in China. She also taught English and conducted first aid courses for both men and women in Chinatown, and, in her capacity as a community worker at the Chinese YWCA, made house visits, wrote articles that were published in the Chinese newspapers, and implemented programs that benefited Chinese women in the community.

Conclusion

In 1931, Chinese women in San Francisco were still not fully emancipated from social restrictions of the past, but they had come a long way from their nineteenth-century subordinate roles as indentured prostitutes and cloistered wives (Hirata 1979b; Yung 1986). As Sieh King King had advocated in 1902, they had unbound their feet and begun to unbind their lives in America. Most, like Law Shee Low and Wong Ah So, had immigrated for a better livelihood but found themselves exploited as prostitutes or working wives at the bottom of a labor market segmented by race and sex. Some, like Jane Kwong Lee, had come from a privileged background yet still had encountered discrimination in the work place, in Chinatown, and in the larger American society. But like many other immigrant women before them, they not only persevered and survived, but took advantage of new circumstances to improve their lives and contribute to the well-being of their families and community.

For women like Law, Ah So, and Jane, a myriad of developments in China and here in the United States impinged upon their lives and enabled them to break away from the traditional roles of Chinese women during the early years of the twentieth century. In China, foreign domination, political disorder, and economic impoverishment had triggered a national movement for reform and modernization in line with the Western model. Elevating the status of women—one-half of the country's population—through education and equal rights could help strengthen and save China from further imperialist encroachment. These sentiments were echoed in Chinatown by newspapers such as *Chung Sai Yat Po* and espoused by feminist orators such as Sieh King King. Chinese Americans, concerned with China's future not only because of strong nationalist feelings but also because their poor treatment in America was directly related to the low international standing of their ancestral homeland, consistently contributed funds and talent to help build a stronger China. At the same time, they worked for changes in their own community in an effort to improve their socioeconomic status in America. Thus, nationalist reformers in Chinatown, following the example of their counterparts in China, advocated emancipation for Chinese women in America, calling for an end to footbinding and prostitution while promoting women's education and rights and the involvement of women in nationalist causes.

Concurrently, the Social Gospel and Progressive movements in America unleashed a fury of activity among middle-class women who made it their crusade to uplift the lives of the "uncivilized" in the four corners of the world, as well as the poverty-stricken in urban areas of the country. Protestant missionary women such as Donaldina Cameron were especially sympathetic toward the plight of women in China as well as in Chinatowns and worked toward saving their souls and improving conditions for them in these places. Although they were often condescending and self-righteous in their attitude toward Chinese women, it was in large part due to their efforts in San Francisco's Chinatown that prostitution declined, abused wives found assistance and refuge, girls and women were educated, and women began to participate in organized activities outside the home—in churches, for example, as well as at the Chinese YWCA.

Encouraged by the call for women's emancipation among nationalist reformers and by the support services of Protestant missionaries, the "new woman" no longer bound her feet, hid her face from the public, or suffered abuses silently by the time Wong Ah So, Law Shee Low, and Jane Kwong Lee arrived in San Francisco in 1922. Women like Ah So, who had been sold into prostitution unknowingly, directly benefited by these new circumstances; among the last to be rescued by Donaldina Cameron, she chose to later marry a Chinese merchant and settle in Boise, Idaho. Immigrant wives like Law continued to assume the double burdens of homemaker and worker, but no longer the role of the oppressed woman. In the absence of the mother-in-law and with the advantage of new resources opened to them in America — the support of other immigrant women, the churches, missionary homes, the Chinese YWCA, the American legal system, and jobs outside the home — they were able to improve their status within the home. Although encumbered by both race and sex discrimination, someone like Jane was still able to acquire a college education and become gainfully employed and socially active within her own community, thanks to the help of relatives and Christian friends, and the call for women's involvement in nationalist and Christian causes.

Even as immigrant women began to enjoy their new roles as emancipated women, economic depression was setting in and war loomed large in their homeland. The challenges of the 1930s and 1940s — economic survival and the war effort on two fronts — would lead to even greater dramatic changes in their lives, allowing them to take the first steps toward fuller participation in American society.

Note

I am especially indebted to the following for their generosity in sharing documentary evidence used in the preparation of this essay: Sucheng Chan for her data on Chinese women in San Francisco from the 1910 U. S. Census; Peggy Pascoe for her file on Mrs. Ng Poon Chew (Chun Fah) from the Presbyterian Mission Home; and Teresa Wu of the Chinese YWCA, historian and architect Philip Choy, and Yee Ling Fong of the International Institute of San Francisco for the correspondence, board minutes, and staff reports of the Chinese YWCA.

References

Asbury, Herbert. 1933. *The Barbary Coast: An Informal History of the San Francisco Underworld.* New York: Alfred Knopf.
Beahan, Charlotte L. 1976. "The Women's Movement and Nationalism in Late Ch'ing China." Ph.D. dissertation, Columbia University.
Cameron, Donaldina. 1925. "The Story of Wong So." *Women and Missions* 11 (5):169-172.
Chen, Helen. 1980. "Chinese Immigration into the United States: An Analysis of Changes in Immigration Policies." Ph.D. dissertation, Brandeis University.

84 Asian Americans

Chesneux, Jean, Marianne Bastid, and Marie-Claire Bergere. 1976. *China from the Opium Wars to the 1911 Revolution.* New York: Pantheon Books.

Choy, Philip P. 1990. "San Francisco's Chinatown Architecture." In *Chinese America: History and Perspectives,* 37-66.

Coolidge, Mary Roberts. 1909. *Chinese Immigration.* New York: Henry Holt.

Dillon, Richard. 1972. *The Hatchet Man: San Francisco's Chinatown in the Days of the Tong Wars, 1880-1906.* New York: Ballantyne Books.

Dobie, Charles Caldwell. 1936. *San Francisco's Chinatown.* New York: D. Appleton-Century Company.

Hirata, Lucie Cheng. 1979a. "Free, Indentured, Enslaved: Chinese Prostitutes in Nineteenth-Century America." *Signs: Journal of Women in Culture and Society* 5 (1):3-29.

———. 1979b. "Chinese Immigrant Women in Nineteenth-Century California." In *Women of America: A History,* edited by Carol Ruth Berkin and Mary Beth Norton. Boston: Houghton-Mifflin.

Hoexter, Corinne K. 1976. *From Canton to California: The Epic of Chinese Immigration.* New York: Four Winds Press.

Issel, William, and Robert Cherny. 1986. *San Francisco, 1865-1932: Politics, Power, and Urban Development.* Berkeley: University of California Press.

Kung, S. W. 1973. *Chinese in American Life: Some Aspects of Their History, Status, Problems, and Contributions.* Westport: Greenwood Press.

Lai, Him Mark. 1987. "The Chinese-American Press." In *The Ethnic Press in the United States: A Historical Analysis and Handbook,* edited by Sally M. Miller. New York: Greenwood Press.

Lai, Him Mark, Genny Lim, and Judy Yung. 1980. *Island: Poetry and History of Chinese Immigrants on Angel Island, 1910-1940.* San Francisco: HOC-DOI Project, Chinese Culture Center.

Lan, Dean. 1976. "Chinatown Sweatshops." In *Counterpoint: Perspectives on Asian America,* edited by Emma Gee et al. Los Angeles: University of California Asian American Studies Center.

Lee, Jane Kwong. n.d. "A Chinese American." Unpublished manuscript.

Light, Ivan. 1974. "From Vice District to Tourist Attraction: The Moral Career of American Chinatowns, 1880-1940." *Pacific Historical Review* 43 (3):367-394.

Lissner, Elsa. n.d. "Investigation into Conditions in the Chinese Quarter in San Francisco and Oakland." In Survey of Race Relations Collection, Hoover Institution on War, Revolution, and Peace. Stanford University, Box 1, "Segregation" file folder.

"Miscellaneous Accounts." In Survey of Race Relations Collection, Hoover Institution on War, Revolution, and Peace. Stanford University, Box 26, file folder 149.

Pascoe, Peggy. 1986. "The Search for Female Moral Authority: Protestant Women and Rescue Homes in the American West, 1874-1939." Ph.D. dissertation, Stanford University.

———. 1989. "Gender Systems in Conflict; The Marriages of Mission-Educated Chinese American Women, 1874-1939." *Journal of Social History* 22 (4):631-652.

Shumsky, Neil Larry, and Larry M. Springer. 1981. "San Francisco's Zone of Prostitution, 1880-1934." *Journal of Historical Geography* 7 (1):71-89.

"Story of Wong Ah So—Experiences as a Prostitute." 1946. In "Orientals and Their Cultural Adjustment," Social Science Source Documents, No. 4. Nashville: Social Science Institute, Fisk University.

Wang, L. Ling-chi. n.d. "An Overview of Chinese American Communities during the Exclusion Era, 1883-1943." Unpublished manuscript.

Whitfield, Ruth Hall. 1947. "Public Opinion and the Chinese Question in San Francisco, 1900-1947." M.A. thesis, University of California, Berkeley.
Woo, Wesley. 1983. "Protestant Work among the Chinese in the San Francisco Bay Area, 1850-1920." Ph.D. dissertation, University of California, Berkeley.
Yamato, Alex. 1986. "Socioeconomic Change among Japanese Americans in the San Francisco Bay Area." Ph.D. dissertation, University of California, Berkeley.
Yung, Judy. 1977. "A Bowlful of Tears: Chinese Women Immigrants on Angel Island." *Frontiers: A Journal of Women Studies* 2 (2):52-55.
————. 1986. *Chinese Women of America: A Pictorial History*. Seattle: University of Washington Press.
————. 1988. "The Social Awakening of Chinese American Women as Reported in *Chung Sai Yat Po*, 1900-1911." In *Chinese America: History and Perspectives*, 80-102.
Zeng Buqui. 1986. "Sun Yat-sen and the Women Members of San Francisco's Tongmenghui" (in Chinese). In *Zhongshan Xiansheng Yishi*. Beijing: Zhongguo Wen-shi Chubanshe.

Racial Order and Contestation: Asian American Internees and Soldiers at Camp McCoy, Wisconsin, 1942-1943

Peggy Choy

> *an enemy is not a person. It is just a word, an idea –*
> Patsy S. Saiki, *Ganbare! An Example of Japanese Spirit*

Minidoka, Tule Lake, and Manzanar; these are some of the names of internment camps – the first located in Idaho, and the other two located in California – commonly mentioned in the media and literature on the Japanese American internment experience. It is less commonly known that Camp McCoy in Sparta, Wisconsin, was an internment camp for Japanese Americans. This site was unique from the standpoint of Asian American history. Not only were Japanese Americans interned at this camp, but the highly decorated 100th Infantry Battalion trained there for six months. In addition, Japanese, Italian, and German prisoners of war (POW) were detained there. The POWs have an important story of their own (Krammer 1983), but for my purposes here, I will focus on the Asian American internees and soldiers.

Camp McCoy epitomized the contradictory nature of the Japanese American experience in World War II – incarceration on the mere basis of race, and the giving of life and limb in military service fighting for principles which should have foreclosed such incarceration in the first instance. I attempt to show that, contrary to much of the existing literature which portrays Japanese American internees and military volunteers as passive subjects of the dominant order, they in fact demonstrated in certain instances actions which exemplified a spirit of resistance and collective self-assertion.

The literature on the Asian American experience during World War II makes relatively little reference to Camp McCoy. Writers who do mention the Camp McCoy experiences of the internees or the 100th Battalion soldiers by-and-large tend to stress the treatment of these Asian Americans by whites around them—camp officials, other camp residents, and the local community. The internees, the literature states, received decent treatment by the commanding officers. The men of the 100th Battalion are described as being well-accepted by the local Wisconsin community. Writers also stress how the commanding officers came to recognize the soldiers' patriotism and loyalty, and to respect their self-discipline and skill. I propose that *both* the Japanese American internees and the soldiers were prisoners of the state, incarcerated at Camp McCoy during a time in which the dominant racial order threatened to dehumanize these men. In fact, this military facility was a bastion of this dominant racial order. Even under oppressive conditions, the men retained a sense of struggle and political awareness. While the internees and soldiers showed acceptance of their situation, they were keenly aware of the limits of what they would tolerate. In both cases, when pushed to the point of intolerance, the men were able to take "collective control"[1] of the situation.

Omi and Winant's discussion of the "racial state" is useful in analyzing this wartime situation at Camp McCoy:

> Since the earliest days of colonialism in North America, an identifiable racial order has linked the system of political rule to the racial classification of individuals and groups... But even at its most oppressive, the racial order was unable to abrogate itself the entire capacity for the production of racial meanings, of racial subjects. Racial minorities were always able to counterpose their own cultural traditions, their own forms of organization and identity, to the dehumanizing and enforced "invisibility" imposed by the majority society... even in the most uncontested periods of American racism, oppositional cultures were able, often at very great cost, to maintain themselves (Omi and Winant 1986:72-74)

The dominant view in the literature surveyed has emphasized the "humane" treatment of the internees and the soldiers *by* the white military at Camp McCoy and the local community. The Japanese Americans—internees and soldiers alike—are described somewhat passively as *recipients* of good will.[2] I maintain that both groups of men actively shaped their situation, and in this way contested the racial meanings which threatened their identities. Rebellions and resistance occurred at other camps—particularly Tule Lake—providing evidence that counters the commonly accepted view of internees as docile recipients of unjust treatment. Counterintelligence reports mention strikes and the November 1943 "riots" that occurred at the Tule Lake "segregation center" for "disloyal Japanese" (Daniels 1989:21-22). When national War Relocation Authority (WRA) director Dillon Myer visited the Tule Lake camp on November 1, 1943, he was greeted by angry demonstrators—2,000 to 5,000 internees—organized by the Daihyo Sha Kai (Saiki 1983:190). Omura describes the "resistance movement" in the camps in his article, "Japanese American Journalism During World War II" (Omura 1989:71-77). In *Prejudice, War and the Constitution* (TenBroek, Barnhart, and Matson 1954: 130-131, 164, 175, 177), there is mention of mass demonstrations and "disturbances" at camps including Manzanar, Poston, and Tule Lake. Thomas and Nishimoto's *The Spoilage* (1946:43, 113-115, 119, 127-129, 133-139, 142-146) gives accounts of organized resistance at Tule Lake involving construction and coal crews, farm worker units, a hospital demonstration, and the November 4th "riot."

With a similar spirit of resistance and consciousness, the Camp McCoy internees (who were later sent to other camps such as Tule Lake) and the 100th Battalion soldiers were able to maintain their own sense of identity and humanity. It was their own struggle and initiative—rather than the attitudes of and treatment by the white military officials and the townsfolk—that determined how they were treated over time.

Although the focus of this paper is what happened on the "inside"—within the confines of Camp McCoy—versus the "outside" world or the "free zone" (Omura 1989:72), it is crucial to realize that for the internees and soldiers to resist the racial order of the camp was to resist the racial order of the military institution, as well as all other political institutions of the state.[3] Those actors crucial to the state's political rule—the president of the United States, the secretary of war, the military establishment, the department of justice, the supreme court, and the U. S. congress—were all active participants in racially stigmatizing Japanese Americans (Dower 1986:79-80). As one former soldier of the 100th Battalion said to the author, the "war was a racial war." To assert one's identity in this context required great endurance and courage.

Background on the Camp McCoy Area

Camp McCoy (now called Fort McCoy) was founded in 1909 by Robert Bruce McCoy for the training of army and national guard troops to "support the nation's needs" (Sorenson 1986:2). In the past century, the Winnebago Indians had been removed from the area by the 1830s and forced by U.S. troops into Minnesota, North Dakota, and Nebraska. The 1886 Homestead provisions, however, allowed the Winnebago to return to their native Wisconsin, confining them to designated homestead lands near Camp McCoy and forcing them to farm forty acres of relatively infertile land. A racist atmosphere prevailed during the early 1900s. Some white residents physically harassed and stole from the Winnebago (John Beaudin, personal communication).

Beginning in 1940 and continuing through the war years, Camp McCoy expanded; ultimately, it included an internment camp, finished in the winter of 1941, new barracks, a hospital, tent frames, and, most significantly, a cantonment *(Sparta Herald* [hereafter cited as *Herald*], January 13, 1941, 1, and March 2, 1942, 1).

The wartime cantonment construction began in March 1942 with a budget of $22,800,000. The project required the confiscation of 9,600 acres of surrounding land *(Monroe County Democrat* [hereafter cited as *Democrat*], January 22, 1942, 1). The government takeover of land for military purposes involved the forced removal of about eighty-five farming families, many of whom were left homeless *(Herald,* September 7, 1942, 1).

The camp's expansion also meant a significant number of new but temporary jobs for local residents. Hundreds of people—including Winnebago from the local and neighboring areas—signed up for these temporary jobs. There was an upsurge in service employment and night club activity, and local taxi business increased *(Herald,* February 17, 1941, 1). However, unemployment compensation statistics from pre-war, wartime, and post-war years suggest a "boom" wartime situation preceded and followed by periods of significant unemployment (Unemployment Compensation Statistics).

I will now address the specific nature of the struggle of the internees and the men of the 100th Battalion. I include the local media rhetoric—in print, film, and audio media—as an important aspect of the dominant "racial order."

The Internees

The arrival of the Japanese American internees at Camp McCoy on March 9, 1942, was shrouded in secrecy. Their train was "old, slow and sooty" (Saiki 1983:77). Japanese American civic leaders, priests, businessmen, and teachers, all from Hawaii, rode on this train. Except for the last car which carried the "old men...too frail to escape," the train coach windows were barred (Miyamoto 1964:358; *Democrat,* March 12, 1942, 1) and the train was heavily guarded by a troop of soldiers and two officers *(Democrat,* March 12, 1942, 1). The internees arrived in what to them felt like "biting cold." They were not let off at the station but had to trudge through deep snow to the camp. Several other mainland Japanese Americans were already at the camp when the group arrived around suppertime.

The arriving internees were housed in the camp's old Civilian Conservation Corps barracks constructed during the depression. A former internee interviewed by the author remembers about forty men being housed in each of the five barracks. Cots were arranged alphabetically according to last names. There was little privacy: toilets located in an enclosed outhouse were long wooden benches with holes. The *Democrat* described the camp as having two barbed wire fences, and six towers with search lights at strategic points along the fences. The towers were manned by heavily armed guards, and the camp was considered "escape-proof" *(Democrat,* January 15, 1942, 1).

The mystery surrounding the Japanese Americans' presence at the camp has continued into the present, due mostly to a paucity of available documentation. According to Fort McCoy public relations representative Mary Binder, the camp's war records were destroyed in a fire during the war (Mary Binder, personal communication).

There is confusion—both in the local papers at the time, and in the postwar literature—as to how many men were in the aforementioned group, and when they arrived at Camp McCoy. Local reporters claimed that the military refused to disclose any information on the new arrivals. The *Sparta Herald* reports that the internees arrived on March 2, 1942. The *Monroe County Democrat* reports that 188 internees arrived on March 12, 1942. Miyamoto says that a group of 188 arrived on March 9, remained for seventy days, then departed on May 29 (Miyamoto 1964:359). Duus mentions that the FBI sent 172 to Camp McCoy (Duus 1983:24). Saiki says a group of 160 left Hawaii for Camp McCoy, the first group of internees to leave the islands (Patsy S. Saiki, personal communication). Some internees remember arriving at the camp on March 3. A list of internees published in a Japanese paper in Hawaii lists 172 men who left Hawaii on February 17, 1942 (Helen Khim, personal communication). An Aliens Division communique of the war department dated February 28, 1942, states that "1 Japanese prisoner of war and 198 internees sailed for San Francisco February 22, 1942" including "173 Japanese, 20 Germans, 2 Italians, 1 Norwegian, 1 Dane and 2 United States citizens" (Daniels 1989). Miyamoto refers to a "mainland" internee, "Rev. Kanow" from Nebraska, who was a graduate in agriculture (Miyamoto 1964:369). "Rev. Kanow" likely refers to the Rev. Hiram Hisanori Kano, who wrote the pamphlet *A History of the Japanese in Nebraska*, in which he mentions internment at a camp in Sparta, Wisconsin (Kano 1984:27).

Beginning with the outbreak of the war, the rhetoric in the local print media helped create a nervous, suspicious, and anti-Asian atmosphere. Local newspapers, filled with racist language about the Japanese, had already created a fearful and hostile anti-Asian atmosphere prior to the arrival of the Japanese American internees. On December 7, 1941, the *Herald* reported that soldiers stationed at the camp listened calmly to Sparta residents who were outraged about the Japanese bombing of Pearl Harbor, and accepted inevitable conflict with "Japs." In this nervous atmosphere, shortly after the internees reportedly arrived at Camp McCoy, the *La Crosse Tribune and Leader-Press* (March 12, 1942, 1) reported that a "Jap" arrested in River Falls while allegedly tampering with some electric wires turned out to be "a Chinaman" and was freed.

Local newspapers described the newly arrived internees as a hostile, "enemy force, presumably mostly Japanese," of "dangerous enemy aliens" (*Democrat*, March 12, 1942, 1; January 22, 1942, 1). The wartime scrap metal campaign was constantly accompanied by racist jargon in the newspapers. For example, an article in the *Herald* (July 6, 1942, 6) headlined, "Cooking Up Trouble for the Japs," included "Something unpleasant is being cooked up for the little brown men of Nippon." In March 1942, the month of the internees' arrival, the *Democrat* (March 26, 1942, 8) featured a racist cartoon depicting a farmer beating a Japanese caricature with a metal bar, with the caption, "Scrap to Slap the Jap, Farmers of America—Uncle Sam Needs Your Scrap Iron!"

Almost a year after the bombing of Pearl Harbor, specifically anti-Japanese films began to show in Sparta movie houses, including *Secret Agent of Japan*, and, starring Humphrey Bogart, *Across the Pacific*. The ad for *Across the Pacific* included the phrase, "Bogart Tops Those 'Maltese Falcon' thrills—as he slaps the Japs" *(Herald,* September 7, 1942, 4, and January 4, 1943, 4). War songs popular at the time included "You're a Sap, Mr. Jap," "Let's Take a Rap at the Jap," "They're Gonna Be Playing Taps on the Japs," and "We're Gonna Have to Slap the Dirty Little Jap" (Dower 1986:81). These songs may well have been aired over the local Wisconsin radio. This was rhetoric the local community was reading and hearing almost daily when the internees arrived (and, for that matter, when the 100th Battalion arrived).

The internees lived in uncertainty during the period of their confinement (Miyamoto 1964:366). During the time they were at Camp McCoy, they were never informed as to how long they could expect to stay there or what would happen next. They were not told where they were going when they left Camp McCoy for Camp Forest by train. Letters were censored, and, in some cases, diaries were confiscated. They were under surveillance. There was a direct line of communication from the camp's commanding officer, Lt. Col. Rogers, to the chief of intelligence in Washington (Saiki 1983:84).

According to internee Suikei Furuya (1964:105), tensions arose particularly between the younger and older internees shortly after their arrival at Camp McCoy. The younger men felt they were being unfairly exploited because they had to perform hard labor such as going out into the cold to gather firewood. There was an understanding that internees were supposed to be paid seventy cents per day, but Camp McCoy internees received no compensation.[5] Internees performed daily menial work such as cleaning toilets and cooking. Many of the men had never performed these kinds of chores in their own homes. Their clothing was inadequate (clothing had been sent from Hawaii by family members but took a long time to arrive). They were always hungry, perhaps due to moving to a cold environment from a warm tropical climate. The strained atmosphere among the prisoners became more relaxed as conditions improved (Furuya 1964:112). The improved conditions, I argue, were mostly due to internee initiative.

Miyamoto (1964:359-360) and Saiki (1983:84, 90) focus on the "fairness," "humaneness," and on the "superb" and "rare" nature of the white commanding officer, Lt. Col. Rogers. They stress that it was because of this man's behavior, and because he "ignored race" (Saiki 1983:90), that the internees' stay was a happy "respite" (Miyamoto 1964:359). However, it is clear that the prisoners themselves took the initiative. The men from Hawaii came together, and, within the bounds of their incarceration, acted to pool their political and cultural resources. They elected Dr. Okimura as their spokesperson (Miyamoto 1964:361), and each barracks elected its own leaders and other officers (Furuya 1964:97).

Internees at that point began to assert their identity as a group. A Mr. Sakamoto, for example, requested permission to celebrate Buddha's birthday. On April 29 (actually the Emperor's birthday), Rev. Takahashi carved Prince Siddhartha from a large carrot, and Rev. Oda created a cherry blossom flower arrangement from toilet paper. Led by Rev. Ninryo Nago, thirty priests took part in the service (Miyamoto 1964:363; Saiki 1983:84-85). The men gave three "banzai" cheers and wore their normal clothing for the first time since their arrest.

Dr. Kohatsu observed that the older men began to quarrel bitterly, and read this as a sign of mental deterioration (Miyamoto 1964:365). Dr. Kazuo Miyamoto observed that the men looked like "zombies" (Saiki 1983:85), and informed Lt. Col. Rogers that the men were deteriorating both mentally and physically, and that it was imperative that they participate in constructive activities of their own choosing. The men then collectively decided upon their activities for the little free time they had—collecting stones with which to play *shogi* (Koetsu Morita, personal communication), listening to news broadcasts, group singing (Miyamoto 1964:363-365; Saiki 1983:85-86), playing baseball, and developing an evening lecture series—the latter two activities being the most popular (Furuya 1964:124).

Internees not only asserted their identity as a group, but as individuals as well. For example, one former internee—a Soto sect priest—informed the author that he practiced daily meditation upon his cot.

When tensions rose over food distribution, internees monitored for themselves what was fair. Furuya describes the incidents:

> we received one potato and two slices of bread without butter for lunch one day. On the same day we had dumpling soup, two slices of bread for dinner. We were supposed to get a slice of meat for each cup, but some people got two or more slices and others didn't get any of it. At last someone complained about it. So a slice of meat was put into a cup first before the soup was served in. Ends of sliced bread were distributed among those that wanted them. The problem was that everybody wanted them. The distribution was not fair because a distributor gave two ends to his friends but ignored those he disliked. The problem of the food was soon resolved when we talked to the Commander-in-Chief Rogers (Furuya 1964:105).

Another instance of overt resistance occurred when some of the younger internees went on a labor strike. A guard used his gun to prod the men working on the road outside the camp's gate. The men threw down their shovels and, refusing to work, returned to the camp. Dr. Okimura argued that the men should be compensated for their work in accordance with the Geneva conference agreement on the treatment of war prisoners. Because they were not being paid, he said, they would not work (Miyamoto 1964:361-362).[5] All of these collective actions were forms of resistance (sometimes quite subtle) to their status as internees, and confirmed their own identity as Japanese Americans.

The 100th Infantry Battalion

The famous 100th Infantry Battalion, or the "Purple Heart Battalion" — as they came to be known — trained at Camp McCoy from June 16, 1942, to January 6, 1943 (Duus 1987:22, 39). After this period of over six months at McCoy, they went on to Camp Shelby for more than seven months of training until August 21, 1943 (Duus 1987:77), when they departed for the front in North Africa, Italy, and France (Commission on Wartime Relocation and Internment of Civilians [hereafter CWRIC] 1982:256).[6]

As was the case for the internees, the 100th Battalion's journey from Hawaii to Camp McCoy was marked by apprehension. As their train pulled into the camp, the barbed wire surrounding the internment area came into view. The men thought they had traveled to Wisconsin to be prisoners in a concentration camp. Five 100th Battalion soldiers the author interviewed expressed this reaction. This view is also documented in "The Boys of Company B" (1981:13) and in Duus's *Unlikely Liberators* (1987:22-23).

As was suspected by members of the 100th Battalion, they were frequently under surveillance. There was much confusion, distrust, and suspicion at the highest government and military levels concerning the soldiers as "Japanese Americans." The 100th Battalion was first organized as an unarmed labor battalion.[7] The soldiers' arms were taken away in Hawaii (Martin Tohara, personal communication) and they arrived unarmed in Wisconsin (Hideo Tokairen, personal communication; Richard Hosaka, personal communication). A radiogram dated February 5, 1942, which was sent to the war department's adjutant general from Fort Shafter, cited the need for such an unarmed labor battalion (Daniels 1989).

One reason why they trained for so long was that no one knew what to do with them (Roland Kotani, personal communication). One former soldier remembers that their training involved the "same thing over and over." Camp McCoy was the means of isolating these soldiers and keeping them out of the Pacific arena. On July 1, 1942, Thomas Handy, the war department's assistant chief of staff, wrote a memo to the assistant secretary of war stating that "the Commanding General, Hawaiian Department was authorized to form all officers and soldiers of Japanese ancestry into a provisional infantry battalion which was moved to the Mainland for training with a view to its employment in some other theater of operations" (Daniels 1989)—that is, other than the Pacific.

This isolation was not unlike the isolation of the Issei internees. Tanaka writes:

> distrust and suspicion followed the Nisei even into their training at Camp McCoy, Wisconsin, and at Camp Shelby, Hattiesburg, Mississippi. All during stateside training a constant flow of secret, periodic reports on the Japanese American unit wended its way to the War Department. In addition, cameras, generally taboo, were issued to a favored few who took pictures of the scenery...and any suspicious or *abunai* (dangerous) *kibei* (Nisei educated in Japan) (Tanaka 1982:9).

A former soldier interviewed said letters he wrote were opened, read, taped closed, and then mailed. He was forbidden to write in Japanese. This same soldier, whose father was also interned, remembers feeling torn by the contradictory situation. He said, "I felt so stupid. I just hoped the war would end...my father in concentration camp, and I in American uniform, and they trust me and not my father."

The battalion was assigned to General Ben Lear of the Second Army in Memphis, Tennessee. He constantly sent inspectors and observers to monitor the troops. James Lovell, Executive Officer of the 100th Battalion, remembers:

> Within the next several months, we were the most observed and inspected unit in the entire army. Then we had the photographers, newsmen, magazine representatives; flocks of them, all curious to see what we were made of (Tamashiro 1980:10).

The soldiers were pressured into "proving themselves," and to be on their best behavior for the "higher ups" in Washington. They were told by a superior officer that consideration for overseas combat depended upon how well they performed in their training (Richard Hosaka, personal communication). Initially, the local community's attitude toward the newly arrived battalion of 1,432 men (Tsukano 1985:82) was one of concern, followed by a general openness. Kenneth Koji, member of the 100th Battalion and a resident of Sparta, remembers that there was at first a general feeling of curiosity and, at the same time, suspicion toward the soldiers (Williams 1979:14). Duus describes the men, off-duty for the first time, taking a bus into Sparta: townspeople stared from afar or peered out of their windows at the soldiers (Duus 1987:25). Former 100th Battalion soldier Martin Tohara (personal communication) described to the author how farmers who met them said with relief, "I'll be darn, all you boys talk English!" The *Herald* (June 29, 1942, 1) reported that, because of their racial features, the "Japanese American" soldiers constituted a "military hazard" in the Pacific, and therefore could not be sent to the Pacific or kept in Hawaii. Certainly the media fueled the fires of suspicion.

Breaking down stereotypes and barriers was not initiated by change in the language of the media, nor by change in the community attitude toward the men. The men of the 100th Battalion answered to a smile or an invitation with their best behavior. They went out of their way to be friendly and gracious. Ben Tamashiro (personal communication), the Club 100 historian and a former battalion member, says in retrospect, "Our own attitude helped," it rubbed off on the other side. The soldiers knew that they were walking a tightrope, that they were being carefully observed in the eyes of everyone from the local townspeople to the military and the Department of War. If they "slipped up," all who watched would have immediately reversed their perceptions.[8]

Duus (1987:25) writes that it was because of Alice Kelly that the "ice was broken"; again, credit is given to a white person for the beginning of friendship between the soldiers and the community. What Duus fails to emphasize is the initiative and the sense of responsibility the men exhibited, which were, finally, the determining factors. The reception would not have been so warm had the men not brought their "aloha spirit" into the homes of the local residents.

As it had for the internees, the media's particular racial rhetoric for the battalion soldiers had an impact on the formation of images in the minds of the community. Newspaper articles referred to the soldiers as "Hawaiian," with the headline "Hawaiian Soldiers Like Sparta and Sparta People Like Them." The article read as follows:

> The Hawaiians are welcome in business places, and recreation centers in Sparta and neighboring cities... And we'll bet they can fight, fight with the same spirit as any good American regardless of color *(Herald,* June 22, 1942, 1).

The print media's use of the word "Hawaiian"—which designated a totally different racial group—and neutralizing terms such as "good American regardless of color," took the focus away from "Japanese"—then a loaded word[9]—and prompted acceptance in the minds of local Spartans. The soldiers mixed with local Sparta women. Being considered "Hawaiian" made them more socially acceptable. According to Murphy (1955:81), a few of the 100th Battalion soldiers called themselves Hawaiian, wishing to avoid awkward situations. Murphy juxtaposes the Hawaiian image with the ubiquitous enemy Japanese stereotype:

> Sparta girls were curious about these boys from the romantic Pacific islands, and found them quite different from the Hollywood portrayals of the bucktoothed, shaven-headed, heavily eye-glassed "Jap." More than one AJA was told that he was "not a bit like the movies" (Murphy 1955:82).

The rhetoric used for the internees, as described previously, contrasts markedly with the Hawaiian soldiers' image. The internees were categorized as clearly "Japanese," and as "enemy aliens." Sources indicate that some of the internees at McCoy were actually fathers or brothers of 100th Battalion soldiers. This contrast of rhetoric for those of the same blood line illustrates the fluidity of racial categories and meanings.

The internees and the soldiers were kept in different parts of the camp. There is confusion in the sources as to whether or not the two groups were residing at Camp McCoy at the same time. Miyamoto says that the internees departed just before the 100th Battalion arrived (1964:369). However, Duus says that the "first assignment of the 100th Battalion was to guard the Issei when they were allowed out for exercise" (1987:24). She also notes that "Kenneth Kaneko recalls hearing that one of the issei detainees was the father of a 100th Battalion soldier." Anthony Stapleton (personal communication), director of security at Fort McCoy, attested to the author that all of the internees had left the camp before the arrival of the 100th Battalion. However, several internees remember that a number of Japanese Americans from the mainland were already at the camp when the Hawaii group arrived, and these Japanese Americans remained behind when the Hawaii group left the camp. On the other hand, former 100th Battalion soldier Abe Alapai (personal communication), a resident of Tomah, Wisconsin, remembers that the internees were there at the same time the 100th Battalion was training. Ben Tamashiro (personal communication) says that communication between internee and soldier was attempted. He recalls that, not long after their arrival at Camp McCoy, a few of the soldiers went to the internment camp to "see people they knew." If these meetings took place, they represented instances of attempts to salvage relations torn apart by the dominant racial order. From interviews conducted by the author, it appears that the soldiers arrived after the Hawaii internees had departed from the camp. There were occasions when the Hawaii soldiers inadvertently came into contact with older Japanese men. These internees were most likely the few "mainland" Japanese Americans who stayed behind after the departure of the Hawaii internees.

While the men of the 100th Battalion were constantly struggling to preserve their dignity and identity—in the community and on-post—they were finally pushed to the breaking point. Provoked by racist attacks from white soldiers of the Texas Second Division, who arrived at the camp in November 1942, the 100th Battalion men fought back (some with martial arts experience), and a "near-riot" broke out. Thirty-eight Texans and one Japanese American were injured (Duus 1987:36-37). A 100th Battalion soldier recalls how the Texans called them names, including "damn Japs." Other minority soldiers—Chicano Americans and Native Americans serving in the Texas division—never touched the 100th Battalion soldiers. There was a sense of solidarity with other soldiers of color.

Duus (1987:28) mentions other fights in town, and notes that there were "a few hell-raisers who always seemed to be getting in trouble...after a few drinks." The possibility that these fights were provoked by the racist remarks and actions of Sparta residents should be recognized. Although these "barroom brawls" were probably isolated incidents frowned upon by the rest of the men in the battalion, they might also be considered a form of resistance against racism.[10]

In the media, and in history written since the war, the 100th Battalion has been referred to as "Japanese American" and as the "Nisei" battalion. With the excuse of expediency, I have used the terms "Japanese American" and "Asian American" in this paper to describe the battalion. In actuality, it was not 100 percent Nisei; Okinawan men, Hawaiian men, men of mixed ancestry, and one Korean American, Young Ok Kim,[11] also served in the battalion (Ben Tamashiro, personal communication). Duus (1987:33) says there were about twenty soldiers with "mixed-blood." This includes those soldiers with Hawaiian blood. She mentions that in addition to the Kaholokula brothers, some of the other soldiers had Hawaiian surnames like Kaleialoha or Kealoha, and some with Hawaiian blood had Japanese surnames. There were also soldiers with Japanese-Portuguese, Japanese-Chinese, or Japanese-Filipino parents. Former soldiers the author interviewed also spoke of other soldiers who were Portuguese-Japanese, and "pure Hawaiian."

Tamashiro said that a few Caucasian sergeants trained the 100th men at Schofield Barracks when they had first joined the National Guard. Six to eight Caucasian officers (all from Hawaii) were with the 100th. The Caucasian-sounding names of men in the 100th Infantry Battalion were actually names of Hawaiian or part-Hawaiian soldiers. For example, one former soldier the author interviewed said that his fellow soldier Charlie Diamond was "pure Hawaiian," and that he had joined the 100th Battalion because he did not want to remain with the Hawaii National Guard's 298th and 299th Infantry Regiments which consisted largely of "haole" (Caucasian) soldiers. Tamashiro offers the view that Diamond had traveled to Japan with his parents, and, in the rush to enlist Japanese American men, someone noticed Japan on Diamond's record and in haste mistook him for a Japanese American. This view contradicts Murphy, who states that two Hawaiian brothers had *claimed* Japanese ancestry to join the battalion (1955:83).

As history writers are prone to gloss and generalize, it is important to acknowledge that the 100th Battalion was made up of men of different racial backgrounds, although predominantly Nisei, who managed to form intimate and enduring ties across racial differences. Other than Kim (who was from San Francisco), the men were all from Hawaii (Duus 1987:40). Many of the men had known each other in Hawaii (Ben Tamashiro, personal communication) and could "talk story" endlessly in the barracks. In my view, "talking story" in this context was a means of resistance that brought the men into a familiar sphere of communication and sustained their sense of collective control. Seeing themselves as "ordinary guys" was perhaps another reason for their closeness. One former soldier told the author, "We weren't born soldiers. We were just drafted three months before Pearl Harbor. They wanted to make a killer out of you. Cannot."

A few of the men found another source of support in their wives, who joined them while they were still training at McCoy. These women lived off-post in Sparta and neighboring towns, such as La Crosse. They went with the men to Mississippi, then followed them to New Jersey just before they left the United States for the front. We need to hear more of these women's stories.

Conclusion

Camp McCoy, as a United States military installation, played its role in American history as an institution upholding the racial order of the state. During the war, Camp McCoy was responsible for detaining two groups of "Asian American" men—the Issei internees and the predominantly Asian American 100th Battalion. Although the groups were there for seemingly different purposes, they were in essence both incarcerated at the camp because of the state's racist, wartime ideology. Both groups—as "prisoners"—also shared similar characteristics: (1) They were isolated on the basis of gender and race. Their lives were radically intruded upon as they were torn from their families and thrust into a climate very different from that of Hawaii. (2) They were distrusted and, as a result, had no privacy and were kept ignorant of state decisions affecting them. They were carefully guarded and their mail was censored. (3) The activities of both groups of men were regimented, monitored, and controlled.

Given these constraints, the internees joined together for collective actions ranging from a Buddhist ceremony to a labor strike. The 100th Battalion consolidated their sense of solidarity, struggled together to survive both in the camp and in the community, and took strong collective action against overt racist attacks. It is in this way that both groups contested the state's racial meanings. By re-reading and re-thinking this bit of Wisconsin history, I have tried to show how internees and soldiers seized some control over their imposed identities and contested the dehumanizing racial order.[12]

Notes

1. I borrow this phrase from Omi and Winant. According to Omi and Winant, throughout the history of the United States racial minorities attempt to achieve "collective control" as part of a racial "war of maneuver" wherein "subordinate groups seek to preserve and extend a definite territory, to ward off violent assault, and to develop an internal society as an alternative to the repressive social system they confront" (Omi and Winant 1986:74).

100   Asian Americans

2. Sources which describe the McCoy internment experience include Patsy S. Saiki's *Ganbare!*, Roland Kotani's *The Japanese in Hawaii*, Kazuo Miyamoto's *Hawaii: End of the Rainbow*, and an unpublished paper by Charles Williams, "Captives and Soldiers: Camp McCoy and the War Years." Brief mention of the internees at McCoy appears in Kano's *A History of the Japanese in Nebraska*, and in sources focusing on the experiences of the 100th Infantry Battalion, including those by Masayo Duus, John Tsukano, Thomas Murphy, and Arnold Krammer. I am indebted to Jan Miyasaki for drawing my attention to the work of Miyamoto, Duus, and Krammer; and to Akira Toki for loaning me the sources by Kano and Tsukano.
3. Because all Japanese Americans were stripped of their constitutional rights, those living outside the camps in the "free zone" were not exempt from military jurisdiction. For example, James Omura, the editor of *Rocky Mountain Shimpo*, wrote articles regarding draft resistance at the Heart Mountain camp—and was subsequently tried for conspiracy. This fact was first brought to my attention by Gary Okihiro, and is described by Omura himself in his article, "Japanese American Journalism During World War II" (Omura 1989:71-77).
4. I thank Gary Okihiro for sharing with me excerpts from the pamphlet by Suikei Furuya, *Haisho Ten-ten*.
5. A diary entry of one of the internees states that this event occurred not at Camp McCoy but during the internees' one-year detention at Livingston, Louisiana: "We refused to work outside of the wire net fence under the provision of [the] Geneva Agreement. But, we reluctantly worked after persuaded by the officials that the cleanness of the surroundings would benefit both sides...[After about five months' service by seventy or eighty men] one of the detainees heard from a sergeant and reported [to] us that the camp site would become an airport. The report created a stir among the detainees. We entirely refused to work at any place except in the fence and reported the reason to the Spanish Consul. There was no reaction taken by the military authorities."
6. They fought in North Africa and Italy, where they engaged in bloody battles which "moved the Allies up the Italian peninsula" (CWRIC 1982:256). The 100th Battalion merged with the 442nd Regimental Combat Team on June 15, 1944, and together—now as the 442nd—moved on to France, then returned to Italy until the war's end in May. In the seven major campaigns, more than 18,000 men fought with the unit, suffering 9,486 casualties (more than 300 percent of its original infantry strength) (CWRIC 1982:257-258).
7. Duus documents this confusion and distrust in her book *Unlikely Liberators*, drawing upon memoranda of the war department. See also Daniels 1989.
8. Thanks to Jan Miyasaki for pointing out the "double-edged sword" situation in which the 100th Battalion men were caught.
9. This idea came from discussion about print media discourse with Mimi Kim.
10. In 1980, between 10,000 and 13,000 Cuban refugees were interned at Fort McCoy *(Monroe County Democrat,* June 5, 1980, 1, and June 12, 1980, 1). The Cuban situation provides a case which substantiates my suggestion that racist comments motivated the bar fights. In a *La Crosse Tribune* article, a Cuban who was interned at Fort McCoy in 1980, Jorge Innes, expressed the following: "We are really concerned about the treatment we are receiving. We are able and want to work. Many of us have an additional problem of being black... We would like to stop the fights, but we don't know how to do it. We like to go to a bar and drink a little beer, but they look at us and start insulting us" *(La Crosse Tribune,* May 19, 1981, 9).

11. Of Young Ok Kim, Tamashiro says: "He was the only Korean who served with the 100th. He was the gutsiest soldier there ever was. He was just that kind of guy. He wasn't afraid of dying" (Ben Tamashiro, personal communication).
12. The author warmly thanks Jan Miyasaki for many helpful conversations throughout the preparation of this essay and for source materials; Mimi Kim and Wendy Ho for their support; and Sara Sunindyo who stressed the necessity of recording occurrences of resistance no matter how seemingly insignificant. The author is also indebted to Helen Khim, an invaluable resource person and translator, and to Abe Alapai, John Beaudin, Mary Binder, Richard Hosaka, Roland Kotani, Koetsu Morita, Patsy S. Saiki, Anthony Stapleton, Ben Tamashiro, Martin Tohara, and Hideo Tokairen, whose personal memories of the matters discussed in this paper, elicited in interviews in 1989, provided invaluable data. Thanks also to Gary Okihiro.

References

Commission on Wartime Relocation and Internment of Civilians [CWRIC]. 1982. *Personal Justice Denied.* Report of the CWRIC. Washington, D.C.: United States Government Printing Office.
Daniels, Roger, ed. 1989. *American Concentration Camps: A Documentary History of the Relocation and Incarceration of Japanese Americans, 1944-1945,* volume eight. New York and London: Garland Publishing.
Dower, John W. 1986. *War Without Mercy: Race and Power in the Pacific War.* New York: Pantheon Books.
Duus, Masayo Umezawa. 1987. *Unlikely Liberators: The Men of the 100th and the 442nd.* Translated from the Japanese by Peter Duus. Honolulu: University of Hawaii Press.
Furuya, Suikei. 1964. *Haisho Ten-ten.* Honolulu: Hawaii Times.
Kano, Hiram Hisanori. 1984. *A History of the Japanese in Nebraska.* Crawford, Nebraska: Cottonwood Press.
Kotani, Roland. 1985. *The Japanese in Hawaii: A Century of Struggle.* Honolulu: The Hawaii Hochi.
Krammer, Arnold. 1983. "Japanese Prisoners of War in America." *Pacific Historical Review* 52 (1):67-91.
La Crosse Tribune and Leader-Press, La Crosse, Wisconsin.
Miyamoto, Kazuo. 1964. *Hawaii: End of the Rainbow.* Rutland, Vermont and Tokyo: Charles E. Tuttle.
Monroe County Democrat, Monroe County, Wisconsin.
Murphy, Thomas D. 1955. *Ambassadors in Arms: The Story of Hawaii's 100th Battalion.* Honolulu: University of Hawaii Press.
Omi, Michael, and Howard Winant. 1986. *Racial Formation in the United States: From the 1960s to the 1980s.* New York: Routledge and Kegan Paul.
Omura, James. 1989. "Japanese American Journalism During World War II." In *Frontiers of Asian American Studies: Writing, Research, and Commentary,* edited by G. M. Nomura, R. Endo, S. H. Sumida, and R. C. Leong. Pullman: Washington State University Press.
Saiki, Patsy Sumie. 1983. *Ganbare! An Example of Japanese Spirit.* Honolulu: Kisaku.
Sorenson, Martha. 1986. "Post Becomes a Reality in 1909." *Triad* 3 (11):2-4.
Sparta Herald, Sparta, Wisconsin.
Tamashiro, Ben. 1980. "A Bastard Outfit—What Else?" *Puka-puka Parade* 34 (1):5-15.

Tanaka, Chester. 1982. *Go For Broke: A Pictorial History of the Japanese American 100th Infantry Battalion and the 442d Regimental Combat Team.* Richmond: Go For Broke, Inc.

TenBroek, Jacobus, E. N. Barnhart, and F. W. Matson. 1954. *Prejudice, War and the Constitution.* Volume three of *Japanese American Evacuation and Resettlement.* Berkeley and Los Angeles: University of California Press.

Thomas, Dorothy Swaine, and Richard S. Nishimoto. 1946. *The Spoilage: Japanese American Evacuation and Resettlement During World War II.* Volume one of *Japanese American Evacuation and Resettlement.* Berkeley and Los Angeles: University of California Press.

Tsukano, John. 1985. *Bridge of Love.* Honolulu: Hawaii Hosts, Inc.

Unemployment Compensation Division. 1938-1951. *Unemployment Compensation Statistics: U. C. Claims Filed Weekly by District in Wisconsin.* Madison: Industrial Commission of Wisconsin.

Williams, Charles M. 1979. "Captives and Soldiers: Camp McCoy and the War Years." Unpublished manuscript.

The Collective Memories of Communities

Wendy L. Ng

The community is central in understanding how individuals derive a sense of belonging, identity, and meaning in their lives. Communities are created by individuals through their interactions with one another, based upon a common history. A part of this creation of community is the history of the community, the memory of the past which individuals bring to the community: a community memory. As Japanese Americans reflect upon the events of forty years ago, and then question the definition and meaning of community in the 1980s, it is time to consider this concept of collective memory in the social discourse of the Japanese American experience.

I use the assumptions of collective memory somewhat broadly; that is, that community history is stored, preserved, and shared as a set of events in the memory of individuals. Included in this definition is the assumption that different generations have different experiences and perspectives of the past. This knowledge of the past is transmitted from one generation to another through culture—traditions, rituals, and folklore (Schudson 1987; Wertsch 1987). The collective memory then is an integral part of identity and belonging within a community, providing a sense of collective identity among individual members of a community. The collective memory is a critical source of knowledge and traditions within the Japanese American experience. This community study approach assumes individuals are responsible for creating their sense of the past and are active participants in creating their own history. Through the collective memory, the continuity of the intellectual, social, and cultural traditions of a community are maintained and perpetuated.

In the present-day Japanese American community, one aspect of belonging involves a sense of what has occurred in the past. In recent years, this history of the "buried past" (Ichioka 1974) has been uncovered. Collectively, Japanese Americans have uncovered the history and stories of the community — through the understanding of relocation camps, incarceration, and redress. All of these have become a part of the vocabulary of the community. In addition, the wartime experiences of the community have brought forth visual reminders in the form of documentaries and films such as *Nisei Soldier, Unfinished Business,* and *The Color of Honor.* The presence of an active collective memory — a past memory — serves as a part of the continual re-creation and linkage to the past. In effect, the collective memory cements the past and the present to one another. History has played an important role in shaping the Japanese American community, and, today, past actions have taken on new and reinterpreted meanings in the context of justice and civil rights.

Memory is selective, and individuals are cautious about what they choose to remember and to not remember. They interpret past experiences to fit their own needs or desires, as well as choosing to conceal their past (memory) to avoid emotional trauma. (A good example of this is incest victims who conceal their past.) Such has been the case with Japanese Americans who were incarcerated in relocation camps during the war. To avoid reliving the trauma of the past, they have as a community collectively chosen to remember the camp experience in selective ways.

Remembering the past is subjective. Relying on memory accounts presents challenges to the accuracy of research on and about historical events. However, selective interpretation of events is important because it reveals how individuals and their community cope with, adjust, and respond to their historical conditions. As such, the transmission of events, as well as the suppression of experiences, is significant today.

Community and individual identity are engaged in a dialectical relationship with history. In this paper, I look at the collective memory of the Japanese American community through the eyes of the third generation, or "Sansei." I focus on the Sansei because they did not directly experience the events of previous generations, and thus they provide evidence as to how history is transmitted within a community from one generation to another.

Hood River is similar to other West Coast Japanese American communities. Settling there during the early 1900s, the Japanese farmed truck garden crops and deciduous fruit orchards. During World War II, they were sent to Tule Lake and Minidoka relocation camps. Following the war, many returned to rebuild their farms and orchards despite the well-known anti-Japanese advertisement campaign by local Hood River residents and the anti-Japanese sentiment of the American Legion of Hood River (Martin 1946; Moore 1945).

Between June 1987 and September 1988, in-depth interviews were conducted with Sansei who were born and raised in Hood River, Oregon.

Subjects were obtained through personal and word-of-mouth contacts; during the interview, they responded to a semi-structured, open-ended questionnaire focusing on family, work, and community life.

In many respects, this research is exploratory because of the limitations of the sample size. Nonetheless, these interviews represent a case study of a community's experience and thereby contribute to a broader, history-based understanding of the contemporary Japanese American experience.

The major themes—the collective memory—of the Sansei lives I describe are responses to the experience of growing up in a minority community which seeks acceptance and assimilation. The experiences of the Sansei are just one facet of Japanese American community life. These themes of their collective memory are "cultural lenses" of a generation: ones from which to view the Japanese American experience, captured at this one moment in time.

Learning the Past

> Now what are they talking about? Camp? And then they'd just call it camp, too. Which was like... we had this very vague vision of summer camp. What are they talking about? Camp? And we had this sort of vague impression of tents or you know, a bunch of young people on a beach or something.

Sansei reacted in a number of different ways to learning about their parents' experiences during the war. Curiosity, indifference, surprise, and anger were some of the responses. They found out about camp through their parents' scattered stories and peculiar behavior, and they were fully aware that the experience had been traumatic as well as dislocating. Most Sansei said that their parents' behavior was an unusual but accepted part of growing up, as their parents tended to privatize the experience by not discussing it openly. During the course of the research Sansei often asked, "Did your mother ever talk about it?" as if to validate their experience of not knowing the details of their parents' internment.

Sansei felt their parents were very casual about mentioning camp, as if it had very little significance or meaning to them at all. As one female Sansei told me:

> Well, he always referred to it as camp... "back when we were in camp," and sometimes he would tell funny stories. And sometimes not. He never talked much about how he felt. We just sort of got that out of the way he talked about it.

Her father's casual approach made her angry. She said, "At one point, I was really angry. I was yelling at him and saying, why didn't you tell us any of this stuff cause it makes a difference!"

In addition to the casual remarks about camp, Sansei had to piece together bits of stories and the fragmented, abstruse behavior of their parents. This is discussed by the following Sansei who remembered incidents where camp was mentioned by her mother and father:

> My Dad would sort of drop these hints. Very subtle things like, he'd say, like, you know how you get those, sometimes, those terrible gift packs where, for Christmas, like Knotts Berry Farms jelly and stuff. One of them was orange marmalade. And he refused to eat any of it. Just refused. He said, "I just don't like it. I refuse to eat it." And we'd just go, "How? How could you, we never saw you eat this before?"
>
> And my mom never made any before. She'd make jams and things, but, how do you know if you don't like it? Then he said, "Well, in camp they made us eat this every single day for breakfast, that's all they had, every single day." And he just goes, "And I can't even look at it. I can't stand the smell of it."
>
> He would say stuff like that and we'd get the message that it was really something unpleasant. It etched an unpleasant memory in him that he wouldn't go as far as to [eat it] now, even he's in his sixties, he wouldn't act on some of that.

Sansei learned that camp had very little positive meaning; their parents rarely talked about it and never directly told them what had happened. As another Sansei added:

> They never did sit down and talk about it They just wanted to kind of forget it I guess. And my sister had a hard time drawing it out of them too. It's terrible, my Dad's never really said anything about the whole community – moved lock, stock, and barrel. He's really never said anything about it. We've asked him about it, he just doesn't – he just won't say much about it.

To other Sansei, their parents would talk about it in the security of their own homes and families:

> He never would talk about it unless he felt safe. There were a couple of times when I had, I remember one guy I was dating, who was white. He was asking Dad about it and it was... I got really uncomfortable because it was quite clear that Dad didn't feel comfortable talking to him about it because the guy was being insensitive and ignorant.

This father's reactions illustrate the private side of the camp experience. Although he was willing to share his experience with his daughter, and did so somewhat selectively, he was reluctant to discuss his experiences with a non-Japanese outsider.

This privatization of the camp experience is reflected in other Sansei experiences. Nisei parents selectively shared bits and pieces of information from their past. When pressed by their children to tell more, they were reluctant to do so. In some cases, this silent side of the camp experience was interpreted as a positive way of dealing with the past. Because Nisei parents presented a positive or neutral picture of camp and of the non-Japanese Hood River community, this attitude reflected better on the Japanese American community as a whole. One Sansei told me:

> There were a lot of "anti" feelings. Grandpa would say, "It does no good to get mad." So I guess my dad had that same feeling. He didn't want to talk about it.

Another Sansei reflected upon her parents' experience:

> It was never a negative comment. It wasn't necessarily a positive one either. It was simply that camp was a part of my mom's life and it may not have been until I started investigating on my own that I realized that camp was a very horrible experience for my parents. They had some very strong feelings about how they'd been treated in the war.

While most parents of Sansei were reluctant to speak about what happened to them during the war, some were open:

> Dad was always talking about it. He'd always go south or something, he'd drive by Tule Lake and he'd say, "That's where we were interned during the war" or something. There was never any effort to keep hiding it or anything like that.

However, this experience was far from the norm. For the most part, Sansei grew up not knowing significant episodes of their parents' past. It was a curious but accepted part of their experience as Japanese Americans. The stories Sansei heard from their parents are a part of the collective memory of the Japanese American community. They provide a link from the past to the present and re-create the camp experience for the Sansei.

Be American, but Remember You're Japanese

> Don't make a big deal about being Japanese. You're American... Work hard, study a lot, mix in, be productive, make money, and everything will be OK.

Repeatedly, Sansei heard the message that they were Americans. This was ingrained in their day-to-day lives at home and in school. Yet, while the language this was communicated to them in was English, they were also reminded they were Japanese—by their parents, and their peers.

Loss of the ability to communicate in the Japanese language is just one cost to the Japanese American community. Although most Sansei grew up knowing their Japanese-speaking grandparents, they could not communicate with them; their parents discouraged the use of Japanese in the household lest they should be handicapped by language problems later in life. Many Sansei lived in extended family arrangements with Japanese grandparents. In these bilingual (Japanese and English) households, they often understood, but never bothered to learn to speak, Japanese. One Sansei said, "They [the grandparents] never bothered to learn English." This resulted in communication difficulties between the two generations, and the Nisei parents had to serve as intermediate interpreters. Furthermore, it was made clear that, "It was kind of like, I shouldn't learn Japanese. Because if I grew up with an accent, that would be held against me in terms of, you know, what society felt. I had to make a real effort to be accepted in mainstream society."

One Sansei said she noticed a difference in the way she grew up as compared to her cousins: They had lived with her grandparents and were at least able to understand the Japanese language:

> I remember being kind of jealous because they [her cousins] got to see grandpa and grandma all the time. And they even, though they didn't speak Japanese, they understood it. And so, you know, all the conversations that went on, I'm sure, it was eighty percent Japanese, they understood everything. I don't think they ever responded in Japanese, because they were never taught it formally. But, they always knew everything that was going on. And I was always envious of that.

As a result she felt left out because she never could clearly communicate to her grandparents:

> I remember when I was really young, just really, I'd go to bed at night and just wish and wish and wish and wish really hard that I could just wake up fluent in Japanese. I just wanted so bad to be part of this communication that I didn't understand.

Despite not being encouraged to speak Japanese, Sansei received messages from their parents that they had to do well in school because they were Japanese:

> My Dad told me, "You have to be the smartest in your class because." Because of what he knew, you know, he just felt that—OK. You're just going to have problems unless you can distinguish yourself early. He'd say, "Well, OK. You're different and you have to establish yourself so no one can make fun of you if you are the smartest one in the class." And so, there's a lot of pressure to do really well.
>
> I remember my parents telling me I always had to do something twice as good as my non-Asian counterparts because, first, we had high visibility within that community [Hood River]. We were less than a percent of the population. But, when you took the time to do something, people you know, would notice. Be model citizens, just like our Nisei parents.

Being the best, the model citizen, and being proud were ways of coping with the racism still present in the community. "It seems like the Japanese are real proud," said one Sansei. "All the parents wanted their kids to be the best, the smartest. Any activity they did, there are other Japanese American families involved, they wanted to be the best."

Sansei talked about their experience of growing up as no different than anybody else's. They competed in sports, were active in school, were elected to student government, were involved in 4-H, and took ballet and piano lessons. They were in many cases the prototypical all-American boys and girls of their community, with one exception: they were Japanese. The result is a contradiction: they felt that they were treated no differently than non-Japanese, but they still felt prejudice toward Japanese (including themselves) within Hood River. As one Sansei stated, "I was treated no differently than anyone else. But you do feel it—some prejudice. I mean, it was still there."

The racism Sansei encountered ran deeply within the social institutions of the community and among the parents of their non-Japanese friends. For example, the Elks Clubs excluded Japanese from their facility until the late 1970s. Friends' parents prohibited their children from dating interracially, despite its commonplace occurrence. There were other reminders of being Japanese: Pearl Harbor Day and being called Jap by non-Japanese peers. Clearly, the Sansei learned that they were different because they were Japanese. "The fact that they think you're different, and therefore, weird. You sort of pick it up and internalize it yourself because there was always the comment about being—JAP," said one Sansei.

Sansei felt that their parents expected them to excel in school because they were Japanese. However, there was still a subtle, anti-Japanese presence within their community. As a result, the consequences of the past, the hidden history of camps and relocation, influenced the Sansei view of themselves as Japanese Americans. The collective memory of the community transmits, not intentionally, but on a subverted level, a less-than-positive attitude about Japanese ethnicity. One Sansei interprets this as denial of ethnicity:

> And I think that kind of mentality gets absorbed by the children, whether or not it's explicit. You pick it up because... I mean the ways that it comes out concretely, is parents encouraging children, Sansei to not confront or deal with being Japanese, not know what your heritage is about, not be that connected to relatives in Japan, things Japanese, or things being done at home, you don't talk about them in school. Seems like a lot of Sansei are really confused about who they are and don't want to deal with being Asian because they don't know how to deal with it.

Consequently, the continued challenges to their identity, the silence of their parents, and the still present racism of the Hood River community presented emotional and identity challenges to the Sansei. They knew that their parents experienced similar challenges from being in relocation camps. "[Camp] breaks down the family structure. I think it's resulted in emotional challenges for our family," said one Sansei.

These emotional challenges are very rarely mentioned and are not discussed within the Japanese American community. As a result, there are invisible costs to the Japanese Americans themselves and to their community:

You know I have an aunt on my mother's side who is—who had a mental breakdown. They admitted her to a medical facility. After the camp, she never fully recovered from that mental state. We don't know if it's attributed to the incarceration or just she had other problems. I think it [camp] *really* affected them psychologically. I mean, no one really wants to say that, but why don't I...why don't you speak Japanese fluently? Right?

Redressing the Past
Is there really any price?

The topic of great concern and of much resistance among Hood River Japanese Americans is the issue of redress and reparations. In Hood River, the campaign for monetary compensation for Japanese American losses during World War II has been a sensitive subject among the Nisei. Redress is a sensitive issue because of Hood River's past anti-Japanese history. Nisei parents are reluctant and cautious to come forward in support of redress because they do not wish to rekindle any ill feelings over the monetary compensation. Among the Sansei, however, redress invoked strong feelings. Unlike their parents, who will benefit from monetary compensation, Sansei would not receive anything. Yet, Sansei were surprisingly in support of redress for their parents. They realized the reasons for their parents' caution, however:

> You'll find most Nisei are very reluctant to talk about redress...especially in Hood River. Because they're still living within that community. Their feeling is, "You know, you people in Portland, you can say all you want about redress and stir waters. But, we have to live here and we have to get along with our neighbors, and so...we can't really say how we feel."

Another Sansei who no longer lives in Hood River realized that her parents' response is based upon what happened over forty years ago. She said:

> I think politically, it's a sensitive issue for the Japanese community in Hood River. Because they remember how difficult it was when the relationship was strained and [they] worked hard to develop a positive relationship with their Caucasian community. So having this issue raised...I'm sure will raise some sensitivities about that because it means that the problems that they faced in the past was from these relationships [with the Caucasians] of that related to the camps, and that's very sensitive for them.

It is unclear whether Japanese will ever see the actual monetary compensation that redress will offer. Because of this, they hold rather doubtful attitudes about redress. Another Sansei added the bitterness she felt over the matter:

> I mean, if someone just said, OK, I mean you don't know if that you'll ever get paid your money or anything. Just the idea of it is sort of strange to me. Like, OK, we've made you suffer, or we did this horrible thing, this horrible act. OK, we made this bad mistake and if we give you some money you could

just forget about it. You know? I mean what is that idea? Is it sort of like, if we give you money then you'll forgive us? Completely. Or that's what it was worth to you? There are these bad memories, certainly bad memories about it.

It's almost this running joke. I mean, everyone goes...they would say things very flippantly. Like they'll say something like, "Oh, we need a new something or other. We need a new—whatever, piece of equipment for the orchard or something." And then my mom would just sort of very flippantly say, "Oh well, you could buy that with your $25,000." And then they'd [parents] both laugh. Just like—oh yea, right. She thinks about it, but whether or not it happens—it will *ever* happen, is just speculation.

One Sansei was entirely indifferent to the issue. He never had to experience what his parents went through, and thus, even with his awareness of the wrong of the wartime internment, it was not a concern of his:

A wrong was created. It was wrong to have evacuation, but it's really none of my business because I wasn't even born at the time of evacuation. I think we've been more accepted by our Caucasian neighbors because we don't really get excited about racial issues or anything. We're really too busy to have anything to do with it, or we really don't care too much about it.

The sensitivity of the redress issue, the inability to talk about the past in public, as well as the indifference to redress, demonstrates a correlation between history (what happened to them) and the present (unwillingness or inability to talk about their experience). These attitudes are a part of the hidden costs to the community. In the same way that Nisei parents were private about the camp experience, they are also reluctant to speak out within the Japanese American community about political issues such as redress.

Conclusion

The collective memory of the Hood River community has been selective memory, filled with the insecurities and ambivalence of relocation and return to the community. The collective response to the relocation was to filter only bits and pieces of the past, thus shielding future generations from any knowledge of what actually occurred. In spite of this, the memory of the wartime experience lingers with their children, the Sansei. Although Nisei parents were cautious in how they talked about their experience, their feelings were nonetheless present in their stories and behavior. These feelings etched a bitter picture of the past. This history of the Nisei parents and the Issei grandparents—the Japanese American community—plays a significant role for individuals, establishing an important sense of collective identification with the group. Despite not having experienced the relocation camps firsthand, Sansei have come to know what their parents experienced through the collective memory of their community.

The Sansei experience is an ambivalent one. It has been shaped by the historical conditions and the collective memory of their community. The collective memory of the community is a component of the sense of individual identity and connections to a group. Even though Nisei parents had a subtle code for suppressing the Japanese-ness of their children, they still expected Sansei to retain ties to the Japanese American community. The Nisei have said, "We didn't even give them Japanese names. We didn't want them to learn Japanese"; and at the same time they imparted a message of, "Because you're Japanese, you have to do better than everyone else." As a result, Sansei find themselves in the curious dilemma of being both alien to the Japanese-ness of their parents and grandparents and separate from the dominant majority-culture social structure of the Hood River community because they belong to a racial minority group. This range of expectations results in stresses for the Sansei who, despite their insistence on their American-ness, have had to live in two environments: the inclusiveness of the Japanese American community's expectations (to be all-American), and the exclusionary non-Japanese community of Hood River.

The meaning of community for Sansei in the 1980s is deeply rooted in their parents' history and in their community's history. Knowing the past is vital to the survival of a community and culture. The events of the past have developed distinctive elements in Japanese Americans: the privatization of personal experience, the abandonment of language, and the emphasis on being "all- American." The collective memory, as it is reconstructed in the present, creates an identity for Japanese Americans which is a unique part of the Asian experience in America. It is a memory continually being transmitted and created through interactions between members of the community, and it is a history and shared past which will never disappear. As "American" as they might be, Sansei are connected to the Japanese American community and share with their parents the collective memory of the community.

References

Ichioka, Yuji. 1974. *A Buried Past: An Annotated Bibliography of the Japanese American Research Project Collection.* Berkeley: University of California.
Martin, R. G. 1946. "Hood River Odyssey." *The New Republic* 115:814-816.
Moore, A. W. 1945. "Hood River Redeems Itself." *Asia and the Americas* 56:208-209.
Schudson, Michael. 1987. "Preservation of the Past in Mental Life." *The Quarterly Newsletter of the Laboratory of Comparative Human Cognition* 9:5-11.
Wertsch, James A. 1987. "Collective Memory: Issues from a Socio-historical Perspective." *The Quarterly Newsletter of the Laboratory of Comparative Human Cognition* 9:19-22.

Coroners' Reports as a Historical Source for Asian American History

Lee S. Hayakawa[1]

The science of demography, the statistical study of human life, includes the fields of genealogy, human eugenics, biometrics, and pathometrics; in the collection of data, it often involves the census and the registration of vital facts and vital statistics. The census is used mainly for the purpose of adjustments in legislative bodies and the formulation of governmental and other policies; registration is "essential as a means of preserving evidence of personal status in order to establish the individual's identity, age, citizenship, and marital condition for the proper determination of the various rights and obligations which arise in connection with life insurance, pension plans, social security, employment, passports, military service, public assistance, etc. and in the settlement of estates and inheritances" (Wolfenden 1954:1-2). Registration records the life cycle; from birth to marriage and then to death. Since the way a person died reveals much about the way that person lived, coroners' reports can be a valuable demographical tool in the study of a people's history.[2]

The coroner's office, first made popular by Japanese American Thomas Noguchi, the former Los Angeles coroner, was begun in California in 1849. This date is very significant because it is also about that time that Asians began to immigrate to California and the West Coast. Santa Clara County, where many of these immigrants settled, possesses a collection of coroners' reports that dates from 1865 to 1930. The decedent's native country, age, marital status, sex, race, residence, time resided in the country, and occupation are listed in these reports. In addition, they document not only the cause of death, but the manner of death—something that has been most revealing. Santa Clara County coroners' reports thus represent a fairly comprehensive documentation of a major part of Asian American history.[3]

As accurate, primary sources of history, however, these coroners' reports fall short. They show a prejudice that was prevalent at that time, and thus lack the objectivity one would expect from a public service office document. The reports' consistent and seemingly accepted use of the epithets "Jap" and "Chinaman" reflect this. Many of the Asian names are grossly misspelled and inaccurate, and the handwriting is atrocious. In addition, the credibility, standards, and practices of coroners during this time period are virtually unknown and undocumented. Objectivity, and perhaps thoroughness and professionalism, are lacking. Nevertheless, the vital statistics provided by these reports give much insight into a historical perspective which otherwise could only be obtained through personal histories, journals, and newspapers of the past.

In reviewing hundreds of Santa Clara coroners' reports, certain cases caught my eye and piqued my curiosity.[4] After further research, I categorized these cases: some seemed to refute stereotypes, some seemed to confirm stereotypes, some confirmed present-day Asian American conditions, and others were just unusual. I will give examples of each.

The first category is crimes of passion. Because of negative portrayals in the media, it is common to think that Asian men are asexual, single-faceted, and, in general, less-than-masculine. Perhaps the cases I have seen are isolated ones, but I see them as incidents that are nevertheless significant. On July 25, 1908, one Hisagi Yamamoto entered the house of S. Sakata and badgered Sakata's wife, Hagime Ishizaki, as he had been doing for some time. Entering the house, he fired a wild shot, and delivered an ultimatum to Hagime. According to Hagime in the coroner's inquest, "He said if I wouldn't live with him he might do something against me." S. Sakata, protecting his wife, drew his gun and shot Yamamoto dead. Hisagi Yamamoto's coroner's report reads, "gunshot wounds inflicted by S. Sakata in self defense and we exonerate said S. Sakata from all blame." Yamamoto, in fact, was wounded by four gunshots in the upper part of the right chest and neck and one shot through the left forearm.

Another case, also a crime of passion, is highly speculative and rather suspicious in appearance. The case concerns the death of a Caucasian woman, Iva Edwards, who was found murdered in her bed. Apparently, a 28-year-old Japanese male, S. Kishi, had entered her bedroom, shot her in bed, and then proceeded to shoot himself, committing suicide. The reasons behind the murder/suicide were not expounded upon in the inquest and leave much to the imagination.

One case in particular refutes the stereotype of the quiet, meek, submissive Asian: this category I have called "belligerent Asians." This may well be an isolated instance, but it still provides another perspective on Asians during this time period.

On December 1, 1908, two Japanese males, Kemyji and Tarada, approached several Caucasian workers at a train station and asked if they could ride in a certain boxcar. The workers replied "no," because of orders from a John Kyne. Returning several times, the two were still turned down for reasons not expressed in the inquest. Later, Kemyji and Tarada, along with a Shiraishi, Okuma, and Yoshimizu, returned intoxicated and attacked John Kyne. One held off the other Caucasian workers with a chisel, while the other four beat Kyne to death with a hammer and hand axe. This gruesome story reflects a "different" Asian.

The third category is that of the quality of life. The case of Chokichi Doi raises many questions, some of them contemporary issues. Chokichi Doi, a 23-year-old male, died of pneumonia and heart trouble on September 21, 1907. The inquest revealed that one T. Kuwahara, a licensed doctor in Japan but unlicensed in the United States, attempted to help Doi. Whether Asian medical practices are inferior to those in America, and in what capacity Kuwahara could practice in the United States, are questions that arose at the inquest. The verdict of the coroner's jury reads, "We the jurors find that the deceased came to his death of pneumonia and heart trouble, without any medical attention. We the jurors recommend that the city physician look after the so-called doctors-nurses who are practicing in Chinatown and vicinity without a license." It is important to note that Asians were not allowed into all-white hospitals, but had a separate facility.

Other quality-of-life cases include Asians in high risk jobs, prone to many occupational hazards. One case reports on a 28-year-old Japanese male, Isaku Tanaka, who was killed while dismounting from a mule after a day's work. His coroner's report reads, "being dragged and kicked to death by a span of mules." This is obviously a sad story of an immigrant worker trying to make a better life.

The last quality-of-life cases deal with automobile and motorcycle accidents. It is apparent that a handful of Asians had a surplus of wealth and were able to afford such luxuries as motorcycles and automobiles. If these accidents were the fault of the Asian drivers, then, unfortunately, the stereotype of the "bad" Asian driver could be substantiated.

The last category is simply a group of cases that I have labelled "unusuals." A very strange case was the death of Sahatachi Uchida, a 37-year-old Japanese male from Hawaii, who was accidentally drowned on October 4, 1906. Mr. Peacock, the chauffeur of the automobile in question, accidentally (?) ran Uchida, who was riding a bicycle, off a country road into a ditch filled with water. Somehow, Uchida ended up pinned underwater beneath the front axle of the car. The verdict of Uchida's coroner's jury reads, "accidental drowning in an automobile collision in the county road ditch, and we exonerate the chauffeur, Mr. Peacock, from all blame."

116 *Asian Americans*

Having a limited educational and research background, I do not, by any means, consider this research conclusive or definitive; I have merely scratched the surface of a resource that requires a closer look and a more profound evaluation. Other studies that could be done, for example, include a statistical analysis of the many Asian suicides in Santa Clara County, given the supposed cultural propensity for suicide. Methods ranging from simple hanging, shooting, or disembowelment to the slitting of the throat with a razor blade (and in one case a cleaver) were seen in the coroners' reports. Another study could be done on Asians' migratory patterns, using the place and length of residence provided in these reports. A study might also be conducted on the interethnic relations between the Japanese and the Chinese by examining any murders that may have occurred between the two.

When combined with supplementary records such as the census, police records, and criminal court cases, coroners' reports represent a potentially rich source for Asian American history. More extensive studies can provide valuable insight and perhaps even a whole new perspective for Asian American Studies.

Notes

1. I would like to acknowledge and express my gratitude to Leslie Masunaga, Robert Fung, and Steven G. Doi, and special heartfelt "mahalo's" to Dr. Gary Y. Okihiro.
2. It is important to note that all deaths that occurred were not examined by the medical examiner/coroner. The regulations and conditions that require an inquiry by the medical examiner/coroner today are described in detail in the California Law Code Sections. Deaths requiring inquiry by the medical examiner/coroner are, in summary, those with unusual circumstances where the causes of death may be other than natural. This means that sudden or immediate deaths, suicides, deaths involving foul play, accidental deaths, and unusual deaths are reported and go through the coroners' office.
3. The Santa Clara County coroners' reports include information on the name of the coroner, the date of the inquiry, name of decedent, native country, age, marital status, sex, race, residence, time resided in the country, occupation, place and date of death, and cause of death.
4. These particular coroners' reports can presently be found at the San Jose Historical Museum under archivist Leslie Masunaga. She informed me that coroners' reports were actually saved by the city historian, Clyde Arbuckle, who received them from various city and county departments that were cleaning out their old files and records. This collection began in the 1950s and includes reports dated as early as 1865 and as late as 1930. Each coroner's report consists of a coroner's subpoena, a coroner's summons of jurors, inquest testimony which decides the specific cause of death, any background from witnesses or persons related in some way to the decedent, and the verdict of the coroner's jury. There are twenty-seven legal size boxes containing the coroners' reports. At the time of this writing, I have been through roughly half of the boxes and have picked out all decedents whose country of origin was Asian, i.e., China or Japan, or those decedents with Asian surnames. I recorded the pertinent information on three-by-five cards and have tabulated the results thus far somewhat quantitatively into twelve categories. The deaths were tabulated by

the year spans that appeared on the labels. A chronological, comprehensive analysis of all of the reports has yet to be done. The categories of causes of death are: suicide, natural causes, train accident, auto accident, murder, fire, drugs, drowning, accidental gunshot, accidental fall, accidental consumption, and unknown. I have looked further into several interesting and unusual cases by reading the inquest testimony and other peripheral background materials.

References

Hollingsworth, T. H. 1969. *Historical Demography.* Ithaca, New York: Cornell University Press.

Smith, T. Lynn, and Paul E. Zopf, Jr. 1976. *Demography: Principles and Methods.* Port Washington, New York: Alfred Publishing Company.

Wolfenden, Hugh H. 1954. *Population Statistics and Their Compilation.* Chicago: University of Chicago Press.

Part Three
Contemporary Asian American Issues

Demographics, Economics, and Politics

Stephen S. Fugita

Given the magnitude and the interconnectedness of the political and economic changes taking place in both the eastern and western hemispheres, it is now even clearer that our approaches to the study of Asian Americans must become more global and comparative. This broadening process, which is well on its way, has seen the field expand from its original, more narrow but critical concerns with recovering the past and understanding the political and economic context in which Asian America found itself. As the papers in this section demonstrate, we need to better comprehend the consequences of global realignments, the rapid increase in the number of people from the eastern and southern hemispheres, and the increasingly multicultural environment of Asians in America.

Tomoji Ishi's paper, on a world-systems perspective of anti-Asian activities, points out that we must go beyond existing race relations theories that focus solely on groups and classes within a nation-state. A good starting point in this regard is world-systems theory, which was initially developed by Wallerstein (e.g., 1974). Ishi's world-system oriented discussion of the precursors to anti-Asian activities suggests that three factors are critical: (1) Asian labor migration; (2) Asian capital migration; and (3) the international political economy. However, Ishi notes that from a local intervention perspective, a weakness of the world-systems perspective is that it is too macrostructural and economic in its orientation.

Yvonne Lau, in her paper on Asian American politics in Chicago, examines the factors that have given rise to increased Asian political participation recently seen in that city. Her case study is important not only because of the dearth of work on this topic, but because of the current ferment in this area. Lau's methodology involved interviewing a group of visible political leaders and community activists. She points out that the destruction of the Democratic machine, marked by Harold Washington's victory in 1983, created new niches which Asians were able to fill. Because of Washington's narrow margin of victory, Asians, as well as many other groups, could credibly take credit for being a critical element in the victory and thus command the attention of larger political interests.

Lau suggests that even though Asians have become more visible in Chicago's government, these leaders have narrow personal, or ethnic-group specific, as opposed to Asian American, agendas. One reason for this is that few viable pan Asian American organizations in Chicago can articulate an Asian American agenda; as a result, homeland issues are frequently pushed and the cohesiveness of the Asian coalition is reduced. Further, there have been no issues which have galvanized the disparate Asian groups in the city.

Jeremy Hein examines the unique situation of the Indo-Chinese refugees whose resettlement was managed by the American social welfare system. This process, for a number of reasons, was often not as productive as it could have been. Since the refugees had no such system in their homelands, they were unfamiliar with its characteristics and their assigned roles in it. Further, there were large disparities in the values and norms on which it was predicated as compared to those held by the refugees themselves.

Using case studies collected as a participant observer and interviewer in New York and San Francisco, Hein nicely illustrates the frequent incongruencies the refugees experienced when they confronted the Western welfare system. These studies highlight the often opaque, to American observers, reasoning behind the choices individuals make and the varied outcomes.

Edward Chang argues that the rapidly changing demographic patterns detailed by Ong have significant consequences not only for American race relations, but for our theories of such as well. Up to this point, the majority of conceptualizing done on the topic has focused on black-white relations. With the recent large influx of Asians and Hispanics, our theoretical attention needs to be expanded to better account for intra-Third World conflict. The latter is frequently embedded in the situational context of Korean small businessmen in black neighborhoods.

Although this conflict is fundamentally an economic one, that is customer-merchant, it is strongly impacted by the unique historical and cultural experiences of both groups. For example, Chang suggests that owning a business is for blacks a symbol of success; for Koreans it is seen in the more prosaic terms of simply earning a living, given that other occupational opportunities are at least partially blocked. Moreover, it should be remembered that the "merchant class" has been historically a low one in Korean society, below that of farmers.

Chang also argues that the general strategy for mobility is different for the two groups. Koreans, like many other Asian groups, have experienced oppressive governments in their homeland and thus are wary of becoming involved in the "risky" political process. Further, to them politics is tangential to dealing with their more pressing concerns of economic security and mobility.

Kyeyoung Park, in the last paper in this section, in part takes up where Chang leaves off by examining, at the more micro, individual level, Koreans' perceptions of other ethnic group members. In particular, she focuses on the development of ethnic perceptions in the workplace. Park shows that small businessmen, workers, and professionals develop markedly different constructions based upon the salient role of relationships involved in their interactions with other ethnic group members. Initially, the Koreans' own cultural orientations have the strongest effects on their perceptions of other groups. With greater exposure to racism in the general society, however, they modify their constructions to more strongly incorporate those of the American mainstream.

Taken as a set, these papers illustrate that the social science area of Asian American Studies is maturing; a synthesis of macro-, meso-, and micro-level analyses can now be profitably attempted. Further, interest is shifting from a focus on Asians' interface with white society to one on their interrelationship with other groups. The next decade for Asian Americanists thus promises some exciting developments as the global and comparative thrust of the field emerges.

Reference

Wallerstein, Immanuel. 1974 [1976]. *The Modern World System: Capitalist Agriculture and the Origins of the European World-Economy in the Sixteenth Century.* New York: Academic Press.

Contemporary Anti-Asian Activities: A Global Perspective

Tomoji Ishi

Introduction

Vincent Chin, a United States citizen of Chinese ancestry, was murdered in Detroit in 1982 by a Caucasian auto-worker who blamed Japanese auto imports for his unemployment. After a series of trials, however, the worker was ultimately acquitted. Racism in Japan against African Americans, including racial remarks made by Japan's former Prime Minister Nakasone regarding the "intelligence" of African and Hispanic Americans, have increased racial tensions in the United States. An assault on a Japanese cemetery in Los Angeles and a call for the boycott of Japanese products on Pearl Harbor Day are some examples of how this tension has been expressed.

In a different context, small Korean businesses operating in inner cities of large metropolitan areas such as New York, Los Angeles, and Washington, D.C., have faced confrontations with low-income African American residents. For example, three Korean merchants were killed and eleven Korean stores were firebombed in the Washington, D.C., area. The animosity of such residents stems from a belief that "foreign" Koreans are exploiting and not contributing to the communities, and that they are receiving government assistance to start businesses.

Anti-Asian activities have also surfaced in middle-class neighborhoods. In Monterey Park, California, where a large number of new Chinese immigrants reside, severe racial hostility between the Chinese and long-term Caucasian residents took place in a political form concerning the policy to make English the official language of the city. A recent, shocking racial conflict involved Southeast Asian immigrants: in Stockton, California, five Kampuchean school children were killed by a Caucasian male. Conflicts between

Vietnamese and Caucasian fishermen in Florida, Texas, and California have flared. The Texas case resulted in the shooting death of a Caucasian fisherman. Animosity between Southeast Asians and long-term residents competing for jobs, public assistance, and housing has been aggravated by misinformation about the United States government providing Southeast Asians with cash grants for resettlement, greater welfare benefits, and low-interest loans to use as start-up money for businesses (United States Commission on Civil Rights 1986:34-36).

Furthermore, the passage of the Immigration Control and Reform Act of 1986 was based upon the assumption that new immigrants, particularly Third World immigrants, have been taking jobs away from United States citizens. Although the validity of the above belief remains in question, animosity against Asians and Hispanics has risen. Senator Simpson, co-author of the immigration bill, stated that since "a substantial portion of these new persons and their descendants [Asians and Hispanics] do not assimilate into the society, they have the potential to create in America a measure of the same social, political and economic problems from which they have chosen to depart" (Rips 1983).

Finally, anti-Asian activities have derived from the popular perception that Asians are a "model minority." The decline in the number of Asian freshmen at the University of California, Berkeley, led to an investigation. The "success" stories of Asian students, while lauded by the media, have at the same time generated hostility against and envy toward Asians among non-Asian students.

All the above incidents and examples illustrate the complexity of contemporary anti-Asian activities in the United States. In fact, both the California Attorney General's office (California State 1988) and the United States Commission on Civil Rights (1986) have published reports on increasing anti-Asian activities (while acknowledging the lack of any mechanism to systematically collect data on this national phenomenon).

Such contemporary anti-Asian activities have largely been related to international events, such as economic relations between the United States and Asia, and the international migration of people from Asia to the United States. Although the "model minority" concept illustrates the presumed "success" of both native- and foreign-born Asians, it is the "success" image of new Asian immigrants that has been largely depicted in the media. It is interesting to note that this image overlaps with the media image of Pacific Rim countries.

The international nature of the situation of Asians in the United States is not, certainly, a contemporary phenomenon. The treatment of Asians in the United States has, since the early migration of Chinese to the United States in the mid- to late-nineteenth century, closely paralleled the nature of U.S.

relations with the ancestral countries of these immigrants. However, there is a clear difference between the past and the present.

In the past, the treatment of Asians in the United States was, to a large extent, related to relationships between the United States and the countries of origin. The 1942 World War II internment of Japanese, both citizens and non-citizens, is an obvious example. Similarly, the repeal of the Chinese Exclusion Act of 1882 was a function of the friendly relationship which developed between the United States and China when the two countries became allies to fight against Japan. Yet, Asians in the United States, with the exception of a few elite groups, had no direct political and economic linkages with their "home" countries. They became the instruments of international politics, serving either as "hostages" captured by the United States or "representatives" sent by their "home" countries; the major concern of both the United States and Asian governments was not the welfare of the Asian immigrants, but relations between the United States and Asia. One example is the outrage of the Japanese government at the segregation of Japanese students in San Francisco in 1905: not because they were concerned about the Japanese immigrants, but because the treatment was similar to that of the Chinese, and this was found to be insulting. In contrast, the Japanese government did not hesitate to issue the Gentlemen's Agreement to restrict Japanese labor immigration to the United States (Cho 1984).

Today, it is different. Asians here hold direct political and economic linkages with their "home" countries. Small Korean businesses and Korean communities directly serve South Korea as its distribution and consumption centers in the United States. South Korean businesses and the government have been interested in maintaining control over the Korean communities in the United States for their own economic sake. The "development" (or "redevelopment') of Chinatowns, Japantowns, and Koreatowns in California were all largely supported by Asian capital. It should be noted that these linkages are not created solely by foreign-born Asians in the United States. Increased interest in Pacific Rim affairs (political, economic, and cultural) by native-born Asians should also be stressed, as pointed out by Nakanishi, who enumerated examples such as the U.S.-Asia Institute and the Japanese American Citizens League, which attempted to serve as "brokers" between the United States and Asian corporations (Nakanishi 1985-1986:32-34).

A World-System Perspective

Given the international nature of anti-Asian activities prevalent in the United States in the 1980s, how can the phenomenon be theoretically conceptualized? The major limitation of the existing theories of United States race relations is that their level of analysis is based on groups and classes within the context of a nation-state. For example, assimilation theorists (Gordon 1964; Park 1950) consider race relations to be part of the assimilation process of new ethnic groups adjusting to the mainstream culture and institutions. This ecological assumption sees eventual harmonious race relations, by means of assimilation, as a matter of time, and ignores historical and macro-structural factors (both national and international). If assimilation does not work, newcomers are blamed for being "unassimilable" – and ofttimes excluded.

Compared to the conventional assimilationist perspective, Marxist class theorists (Reich 1971; Bonacich 1972) view race relations as the product of a tripartite class conflict among capital (employers), dominant labor, and subordinate labor. Apart from the problem that they focus solely on the labor market, their level of analysis is limited to either a firm or a nation-state (capital as a whole). Hence, they miss both the internal division within subordinate labor (ethnic labor market) and the role of transnational actors in intervening in the class conflict among the three actors mentioned.

Internal colonial theorists (Blauner 1972; Hechter 1975) see race or ethnicity as an independent variable which determines the status of a particular racial or ethnic group in developed countries. The concepts of "colonialism" and "core-periphery," which define unequal relationships between developed and underdeveloped countries, are meticulously employed by internal colonial theorists. The application of these international concepts to race relations within developed countries is, no doubt, an advancement in the examination of contemporary race relations. However, since the theory attempts to explain race relations as based on the historical legacy of particular racial or ethnic groups, whose statuses are derived from their colonial or peripheral statuses in the past, it lacks an analysis of contemporary world political economy and interactions among both developed and underdeveloped countries. Moreover, internal colonial theory tends to view race relations as dichotomous relations (e.g., whites versus colored) while overlooking the multiplicity of race relations among diverse groups.

The theoretical perspective best able to capture the "international" characteristics of present race relations in the United States is the world-system one. This, to be sure, does not imply that the world-system theory explains all cases of race relations in the United States; instead, this approach brings a new look to our understanding of contemporary race relations. It also resolves some theoretical problems associated with the existing theories of race relations, and poses different policy implications for the elimination of racial conflicts.

The theory of the modern world-system, developed by Wallerstein (1974), has two propositions crucial to my argument on race relations. First, it raises a question about level of analysis. The theory considers the world-system, instead of nation-states or groups/classes, as the single unit of analysis; thus, it allows us to view domestic race relations first within a world-system context. This leads us to a second proposition embedded in the world-system theory:

> the capitalist world-economy was built on a worldwide division of labor in which various zones of this economy (that which we have termed the core, the semiperiphery, and the periphery) were assigned specific economic roles, developed different class structures, used consequently different modes of labor control, and profited unequally from the workings of the system (Wallerstein 1974:162).

This proposition suggests that we must distinguish "semiperipheral" groups from "core" and "peripheral" groups. The concept of the "middleman minority," developed by Bonacich (1973), which stresses the role of a particular minority group serving as a "buffer" or a "broker" between dominant and subordinate groups, can be expanded into a broader context. An important question can then be raised as to how race relations are formed when people of different spatial zones meet each other. The encounter of people through transnational migration can be classified according to migrants' status – both in their countries of origin and in their destinations within the world economy.

The following discussion will deal with the international nature of anti-Asian activities, a product of three factors: (1) Asian labor migration; (2) Asian capital migration, and (3) the international political economy. All of these affect the ways in which Asians are treated in the United States.

An increasing number of empirical studies on international labor migration appear to be developed within the world-system framework. Students of this field (Portes and Walton 1981; Sassen-Koob 1981; Cheng and Bonacich 1984; Ishi 1988a) treat the international migration of labor as a consequence of how the world-system has been shaped. To put it differently, immigrant labor from periphery countries is compelled to go to core countries because of direct and indirect linkages between the two regions, which, in turn, continue to perpetuate the core-periphery relationships. At the same time, the international migration system creates a distinct type of labor system for immigrants within developed countries.

The consequence of the above development has been conflict between native dominant workers and immigrant subordinate workers. However, new waves of international migrants generate further complex race relations in core countries. Sassen-Koob (1981) discusses the potential competition in the United States between native-born minorities and foreign-born immigrants. Contrary to the pre-World War II period when immigrants of color were subjected to severe labor exploitation and racial exclusion, a large number of immigrants of color in the postwar period entered the United States as elite refugees, professionals, and entrepreneurs, a reflection of the transformation of national economies abroad and in the United States. Thus, we see different types of Asian immigrants—from low-income, welfare recipients to well-off business executives. Both types of immigrants face different racial realities which cannot be explained solely by a white versus colored dichotomy.

If we are able to discuss how the international migration of labor affects racial relations here, the international migration of capital can be examined in the same manner. Foreign capital accompanies the movement of managerial personnel to other countries. As long as investors were limited to Europeans and Canadians, racial antagonism between managers of foreign corporations and local communities was minimized. A current trend, however, is the growth of Asian investors, particularly the Japanese. A recent *Wall Street Journal* article (Boaz 1989) warned of the tendency toward Japan- or Asia-bashing (or xenophobia toward a new "yellow peril") against Asian investors. Similarly, the *U.S. News and World Report* published survey results in 1988 which showed greater U.S. public resentment toward Asian, as compared to Canadian and European, investors: fifty-eight percent of the respondents objected to Asian investment in the United States, while thirty-seven and twenty-two percent respectively opposed European and Canadian investment.

On the other hand, Asian multinational corporations have racial problems of their own in the areas of equal employment opportunities and community relations. African American communities have accused Japanese corporations of unfair hiring practices in the United States. A number of litigations involving the United States Equal Employment Opportunity Commission and research findings indicated racially biased hiring on the part of Japanese companies doing business in the United States. Under these circumstances, the Congressional Black Caucus held a public hearing on this matter and called for a "Buy American" campaign and encouraged African Americans not to buy Japanese products.

On the other hand, smaller Asian investors, who are involved in garment factories, restaurant enterprises, janitorial services, motels, electronic firms, etc., have not faced this same type of racial conflict in their businesses because these ethnic enterprises tend to employ family members and a small number of immigrant workers from their own ethnic groups. Also, non-Asian communities do not tend to target small Asian firms for complaints of discriminatory hiring practices. However, a different type of racial tension is raised at the community level. The Chinese-Caucasian conflict in Monterey Park is a clear example; the Korean-African American conflict in Los Angeles and Washington, D.C., is another.

We need to consider the international political economy as the third factor affecting race relations here. A decline in the competitiveness of United States industries in the world economy has generated American economic problems such as plant closings and the lay-off of workers. It is probably unavoidable that displaced workers and communities become antagonistic toward the importation of foreign products. The peoples of the country where the imported products originate are accused of offering "cheap labor," being "economic animals," and exercising "unfair practices." This issue becomes heated when people of the same race/ethnicity or nationality as those of the competing foreign country reside within the United States; such groups become the target of attack and the "hostages" of the international political economy.

Stack (1981:9) correctly stated that the economic and political strain between two states "infuses these conflicts with the potential for mobilizing collective group fears against the 'foreigners'." This explains Chin's murder and the boycott of a Japanese restaurant in Oakland. Kwong (1979:13) aptly put it:

> a "national" approach assumes that there will be a close correspondence between a group's treatment in this country and the international standing of the group's homeland.

Conceptual Clarification

Now that we have come to realize how significant it is to examine the international context in understanding anti-Asian activities, we need to further elaborate on the meaning of "international." Definitional clarification is crucial, given the increasing and confusing usage of the terms "international," "global," "transnational," and "comparative." The present treatment owes a lot to Nakanishi (1985-1986) and Stack (1981). Nakanishi, by emphasizing the nondomestic nature of "Asian American" politics, classified five persistent international political processes. They are (1) transnational political activities of Asian Americans over Asia, (2) transnational political activities of Asian homeland governments over Asian Americans, (3) the impact of bilateral United States-Asia relationships on Asian Americans, (4) Asian Americans influencing bilateral United States-Asia relationships, and (5) the impact of global mobility on Asian Americans. Stack (1981:19-20) differentiated three levels of analysis with regard to the international nature of ethnicity today. They are, first, an intrasocietal level in which an "evolving transnational system" increasingly affects ethnicity in the domestic arena of the state; second, a state level in which ethnic groups directly participate in world politics through the state system; and, finally, a global level in which ethnicity becomes an independent transnational actor. There appear to be three levels of conceptualization on the international dimension as considered in the present paper.

The first is an *extra-national* level at which we can conceptualize a direct linkage between a foreign country and its own nationals abroad, as in the case of Asian countries influencing the communities of their nationals in the United States, as well as those of nationals influencing their Asian countries abroad. These cases do not usually generate race relations problems in the United

States because the ethnicity of the nationals is usually the same as the people of their home countries. For example, the murder of a naturalized Chinese American in the United States by a Taiwan mercenary allegedly tied to the Taiwan government was treated by the United States media as a Taiwanese issue, not an American one. However, the fact that a United States citizen of Chinese ancestry was killed in the United States was largely ignored. The assumption that Asians in the United States are "foreigners," regardless of nativity, gravely neglects their civil rights.

To be sure, this extra-national relationship is frequently influenced by government policies in the country where the nationals reside. Activities of extra-nationals may be either encouraged or discouraged. For example, when Iran took U.S. hostages at the American Embassy in Tehran in 1979, militant anti-American activities by Iranian students in the United States, and mounting U.S. hostility toward Iran, caused President Jimmy Carter to order an investigation on the status of all Iranian students, regardless of the reason for their presence in the United States. In addition, many Middle Easterners in the United States were harassed by angry United States citizens.

The second level of conceptualization may be called *inter-national*. Here, we see how the relationship between a foreign country and the United States both affects and is affected by the situation and activities of an ethnic group whose ancestral land is that foreign country itself. U.S. policies and general public concern toward the ancestral lands of Asians in this country have been crucial factors associated with how Asians have been dealt with in the United States.

In these cases, Asians in the United States can simply dissociate themselves from United States-Asia relationships to show that they should not be held accountable for bilateral relations. Most non-Asians in America adhere to the widely-held misconception that Asians in the United States are "accountable" for the doings of their ancestral lands. This fact creates an uneasy and difficult situation for these Asians.

It is interesting to note here that while the Japanese in America have been "reluctant" to talk about Japan, the Jews insist on a strong tie with Israel. The relationship between the United States and Japan, for example, has undergone a series of changes beginning with the forced opening of Japan by the United States, continuing through the Pacific War and U.S. occupation of Japan, and culminating in today's trade and investment frictions. Generally speaking, while Japan was kept dependent upon the United States, the relationship between the two countries remained rather calm and did not negatively affect the treatment of American Japanese. However, when Japan's economic and military ascendency became evident, the relationship worsened, and the status of Japanese Americans, who were already victimized by racism, was further aggravated.

In contrast, Jews in the United States have, as a symbol of "freedom" against such "tyrannies" as Nazi and communist rule, remained eminent since the 1930s. American support for Israel and Jews in the Eastern Bloc has further strengthened the power of Jews in the United States. Undoubtedly, this symbol of freedom from communism has positively affected their status. Whereas a tie to Israel has been an asset for United States Jews, a tie to Japan has been a liability to the Japanese in this country.

Finally, a *trans-national* level of analysis should be considered. Contrary to the first two levels, which still consider the country as a viable unit, this level ascends from the nation-state analysis into a global one. Different from the second analytical level in which a racial or an ethnic group in the United States is not responsible for a particular relationship between its ancestral land and the United States, the trans-national analysis allows us to examine the impact, in both racial and economic terms, of foreign-born Asians doing business or working in the United States. These foreign-born Asians, reflecting the economic realities of their homelands and their homelands' relationships with the United States, shape distinct economic relationships with U.S. non-Asian ethnic groups. These relationships in turn lead to particular race relations between Asian and non-Asians because of their direct contacts — competitive at one time, and hierarchical at another — in workplaces and in communities in this country.

Distinguishing among the three levels of analysis discussed will facilitate the establishment of research problems and avoid confusion in the development, as well as the practical implications of, the world-system theory.

Practical Implications

Using the world-system perspective, the murder of Vincent Chin can be explained by international competition in the automobile industry — an explanation that goes beyond Ronald Ebens's racism. Similarly, the reactions of some segments of African Americans against the Japanese can be explained by the fact that Japan, due to its increasing influence over the people of the United States, has been scrutinized. However, such explanations are not satisfactory in dealing with actual race relations.

A major weakness of the world-system perspective is that it is too economic and too macro-structural. Although it is strong in explaining the context in which race relations take place, it only gives a "passive" picture of the people involved. It tends to explain racial antagonism simply as an impulsive response to changes in the world-system. This perspective inhibits investigation on by whom, for what interest, and in what way a particular race relationship is formed and transformed.

Civil rights education, cross-cultural efforts to break myths and stereotypes, stiff penalties against offenders, and empowerment have in the past been major instruments in remedying anti-Asian activities. Some programs have encouraged a dialogue between Koreans, Vietnamese, and African Americans in Philadelphia and Oakland (Laslett 1987). The establishment of hate crime legislation has gained momentum, particularly in California (California State 1988). The Oscar nomination of *Who Killed Vincent Chin?*, a film produced by Asian Americans, was a remarkable accomplishment. Despite an increasing number of anti-Asian activities, the political strength of Asians in the United States has been noted at both the legislative and grassroots levels.

There are, however, limitations to these approaches: namely behaviorism and the lack of a macro-economic, international analysis. This is not to suggest that a behavioral approach or a domestic solution is not fruitful, but that a structural approach, or an international solution which the world-system perspective can bring, should be sought in addition to conventional means to deal with race relations.

For Asians in the United States, some practical implications derived from the world-system perspective are in order. First of all, the extra-national framework highlights the importance of defending the civil rights of foreign-born immigrants in the United States with regard to their activities toward their home countries, as well as the home country's interventions in their lives in the United States.

The action that the Japanese American Citizen's League took to defend Iranian students in the late 1970s is a fabulous example, particularly in light of the strong anti-Iranian sentiments then present in the United States. In this case, whether or not the Japanese American Citizen's League supported the cause of the Iranian people against "U.S. imperialism" is not important; the civil rights of Iranian students vis-à-vis discriminatory legislations and racial attacks is of primary concern. The civil rights of immigrants must be defended at all times, even if their home countries are at odds with the United States; otherwise, a situation of wartime internment may be repeated.

With regard to the inter-national level of analysis, as mentioned earlier, Asians in the United States have rightfully dissociated themselves from international relations between the United States and Asian countries. However, because of increasing business relations, United States Asians have been wrongfully treated by non-Asians. To remedy this situation, Asians in the United States must go beyond reactive responses.

The growth of Pacific Rim studies in this nation may threaten the existence of Asian American Studies by proceeding beyond business-related matters to introduce and examine Asian cultures. It is the responsibility of Asians in the United States to present their own views about Asian and Asian American cultures and histories since the images of Asians and Asian Americans overlap one another. The misunderstandings of U.S. scholars, policy makers, and the media about Asian peoples and cultures affect Asians here. On the other hand, the Asian American perspective can shed positive light on the way Asian cultures in Asia are viewed. Dialogue between Asian American Studies and Pacific Rim Studies must start now.

The most pressing needs probably come from the third level: a transnational one. Apart from an international context, contemporary anti-Asian activities illustrate the nature of racial antagonism arising both from Caucasians and other racial minorities, and the vast areas of conflict among diverse class strata. This means that we must look into economic issues that reflect global stratification, as the key factor affecting the rise of anti-Asian activities. The friction between Korean merchants or Japanese corporate managers and African Americans as well as Caucasians is, to be sure, cultural and racial. Civil rights awareness on both sides must be promoted. This is particularly important since many of these business people have been educated in Asia; their understanding of United States culture and history is therefore limited.

However, it is not enough to say that cross-cultural misunderstandings or stereotypes are the sole causes of racial tensions. Economic justice must come with racial justice. Asian business communities in the United States must, by practicing equal employment and "good corporate citizenship," be responsible for the communities where they do business. In this respect, Asians in the United States can contribute to the remedy of racial frictions by educating Asian immigrants.

Asians in the United States and Asian American Studies face numerous challenges today. We are no longer living in the 1960s, a time characterized by "white versus colored" stratification. Asians in the United States can no longer afford to see themselves merely as victims of racism, but must move forward to educate both the "mainstream" and newcomers from Asia. In this respect, the expulsion of Asians from Uganda should not be viewed nonchalantly.

Note

The author is indebted to Mario Barrera, Bob Blauner, Edward Chang, Stephen S. Fugita, Hiroshi Kashiwagi, Virginia Louis, and Michael Omi for their helpful comments. He is also solely responsible for the content of this paper and not the Japan Pacific Resource Network with which he works.

References

"Asian-Americans: The Drive to Excel." 1984. *Newsweek*, April.
Blauner, Robert. 1972. *Racial Oppression in America*. New York: Harper and Row.
Boaz, David. 1989. "Yellow Peril Reinfects America." *Wall Street Journal*, April 7.

Bonacich, Edna. 1972. "A Theory of Ethnic Antagonism: The Split Labor Market." *American Sociological Review* 37:547-559.

———. 1973. "A Theory of Middleman Minorities." *American Sociological Review* 38:583-594.

California State, Office of the Attorney General. 1988. *Attorney General's Asian and Pacific Islander Advisory Committee Final Report*, December.

Chang, Edward. 1985. "Korean-Black Conflict: A Global Perspective." Unpublished manuscript.

Cheng, Lucie, and Edna Bonacich, eds. 1984. *Labor Immigration under Capitalism: Asian Immigrant Workers in the United States before World War II*. Berkeley: University of California Press.

Cho, Masa. 1984. "San Francisco Japanese Pupils Segregation and Japanese Government Intervention." Japanese Immigrant Educational Network, *Immigrant Network* 3 (2).

Chung, L. A. 1985. "Rising Assaults on Oakland Asians." *San Francisco Chronicle*, July 8.

Gordon, Milton. 1964. *Assimilation in American Life: The Role of Race, Religion, and National Origins*. New York: Oxford University Press.

Hechter, Michael. 1975. *Internal Colonialism: The Celtic Fringe in British National Development, 1536-1966*. Berkeley: University of California Press.

Hsu, Evelyn. 1986. "Influx of Asians Stirs Up L. A. Area's 'Little Taipei'." *San Francisco Chronicle*, August 1.

Ichioka, Yuji. 1977. "Japanese Association and the Japanese Government: Their Special Relationship, 1909-1926." *Pacific Historical Review* 46:409-438.

Ishi, Tomoji. 1987. *Nakasone's Racial Remarks and International Dynamism in Race Relations*. Berkeley: Japan Pacific Resource Network.

———. 1988a. "International Linkage and National Class Conflict: The Migration of Korean Nurses to the United States." *Amerasia Journal* 14 (1):23-50.

———. 1988b. *Japanese Automobile and Television Assembly Plants and Local Communities: County Demographic Correlates*. Berkeley: Japan Pacific Resource Network.

Japan Pacific Resource Network. 1986. *JPRN Bulletin* 9. San Francisco.

Kasindorf, Martin. 1982. "Asian-Americans: A 'Model Minority'." *Newsweek*, December 6, 39-51.

Kim, David S., and Charles Choy Wong. 1977. "Business Development in Koreatown, Los Angeles." In The *Korean Diaspora: Historical and Sociological Studies of Korean Immigration and Assimilation in North America*, edited by Hyung-chan Kim, 229-245. Santa Barbara, California: ABC-Clio.

Kim, Illsoo. 1981. *New Urban Immigrants: The Korean Community in New York*. Princeton: Princeton University Press.

Kwong, Peter. 1979. *Chinatown, New York: Labor and Politics, 1930-1950*. New York: Monthly Review Press.

Laslett, Michael. 1987. "Inter-Racial Violence: Conflicts of Class and Culture." *The Minority Trendsletter* 1 (2).

Manzagol, Michael. 1986. "Asian Enrollment Figures Subject of Federal Inquiry." *Daily Californian*, October 31.

Mar, Don. 1982. "Have Asians Made It?" *East Wind* 1 (2):21-22.

Nakanishi, Don. 1985-1986. "Asian American Politics: An Agenda for Research." *Amerasia Journal* 12 (2):1-27.

Nakano, Annie. 1985. "Anti-Asian Racism Rising." *San Francisco Examiner*, October 30.

Omi, Michael, and Howard Winant. 1986. *Racial Formation in the United States: From the 1960s to the 1980s.* New York: Routledge and Kegan Paul.
Park, Robert Ezra. 1950. *Race and Culture.* Glencoe, Illinois: Free Press.
Portes, Alejandro, and John Walton. 1981. *Labor, Class, and the International System.* New York: Academic Press.
Reich, Michael. 1971. "The Economics of Racism." In *Problems in Political Economy: An Urban Perspective,* edited by David Gordon, 107-113. D. C. Heath and Company.
Rips, Geoffrey. 1983. "The Simpson-Mazzoli Bill: Supply-Side Immigration Reform." *Nation* 237 (10):289, 303-308.
Sassen-Koob, Saskia. 1981. "Towards a Conceptualization of Immigrant Labor." *Social Problems* 29 (1):65-85.
Stack, John F., Jr., ed. 1981. *Ethnic Identities in a Transnational World.* Westport, Connecticut: Greenwood Press.
Survey of Current Business. 1984. October.
──────. 1986. August.
United States, Commission on Civil Rights. 1986. *Recent Activities Against Citizens and Residents of Asian Descent.* Washington, D.C.
Wallerstein, Immanuel. 1974 [1976]. *The Modern World-System: Capitalist Agriculture and the Origins of the European World-Economy in the Sixteenth Century.* New York: Academic Press.
──────. 1979. *The Capitalist World-Economy: Essays.* Cambridge: Cambridge University Press.
Wang, Ling-Chi, 1976. Review of *Ethnic Enterprise in America,* by Ivan Light." In *Counterpoint: Perspectives on Asian America,* edited by Emma Gee et al. Los Angeles: University of California Asian American Studies Center.

Political Participation among Chicago Asian Americans

Yvonne M. Lau

With new favorable demographics and politicized generations, Asian Americans are increasingly choosing politics as careers or avocations. For one group of Asian American political participants in Chicago, the road to empowerment crosses numerous intersections leading to different combinations of political outcomes and players. This paper examines the effects of one city's changing political context on one group of Asian Americans through their perspectives on the politics of inclusion and consequences of exclusion. While Chicago Asian Americans have borrowed tactics from African American and Hispanic communities, they have yet to voice their own rhetoric or outline their vision of an agenda for social, political, and economic change.

In an attempt to understand this group's motivations and behavior, as well as the dimensions of their political participation, I have developed a working typology of political participants – "careerists" and "activists" – as an initial conceptual tool. Most often assuming appointed offices or activist roles, this group of Asian American political participants is highly motivated to transform their generally token positions into key political slots. Given continuing factionalism within minority coalitions in racially and ethnically segregated cities like Chicago, Asian Americans may wield greater power in roles where they effect the balance of power among those historically disenfranchised. Even representing small numbers, Asian Americans can be targeted by mainstream politicians to play a role in breaking the balance between African American and Hispanic American coalitions; and they may be caught in the escalating rivalries between minority factions.

Variants of Political Participation

While the local press continues to praise Asian Americans as high educational achievers and, generally, successful fast-trackers in businesses and professions *(Chicago Sun-Times,* October 23, 1988), seldom do they target Asian Americans (hereafter abbreviated as "AAs") as potential players in mainstream politics. Assuming that this lack of attention stems from small numbers alone, and given that AAs are the fastest-growing minority group in the nation, it would be timely to investigate whether increasing numbers alone—especially in regions where AAs are widely dispersed—will bring increased political participation.

Traditional types of political involvement include electoral participation, which encompasses voting behavior, campaign support, and pursuing office (Jo 1980). Yet, until recently, most exit polls failed to identify Asian American voters. Data on Asian American electoral behavior are scarce and sometimes surface as anecdotal, first-hand accounts of political experiences. Some empirical studies on the California electorate pioneered analyses of Asian American registered voters, using sight recognition of Asian surnames (Din 1984; Nakanishi 1985-1986). Such studies are invaluable for obtaining detailed information on ethnic population ratios, electorate party affiliations, and potential voter eligibility.

For regions with low ratios of AAs or diffused geographical concentrations, however, survey research techniques yield categorical data at high costs. By focusing on the electorate in the local community, political linkages to the larger municipality are overlooked. To examine Asian American politics in Chicago, for example, without considering the influence of Chicago's Democratic machine or the context of Chicago's ethnic coalitions, leads to a cursory overview. Because Asian American communities in Chicago are often too small or scattered to constitute self-sufficient, independent neighborhoods, their social, economic, or political lives need to be examined against the larger backdrop of urban institutions and their changing leadership.

Tracing the roots of Asian American political movements to the civil rights and the Asian American movements, a second dimension of political participation emerges. Non-electoral participation extends the range of legitimate political strategies to: (1) protest movements (Moriyama 1976; Wang 1976); (2) recognition politics (Morimoto 1989); and (3) ideological literature (Wong 1988; San Juan 1976). Nakanishi (1985-1986) suggests that more studies are needed for the second form of politics, exploring advocacy and lobbying efforts which seek recognition for many Asian American interests.

Rationale for Study

Part of this study attempts to address this need for more data on a growing infrastructure of advocacy and leadership groups which, as later discussed, espouses coalition politics reminiscent of the Asian American student movement, instead of the ethnocentric agendas common to ethnic enclaves. Another impetus for this study stems from explaining new forms and growing levels of political participation among AAs in the Chicago metropolitan area. While political activities have not resulted in elected office for AAs in Chicago's Cook County, the last decade reflects increased electoral participation, from grassroots organizing to major fund-raising. AAs have also received recognition as a minority group, with select professionals and businesspeople being invited to participate on municipal and state boards, commissions, and councils.

While this may be generally viewed as a community study because of its emphasis on shifting relationships between competing political factions within Asian American communities, my analysis contains different assumptions about the nature of contemporary ethnic communities. Past community studies concentrated on portraying elitist power structures, e.g., The Chinese Consolidated Benevolent Association, or Six Companies, as monopolizing control over residents (Lyman 1970; Kwong 1987). Today, these traditional power brokers no longer dominate, given the influx of new immigrants, outside funding, and shifting neighborhoods. The images of self-governing ethnic enclaves have fallen to the realities of neighborhoods linked socially and culturally, but dependent on city services and government funding.

My study examines the status of Asian American political activities in Chicago, generally from the perspectives of a small group of highly visible political leaders and community activists. Earlier community studies focused on politics within ethnic enclaves, isolated from city hall. This investigation attempts to locate Asian American political activities in Chicago on a continuum of political empowerment. Marked by the 1983 victory of Mayor Harold Washington, a political watershed launched by a mobilized black electorate, the changing political context created new niches for AAs. Invited into the "Rainbow Coalition" along with other disenfranchised groups—Hispanics, Jews, progressives, gays, and lesbians—AAs traded their discounted status for group recognition. Integrated with city and state politics, the evolution of political participation for the Asian American community reflects its roots in the Midwest. Whether the "Chicago" factor influences political forms and strategies is one subject for debate.

Given different forms of political participation from electoral to non-electoral, ethnic groups find themselves at different points of political maturity. Often, minorities are more vulnerable to institutional shifts of power, and have fewer choices of optimal political strategies. For example, among Chicago Hispanics, a ward "remap" in 1981 diluted Hispanic voting power among several wards, while restoring white majorities to other wards. Only after court action were the Hispanics able to regain four Hispanic majority wards several years later.

A Staple of Asian American Political Diets: Rice-bowl Issues

Though the entry of AAs into the "minority" doors of city hall was not as dramatic as that of the Hispanics, they too encountered changes in the opportunity structure. The declining significance of the Democratic machine, political party, and traditional white ethnic voting blocs created access for those formerly denied. With the new Washington administration entrenched, AAs as one of the fastest growing groups (see Table One) — rising by over thirty-five percent in Cook County in the first half of the 1980s — were embraced for the first time as disadvantaged, underrepresented minority members who were entitled to meetings with the executive office in city hall. With a sympathetic mayor promising reforms and increases in city hirings through affirmative action programs, for the first time AAs experienced inclusion as a group. The Mayor's Advisory Committee on Asian American Affairs was established with a dozen slots for voluntary, unpaid advisers to be advocates on behalf of their Asian communities and to serve as consultants to the mayor's Asian American liaison and paid staff.

Similarly, advisory councils to state executives and legislative offices were formed in rapid succession starting in 1984. As a core group of suitable commissioners and advisers were recycled into the mills of advocacy, political "success" became associated with high counts of AAs sitting on as many government commissions as possible. As one informant remarked, "Naming names became an end in itself...Body counts became the thing, like tallying up Nobel prizes." (Mr. Wu) (Note: All respondents' names are changed, along with identifying characteristics.)

In evaluating the prizes of recognition politics, it becomes important to distinguish between short-term gains and long-term solutions. In early stages of political awareness, gains may be eagerly embraced as signs of success, especially when they include "rice bowl" issues (adopting the Asian metaphor for sources of livelihood; akin to "bread and butter" issues). Higher numbers in available jobs, funding sources, or prestigious appointments provide new symbols of change.

Political rewards favoring a select few, however, do not signify the presence of a political movement. My hypothesis argues for the development of a social agenda before a political movement can take root. Without articulating a larger social agenda, aspirants to a Pan-Asian or Asian American coalition will find it difficult to sustain group solidarity. Lacking Pan-Asian organizations to research and mobilize on issues arising from institutionalized discrimination or systematic inequities, AAs in Chicago remain in the early stages of political maturity. While they may admire successful efforts by national organizations like the Japanese American Citizens League, which lobbied for redress and mobilized many AAs, Chicago AAs show more evidence of adopting personal or ethnic agendas rather than Asian American agendas.

To pursue questions revealing more about the possibilities of Asian American political movements, interethnic coalitions, and the political attitudes of AAs in Chicago, I will review the comments made by a group of informants immersed in regional politics. Their experiences in this highly politicized metropolis serve as micro-indicators of Midwestern political maturity and of regional constraints on political growth.

Research Design and Selected Characteristics of Informants

This study is based on semistructured interviews with twenty-two political leaders and community activists. The snowball sample was generated through key informants and personal referrals. In order to probe for details on political participation, career history, political philosophy, and ethnic orientation, this exploratory study incorporates field observations, as well as interviews. Though survey research would have provided a larger sample, I welcomed the textured responses, revealing political choices and values, available from in-depth sessions.

Interviews averaged two to three hours and were usually conducted at the informants' offices. The group included three Filipino Americans, five Japanese Americans, eight Chinese Americans, four Korean Americans, one Vietnamese, and one Asian Indian American. Both women (ten) and men (twelve) participated, with native-born (ten) and foreign- born (twelve) groups. Most of the sample are considered professionals (eighteen), with some businessmen (two), and low-level workers (two). A majority of the sample (eight) have careers in political advocacy, mainly in government institutions; some are heads of social service agencies (three).

Other components of the study relied on observations made by attending political meetings and rallies, mostly in local communities, during a six-month period, and on content analyses of Asian American publications. Later, using dimensions of career and political agenda, I will offer a tentative typology of four groups of participants.

Transforming AAs into a Recognized Minority Group: City Politics and the Mayor's Advisory Committee on Asian Americans

The 1980s brought a new goal for all minority groups in Chicago – political empowerment. With the passing of Mayor Richard J. Daley's reign in 1976, traditional ruling coalitions changed and the Democratic machine weakened. In addition, patronage jobs were devalued and diminished in number by shifting secular trends as well as by judicial decisions curtailing the politicized recruiting and firing of public employees (Squires et al. 1987). Under the machine, the main objective of political activity was to fuel it; votes were exchanged for services and jobs.

As both the Democratic mayor of Chicago and party chairman of Cook County, Daley exerted total control over city and county patronage. The twenty-one years under Mayor Daley resulted in white dominance institutionalized by the Democratic party (Kleppner 1985). Political analysts have described the Chicago Democratic organization as one assigning subordinate roles for blacks and subsuming their political interests to the needs of white ethnics (Squires et al. 1987). Race dominates Chicago city politics.

When Daley passed away, Michael Bilandic, alderperson from Daley's South Side ward, became acting mayor and eventually won the general election. Criticizing a lackluster Bilandic administration, Jane Byrne entered city hall in 1979, after the machine could not deliver the mayoral nomination to its slated choice in the primary. When her reform facade had faded away and business as usual took over – favoring white neighborhoods over black and Hispanic – blacks became politicized in the common goal of political empowerment. Between November 1982 and the 1983 general election, black voter registration jumped to eighty-nine percent with a seventy-three percent turnout. This resulted in the election of Mayor Harold Washington, the first black mayor of Chicago.

Though this is a sketchy account of Chicago mayoral history, it serves to demonstrate how Chicagoans have consistently voted along ethnic and racial lines. (In the latest mayoral race, won by Richard M. Daley in 1989, fewer than ten percent of the voters crossed racial lines.) The Washington campaign became a movement as well as a campaign, marked by an intense degree of racial polarization. When, for the general election, Washington ran against Bernie Epton, a Republican backed by the white power structure, ninety-two percent of Washington's votes came from blacks, while eighty-eight percent of whites voted for Epton (Kleppner 1985).

AAs in Chicago were affected by one major consequence from the Washington election – that victory stemmed from a small number of votes (46,250; Kleppner 1985), giving any group a chance to claim that they made the difference. Washington won the primary with only a plurality of votes, with results being highly polarized along racial lines. Given that Washington was elected from only 4.1 percent of white ethnic ward voters (Kleppner 1985), AAs at 2.5 percent of the city's population were taken seriously by Washington. Most of the informants agree that his administration marked a turning point for AAs.

Mr. Aki, a bureaucrat, reflects on Washington's attitudes toward AAs:

> The change in the mayor's attitude meant that Asians would be recognized as a community... First Ward [the site of Chinatown] politicians didn't talk about AAs. Washington was concerned about our community's inclusion... rules that helped them [blacks], helped us. He was the first to give out grants to neighborhoods. When he died, he left Sawyer [Washington's successor] in the position of increasing hiring from less than one percent to four percent.

An organizational leader noted that "symbolic gestures were much more important than what he did." Another professional woman, Ms. Takasugi, reminded us that in progressive thinking, "we are entitled to be empowered." Ms. Lopez, a professional, felt that Washington brought Asians into a multiethnic, bipartisan coalition, saying that he opened "government for everyone."

The dismantling of the machine spurred hopes that Asian American empowerment would move closer to reality. As one attorney said, "After 1983, every politician included AAs." Washington's administration produced a political climate conducive to coalition activities, especially between blacks and Hispanics. Mr. Doi, an activist, remembers that "there was no Asian American political movement but 'consciousness' leading to participation." Some informants point to the movement to remember Vincent Chin as coinciding with these new activities, as well as redress. Mr. Wada feels that "the Asian Unity Dinner was a highlight of 1984, with attendance close to 1,000." In the 1980s, remarks Mr. Gow, a businessman, "each community alone didn't have the numbers to make a difference. Each community has its own agenda – the AA community is not mature yet... [Unity] will come when we become more comfortable with each other."

The majority of the group does not feel that Washington worked personally to enhance Asian American unity, though he was famous for eloquent speeches. There are some disagreements among the informants over Washington's true contribution to the Asian American community. His policies did include for the first time AAs as minorities, eligible for affirmative action and minority set-aside contracts. Ms. Bao comments that he often promised more than he delivered:

144 Asian Americans

He was a nice man so people forgave him for not following through. But while he gave us an advisory committee, he didn't give it "commission" status, placing us under the Commission on Human Relations. Likewise, he promised to appoint AAs to several of the major boards, like school or library, but he kept delaying it. It wasn't until Mayor Sawyer came into office that he followed through on what Harold promised. Whether he [Washington] was disorganized or tried to put us off is hard to say. All these people wanted things from him.

Of all the advisory groups to major politicians, the Mayor's Advisory Committee on Asian American Affairs has been the target of some bitter ethnic rivalries, provoking cries of foul play. Some of this arises from the disproportionate representation of some ethnic groups over others, while another source of strain is said to be linked to the inclusion of homeland politics during the group's closed meetings. As one committee member argues:

Is it right that the Chinese get extra representation because they want to count Taiwan, and the PRC, and Hong Kong? I think it's because those guys gave big donations so they want to come here and introduce their foreign-agendas and mess things up. They should have representation on the basis of population ratios here so we can get our fair share... The new immigrants shouldn't think they're better than anyone else and try to dominate the Asian American political movement.

Lee (1980) and Nakanishi (1985-1986) address the importance of including domestic and non-domestic issues when analyzing political participation. Committee members' conflicts about defining legitimate agendas attest to the need to consider the political ideologies of participants and their effects on committees or organizational members. As Nakanishi points out, concern for homeland politics is not exclusive to foreign-born members (e.g., the recent Chinese student movement drew sympathizers from native- and foreign-born).

Given the formal role of a mayor's advisory committee (to remind the administration to follow affirmative action guidelines, to match services with clients and different city agencies, and to publicize government and community programs), however, debates on homeland agendas are intensely contested. With the majority (about seventy-five percent) of committee members being foreign-born, dissension on appropriate mandates further threatens the cohesiveness of the group.

The five who served on this mayor's advisory committee also alluded to generational problems among the members, expressed through clashes in work and communication styles. Mr. Wada complains:

I don't believe "X" was utilized properly. The members of the Committee have to understand their roles and understand his staff roles. This committee expected to be taken care of, but they should've expressed their goals. It's easier to be operational than be a good committee. So we got caught in community squabbles. The first-generation Asians are sensitive to cultural things. Their type of consensus takes a few years. For us [second-generation], we'd get it done. Everyone has their own agenda. Maybe I'm not surprised that in all these years, not a lot happened. Maybe that's OK – part of the process.

Mr. Wada's last comment addresses the debate about empowerment: empowerment for whom? If the mayor's committee could not agree upon a unifying issue and set aside personal interests and internal conflicts, then should it be satisfied with politicizing newer members to the ways of participatory democracy? Or should foreign agendas or any issues provoking conflicts within such groups be dismissed from consideration in order to hone consensus-reaching techniques? Those familiar with the internal politics of the Mayor's Advisory Committee on Asian American Affairs saw an absence of group consciousness that gave way to individual agendas and intercommunity conflicts.

With the newly approved status of "commission" instead of "advisory committee," this body will soon expand in staff and number of commissioners, with the mission of incorporating Asians into city government and advising the mayor and city departments on city policies affecting the Asian community. While more AAs work for the city than ever before – about 1.4 percent of the total workforce – they continue to be treated as token minorities and receive symbolic recognition. Given the dissension among committee members over legitimate agendas, this highly visible body of leaders needs to articulate goals and strategies before the potential for cooperation disappears.

Roles and Agendas: Arriving at a Working Typology of Asian American Political Participants

In trying to differentiate Asian American political participants, I have developed a working typology as one conceptual tool. Four career patterns emerge along the dimensions of agendas and career choices (see Table Two). First, two types of career roles may be distinguished. Careerists refer to those professionals whose primary career matches their political career. They are usually institutionally-based and derive salaries from promoting their agendas.

Careerists with Asian American agendas (hereafter abbreviated as "CAAs") usually serve in advocacy roles in municipal or state government, or in organizations supported by local or federal funding. CAAs immerse themselves in recognition politics, advancing the well-being of Asian Americans and their inclusion into all occupational strata. Their commitment to an Asian American agenda focuses their energies toward protecting the civil rights of AAs, including parity in private and public domains. Because Asian American unity represents a major value, other agendas which disrupt coalition-building are avoided, i.e., foreign agendas.

Careerists with ethnic agendas (hereafter abbreviated as "CEAs") are salaried professionals who are often integrated into institutions within one ethnic community. Commonly, organizations that offer social service programs such as counseling and adjustment services, manpower services, or community economic development programs are likely to nurture such individuals. Because their values and funding sources are usually supported by service to one dominant ethnic group, their political orientations tend to focus on cultivating one ethnic agenda. When expedient, CEAs will also take on the more public Asian American agenda as a springboard for the ethnic agenda. They also tend to focus on recognition politics.

Activists are those political participants whose political activities represent their avocations. Fully-employed or supported by their own businesses, they engage in political work as a sideline or hobby. Their commitment to community political struggles may be just as intense as that of careerists. Because they are likely to be less personally concerned about rice-bowl issues, they are more attracted to other forms of political participation, including protest politics and elected offices.

Asian American activists (hereafter abbreviated as "AAAs") tend to favor protest movements to mobilize larger numbers of supporters and field workers. AAAs seek Asian American unity as a vehicle for political empowerment. They are likely to pick issues limited to a domestic agenda and to develop umbrella organizations to carry out agendas.

Activists with ethnic agendas or homeland concerns (hereafter abbreviated as "AEAs") tend to favor electoral participation or pursue elected offices themselves. Their self-identification as ethnic Americans or Americans with foreign interests reveals more conservative ideals. If attempts at elected office fail, they would be most likely to endorse the formation of political action committees.

The majority of this study's informants are CAAs (eight), followed by AEAs (six), AAAs (five) and CEAs (three). While this typology can be considered only a preliminary differentiation of modal types, it allows some discussion of the contrasts in political styles and agendas.

In reviewing my small sample, several generalizations might be made. AAAs are mainly native-born. Concerned about parity and affirmative action for AAs, they gravitate toward gaining skills to implement democratic ideals. Ms. Song says, "The political process leads to a dialogue which leads to consensus-reaching." "We've learned that we don't give till we get, no more trusting politicians...we use the American way, not the Asian way," snaps Ms. Lopez.

CEAs are foreign-born, and excel in wearing more than one hat. They appear to be more ethnocentric and bipartisan. "You have to be on both sides because you never know who's going to win," laments Ms. Bao.

CAAs tend to be native-born bureaucrats. Being institutional leaders, they use institutional resources, including legislative action, to support social agendas. "There are no more strictly Chinese issues or Japanese issues—we have to use our roles as advocates to get more respect...then the whole community benefits," says Mr. Shito.

Finally, AEAs have multiple agendas. Mainly foreign-born, they retain foreign agendas while pursuing political empowerment. But as Mr. Desai cautions, "When we seek political empowerment, we must be aware of accountability and responsibility to community...must not take a visible role, but rather be part of a broad and deep coalition."

Chicago: Where Is the Pan-Asian Vision?

Most of the informants speak about different political expectations and pragmatic concerns for AAs in Chicago. They address the low population ratios and risk-adverse attitudes rooted in the Midwest. Mr. Gow, an AEA, comments: "Our numbers are less here so the friction's less. But Asians here are weak—they need to get past the survival mode." Mr. Wu, an AAA, offers:

> Chicago faces the reality of number games. On the coasts, they're preoccupied with political power. In that sense, in the Midwest, we're less frustrated because we cannot play the game as an Asian—we're not part of a self-sufficient community. We're less concerned about the census. There are major conceptual differences.

Yet the Chicago region is not politically like other regions of the Midwest. Ms. Song, a CAA, says, "For being Democratic, we have one of the most conservative Asian communities; we are not perceived as being a player though we could be an important bloc if we can pull above the volatility." Few AAs tackle elected office because, according to Ms. Takasugi, "We're more underdeveloped, more conservative, and we need exposure to get away from the 'only and the first' mentality."

One CEA, Ms. Tran, is optimistic about her Chicago roots. She feels, "Asians are stronger here because of the history of participation of grass-roots people, compared with the West Coast where prominent individuals are in control."

Others, however, point to the limited pools of manpower. Ms. Chong believes, "We don't have the resource pool of talent and motivation. We have self-promoters showing up as reps." Mr. Young, an AEA, summarizes, "Yes, we're different here because we never generated our own momentum. Our consciousness was stirred by outsiders—our middle class got co-opted to fill the slots...We don't have power brokers here—just conduits."

The dearth of political programs or Pan-Asian PACs shows why a Pan-Asian vision is still being formed. Political philosophies adopted here are often borrowed from California. Controversies, including the furor over census categories, are almost ignored here. While a benefit for Vincent Chin was held, there were no organized protests or other activities. In trying to understand the "local" orientation of Chicago, I suggest we first discuss the political maturity of Chicago's Asian American community.

Political Strategies and Ideologies

After investigating the range of subjects prioritized by this study's informants, rice-bowl issues predominate. Concern for services and funding, along with token appointments and jobs, constitutes the common vocabulary in political negotiations. A social agenda, on the other hand, has not been the focus of debates, whether in addressing civil rights issues like questioning institutional standards for categorizing AAs as minorities, or changing employment practices unfair to larger numbers through the political process. Manifested in electoral support, the higher value placed on immediate, tangible rewards leads to major support for political candidates who are likely winners. Rather than deciding on the candidates' issues, there is little conviction on "who I should vote for."

This emphasis on selecting the winning candidate only, without regard to individual merit, is reminiscent of how political action committees choose their candidates. In close elections, PACs will cover both ends to assure themselves of backing the winner. As one AEA, Mr. Lee, puts it, "At the meeting, we decided that half would support Mr. X, and the other half would raise money for Y... It's all very friendly—we learn that from the big boys; it's a game." As contributors hit both sides, they remain indifferent to the candidates. Mr. Doi, a Chinatown businessman and AEA, reveals:

> Chinatown leaders are pragmatically determined. They're not staunch Democrats, they don't fight city hall, but when it's up for grabs, you better find out who's got a good chance of winning. They don't think blacks are any worse than whites. Under Byrne or Washington, it was business as usual.

A strong bipartisanship prevails for AAs who feel they have never been included in any camp. Voting for the candidate who shows the most sensitivity, "Asians are not secure enough or mature to feel safe with one party," comments a CAA. And in Illinois, Republicans have Democratic values too, "especially if a Republican governor wants to peel off one percent of the city vote," quips Mr. Aki, a CAA. A colleague, Mr. Shito adds:

> AAs used to be all Democrats. Now it depends on what we're doing. It all depends if it gets in the way of political ambition. If you're out in Du Page [the county west of Cook where AAs have increased in large numbers], it makes sense to be a Republican.

Reviewing the political savvy of AAs, many of them express frustration that they have not been able to negotiate dollars into commitments. Some observers feel that political maturity will come when enough gains accumulate.

"You need to be politically sophisticated to ask for something in return," says Ms. Moy, an AAA attorney. With a second politically active generation entering the field, changes in political behavior are likely to occur. Commitments for electoral rewards will be more openly solicited. Among this second cohort, a quid pro quo strategy for political support follows from their goal of political empowerment.

As Mr. Ramos, a CAA, projects:

> The Asian community makes big contributions, especially those business folks, but we don't make enough waves to get the politicians' attentions. If they want our dollars though, and there are alot of campaigns, the candidates are going to have to listen to us and what we need. If you don't ask, you're letting the politicians off. We've got to turn those banquets into something tangible.

Like other professionals who feel committed to the "American-style" of politicking and to an Asian American agenda, Mr. Ramos believes that politicians need to be made accountable to the concerns of AAs. As competition for fund-raisers becomes keener, this second-generation group will attempt to channel funds toward candidates who support Asian American issues.

Yet with strong mayors like Richard M. Daley in office, it is unlikely that the needs of Asian communities in the city will be met without pressuring, organizing, and lobbying for them. More important will be whether a consciousness of group identity develops for AAs, enabling them to work for social change. Asked about the kinds of rallying issues that would ignite a group consciousness, a CAA replied:

> A loss of life would be an organizing issue. A strong clear case of discrimination would be enough. If we got evidence that a local college had hidden ceilings for Asian students, that would be great... Vincent Chin was a perfect case because on top of everything, they thought he was Japanese, letting us know that no matter how we think we're different, outside they don't realize that. As long as they treat us the same, there's value for us to work together and fight back.

Mr. Wu, an AAA, begins by commenting on the one umbrella group whose main function is to sponsor a Lunar New Year banquet, hosted by rotating ethnic service organizations:

> We need a focus, not just an annual coalition dinner. Perhaps one EEOC case like where a small businessman is told he can't hire all his relatives, and then, all Asians would come and fight in court! If an Asian firm is cited for hiring more Asians than whites, then, this is an issue that all AAs can identify with.

Without some catalytic incident of discrimination or loss of civil rights provoking a common outrage, AAs in Chicago politics will remain self-absorbed in filling their rice bowls.

Overview

With about four percent of the population, AAs in Chicago have experienced decisive gains in the past decade, without attaining elected public office. Witnessing a doubling of the city hiring rate, the Asian American community has also applauded many firsts: the first Asian American on the school board (who just recently became the only member to be retained on Daley's School Reform Board), library board, park district board, board of health, and in the mayor's cabinet.

Some may criticize such appointed offices as window-dressing or token slots, tainted by partisan affiliations or personal agendas. Similar to the majority of AAs in corporations and other bureaucracies, AAs in the public sector most likely hold staff positions, not line positions which would confer decision-making power. Yet when a critical mass of city, state, and federal appointees or "special assistants" interact, the net effect may not capture front-page headlines, but subtly changes the perceptions of government officials and media. Mayor Washington left a legacy of inclusion, especially of those disenfranchised, allowing the Asian American community visibility, representation, and potential to become the swing vote in close races.

As a strategy for greater participation in higher levels of decision-making, appointed office serves to rapidly heighten visibility in the executive branch. Similar to the experiences of California politicians where "identifiability" may be an asset (Jo 1980), AAs on boards and commissions may find that increased recognition leads to greater opportunities. Just recently, the special assistant to the governor on Asian American Affairs was promoted to a cabinet post in the state of Illinois, another first that resulted from serving on a state advisory council.

While AAs in Chicago have just started to develop Pan-Asian political organizations or coalitions, they are exploring different forms of political life accessible to them. Activists and careerists alike, who are building the foundations for a political movement, will make choices regarding whether getting the first Asian American in public office (within Chicago; in Du Page County, several AAs already hold elected office) takes priority over demanding more commission appointments. Both choices contribute to the political process, enhancing the credibility and clout of AAs.

Although rice-bowl issues reflect the majority of concerns at this stage, with growing ratios of registered voters combined with increasing numbers of institutional leaders and grass-roots activists—all within Asian American communities—organized activities will flourish. When the right, mobilizing issue arrives, Asian Americans in Chicago will have the opportunity to test their political maturity, and take on the challenge of articulating a social agenda.

Table One
Population by Race; Chicago Region, City, and Suburbs: 1980, 1985

1985	Region	City	Suburbs
White	4,830,659	1,180,132	3,650,527
Black	1,521,087	1,234,211	286,876
Spanish	693,562	483,765	209,797
Asian	229,192	109,495	119,697
Total	7,274,500	3,007,603	4,266,897
1980			
White	4,944,343	1,321,359	3,622,984
Black	1,427,826	1,187,905	239,921
Spanish	580,609	422,063	158,546
Asian	150,846	73,745	77,101
Total	7,103,624	3,005,072	4,098,552
1985			
White	66.41%	39.24%	85.55%
Black	20.91%	41.04%	6.72%
Spanish	9.53%	16.08%	4.92%
Asian	3.15%	3.64%	2.81%
Total	100.00%	100.00%	100.00%
1980			
White	69.60%	43.97%	88.40%
Black	20.10%	39.53%	5.85%
Spanish	8.17%	14.05%	3.87%
Asian	2.12%	2.45%	1.88%
TOTAL	100.00%	100.00%	100.00%

The Chicago Region is defined as the Chicago Standard Metropolitan Statistical Area and comprises the counties of Cook, Du Page, Lake, Kane, McHenry, and Will. Source: Department of Planning, *Population by Race, Chicago Region,* 1980-1985 (May 1987).

Table Two
Working Typology of Asian American Political Participants
Dimensions of Leadership Roles

	Agendas	
Roles	Asian American	Ethnic
Careerists (institutionally-based: primary rice bowl feeds the agenda)	**CAA**	**CEA**
Activists (political work represents avocation: primary rice bowl remains distinct)	**AAA**	**AEA**

References

Chicago Sun-Times. 1988. October 23, 4.
Din, Grant. 1984. "An Analysis of Asian/Pacific American Registration and Voting Patterns in San Francisco." MA thesis, Claremont Graduate School.
Gee, Emma, Bruce Iwasaki, Mike Murase, Megumi Dick Osumi, and Jesse Quinsaat, eds. 1976. *Counterpoint: Perspectives on Asian America.* Los Angeles: University of California Asian American Studies Center.
Jo, Yung-Hwan, ed. 1980. *Political Participation of Asian Americans.* Chicago: P/AAMHRC.
Kleppner, Paul. 1985. *Chicago Divided: The Making of a Black Mayor.* DeKalb: Northern Illinois University Press.
Kwong, Peter. 1987. *The New Chinatown.* New York: Hill and Wang.
Lee, Hwasoo. 1980. "Toward Korean-American Participation and Representation in American Politics: The Case of Los Angeles." In *Political Participation of Asian Americans*, edited by Yung-Hwan Jo, 74-89. Chicago: P/AAMHRC.
Lyman, Stanford. 1970. *The Asian in the West.* Reno: Desert Research Institute.
Morimoto, Joy. 1989. "Where Do We Go after Redress?" *Asian Week*, April 7, 16-17.
Moriyama, Alan. 1976. "The 1909 and 1920 Strikes of Japanese Sugar." In *Counterpoint: Perspectives on Asian America*, edited by Emma Gee et al., 169-180. Los Angeles: University of California Asian American Studies Center.
Nakanishi, Don. 1985-1986. "Asian American Politics: An Agenda for Research." *Amerasia Journal* 12:1-27.
San Juan, E. 1976. "From Carlos Bulosan and the Imagination of the Class Struggle." In *Counterpoint: Perspectives on Asian America*, edited by Emma Gee et al., 190-194. Los Angeles: University of California Asian American Studies Center.
Squires, Gregory, Larry Bennett, Kathleen McCourt, and Philip Nyden. 1987. *Chicago—Race, Class, and the Response to Urban Decline.* Philadelphia: Temple University Press.
Wang, Ling-chi. 1976. "Lau V. Nichols: History of A Struggle for Equal and Quality Education." In *Counterpoint: Perspectives on Asian America*, edited by Emma Gee et al., 240-263. Los Angeles: University of California Asian American Studies Center.
Wong, Sau-ling. 1988. "Tales of Postwar Chinatown: Short Stories of the Bud, 1947-48." *Amerasia Journal* 14:61-80.

Indochinese Refugees' Responses to Resettlement Via the Social Welfare System

Jeremy Hein

How do international migrants respond to a host society institution that has no parallel in their home countries? This question has been raised for Asian migrants in the United States in two areas. The first, and more widely recognized, is Chinese migrants' reaction to democratic political institutions. One of the paradoxes of Asian American politics has been the comparatively low levels of political mobilization in American Chinatowns. These neighborhoods experience many social problems—illegal working conditions, overcrowding, poverty, and inadequate municipal services—that should generate mobilization. However, mobilization is inhibited by a range of factors: the transplanting in the United States of feudal political institutions; traditional elites, particularly in the restaurant business, who resist change; and a perception of politics as a high risk/low gain confrontation due to prior experience of communist-nationalist conflict in China, as well as life under communist and authoritarian governments (Kwong 1979, 1987; Light and Wong 1975; Lyman 1986).[1] Those Chinese immigrants who are politically active tend to have learned about the use of strikes, petitions, and demonstrations after arriving in the United States (Kuo 1977; Wong 1982, 1987). Thus, lack of democratic political institutions in their homelands accounts in part for difficulties in mobilizing Chinese immigrants to seek change in the United States

The second aforementioned area, less recognized, is the case of Indochinese refugees and the American welfare state.[2] Public and private social welfare institutions have managed the resettlement of these refugees since the arrival of the first Vietnamese refugees in 1975. In this paper I examine some of the responses among refugees from Vietnam, Laos, and Cambodia to resettlement via the social welfare system. By analyzing the responses of Indochinese

154 *Asian Americans*

refugees to the resettlement program, we can begin to determine how Asian migrants adapt to a host society institution with which they have had no prior experience: the Western welfare state.[3]

I begin by arguing that analysis of refugees' use of public assistance and entry into the labor force is incomplete without an examination of their help-seeking behavior, and I discuss three factors which shape this behavior: kinship ties, survival strategies, and cultural norms. I then describe the use of social welfare programs in the resettlement of Indochinese refugees: what I term *state incorporation of allied aliens*. Finally, I present four detailed ethnographic cases illustrating each of the factors which mediate refugees' use of the resettlement program.

Refugees' Use of Public Assistance, Labor Force Participation, and Help-seeking Behavior

It is important to analyze Indochinese refugees' responses to the American social welfare system for two reasons. First, since 1975, public assistance has been an integral feature of the refugee resettlement program (Feen 1985; Haines 1985a). A study of upward social mobility among Vietnamese refugees (Caplan, Whitmore, and Choy 1989:215) found that "only 2 percent of the households in our sample [N = 1,384] had managed to climb out of poverty after six months or less on cash assistance and without benefit of specialized refugee programs and services." Rates of cash assistance use among Indochinese refugees climbed from 1975 to 1980 and then remained fairly constant throughout the 1980s; sixty-five percent of the refugees who arrived between 1983 and 1988 receive public cash assistance, and rates tend to be higher in states with large Indochinese communities, such as California (U.S. Office of Refugee Resettlement 1989). Indochinese refugees are unique among recent immigrants to the United States in having rates of public assistance above those of natives (North 1983; Jensen 1988). This finding is significant because there is evidence that Indochinese refugees are increasingly stratified into two populations: those who have entered the stable working class or started small businesses, and those who live in the areas of initial settlement (such as the Tenderloin in San Francisco and Uptown in Chicago) and continue to receive cash assistance (Bach 1986, 1988; Bach and Carroll-Seguin 1986). Although it may be premature to speak of an "Indochinese underclass," given the refugees' reliance on public assistance for resettlement and then for income support, it is important for social scientists and policy makers to understand how refugees respond to the social welfare system.

The employment rate among Indochinese refugees is the second reason their social welfare behavior deserves attention. Indochinese refugees who arrived between 1983 and 1988 had a labor force participation rate of thirty-two percent and an unemployment rate of eleven percent; the figures for the total United States population are sixty-six percent and five percent, respectively (U.S. Office of Refugee Resettlement 1989). Although there are significant differences among the various ethnic groups (Haines 1985c), among migration cohorts (Montero 1979; Nguyen and Henkin 1982), and between men and women (Haines 1986), Indochinese refugees share traits that hinder their entry into the American labor force: languages quite different from English, few transferable job skills, large families, poor health, and traumatic experiences (Haines 1985b; Stein 1979). More detailed studies of the issue reveal that refugees' reliance upon public assistance declines with time (Fass 1986; Montero and Dieppa 1982; Haines 1987); decreases when the refugees are sponsored by native groups and organizations rather than relatives (Bach and Carroll-Seguin 1986); and is closely related to their high fertility rate (Rumbaut and Weeks 1986) and lack of English skills (Strand 1984; Strand and Jones 1985). Although the transition from public assistance to participation in the labor force cannot be understood without these variables, such analysis is incomplete without an examination of refugees' interpretations of the social welfare system.

I employ the concept of help-seeking behavior—the matching of social solutions to one's social problems—to analyze Indochinese refugees' use of the social welfare system (Moon and Tashima 1982). Like natives, refugees select among market, family, and public forms of aid to meet their social needs (cf. Rose 1986 on the "welfare mix"). However, refugees differ from natives in that the American social welfare system makes assumptions about client behaviors and beliefs based on the native rather than the refugee population (cf. Haines 1980 on Vietnamese refugees and the housing market). My thesis is that refugees' use of public assistance, the casework process, and other features common to both the resettlement program and the national social welfare system are mediated by a range of factors derived from past experience and socialization. While both refugees and natives make selective use of the social welfare system, refugees make their selections on the basis of a different set of interpretations and contexts.

I have identified three factors that mediate refugees' use of the social welfare system: kinship ties, survival strategies, and cultural norms. *Kinship ties* are the social bonds among an extended network of blood and fictive kin that orient individuals and nuclear families to a group that may be spread across the country and in some cases the globe. In this context, social welfare decisions and outcomes are frequently collective, although the American social welfare system presumes they will be individual. Second, refugees are adapting to life in the United States after years of hardship and thus have developed *survival strategies:* plans for progress that are unbalanced in that to assure attainment of one goal (such as sending money to relatives overseas), others are sacrificed (such as purchasing clothes suitable for a job interview). This orientation is in conflict with the American social welfare system which assumes that individuals' priorities are sequential ("good clothes lead to a good job") rather than multiple. Finally, *cultural norms* are involved: rules specific to an ethnic group that prescribe behavior for individuals on the basis of statuses like gender and age. Cultural norms from mainland Southeast Asia—profound inequality between men and women and strict seniority by age—are at odds with the cultural norms that the American social welfare system assumes to be operating among natives.

Although other mediating factors could be listed, these three are the most prominent encountered during my fieldwork and from an examination of the literature on help-seeking behavior among Indochinese refugees (Egawa and Tashima 1981; Finnan 1981; Gold 1987; Haines, Rutherford, and Thomas 1981; Khoa 1981; Moon and Tashima 1982).[4] Before presenting the ethnographic case studies, I describe the social welfare programs created by the United States government to manage the resettlement of Indochinese refugees: what I term *state incorporation of allied aliens*.

State Incorporation of Allied Aliens

The admission of Indochinese refugees beginning in 1975 represents the classic United States refugee scenario of strong executive branch support for populations fleeing communism (Loescher and Scanlin 1986). Despite public opposition to the admission of the Indochinese (Stern 1981; Simon 1985), the American government relocated the refugees to the United States because they are what I term *allied aliens*. Enemy aliens are residents or citizens believed by their government to be disloyal on the basis of their ancestry. The 120,000 Japanese Americans interned by President Roosevelt during World War II are the most celebrated case of enemy aliens; even though the legal term was applied only to the Issei, the loyalties of the entire group were called into question. Similarly, President Wilson interned 6,300 German residents during World War I, but the belief that all citizens of German ancestry were suspect led to the banning of German language instruction in public schools, the closing of German newspapers, and the disbanding of German cultural organizations (Higham 1973). Conversely, allied aliens are foreign populations for whom an interventionist state assumes responsibility in the aftermath of failed foreign policies in their country. Vietnamese and other refugees from former Indochina are the paramount cases in this respect. According to the U.S. Department of State (1982:57): "we accept only refugees of special concern to the United States, who meet our admissions criteria, for whom there are no alternative solutions, and whose admission is required by compelling foreign policy considerations." Indochinese refugees represent approximately seventy-five percent of all refugees admitted to the country between 1975 and 1988 (Refugee Reports 1988b).

The Indochinese migration is unique not only for its rapidity, size, and duration, but because the American government has sought to manage the resettlement of these refugees through what I term *state incorporation:* the use of social welfare programs to promote the adaptation of select groups of émigrés (for a more complete discussion of this process see Hein 1989). The Bureau of Refugee Programs in the State Department sets criteria for refugee status and provides a per capita grant to voluntary agencies for the reception and placement services they supply to each refugee they resettle in the United States. Such services range from meeting arrivals at the airport, to registering children in school, to job placement. If the case has been sponsored by a stateside relative, she or he helps with these tasks. The contract is for a minimum of ninety days, although voluntary-agency contact with clients often continues much longer.

Before and after World War II, voluntary agencies had to guarantee the government that arriving refugees and displaced persons were not "likely to become a public charge," and would thus not violate a provision of the Immigration and Nationality Act of 1917 (Dinnerstein 1982; Morse 1967). This adversarial relationship has changed to one of partnership and even dependence. Voluntary agencies have moved from being parochial participants to being buffer organizations between the federal government and their refugee clients (Wright 1981). As refugee admissions and federal assistance have increased, these private organizations have found their budgets made up of greater proportions of government dollars. There are currently ten voluntary agencies that receive federal funding to resettle Indochinese refugees (U.S. Office of Refugee Resettlement 1989: Appendix C).

In addition to the voluntary agencies, Indochinese refugees also receive resettlement assistance through federally funded income support, medical aid, and social service programs. The Refugee Act of 1980 established an Office of Refugee Resettlement in the Department of Health and Human Services to fund resettlement services at the state and local level (Kennedy 1981; Leibowitz 1983). Two special categories of public assistance, Refugee Cash Assistance and Refugee Medical Assistance, were tailored for refugees and initially exempted them for three years (by 1989 it was eighteen months) from local assistance criteria. For example, many states restrict Aid to Families with Dependent Children (AFDC) to single-parent families—but this rule is waived in the case of Indochinese refugees. States are encouraged to allow the Indochinese and other refugees to obtain public assistance by the guarantee of one hundred percent federal reimbursement for the cost of a refugee's first thirty-six months (by 1989, it was twenty-four months) of public aid and medical assistance. In creating these programs, the American government linked the political status of refugees to a social welfare client label. As stated in section 101(b) of the Refugee Act:

The objectives of this Act are to produce a permanent and systematic procedure for admission to this country of refugees of special humanitarian concern to the United States, and to provide comprehensive and uniform provisions for the effective resettlement and absorption of those refugees who are admitted (U.S. Congressional Research Service 1980:63).

How Indochinese refugees have responded to the use of the social welfare system to ensure their "resettlement and absorption" is the subject of the remainder of this paper.

Methods, Field Settings, and Case Selection

The following case studies are based on extensive fieldwork in New York City and San Francisco. During 1982, I was a participant observer in a New York City voluntary agency and then conducted interviews at five agencies during the summer of 1983. During 1984 and 1985, I was a participant observer in the sister voluntary agency in San Francisco, and conducted interviews at six agencies in the spring of 1985. As a participant observer I assisted staff with their work, attended office meetings to discuss cases and policy, worked with agency records, and conducted interviews. Altogether I interviewed thirty-six Indochinese paraprofessionals, twelve native, white supervisors, and two Vietnamese supervisors at a total of fourteen voluntary agencies. Throughout this paper, I use the term VOLAG (the acronym for voluntary agency) to name all agencies, and of course have given fictitious names to all participants.

The four cases discussed below were selected to satisfy two criteria: (1) to represent the range of resettlement issues encountered in the field, and (2) to have a high degree of accuracy in terms of ethnographic detail. To meet these criteria has meant some loss in the cases' demographic representativeness. First, too many of the refugees are ethnic Chinese from Vietnam (approximately twenty percent of the total Vietnamese population). Second, Indochinese paraprofessionals handle the vast majority of cases and obviously only a handful actually worked in the American embassy in Saigon. Many others, however, were employed by Americans in other capacities, and the ethnic Chinese are strongly overrepresented in this job (Hein 1988). The generalizability of the cases will thus be affected: (1) to the degree that the help-seeking behavior of these refugees is not representative of the larger population, and (2) to the degree that the native caseworkers are more or less culturally sensitive than Indochinese paraprofessionals. In fact, the cultures of mainland Southeast Asia share many helping traditions (Khoa 1981; Moon and Tashima 1982). Furthermore, Indochinese paraprofessionals often take their resettlement agency as a reference group and thus tend to expect more acculturation of clients than do native caseworkers, who are heavily influenced by the post-1960s tolerance for cultural pluralism described by Glazer (1983). Thus, the cases below can provide important evidence on how refugees respond to the American social welfare system.

Refugees' Responses to the Resettlement Program
Case A. Kinship Ties: Social Bonds from the Past[5]
During the third visit to his case worker (a native woman named Joan), a Khmer man (Dara) mentioned that he might be leaving New York City. He explained through a Cambodian paraprofessional that he had received a letter from his "sister" (actually his cousin) in Louisiana asking him to join her family. Since Dara was successfully resettled, Joan was reluctant to see him risk a new start. Dara already spoke some English, had found himself a part-time job, was in a building slated for a federal improvement program, and the paperwork for numerous public social welfare bureaucracies had already been completed. He was twenty-seven, spoke some French, and had studied engineering in college before 1975.

Joan pointed out that "this is the United States and you're free to go where you want," but that welfare and food stamps were less in Louisiana and that the VOLAG had already spent close to $2,000 to bring his family to this country and resettle them. At one point Dara tried to explain more clearly to Joan why he had to move: "My sister's family asked me first and also helped me in the [Thai refugee] camps. If I don't go there I'll have a bad name with my family." Here Dara made reference to Khao I Dang, a refugee holding center in Thailand where refugees are interviewed by United States officials to establish their eligibility for admissions. Life in the camps is austere at best, and aid from kin is not quickly forgotten. Joan again stressed that he was free to leave but that she would not help him make arrangements: "It's against our policy to make their departure plans—it might encourage them." Later she confided to me that: "The client's culture can often work against us as a type of counter-culture." Joan had worked in the New York City welfare department for many years before joining the VOLAG. Pictures of the flight from Saigon in 1975, bringing to mind her grandparents' experiences in Czarist Russia, had initiated her desire to work in refugee resettlement.

This seemingly zero-sum conflict was resolved when a friend of Dara's suggested that he talk to a Cambodian paraprofessional (Chanda) who lived several blocks from Dara's Bronx apartment. Chanda worked at a refugee resettlement agency near the VOLAG and was familiar with their staff and activities. He was a quiet, single man who liked to keep to himself, although he was frequently called upon after hours to handle the problems of refugees in his neighborhood. According to the first Cambodian paraprofessional, Chanda convinced Dara that it would be best if he stayed in New York. Dara did not join his relatives in Louisiana.

160   *Asian Americans*

Case B. Survival Strategies: Entrepreneurship in an Ethnic Enclave[6]

Shortly after their arrival in New York City, an extended Chinese Vietnamese family tried to establish a contractual relationship with their case worker (a Chinese Vietnamese woman named Vinh). The leading members of the family told Vinh that they knew she was going to spend "x" amount of money on their case for furniture, rent, clothing, and other immediate needs, and that all would be better off if she gave them the whole sum then. Like many refugees, this family probably learned about resettlement practices in the Thai camps, where knowledge of public assistance payments and the aid provided by each VOLAG is common. Lacking an analogous institution in their homelands, refugees treat contact with social welfare agencies as they would a commercial transaction.

Vinh refused to simply give them money explaining that the "VOLAG has no obligation to serve you — I am here to help you build your new life." The family then declined the apartment Vinh had found for them, and even the jobs, because they wanted to live and work in Chinatown. Some time later, she discovered that they had taken out of Vietnam considerable wealth in gold and opened (in Chinatown) a Chinese restaurant supply store. The vast majority of Indochinese refugees do not come to the United States with capital, but arriving with some valuables was not infrequent among the early groups of boat people who tended to come from Vietnam's commercial class.

Vinh is an American citizen and a former employee of the United States embassy in Saigon. Evacuated in April 1975, she spent several months in Fort Chaffee, Arkansas, one of four mainland reception centers used to house the first wave of Vietnamese. There she was spotted as "ideal social work material" by the VOLAG director. On her use of American casework methods she once commented: "I've been doing it a few years and have adopted the American way a lot. I've learned a lot from American social workers."

Before she finally terminated the case, Vinh had been having problems for close to a year adjudicating between her clients' entrepreneurship, their resettlement needs, and the role of the VOLAG. During that time, the family had been so concerned with business that the needs of the children and grandparents had been neglected. Someone from the family called Vinh asking that she intervene. Since the family was well-off financially, she decided not to take time away from her many other clients. The incident that ultimately caused Vinh to close the case was the family's putting an aged grandmother in a convalescent home. This affronted Vinh's conceptions of kinship and respect for the elderly. It is revealing that it was the violation of Chinese customs, and not the transgression of the case worker/client relationship, that ultimately moved Vinh to break relations.

Case C. Cultural Norms: Female Subordination[7]

The day before her (extended) family of twelve was due to arrive in San Francisco, the sponsoring cousin (a Chinese Vietnamese woman named Dinh) went to her caseworker (a Chinese Vietnamese woman named Oanh) to receive instructions. Oanh is a United States citizen and former employee of the U.S. embassy in Saigon. She arrived in 1975 at Camp Pendleton in California and soon began working for the VOLAG. Oanh told Dinh that she would be responsible for meeting them at the airport and helping them learn about transportation, housing, hospitals, shopping, and banks, and generally taking charge of the family's resettlement plans.

Dinh had made a good start in San Francisco. She earned $11,300 a year as a secretary for a dentist in Chinatown and had moved out of the run-down Tenderloin area to the more affluent Sunset District. The day after the family arrived, Dinh brought them to Oanh. After providing the family with the per-case cash grant, Oanh began discussing their resettlement plans. She told Dinh "to share her experiences about living in the United States with them," implying that as a well resettled refugee she should be able to ensure that her relatives followed a like path. On the following day Dinh returned with the family and Oanh explained the importance of work, especially for the single brothers and sisters, since welfare would not provide them with much to live on. She also pointed out that they could take English classes at night while working during the day. Dinh said she would talk this over with her family during the week and then return to the agency.

A week later Dinh returned with her uncle, the head of the family. Despite her more assimilated position and the recency of the family's arrival, Dinh sat quietly while the uncle explained the family's position: the patriarchal role of the eldest male was being asserted. They had discussed the issue of work and welfare, the uncle reported, and believed that it would be appropriate for them all to temporarily receive welfare so that they could improve their English. Oanh had been having trouble finding jobs for some of her other clients and had begun to believe that this family might indeed profit from language training. Because the cousin was working and might provide a good example for the others, she explained, she would get them an appointment at the welfare department.

Case D. Cultural Norms: Male Primogeniture[8]

Within several weeks of arriving in San Francisco, Lai, one of two Chinese Vietnamese brothers who arrived together, had found work through the county Economic Development Department (EDD). At the time, refugees were interviewed by EDD to see if a job could be found for them before they qualified for any form of public assistance. Lai's caseworker at the VOLAG, Bob, was pleased because jobs for refugees were scarce and this one was with an electronics firm in Chinatown. Lai had completed tenth grade in Vietnam, had "radio and TV repair background," and this was a "skilled job" in line with his ambitions.

Lai's older brother, Van, was not so happy. EDD had referred him to a dishwashing job, which he had refused to take. During a subsequent meeting, Bob relayed the VOLAG's philosophy about the chances for upward social mobility in the United States. Unlike Vietnam, Van was informed, people in the United States usually did not stay in their first job for life. Van was referred back to EDD, and Bob noted that he "thought we had come to terms." Again, Van told the EDD interviewer that he wanted to study English full-time and such restaurant jobs would not do. Bob was very qualified to handle this case. He had worked at the U.S. embassy in Saigon and was fluent in Vietnamese. He thus suspected a deeper level to Van's objections and called on a Vietnamese paraprofessional to help work on the case. After over an hour of discussion at another meeting, Bob realized that the problem had more to do with Vietnamese conceptions of male primogeniture than expectations of job status. Bob noted in the case file:

> Van only completed fifth grade schooling, whereas his younger brother went through tenth grade. Thus, according to Van, he must get schooling before his brother... Van seems sincere, though I think it's mainly a matter of "face," that with the younger brother working in a skilled job, the older cannot take a dishwashing, unskilled job.

Bob now had to decide how to arrange the household's budget, comply with EDD rules, and support Vietnamese conceptions of sibling seniority. As recently arrived refugee households went, the one brother with full-time employment was a good situation. After another interview it became apparent that the brothers had worked out their own solution: "Lai, because he has a skill, will work and support Van to study English." Bob decided to request that EDD grant Van food stamps with the hope that a better job could be found in the future once he spoke more English. Until that was arranged, the VOLAG would provide small funds to maintain the household.

Conclusion

Since 1975, the American government has sought to incorporate into American society allied aliens from Vietnam, Laos, and Cambodia, and the social welfare system has been the primary mechanism for managing their resettlement. The result is an encounter between Indochinese refugees and the Western welfare state. Not only is this institution absent from the refugees' home countries, but the American social welfare system is based on the help-seeking behavior of the native rather than the refugee population. The outcome of this encounter is significant because these refugees use public cash assistance and experience unemployment at high rates, and also have low rates of labor force participation. I have explained Indochinese refugees' responses to the social welfare system by describing the operation of three mediating factors: kinship ties, survival strategies, and cultural norms. These factors shape how refugees selectively use features of the resettlement program such as public assistance and the casework process. By focusing on their help-seeking behavior, I have emphasized the choices refugees make as they confront a new institution; the case studies portray a range of outcomes to this confrontation.

Extensive kinship ties mean that refugees' decisions about social welfare involve more people than the immediate individual or nuclear family. In Case A a fictive kin relative in Louisiana was nearly successful in pressuring a Cambodian family in New York City to move despite the fact that this family was well resettled and that the head of the family was reluctant to move. The survival strategies that refugees have developed to cope with scarcity in their home countries and in countries of first asylum mean that refugees arrive in the United States with a set of objectives at odds with those of the resettlement program: many will plan for the next day only or have plans that can only be realized over several years. In Case B, a Chinese Vietnamese family disregarded the resettlement plans of their voluntary agency caseworker and sought to establish a business in New York's Chinatown at the expense of the children and senior citizens in the family.

Finally, cultural norms shape refugees' use of the social welfare system because seniority, and thus the authority to make key decisions about household economic issues, is often determined by age and gender rather than by knowledge of conditions in American society. In Case C it was the senior male in an extended Chinese Vietnamese family, rather than a woman in the family who had lived in San Francisco for several years, who made key decisions about the household's social welfare plans. Similarly, in Case D, asserting elder brother status meant taking classes in English as a second language and getting food stamps while a younger brother worked. In all four cases, preexisting beliefs and behaviors shaped refugees' use of the resettlement program.

Four ethnographic cases cannot predict which refugees will use public assistance and which will enter the labor force. However, there is an abundance of government statistics on this aspect of Indochinese refugee resettlement. Indeed, one result of this supply of data is that social scientists have provided an overly objective account of the refugees' experiences. The cases in this chapter indicate that refugees bring a set of subjective responses to their encounter with the social welfare institutions seeking their incorporation into American society. Indeed, to expect Indochinese refugees to respond differently is to presume their acculturation to the norms of the Western welfare state.

Notes

1. Similar observations have appeared in the press regarding political mobilization among Indochinese refugees in the United States (Nguyen 1988; Smith 1989).
2. I employ the term "Indochinese refugees" rather than "Southeast Asian refugees" for two reasons. First, Southeast Asia currently has refugee populations other than those from Vietnam, Laos, and Cambodia: Burmese students in Thailand, the Karen and other ethnic minorities displaced within Burma (recently renamed the Union of Myanmar), and residents on the island of Timor seeking independence from Indonesia. As more refugee groups develop in the future, the use of the term "Southeast Asian refugees" to mean political migrants from the three countries of former Indochina will be increasingly misleading. Second, although Indochina ceased to exist as a political unit when Vietnam, Laos, and Cambodia gained independence from France in 1953-1954, using the term "Indochinese refugees" serves as a useful reminder of the historic origins of this refugee crisis. The term "Indochinese" does, regrettably, deemphasize the cultural autonomy of the Vietnamese, Lao, ethnic groups of highland Laos (such as the Hmong), and the Khmer by assuming that the area merely represents the meeting of India and China. The term Southeast Asian, on the other hand, is simply a geographic designation and thus presumes that all groups share the same culture. On balance I believe the term Indochinese refugees is more accurate.
3. In 1988, the Indochinese refugee population in the United States numbered 884,000: sixty-three percent Vietnamese, seventeen percent Cambodian, thirteen percent lowland Lao, and seven percent highland Lao, such as the Hmong (Refugee Reports 1988a). In addition, some 250,000 children have been born in the United States to Vietnamese, Laotian, and Cambodian parents, thus making the Indochinese the third largest Asian group in the country (after the Chinese and the Filipinos) when these offspring are included (Gordon 1989; Rumbaut and Weeks 1986).
4. The reconstruction of ethnic communities also influences refugees' use of the social welfare system. In the rebuilding process, refugees who have been in the United States longer become dispensers of information to newer arrivals: how to use public assistance is a core component of their stock of local knowledge. When asked to describe this phenomenon one Indochinese caseworker replied: "For example, one client said he would go to work but then other refugees told him not to, they told him that since he had a large family he could get welfare. So he avoided coming to see me."
5. Source: observation, participation, and interviews with an American caseworker and a Cambodian paraprofessional in New York City, 1982.
6. Source: interview with a Chinese Vietnamese paraprofessional in New York City in 1982 concerning events in 1981.
7. Source: a 1981 case file followed by an interview with the Chinese Vietnamese paraprofessional, San Francisco, 1985.
8. Source: a 1978 case file in San Francisco, read in 1985.

References

Bach, Robert L. 1986. "Immigration: Issues of Ethnicity, Class, and Public Policy in the United States." *Annals of the American Academy of Political and Social Science* 485:139-152.

―――. 1988. "State Intervention in Southeast Asian Refugee Resettlement in the United States." *Journal of Refugee Studies* 1:38-56.

Bach, Robert L., and Rita Carroll-Seguin. 1986. "Labor Force Participation, Household Composition and Sponsorship among Southeast Asian Refugees." *International Migration Review* 20:381-404.

Caplan, Nathan, John K. Whitmore, and Marcella H. Choy. 1989. *The Boat People and Achievement in America: A Study of Family Life, Hard Work, and Cultural Values.* Ann Arbor: Michigan.

Dinnerstein, Leonard. 1982. *America and the Survivors of the Holocaust.* New York: Columbia.

Egawa, Janet, and Nathaniel Tashima. 1981. *Alternative Service Delivery Models in Pacific/Asian Communities.* San Francisco: Pacific Asian Mental Health Research Project.

Fass, Simon. 1986. "Innovations in the Struggle for Self-Reliance: The Hmong Experience in the United States." *International Migration Review* 20:351-380.

Feen, Richard H. 1985. "Domestic and Foreign Policy Dilemmas in Contemporary U. S. Refugee Policy." In *Refugees and World Politics,* edited by Elizabeth G. Ferris, 105-119. New York: Praeger.

Finnan, Christine R. 1981. "Occupational Assimilation of Refugees." *International Migration Review* 15:292-309.

Glazer, Nathan. 1983. *Ethnic Dilemmas, 1964-1982.* Cambridge: Harvard University Press.

Gold, Steven J. 1987. "Dealing with Frustration: A Study of Interactions between Resettlement Staff and Refugees." In *People in Upheaval,* edited by Scott Morgan and Elizabeth Colsen, 108-128. New York: Center for the Study of Migration.

Gordon, Linda W. 1989. "The Missing Children: Mortality and Fertility in a Southeast Asian Refugee Population." *International Migration Review* 23:219-237.

Haines, David W. 1980. "Mismatch in the Resettlement Process: The Vietnamese Family Versus the American Housing Market." *Journal of Refugee Resettlement* 1:15-19.

―――. 1985a. "Refugees and the Refugee Program." In *Refugees in the United States: A Reference Book,* edited by David W. Haines, 3-16. Westport, Connecticut: Greenwood.

―――. 1985b. "Initial Adjustment." In *Refugees in the United States: A Reference Book,* edited by David W. Haines, 17-35. Westport, Connecticut: Greenwood.

―――. 1985c. "Toward Integration into American Society." In *Refugees in the United States: A Reference Book,* edited by David W. Haines, 37-55. Westport, Connecticut: Greenwood.

―――. 1986. "Vietnamese Refugee Women in the U. S. Labor Force: Continuity or Change." In *International Migration: The Female Experience,* edited by Rita J. Simon and Caroline B. Brettell, 62-75. Totowa, New Jersey: Rowman and Allanheld.

―――. 1987. "Patterns of Southeast Asian Refugee Employment: A Reappraisal of the Existing Research." *Ethnic Groups* 7:39-59.

Haines, David W., ed. 1985. *Refugees in the United States: A Reference Book.* Westport, Connecticut: Greenwood.

Haines, David W., Dorothy Rutherford, and Patrick Thomas. 1981. "Family and Community among Vietnamese Refugees." *International Migration Review* 15:310-319.
Hein, Jeremy. 1988. "State Incorporation of Migrants and the Reproduction of a Middleman Minority among Indochinese Refugees." *The Sociological Quarterly* 29:463-478.
———. 1989. "States and Political Migrants: The Incorporation of Indochinese Refugees in France and the United States." Ph.D. dissertation (sociology), Northwestern University.
Higham, John. 1973. *Strangers in the Land: Patterns of American Nativism 1860-1925*. New York: Atheneum.
Jensen, Leif I. 1988. "Patterns of Immigration and Public Assistance Utilization, 1970-1980." *International Migration Review* 22:51-83.
Kennedy, Edward. 1981. "Refugee Act of 1980." *International Migration Review* 15:141-156.
Khoa, Le Xuan. 1981. "Southeast Asian Social and Cultural Customs: Their Contribution to Resettlement." *Journal of Refugee Resettlement* 1:27-47.
Kuo, Chia-ling. 1977. *Social and Political Change in New York's Chinatown*. New York: Praeger.
Kwong, Peter. 1979. *Chinatown, New York: Labor and Politics, 1930-1950*. New York: Monthly Review.
———. 1987. *The New Chinatown*. New York: Hill and Wang.
Leibowitz, Arnold. 1983. "The Refugee Act of 1980." *Annals of the Academy of Political and Social Science* 467:163- 171.
Light, Ivan, and Charles C. Wong. 1975. "Protest or Work: Dilemmas of the Tourist Industry in Chinatown." *American Journal of Sociology* 80:1342-1368.
Loescher, Gil, and John Scanlin. 1986. *Calculated Kindness: Refugees and America's Half-Open Door, 1945-Present*. New York: Free Press.
Lyman, Stanford M. 1986. *Chinatown and Little Tokyo: Power, Conflict, and Community among Chinese and Japanese Immigrants in America*. Millwood, New York: Associated Faculty.
Montero, Darrel. 1979. *Vietnamese Americans: Patterns of Resettlement and Socio-Economic Adaptation in the United States*. Boulder: Westview.
Montero, Darrel, and Ismael Dieppa. 1982. "Resettling Vietnamese Refugees: The Service Agency's Role." *Social Work* 27:74-82.
Moon, Anson, and Nathaniel Tashima. 1982. *Help Seeking Behavior and Attitudes among Southeast Asian Refugees*. San Francisco: Pacific Asian Mental Health Research Project.
Morse, Arthur. 1967. *While Six Million Died: A Chronicle of American Apathy*. New York: Hart.
Nguyen, Duc Qui. 1988. "California's Southeast Asians Enter the Political Arena." *Refugee Reports* 9 (11):10-12.
Nguyen, Liem T., and Alan B. Henkin. 1982. "Vietnamese Refugees in the United States: Adaptation and Transitional Status." *Journal of Ethnic Studies* 9:101-116.
North, David S. 1983. "Impact of Legal, Illegal, and Refugee Migrations on U.S. Social Service Programs." In *U.S. Immigration and Refugee Policy: Global and Domestic Issues,* edited by Mary M. Kritz, 269-285. Lexington, Massachusetts: Lexington.
Refugee Reports. 1988a. "Southeast Asian Arrivals in the United States by Nationality, FY 75-88." *Refugee Reports* 12 (12):10.
———. 1988b. "Actual Refugee Admissions to the U.S. and Ceilings on Refugee Admissions, FY 75-88." *Refugee Reports* 12 (12):9.

Rose, Richard. 1986. "Common Goals but Different Roles: The State's Contribution to the Welfare Mix." In *The Welfare State East and West,* edited by Richard Rose and Rei Shiratori, 13-39. New York: Oxford.

Rumbaut, Ruben, and John R. Weeks. 1986. "Fertility and Adaptation: Indochinese Refugees in the United States." *International Migration Review* 20:428-466.

Simon, Rita. 1985. *Public Opinion and the Immigrant: Print Media Coverage, 1880-1980.* Lexington, Massachusetts: Lexington.

Smith, Jill R. 1989. "14 Years Later, the War Rages on: Violence among Vietnamese Here Prompts Call for Self-Reflection." *News Star,* April 29, 1-2.

Stein, Barry. 1979. "Occupational Adjustment of Refugees: The Vietnamese in the United States." *International Migration Review* 13:25-45.

Stern, David. 1981. "Responses to Vietnamese Refugees: Surveys of Public Opinion." *Social Work* 26 (July):306-312.

Strand, Paul J. 1984. "Employment Predictors among Indochinese Refugees." *International Migration Review* 18:50-64.

Strand, Paul J., and Woodrow Jones. 1985. *Indochinese Refugees in America: Problems of Adaptation and Assimilation.* Durham: Duke.

United States Congressional Research Service. 1980. *Review of U.S. Refugee Resettlement Programs and Policies.* Washington, D.C.: United States Government Printing Office.

United States Department of State. 1982. "Proposed Refugee Admissions for fy 1983." *Department of State Bulletin,* December, 56-63.

United States Office of Refugee Resettlement. 1989. *Report to Congress: Refugee Resettlement Program.* Washington, D.C.: United States Office of Refugee Resettlement.

Wong, Bernard. 1982. *Chinatown: Economic Adaptation and Ethnic Identity of the Chinese.* New York: Holt, Rinehart, Winston.

―――. 1987. "The Chinese: New Immigrants in New York's Chinatown." In *New Immigrants in New York,* edited by Nancy Foner, 243-271. New York: Columbia.

Wright, Robert. 1981. "Voluntary Agencies and the Resettlement of Refugees." *International Migration Review* 15:157-174.

New Urban Crisis: Intra-Third World Conflict

Edward T. Chang

Introduction

During the twenty-five years since the passage of the 1965 Immigration and Nationality Act, the demographic composition of urban cities in America has undergone rapid change. Immigrants from Latin and Central America and Asia accounted for seventy-five percent of the total immigration into the United States between 1970 and 1979, and 83 percent between 1980 and 1984. More importantly, these new immigrants have settled in urban areas such as New York, Chicago, San Francisco, and Los Angeles. According to the Census Bureau projection, California will be a minority-dominated state by the year 2000. In the city of Los Angeles, whites constitute less than half of the city's population (forty-eight percent as of 1980).

The focus of interest in race relations in America's cities has begun to shift from white-black to intra-Third World (minority-minority) relationships because of these rapid population shifts. However, existing theories of race relations are oriented principally to explaining the relationship between the white majority and black minority (Gordon 1964; Glazer and Moynihan 1970; Blauner 1972; Bonacich 1973; Lieberson 1980). The usefulness of these theories of race relations in understanding and analyzing intra-Third World conflicts is highly questionable. If the frame of reference is always the white majority, researchers are unable to explain intra-Third World conflicts that do not directly involve the white majority in the large cities of America.

The purpose of this paper is to review theories of race relations in America and examine their applicability to the new urban phenomena of intra-Third World conflicts. It will not develop a new theory of race relations, but will suggest possible directions for future research on theories of race relations involving intra-Third World relations. This paper will also attempt to raise questions as to how we look at intra-Third World conflict in relation to the declining number of whites, whose power remains dominant but is being transformed.

Theories of Race Relations

The sociological literature on race relations in America has been concerned primarily with two major issues: first, the factors accountable for racial inequality in America, and second, the causes of racial and ethnic antagonism when people meet.

The ethnic succession theory attempts to explain why black Americans have "failed," while European Americans or Asian Americans have "made it." Succession is defined as "the process by which members of one ethnic group or racial group (the departing group) move up a notch on the socioeconomic ladder and are succeeded in their old position by a less affluent group (the successors)" (Gans 1973:1). It can also be ecological succession, which is described as "the series of events involved in the replacement of one neighborhood population or land use by another" (Aldrich 1975:327; Park 1936). Thus, the successionist views conflict or *competition* between ethnic groups as the inevitable consequence of ethnic minorities striving to achieve success in America. The successionist theory seems to have combined elements of Social Darwinism *(competition* between individuals or groups) with assimilationist theory (Park and Burgess 1921; Glazer and Moynihan 1970; Gordon 1964; Glazer 1975). "The driving force behind succession is *competition* between culturally defined groups over land use, with competition often assuming the form of conflict [emphasis added]" (Aldrich 1975:328; Park and Burgess 1921). According to Sowell (1980), all immigrant groups experience discrimination, but some of them (Asians and Jews) are able to overcome these barriers and move up the economic ladder more quickly.

"Ethnic small business is seen as a major avenue for economic mobility for minority groups, especially for immigrant groups" (Glazer and Moynihan 1970:30). Ethnic succession theory thus portrays Koreans as one of the latest immigrant groups to arrive in search of the American dream. To achieve success in this new society, they must overcome traditional barriers such as prejudice, discrimination, and other forces of antagonism. The successionist model views blacks' antagonism and violence toward Korean merchants as part of a natural, but inevitable, temporary process that must and should be overcome if success is to be achieved.

A major weakness of successionist theory is that it totally ignores the historical perspective of racial relations in America. Dismissing racial discrimination as the central determining factor explaining socioeconomic advancement, it tends to emphasize the importance of "proper" values such as hard work, ethics, discipline, diligence, frugality, and self-reliance.

Class-based theory (Cox 1948; Edwards 1979; Reich 1981) explains interethnic conflict as a consequence of capitalists' "divide and rule" strategy to discipline labor and maximize profits. Breen (1973), in his analysis of the changing composition of the labor force in Virginia between 1670 and 1710, documented white capitalists' promotion of racist beliefs and policies in order to separate white indentured servants from black slaves. For example, white workers had the right to bear arms while blacks were denied the same right. Persistence of the dual labor market in late nineteenth-century California also affected racial and ethnic relations: white Irish railroad workers did not protest the importation of Chinese workers because their influx elevated the status of the Irish workers (Saxton 1971:63). Reich (1981) also argues that "white workers are hurt by racism" rather than benefitted, because labor unions lose their effective bargaining power when their labor force is divided. Reich thus concludes that racism benefits the interests of capitalists rather than those of the working class.

Bonacich (1973) advanced class theory by developing the split labor market theory, which traces the source of ethnic antagonism to the desire of higher-paid labor to protect its own class interests from cheaper labor (usually immigrant labor). "If an expensive labor group is strong enough (strength is generally dependent on the same factors that influence price), they may be able to resist being displaced. Both exclusion and caste systems represent such victories for higher paid labor" (Bonacich 1972:548).

These two theories may provide some insights into the absence of class-based politics and the decline of union membership in the United States as compared to European countries. Katznelson's *City Trenches* (1981) argues that the primary cause of the absence of class-based politics is the division between work and community. American workers think of themselves as workers at the workplace, but as whites, blacks, Latinos, or Asians at home. America's political parties rely upon ethnic and racial affiliation instead of class interests; workers thus tend to align and identify themselves as members of ethnic and racial groups rather than as participants of class-based union movements. "We go our way and they (the blacks) go their way. In blue-collar life the division between the world of work and the world of neighborhood, home, and the family is particularly marked. Thus white workers are likely to feel very strongly about maintaining white neighborhoods" (Blauner 1989:124).

The internal colonial model is useful in analyzing white and non-white relationships in American society. Black ghettos are seen as an internal colony of white America where whites dominate and control the economic, political, and cultural lives of blacks—much the same way that colonizers conquer foreign peoples and use their culture to socialize the colonized elites (intellectuals, politicians, and middle class) into identifying their interests with that of the colonial system (Blauner 1972:90). However, as Blauner admits, the applicability of the internal colonial model to Asian American experiences remains problematic. Most Asian immigrants came here voluntarily and their experiences differ from that of blacks, Native Americans, and Latinos (Blauner 1972:54).

Recently, Bonacich (1987) modified the internal colonial model and middleman minority theory and argued that immigrant entrepreneurs are "oppressed" in addition to being the "oppressors." Middleman minority theory makes several predictions about the role of the middleman minority. According to Bonacich, middleman minorities concentrated in retail and service-oriented industries serve as a "buffer" between the dominant and subordinate populations. In addition, ethnic ties do play a vital role in business development. Bonacich's modified model states that immigrant entrepreneurs are not only exploited by American capitalism, but are also involved in the oppression of the underclass. "One important example is their willingness to operate in high-crime areas, in poverty neighborhoods evacuated by larger stores" (Bonacich 1987:455). Furthermore, this model identifies "immigrant" status as a unique situation that adds two dimensions to the exploitative condition of small business: ethnicity and a legal condition. In other words, immigrants are subject to discrimination because of their cultural and physical differences as well as their legal status (permanent resident) as defined by the state. Unlike other perspectives, this model contributes important theoretical research on the role of "immigrant entrepreneurs" in American society by combining the two important factors of race (internal colonial model) and class (middleman minority). Although its applicability is still uncertain, in my view this model provides a unique perspective in understanding the Korean-black conflict within the context of American capitalism.

Banton's (1983) rational choice theory suggests that competition is the root cause of interethnic conflict. He argues that "competition is the critical process shaping patterns of racial and ethnic relations." Rational choice theory makes several assumptions about racial and ethnic relations. "Physical and cultural differences do not of themselves create groups or categories, but only when these differences are given cultural significance do social forms result"; and ethnic groups result from inclusive processes while racial categories are formed by exclusive processes. Group boundaries tend to dissolve or be reinforced by the form and intensity of competition. In other words, when people compete as individuals, this tends to dissolve the boundaries that define groups; when they compete as groups, this reinforces those boundaries. Group competition is, therefore, the process that dominant groups use to exploit subordinate groups and thereby maintain their status-quo, their privileges, and their power. However, the applicability of rational choice theory to the Korean-black conflict remains questionable; it is not clear if Korean merchants and black residents are competing for the same scarce resources—power or privileges.

Omi and Winant's *Racial Formation in the United States* (1986) challenges existing theories of race relations: "the existing literature has not grasped the uniqueness of race, its historical flexibility and immediacy in everyday experience and social conflict" (Omi and Winant 1986:ix). Omi and Winant thus diverge from previous racial theories by emphasizing the "uniqueness" and the "fundamental" aspect of *race* in the United States. According to their view, America is and has been a color-conscious rather than color-blind society. For Omi and Winant, it is impossible to discuss intergroup relations without treating "race" as an important variable. Furthermore, it is particularly important to reemphasize here that because of rapid demographic changes during the 1980s, which created a multi-racial society, the meaning of "race relations" includes more than white-black relations.

All the theories I have discussed have contributed to the understanding of the dynamics of racial and ethnic relations in the United States. The question which needs to be raised is one involving the best way to analyze a multiracial society in transition while the basic power structure remains intact. Existing theories must be reinforced by taking into account other variables such as the formation of ethnic communities (historical approach), racial ideologies, and the changing nature of the global economy that has had a fundamental impact on intergroup relations in urban America.

Directions for Future Research

To begin the process of searching for an alternative model that will accurately explain intra-Third World conflicts, we can look at Korean-black conflicts as a case study. Tensions and conflicts between these two racial minorities have been reported in many major metropolitan cities of the United States such as New York, Washington D.C., Philadelphia, Chicago, and Los Angeles. In a series of articles and editorials published in August and September 1983 by the *Sentinel*, the largest black newspaper in the Los Angeles area, executive director James H. Cleaver focused on allegations that the black community had literally been taken over by Asian businesses in the last five years. Cleaver charged that Asian merchants were treating black customers with disrespect, overcharging them, failing to hire blacks, and diverting profits from the community. He urged a boycott of Asian (Korean) merchants who take advantage of blacks. This type of intra-Third World conflict has emerged as perhaps the most important and urgent issue facing urban America today.

The Korean-black conflict is different from the traditional white-black relationship in many aspects. First, Korean merchants and black residents are not competing for the same scarce goods and resources. Instead, Korean immigrants and black residents are pursuing their own unique strategies to "survive" in American society according to their own historical, economic, political, and cultural conditions. My hypothesis is that Korean immigrants are taking an individual approach to the very essential issue of "economic survival," whereas black Americans are pushing for a group approach in gaining economic security through political activism. Recent Korean immigrants are more likely to seek individual opportunities to succeed because economic survival is the most important and pressing issue. Most do not have a historical context regarding racial discrimination against which to place their own experiences. Sometimes, they rely upon one another (ethnic solidarity), but they are also willing to compete intensely with fellow Koreans in the United States to get ahead. In other words, recent Korean immigrants are more likely to be involved in ethnic enterprises (individual) than in political activities (group).

The Korean-black conflict may be further explained by *symbols* of "entrepreneurship." Shaped and formulated by historical and economic experience, these symbols are quite different for each group. For black Americans, for example, "entrepreneurship" symbolizes the road to a success they have been denied—that is, the opportunity to establish their own ethnic enterprises in their own neighborhoods. Black residents perceive Korean merchants as a symbol of a "success." Recent Korean immigrants, however, regard ethnic enterprises simply as a means to survive, a way of making a living in a strange land. During the Yi dynasty (1392 to 1910), the Korean "merchant" class was considered the lowest segment of society, inferior even to farmers; for many Korean immigrants, then, owning a small business in a black community symbolizes a step down.

There are some other possible reasons why Korean immigrants tend to be apolitical. The number of Korean (Asian) Americans has been too small to be effective in the domestic electoral political process until recently. Thus, they have not had a chance to develop a tradition of political activism. In addition, many Korean immigrants came to America to avoid a dictatorial regime, corruption, and war; thus, they do not wish to be involved with political activities. Furthermore, the Korean government has kept close watch of the political activities of Korean Americans. Many Korean Americans avoid active participation in politics because they are intimidated, and politics are irrelevant in comparison to their immediate goal of achieving economic security (Chang 1988; Kim 1981). Lastly, many Korean immigrants still regard America as an unfamiliar country where they do not yet feel at home.

Black Americans, on the other hand, carry on their tradition of political activism in order to hold on to the gains they made during the 1960s and push for economic equality at the same time. Due to their experiences in the civil rights movement of the 1950s and the 1960s, black Americans understand the importance of political activism in retaining their rights as American citizens. Therefore, the issues of survival for black Americans and Korean immigrants are different, and are influenced by their historical and political experiences in the United States.

In viewing the Korean-black situation, Koreans are neither dominant nor subordinate compared to indigenous groups, e.g., blacks. This situation is different from earlier contacts between newly arrived groups and indigenous groups. The unequal distribution of power between two groups often determined the form, intensity, and position of relationship. For example, white European settlers were able to nearly exterminate the American Indian population and push them onto reservations. Incoming black slaves, on the other hand, were immediately placed in a subordinate position economically, politically, and racially. The form and intensity of competition depends upon the strength of the incoming group and that of the indigenous population. When the perceived or real power of the two groups is equal, and one group believes it is superior to the other group, there is a high probability that tensions will escalate and turn into violent confrontations. Since theories of racial and ethnic relations in America deal with situations where incoming groups are either powerful or subordinate relative to indigenous populations, the Korean-black situation is unique in that Koreans have an "economic" advantage while blacks have greater "political" power.

The restructuring of the American economy from manufacturing to high-tech industries has had a profound impact on race relations in the United States. This deindustrialization of America (Bluestone and Harrison 1982), accompanied by plant closings, the polarization of class structure, and the internationalization of labor and capital, has intensified the conflict between the various groups of "have-nots" (Portes and Walton 1981; Wallerstein 1974). During the civil rights era, residents of the ghetto had a sense of hope for a better future. However, the black "underclass" of the ghetto in the 1980s is faced with the harsh realities of poverty, unemployment, drugs, and crime that seem to be permanent features of American capitalism (Wilson 1987; Auletta 1982; Glasgow 1980). In fact, the gap between whites and blacks has widened in Los Angeles where more than half of the black adults in the poorest neighborhoods are jobless. Between 1970 and 1987-1988, labor force participation of blacks declined sharply (83.2 percent to 69.1 percent), and the proportion of persons not in the labor force increased from 10 percent in 1970 to 23.5 percent in 1987-1988 (Ong et al. 1989:88).

Lastly, besides economic and political factors, a root cause of Korean-black conflict is the "clash of ideologies" between Korean immigrants and black residents. The ideologies of Korean immigrants and black residents are formed, shaped, and constructed by their own unique historical, cultural, and racial experiences. Korean immigrants must believe in the American *dream;* they *have to* have a firm conviction that they can make it here. If they do not, they probably have no purpose for living a hard life in America. Black Americans, in contrast, have been so profoundly impacted by racism that their views are not as optimistic as those of Korean immigrants. The historical legacy of racism still affects black Americans greatly. In fact, they must yet endure its painful results—poverty, unemployment, drugs, crime, and ghetto life.

In conclusion, no single theory can possibly explain the rapidly changing dynamics of race relations in America today. During the past twenty-five years, the composition of urban populations in America has undergone profound change. Whites no longer constitute the majority in some large metropolitan cities. In addition, Latino and Asian American populations have soared, changing the face of race relations in America's cities from white-black to multiracial. Unfortunately, scholars continue to apply theories of race relations that were developed to understand white-black interaction rather than intra-Third World relationships that sometimes do not involve the white majority.

In this paper, I have tried to enumerate the weaknesses of existing theories of race relations and question their applicability in understanding intra-Third World conflicts. In addition, by utilizing Korean-black conflicts as a case study, I have attempted to provide some possible variables that need to be taken into account for future research on this topic. I hope this paper will generate debate and inspire the further development of theories that can adequately explain and represent the dynamics of multiracial relations in urban America.

References

Aldrich, Howard. 1975. "Ecological Succession in Racially Changing Neighborhoods: A Review of Literature." *Urban Affairs Quarterly* 10 (3):327-348.

———. 1976. "Continuities in the Study of Ecological Succession: Changing in the Race Composition of Neighborhoods and Their Businessmen." *American Journal of Sociology* 81:846-866.

Auletta, Ken. 1982. The Underclass. New York: Random House.

Banton, Michael. 1983. *Racial and Ethnic Competition.* Cambridge: Cambridge University Press.

Blauner, Robert. 1972. *Racial Oppression in America.* New York: Harper and Row.

———. 1989. *Black Lives; White Lives: Three Decades of Race Relations in America.* Berkeley: University of California Press.

Bluestone, Barry, and Bennette Harrison. 1982. *The Deindustrialization of America.* New York: Basic Books.

Bonacich, Edna. 1972. "A Theory of Ethnic Antagonism: The Split Labor Market." *American Sociological Review* 37:547-559.

———. 1973. "A Theory of Middleman Minorities." *American Sociological Review* 38:583-594.

———. 1987. "Making It' in America: A Social Evaluation." *Sociological Perspectives* 30 (4):446-466. Special Issue: *The Ethnic Economy*, edited by Jose A. Cobas. Newbury Park, Beverly Hills, London, New Delhi: Sage Publications.
Bonacich, Edna, and Tae Hwan Jung. 1982. "A Portrait of Korean Small Business in Los Angeles: 1977." In *Koreans in Los Angeles*, edited by Eui-Young Yu, Earl H. Phillips, and Eun Sik Yang, 75-98. Los Angeles: Koryo Research Institute and Center for Korean-American and Korean Studies, California State University.
Bonacich, Edna, and John Modell. 1981. *The Economic Basis of Ethnic Solidarity: A Study of Japanese Americans*. Berkeley: University of California Press.
Breen, Thomas. 1973. "A Changing Labor Force and Race Relations in Virginia, 1660-1710." *Journal of Social History* 7:3-18.
Chang, Edward T. 1988. "Korean Community Politics in Los Angeles: The Impact of the Kwangju Uprising." *Amerasia Journal* 14 (1):51-68.
Chung, Joseph. 1979. "Small Ethnic Business as a Form of Disguised Unemployment and Cheap Labor." In *Civil Rights Issues of Asian and Pacific Americans*, March.
Cox, Oliver. 1976. *Caste, Class and Race: A Study in Social Dynamics*. New York: Doubleday.
Dixon, Marlene, Susanne Jonas, and Ed McCaughan. 1982. "Reindustrialization and the Transnational Labor Force in the United States Today." In *The New Nomads: From Immigrant Labor to Transnational Working Class*. San Francisco: Synthesis Publications.
Edwards, Richard. 1979. *Contested Terrain: The Transformation of the Workplace in the Twentieth Century*. New York: Basic Books.
Gans, J. H. 1973. "Negro-Jewish Conflict in New York City." In *Ethnic Conflicts and Power: A Cross-National Perspective*, edited by D. E. Gelfand and R. D. Lee, 218-230. New York: Wiley.
Glasgow, Douglas G. 1980. *The Black Underclass: Poverty, Unemployment and Entrapment of Ghetto Youth*. San Francisco: Jossey-Bass.
Glazer, Nathan. 1975. *Affirmative Discrimination: Ethnic Inequality and Public Policy*. New York: Basic Books.
Glazer, Nathan, and Patrick Moynihan. 1970. *Beyond the Melting Pot: The Negroes, Puerto Ricans, Jews, Italians, and Irish of New York City*. Second edition. Cambridge: M.I.T. Press.
Gordon, Milton. 1964. *Assimilation in American Life: The Role of Race, Religion, and National Origins*. New York: Oxford University Press.
Gossett, Thomas. 1963. *Race: The History of an Idea in America*. Dallas: Southern University Press.
Havens, A. Eugene. 1970. *Internal Colonialism and Structural Change in Columbia*. New York: Praeger.
Hofstadter, Richard. 1944. *Social Darwinism in American Thought 1860-1915*. Philadelphia: University of Pennsylvania Press.
Jordan, Winthrop. 1968. *White Over Black: American Attitudes toward the Negro, 1550-1812*. Chapel Hill: University of North Carolina Press.
Katznelson, Ira. 1981. *City Trenches: Urban Politics and the Patterning of Class in the United States*. New York: Pantheon Books.
Kim, Illsoo. 1981. *New Urban Immigrants: The Korean Community in New York*. Princeton: Princeton University Press.
Lieberson, Stanley. 1980. *A Piece of the Pie: Blacks and White Immigrants since 1880*. Berkeley: University of California Press.

Light, Ivan. 1972. *Ethnic Enterprise in America: Business and Welfare among Chinese, Japanese, and Blacks.* Berkeley, University of California Press.

Marx, Gary T. 1967. *Protest and Prejudice: A Study of Belief in the Black Community.* New York: Harper and Row.

Omi, Michael, and Howard Winant. 1986. *Racial Formation in the United States: From the 1960s to the 1980s.* New York: Routledge and Kegan Paul.

Ong, Paul, et al. 1989. *The Widening Divide: Income Inequality and Poverty in Los Angeles.* Los Angeles: The Research Group on the Los Angeles Economy, UCLA.

Park, Robert E. 1936. "Human Ecology." *American Journal of Sociology* 42 (1):1-15.

Park, Robert E., and Ernest W. Burgess. 1921. *Introduction to the Science of Sociology, Including the Original Index to Basic Sociological Concepts.* Chicago: University of Chicago Press.

Portes, Alejandro, and John Walton. 1981. *Labor, Class, and the International System.* New York: Academic Press.

Reich, Michael. 1981. *Racial Inequality: A Political-Economic Analysis.* Princeton, New Jersey: Princeton University Press.

Rex, John. 1983. *Race Relations and Sociological Theory.* London and Boston: Routledge and K. Paul.

Sassen-Koob, Saskia. 1982. "Recomposition and Peripheralization at the Core." In *The New Nomads: From Immigrant Labor to Transnational Working Class.* San Francisco: Synthesis Publications.

Saxton, Alexander. 1971. *The Indispensable Enemy: Labor and the Anti-Chinese Movement in California.* Berkeley: University of California Press.

Sowell, Thomas. 1980. *Ethnic America: A History.* New York: Basic Books.

Takaki, Ronald. 1979. *Iron Cages: Race and Culture in Nineteenth-Century America.* New York: Knopf.

Wallerstein, Immanuel. 1974 [1976]. *The Modern World-System: Capitalist Agriculture and the Origins of the European World-Economy in the Sixteenth Century.* New York: Academic Press.

Wilson, William Julius. 1978. *The Declining Significance of Race.* Chicago: University of Chicago Press.

―――. 1987. *The Truly Disadvantaged: The Inner City, the Underclass, and Public Policy.* Chicago: University of Chicago Press.

Wong, Charles. 1977. "Blacks and Chinese Grocery Stores in L.A.'s Black Ghetto." *Urban Life* 5 (4):439-464.

Young, Philip K. Y. 1983. "Family, Labor, Sacrifice and Competition: Korean Greengrocers in New York City." *Amerasia Journal* 10 (2):53-71.

Yu, Jin H. 1980. *The Korean Merchants in the Black Community: Their Relations and Conflicts with Strategies for Conflict Resolution and Prevention.* Elkins Park, Pennsylvania: Philip Jaisohn Memorial Foundation.

Conception of Ethnicities by Koreans: Workplace Encounters

Kyeyoung Park[1]

As Koreans arrive at John F. Kennedy International Airport, they are impressed with the diversity of peoples. When they settle in a multiethnic community such as Queens, they often ask not only "who are the others?," but "who are we?" In this paper, I would like to explore the answers that are generated as Koreans meet and experience people of other ethnic backgrounds.

In short, Koreans develop their own understanding of polyethnic community. By categorizing the people they come across in their daily lives, some develop very elaborate conceptualizations of this multiethnic society; others have simpler ones. For example, all Koreans living in America observe that the lighter one's skin color, the better one is treated. Koreans living in New York City, however, find that there are white and black Hispanics; and to their surprise, they learn that the typical description of blond hair and blue eyes does not seem to apply to very many whites in New York. These numerous and heterogeneous descriptions are responsible for shifting Koreans' perceptions from a narrow racial understanding to a broader ethnic analysis.

With regard to the study of ethnicity, Barth provided a classic formulation: "The critical focus of investigation...becomes the ethnic boundary that defines the group, not the cultural stuff that it encloses" (1969:15). Along these lines, an ethnic population is often best understood as a category rather than as a group with reciprocal relations (Vincent 1974).

Subsequently, the focus defined by Barth shifted to whether subjective claims to ethnic identity derived from the affective potency of primordial attachments (e.g., Geertz 1963; Isaacs 1975) or the instrumental manipulation of culture in service of collective political and economic interests (e.g., Wallerstein 1960; Despres 1967; Cohen 1969). This dichotomy, usually labeled primordialist-instrumentalist, continues to orient studies of ethnicity despite a growing sense that it obscures important aspects of the phenomena under study (Bentley 1987:25). While both the primordialist and instrumentalist models possess an appealing simplicity, they also share a critical gap in their explanatory logic. Neither addresses the question of how people recognize the commonalities (of interest or sentiment) underlying claims to common identity. In this sense, my discussion will address the issue on the level of individuals.

At its base, ethnicity involves a claim to be a particular kind of person belonging to a particular social group. Bentley maintains that the impetus to such a claim lies in ecological adaptation, emotional sustenance, an innate tendency to favor kin (and fictive kin), or shared positions in structures of production and distribution. All of these claims to ethnic identity involve symbolic construal of sensations of likeness and difference, and these sensations must be accounted for somehow (1987:27). He also thinks that the "theory of practice," as formulated by Bourdieu (1977), provides a way to address this problem. Bourdieu argues that objective conditions of existence, mediated by systems of symbolic representations, generate, in different persons, dispositions to act in different ways. Extrapolating from Bourdieu's analysis, we may hypothesize that consciousness of affinities of interest and experience embodies subliminal awareness of objective commonalities in practice. My study finds this reasoning completely valid.

Bentley showed how a woman negotiates her own ethnicity. Here, using a working definition of ethnicity as "cultural beliefs beyond and including affinities of common origin," I would like to add two other dimensions which come from how one conceives other ethnicities, particularly in everyday work situations. While Bentley examined how one individual identifies herself with commonalities of her ethnic group, my discussion will examine how individual members of ethnic classes identify themselves with an ethnic commonality — but only after familiarization with markers of other ethnic groups.

Work as the Context of Ethnic Encounter

In analyzing the ethnic encounters of Koreans and, in particular, ethnic construction at the workplace, I found that class affiliation determines quite different ethnic experiences and conceptions. The cognitive categories of class created by Korean Americans focus on power and prestige. It is this type of class that Korean Americans relate to, rather than the classes of production. These classes — worker, businessmen, and professional — create separate ideologies of racism and ethnicity derived from different spheres of interaction at the workplace. This finding is based on my research on the Korean community in New York City from July 1984 to December 1985. Out of my stratified sample, 53 interviewees out of 108 are classified as workers; 36 belong to the category of small-businessmen; 19 are professionals.

For most Koreans, ethnic encounters usually begin in the day-to-day operations of small businesses. For the most part, these businesses provide a setting in which Koreans serve non-Korean customers. These businessmen and workers are acutely aware that they are subordinate to white Americans in this system of ethnic stratification. In a neighborhood newspaper (*The Woodsider*, June 1987), Koreans were invited to run an Italian deli. They were portrayed as the only people able to operate such businesses:

> [F]or some reason it closed, reportedly and understandably because the children did not want to put in the long hours their parents did. I have a message for the Korean community—Please, please open an *Italian deli in Woodside! I won't put in the long hours to do it. But you will.*

From this, one notices the exploitation of ethnic stratification. After the Immigration Reform and Control Act of 1986, Korean businessmen began to hire non-Koreans, who now compose one-third of this workforce. These circumstances made Koreans aware of which ethnicities they could consider subordinate.

Ethnic Construction and Class Affiliation

Newspaper coverage of black allegations of Korean racism deals mostly with small-businessmen; Korean American professionals and workers are almost never mentioned. I will show that their attitudes contrast markedly with those of small-businessmen.

Small-businessmen

At their workplaces, Korean small-businessmen encounter various ethnic groups either as suppliers or customers. They consider Hispanics the best customers and white Americans problematic in being difficult to please and in threatening to initiate law suits. Due to previous experience, Korean shopkeepers suspect black Americans as potential shoplifters at their stores. Their evaluations of other ethnic groups derive from different cultural traditions about ways of doing business.

Hispanics as the Best Customers

Many Korean small-businessmen say that Hispanics are the best customers. Some express it more clearly: the best business area is a half-Hispanic and half-black neighborhood. It is unclear why Koreans prefer these neighborhoods of minorities, and in particular, Hispanics. One positive rationale comes from this explanation: although Korean businessmen can make more money in a white neighborhood, they prefer the friendliness of Hispanics and blacks. In other words, they do not feel the same warmth from white customers. Another rationale is their explanation that Hispanics and blacks are easy to deal with as customers. That is, they do not take much time to buy goods and are not difficult to please. They complain less than white customers.

Both explanations have their own validity. In the neighborhood of Elmhurst, for example, where most whites are older and in many cases less prosperous than the new immigrant groups, Korean immigrant businessmen do not extend credit. In the following examples, all three business people consider Hispanics to be the best customers and whites the most difficult. However, they have different explanations.

Mrs. Choi runs a Western grocery. Among her customers, she said:

> Hispanics are the best; they are easier to deal with, without complaint. I have such customers as Colombian, Puerto Rican, German, Italian, and Jewish. Colombians they do just as they want, whereas Germans are very particular and bargain over one penny.

Mrs. Lee runs a dry cleaner. According to her analysis:

> Seventy percent of my customers are Spanish and the rest are Asians. Spanish people are good customers: they behave as gentleman, kind, and friendly, with whom I feel intimacy. Among Asians, Indians are ugly: they bring filthy clothes; they bargain over price. Filipinos are clean. There are also some Chinese and Japanese. Among the Spanish, Colombians are a majority. In particular, those elderly Whites who could not leave this neighborhood. They are very difficult to please: they are stingy; at first they try to ignore you; later if you perform well, they accept it, giving even advice to me. In the past I felt inferior to them because of their racism. Now I do not care any more.

Mr. Chung runs a fish market in Washington Heights and lives in Sunnyside.

> Now I hire two black workers. Both of them are very good. Since I have a store around Washington Heights, sixty percent of my customers are Dominican, twenty-five percent are Puerto Rican, ten percent are black, and the rest are others like Chinese, Japanese, or Korean. From my observation, Dominicans are a little bit richer than Puerto Rican. Dominicans are moody people. There are a few Greek and Jewish customers, but I do not want to treat those who are very particular.

Wary of white customers who might make false charges, and black customers who might attack him, Mr. Kim mentions some other aspects of doing business:

> I have run a shoe repair shop in the Bronx. I could make $500 or $600 per week. However, as it was a Jewish neighborhood, they were very stingy. Even now I do not want any business in their neighborhood. After that I have run a general merchandise store in Brooklyn with my savings, $20,000 for one year. Although it was a good business area, I was always worried that they would quarrel with me and that they would attack me. Now I began a body shop in Corona.

Different Business Practices

In many cases, Korean businessmen arrive at different conclusions about their various ethnic customers, including Koreans, due to different business practices. For instance, while Koreans do not ask for a discount at beauty salons, at drug stores they do. Korean customers are considered the best by Korean hair stylists, but the worst by druggists. Moreover, Korean merchants have a positive view toward big-spending customers. There is no doubt that Koreans buy much more than any other customers at Korean grocers. Mrs. Hong, a hairdresser and beauty-salon owner, says:

> Seventy percent of my customers are Korean and the rest are Hispanic, Jewish, Chinese and Indian. Among them the Jewish are usually elderly and Hispanics are both young and old. [When I asked further, she said,] by Hispanics I mean Colombians. Among them, she said, Koreans are the best customers, because they are very generous about price and they are not difficult to please. Jewish people are often bargaining over price. Hispanics are fine, too. Those who used to bargain over price tend to complain a lot, also.

According to Mr. Kim, who runs a drug store:

> Eighty percent of my customers are Korean and the rest are Hispanic and whites. In my opinion, there is little difference between them. However, Koreans are used to bargaining over price and want to buy things on credit. Whereas other ethnics accept my price: if it is too high, Koreans simply do not buy it. Besides, Koreans ask for medicine without doctors' prescription. They do not know that in America there is strict division of labor between doctors and pharmacists. My suppliers are "delivering companies" such as pharmaceutical company and medicine wholesalers who are Jewish or Italian.

Mr. Kim runs a Korean supermarket. He said:

> Eighty-five percent of customers are Korean and the rest are Japanese, Chinese, Indian, and Hispanics. Non-Korean customers do not tend to buy a lot unlike Korean customers, but they do not complain, greeting me well.

This next case is more complicated. Why do Hispanics not work hard at a Korean sewing factory when Koreans do? One answer might be that Asian workers are said to be better educated than non-Asians.[2] Another more important answer is that Koreans might receive internal pressure from members of their ethnic group. Mr. and Mrs. Won run a garment factory. Mr. Won said:

> For the time being, there are fifty workers including those with home work only, around ten workers. Among them thirty are Korean; eight Chinese; five Hispanics; two Indians. Usually those who want work, come to us, then we screen them. In our case, this garment factory has had contact with just one Jewish manufacturer since we have opened this factory through a friend with whom I came to be familiar when I did trucking. As I hire different ethnic workers, he told me his impressions about them: Chinese are very diligent, working patiently; Hispanics do not seem to deal with big pressure from work, working exactly for eight hours a day and five days a week. They do not seem to be quick at understanding work, either. On the contrary, in my thought, Koreans are very quick to learn work, making fast progress and they are sensitive to their own interest. But they are not persistent: if it is not good to their profit, they immediately leave work. However, as the members of the

same ethnic group they are very kind to their employers, working more than what they are required.

Mr. Pai makes it very clear that it is a matter of capital, not a matter of nationality:

> I distribute beer and other drinks to 150 or 200 retailers: half are Western stores and another half are Korean ones. In my comparison, although there seems to be a little difference, Korean stores tend to write bad checks, buy on credit, or get nervous about prices, because of lack of capital.

Workers

Workers understand ethnicity far differently than their employers do. First of all, they emphasize the comparison of Korean workplaces with American workplaces. While they often perceive that Korean employers exploit workers more, they also see that American employers do not trust Korean workers. In some cases they develop friendships with their fellow workers who are not Korean.

The American Workplace

As many Koreans are involved in small businesses either as employers or employees, their workplace is generally a Korean business establishment. However, an increasing number of the second or so-called "knee-high" generation work for Americans. Korean workers at American workplaces feel that they are not trusted by white employers; Mr. Chun, Mr. Chung, and Mr. Park's cases illustrate. Mr. Chun, who worked at a body shop, said:

> At that time I was skilled and worked sincerely so they treated me well because they needed me. There I had both white and black colleagues: whites were very jealous of me, as an Oriental; blacks were very friendly and got along well with me. In my analysis, since whites know only themselves and their family, they are ethnocentric and arrogant.

Mr. Chung, now a fish market owner, said:

> When I was working at an American body shop, the boss lost something. From then on I was treated peculiarly. I was investigated three times. That did not happen to the other workers. I felt dishonored. And I was very upset. Finally, I called the police, and asked them to investigate me and my residence, otherwise how could I clear myself from dishonor? Eventually I quit the job.

Mr. Park worked at an American gas station. He figured:

> While the former Korean employers trusted me fully, this American employer watched me carefully and did not trust me. Well, I admit that we had difficulty with communications. For instance, with other jobs when Korean employers had to leave, they left the counter with me without any reservation, but the Americans would not. To make matters worse, a Spanish worker lorded it over me, a newcomer, in the absence of the employer, and used to order me a lot

to do this and that. After taking this treatment from the other employees and arguing with them for three months, I decided to end this exploitation so I left.

Although they sometimes reported having a hard time with other minority employees, Korean workers felt friendly toward fellow minority workers; this is seen in Mr. Ho's case.

> Ordinary Americans seem to be backward, as they have to make payments for many reasons and try to enjoy weekends. Contrarily enough, Koreans toil in order to make savings 16 or 18 hours per day. Therefore, Americans make fun of us. At the bakery I saw a second generation Puerto Rican who has both a strange inferior feeling and American pride, who tended to hurt others. When I used to work hard including overtime, he used to say, "Damn Chinese, you never know how to rest." But, after weekends, he spent all the money. Then he asked me to lend $10, or $20. While lending money to him, I used to say, "You see, I am not a slave to money. I make efforts at working hard in order to make savings for the future. Do you understand?"

The Korean Workplace

Many Korean employers hire non-Koreans, but they hire them for specific jobs. Some also seem to vary wages according to ethnicity and gender. It is clear that Korean businessmen are aware of the multiethnicity of the community and try to save wages, if possible, by paying different ethnic group workers different wages.

One worker expressed relief that he was not born a Mexican and therefore paid less and exploited a great deal. At a Korean green-grocery where he worked, he and his Mexican fellow worker shared a night shift, twelve hours, six days a week. While he was paid $350 as cashier, his Mexican fellow worker was paid $200.

At a Korean-run wholesale store, Mr. Mo reports that women and different ethnic groups have varying job descriptions:

> Besides the employer and his wife, there are twelve workers: three are Spanish; two are female accountants. I am supposed to do various jobs such as sales, shipping, and arranging stock. Whereas Spanish workers do only sales for Spanish speaking customers, Korean workers do various jobs. Especially because I apparently look very strong, I am usually asked to do very tough jobs.

Mr. Kim tells of the wage differential at a garment factory run by a Korean. Before working at this factory, he worked at an American firm. He said:

> Americans are just and fair about working hours and payment. Whereas in my opinion, Koreans just try to exploit other Koreans, taking advantage of their weak aspects. Once I start to work, I am soon covered with dust. Moreover, Koreans are too cold toward each other, compared with Chinese and Japanese on subway. As I see it, Korean women seem to remain at garment factory almost forever. I see Spanish workers, who work only for an hourly rate not piece work. Although they are little bit lazy, they are kinder than Koreans. If I can command English better, they can be good friends to me.

As illustrated in the above examples, Koreans who work with non-Koreans frequently become sympathetic to their co-workers' problems as they talk and share work and leisure time.

(It is also interesting to note that employees who are supposed to deal with those who shoplift or commit armed robbery are perceived as having negative feelings toward bad customers. In fact, it is store owners who care much more about robbery and are unhappy about shoplifting. Employees often complain that their employers want them to watch the customers.)

Some workers do not see the ethnic or racial differences among customers and express difficulty working for relatives as employers. Mr. Lee's first job was to work at a green-grocery in Brooklyn, where most customers were black. After that job, he helped his uncle in a Western grocery doing odd jobs. This time, most customers were Italians. I asked him to compare Italian customers with blacks at the former green-grocery, and he saw little difference. He did say he had to work harder for his uncle than he did at the first store.

Professionals
Special Demands on Immigrant Professionals
Interestingly enough, two doctors, one a pediatrician and the other a physician, arrived at different evaluations of Korean patients and patients of other ethnicities.

In the case of Dr. Yoon, eighty percent of her patients are Korean and twenty percent are American. I asked her for a breakdown of her American clientele. She said that she meant white, Indian, and Spanish, etc. In her comparison, American patients tend to ask why they must take a drug, but Korean patients do not. Korean patients do not speak out in front of their doctors even if they have questions. In her analysis, Koreans are preoccupied with deference to authority; they are as afraid of coming to doctors as a wife is of moving in with her mother-in-law.

Seventy-five percent of Dr. Lee's patients are black, ten percent are white, and the rest are Korean or Hispanic. Non-Korean patients, says Lee, "do not call the doctor for matters other than treatment, whereas Koreans call to talk to me for personal advice." Lee therefore has to spend more time on Korean patients. However, due to the language barrier, he needs substantial time to treat non-Korean patients. Although he deals with specific medical terms, it is sometimes hard to clarify patients' elaborate expressions or nuances; Lee therefore has to ask several questions and examine very carefully. Ironically, his American patients like his attitude. They feel they get a very careful examination.

Mr. Na, a CPA, also feels that Korean clients ask for more than merely professional service. It is interesting to note that despite the extra service that Koreans demand, the pediatrician above charges them lower fees while CPA

Mr. Na charges them higher fees. This may have to do with the CPA's greater socialization in American ways. Most of Mr. Na's clients are Koreans; few are American. In the case of Koreans, more than half the service is beyond a CPA's obligations—for example, helping them open a bank account. Therefore he charges his Korean clients more.

Ethnic Discrimination toward Korean Professionals

Professionals, like medical technician Mr. Pyo, face racism in terms of promotion:

> Although there is racism, things remain calm on the surface. Employers prefer Americans educated in the U.S., when they are considering promotion. Especially, Koreans tend to advance quickly as professionals, which make people of other ethnicities jealous. However, other Asians facing less language difficulty like Filipinos or Indians get better treatment than Korean and Chinese professionals.

Different Cultural Traditions

Dr. Park is a Korean herb doctor and acupuncturist. He finds Korean patients to be more argumentative than his American clients. This situation reflects a different doctor-client interaction in Korean cultural tradition. In the Korean system of medicine, patients are expected to have more dialogue with their herb doctor. According to Park, Korean medicine was considered common sense in Korea, but here it is in the beginning stages. His American patients often have problems with the back, neck, and neuralgia. They also listen to the doctor quite well and try to get continuous treatment, perhaps because they have lived in this society for a long time. Korean patients, however, do not seem to listen to what doctors say and stop their treatment suddenly or visit the doctor without an appointment.

This explanation can be extended to other professions, such as lawyers and insurance brokers, who complain that Korean customers are more argumentative than American clients.

The Importance of Experience in the Modification of Ethnic Construction

With experience, Korean Americans begin to modify their conceptions of ethnicity. Mr. Park, for example, could not understand the different life-style of Hispanics until he met Hispanics of higher social classes; then he modified his views.

Mr. Park worked at a general merchandise store in Brooklyn. As a watchman, he had to stand ten hours a day, and even ate lunch while standing. Although such a schedule was fatiguing and painful, Park recalls, he soon got used to it. Eighty percent of the store's customers were Spanish (e.g.,

Puerto Rican and Dominican). As a watchman he had many chances to observe them: from early in the morning they drank or took drugs, and they frequently were divorced. They were always having fun. He said, "At that time I tried to work hard, clenching my teeth. So it was very difficult for me to understand them: they looked like lazy, dirty, pleasure seekers, and looked disgusting to me." Later Park was hired as a manager at a general merchandise store in Yonkers, through somebody whom he had worked with in Brooklyn. For more than 1½ years he encountered customers who were Jamaican, Indonesian, or Filipino. In his view, Jamaicans were different from the Spanish he had observed in Brooklyn: they could live better. When they made a purchase, it was after a careful examination of the goods.

Mr. Su provides another example of changing one's attitudes with more experience. Mr. Su worked for three years at a Manhattan sewing machine store run by his brother's friend. There he had the tough job of being on his feet all day delivering heavy sewing machines. He reported that he could not trust Hispanics, who reputedly stole a great deal. Later, operating a store by himself, he was not only helped by the Chilean former owner, but also patronized by Hispanic customers, whom he appreciates. Reports Su, "local Hispanics do not speak English well, either. Therefore I have less problems dealing with them. Furthermore, I feel that Colombians are better customers than Koreans who often bargain over price."

Some Koreans have experienced racial or ethnic discrimination from white Americans and later apparently transfer this racism to black Americans. Mr. Kim, a pharmacist, said:

> From my own experience, I feel a kind of discrimination as a minority, visibly or invisibly. When I lived in Yonkers, a white store owner assumed that kind of attitude, seeing me as Oriental. Now, I feel that sometimes I, myself, imitate that kind of attitude toward black customers, suspecting them all of shoplifting, which is a shame. When I worked at the hospital, I was treated as a professional pharmacist, but not beyond the workplace: they knew nothing about me. They think that Chinese, Japanese, and Koreans use the same language.

Conclusion

Through the process of identifying and interacting with other ethnic groups, Korean Americans create their own new identity. Construction of one's own ethnic identity arises from ascription of other ethnicities. This process is evident in everyday work situations of individuals, and varies according to class and ethnic group. When these individuals are grouped as some kind of class, the artificial construction of ethnicity becomes apparent. Simultaneously with their claim to the unity of their ethnic identity, they maintain the claim to the privilege of constructing their class ranking.

Koreans not only discover new categories of people in New York, they also experience and conceptualize other ethnicities with new value judgements. For Korean Americans, the most important ethnic encounters take place at work. This raises questions about Katznelson's (1981) analysis of the American political system, focused on Washington Heights. He maintains that "class marks political organization at the workplace, but ethnicity reigns organizationally in neighborhoods." For Koreans, any ethnic solidarity in their neighborhood clearly builds on the day-to-day interethnic confrontation at the workplace.

Moreover, for Koreans, ethnic encounters and ethnic constructions depend on their class affiliation within the Korean American community. Professionals are more involved in the American mainstream and thus experience more racial or ethnic discrimination from white American society. In contrast, workers, more than professionals, experience the distrust and discrimination of the American workplace. It is these workers, however, who have more contact with other minorities and thus more empathy and understanding for the ethnic disadvantaged. Some Koreans, experiencing discrimination as an ethnic minority for the first time in the United States, unfortunately reapply this attitude to other minorities.

Finally, this ethnic construction is related to culturally-based notions about the split labor market. As the workforce of Korean business establishments becomes increasingly multiethnic, it uses different wage scales for different ethnicities. However, this ethnic hierarchy is highly dependent upon situational specifics.

Notes

1. This is a revised version of the paper that was presented at the sixth national conference of the Association for Asian American Studies, Hunter College, 1989. I would like to thank Thomas Burgess and Dr. Steven S. Fugita for their editorial help on this paper.
2. There have been studies supporting this. For instance, Roger Waldinger (1986:181), who studied immigrants and enterprise in New York's garment trades, found that Dominicans and Chinese brought with them different levels of professional and managerial experience and education. "Dominicans in New York have a considerable educational deficit when compared with their Chinese neighbors; though the difference among those immigrants employed in the garment industry is not so great, the Chinese still have a preponderance of newcomers with an educational background that is relevant to business success."

References

Barth, Fredrik. 1969. *Ethnic Groups and Boundaries: The Social Organization of Culture Difference.* Boston: Little, Brown.

Bentley, Carter G. 1987. "Ethnicity and Practice." In *Comparative Study of Society and History,* 24-55. Cambridge: Cambridge University Press.

Bourdieu, Pierre. 1977. *Outline of a Theory of Practice.* London: Cambridge University Press.

Cohen, Abner. 1969. *Custom and Politics in Urban Africa: Hausa Migrants in Yoruba Towns.* Berkeley: University of California Press.

Despres, Leo A. 1967. *Cultural Pluralism and Nationalist Politics in British Guiana.* Chicago: Rand McNally.

Geertz, Clifford, 1963. "The Integrative Revolution: Primordial Sentiments and Civil Politics in the New States." In *Old Societies and New States,* edited by Clifford Geertz, 105-157. New York: Free Press.

Isaacs, Harold P. 1975. *Idols of the Tribe: Group Identity and Political Change.* New York: Harper and Row.

Katznelson, Ira. 1981. *City Trenches: Urban Politics and the Patterning of Class in the United States.* New York: Pantheon Books.

Vincent, Joan. 1974. "The Structuring of Ethnicity." *Human Organization* 33 (4):375-379.

Waldinger, Roger. 1986. *Through the Eye of the Needle: Immigrants and Enterprise in New York's Garment Trades.* New York: New York University Press.

Wallerstein, Immanuel. 1960. "Ethnicity and National Integration." *Cahiers d'etudes africaines* 1 (3):129-139.

Part Four
Literature and Art in Comparative and Global Perspectives

"Emerging Canons" of Asian American Literature and Art

Amy Ling

In a brief essay, "Asian Americans Emerge," Teru Kanazawa Sheehan (1988) writes of her shock at several unexpected sights she encountered during walks around New York City: at Herald Center on Thirty-Fourth Street, the loudly-declaiming, Bible-toting sidewalk evangelist turned out to be a handsome, totally unself-conscious Asian American man; just north of Fourteenth Street, on a Fifth Avenue crowded with passersby, a couple entangled in a passionate embrace was Asian; and finally on the flip side of the coin, at a construction site in her neighborhood, a non-Asian construction worker was eating a Japanese lunch with chopsticks. Teru Kanazawa Sheehan interprets these unusual sights as attempts to satisfy "three types of human hunger – spirituality, love, and sustenance" and sees in their Asian American element evidence of "the arrival of the Asian American" as an accepted and integral part of American culture and society. Whether or not Ms. Sheehan is overly optimistic in the conclusion she draws, she is certainly correct in noting a change in the wind.

If my own experience is any indication of the prevailing winds, then without doubt the wind from the East is "in." Only five years ago, I had been told by a close friend, "You're a trailblazer, but you're blazing a trail to a place no one else wants to go." Since most English departments tend to be bastions of cultural colonialism, I usually feel like a lonely scout exploring an uncharted territory; but the tide seems to be turning. Recently, I have been invited to speak on some aspect of Asian American literature at Brown, at Harvard, and at the Modern Language Association's (MLA) annual convention in Washington, D.C. This same convention celebrated the publication of *The Heath Anthology of American Literature* that expands the notion of American literature to include more work by women and "minority" writers. The editor, aglow, reported that interest in this book, for which I was a member of the editorial board, was so great that people from McGraw Hill and other publishers had come to the Heath booth to congratulate him.

In the past two decades, we have been witnessing a great "emergence" in the area of Asian American arts and letters. In reclaiming the past, the University of Washington Press has republished out-of-print texts and has kept others in print, such as John Okada's *No-No Boy,* Carlos Bulosan's *America Is in the Heart,* and Monica Sone's *Nisei Daughter.* The first two titles have become unquestioned classics in Asian American literature courses all over the country. A few years ago, Northeastern University Press reprinted *Crossings* by Chuang Hua, and recently Beacon Press reissued Wendy Law-Yone's *The Coffin Tree.* Since Maxine Hong Kingston's *The Woman Warrior* won the National Book Critic's Circle Award in 1976, it has been the Asian American text most often written about in journals and discussed at conferences. As a gauge of its acceptance by the academic literary establishment, the MLA plans shortly to publish "Approaches to Teaching Kingston's 'Woman Warrior' " putting Kingston in the company of Momaday, Chopin, Chaucer, Dante, and Shakespeare. From October 1989 to April 1990, the National Portrait Gallery in Washington showed "To Color America: Portraits of Winold Reiss" (Reiss was a German who painted multicultural Americans in the early decades of this century). In conjunction with this exhibition, the gallery held a three-day symposium, "The Politics of Portraiture: Icons, Stereotypes, and Other Approaches to Multi-Cultural Imaging."

Poets and playwrights, too, have been gaining recognition: Cathy Song won the Yale Younger Poets Competition in 1983; and Garrett Hongo's two volumes of poetry have both won awards: *Yellow Light,* the Hopwood Prize in 1981, and *River of Heaven,* the 1988 Lamont Poetry Award. David Henry Hwang's "M. Butterfly" received the Tony Award for the best dramatic play on Broadway in 1989. His earlier plays, "F. O. B." and "The Dance and the Railroad" won Obie awards. Genny Lim's play based on the poems carved by Chinese immigrants detained at Angel Island during the early part of this century aired on National Public Television. We have all witnessed the media attention given Amy Tan's novel, *Joy Luck Club,* almost overshadowing Maxine Hong Kingston's *Tripmaster Monkey,* which also emerged in April 1989. All this attention and acclaim is creating a climate hospitable to the development of new Asian American writers. And we may say with great excitement and anticipation that we are now on the brink of an Asian American literary and artistic renaissance. It is a renaissance in which women are playing a prominent, if not dominant part.

"It took forever," Mitsuye Yamada wrote in 1981 of Asian American women's emergence as a vocal force in American society. Susan Schweik in her essay on Yamada's *Camp Notes* writes that " 'forever' here is an unabashed hyperbole, a sign of the emotional eternities of silence undergone by the women of whom Yamada speaks" (1989:226). Schweik asks why *Camp Notes* took so long to be "coaxed out of mothballs" and attributes its lengthy gestation—thirty years from the writing of the central poems about the relocation experience to their publication—to the depth of the silencing of Asian American women, both by the dominant culture and within the Asian communities themselves. In fact, Asian American women's double silencing may explain their greater need to become vocal, as well as their subsequent greater prominence.

The very topic, "Emerging Canons," on which I was asked to speak at the MLA conference and which I chose for the title of this paper, is ambiguous and somewhat problematic. If we examine the implications of both words, we find that "emerging" may be understood to have undertones of condescension, like the term "developing," in "developing nations." The namer/speaker is obviously not from the nation so designated but from a fully "developed" one. She or he is looking down on the object of study and attempting to be polite, not to rub it in that she or he is looking down at all, but nonetheless making his/her superiority clear by the very choice of name for the other. Such a person is employing the distasteful definition of "emerge": "to issue from a state of subjection, suffering, embarrassment" ([*O. E. D.*] 1971).

On the other hand, I like the idea of "emerging" as a gradual disclosure, as a butterfly emerges out of its cocoon, or an object rises "by virtue of buoyancy from or out of a liquid" ([*O. E. D.*] 1971). If we realize that Asian American literature and art have been immersed/buried/hidden because of historical/scholarly/critical neglect and are presently being freed/unburied/revealed by scholarly attention, as well as by virtue of their own irrepressible buoyancy, then the term "emerging" is appropriate. In fact, excitingly, Asian American literature is growing in two directions at once: backward, as scholars are unearthing past writers hitherto forgotten and neglected, like Sui Sin Far and her sister Onoto Watanna; and forward as Asian American writers, both established and new, produce new work. (Asian-British literature is growing and gaining recognition of late as well, with Timothy Mo being recently joined by the much acclaimed Kazuo Ishiguro, whose *The Remains of the Day* has received rave reviews.)

Now we come to the second term of our title—"canons," another highly charged word, which brings out big guns on both sides of the conflict. Though the original definitions of "canon" have to do with the church and particularly with the authenticity of books of the Bible, what is commonly called a literary canon has taken on the authority of the church to support its privileged status as a standard of judgment. Against these "canonical" works others are measured; if found wanting, they are "excommunicated," excluded from participation in the rites and services of the academy, and relegated to the void.

Old enough to have been educated in the traditional "English and American literary canon," I saw myself, when I began to teach, as a bearer of the "sacred torch" to be passed down to future generations. It never occurred to me in those early days, I am ashamed to admit, to look closely at this torch or to question why there were not more "great books" by women or any by minority Americans. After the civil rights and women's liberation movements opened our eyes, however, we women and people of color began to ask these questions and we were told, "Because there were not any," and later, when we discovered them, the response was modified to, "There were not any worth passing down." So the notion of canon carries with it the negative impact of exclusion for women and particularly for people of color.

Under these circumstances, for a woman of color, the most logical stance to take on the question of canons is to explode them altogether. Why have canons? They are an outdated, elitist, exclusionary concept antithetical to our health and well being. On the other hand, all of us who have ended up as scholars and academics tend to be conservative in the sense of wanting to conserve/preserve what was good in the past. We admire things well made, thoughts beautifully expressed. Coming into the dining room, we prefer to find or make ourselves a seat at the table rather than overturn the entire table and not allow anyone to eat. Not only do we take a seat, however, we also want to change the menu and to introduce new foods to the table; instead of an unrelieved diet of boiled meat and potatoes, we bring with us stir-fried vegetables, enchiladas, sushi, and a host of other new and exciting tastes and methods of preparation. "Emerging canons," then, in its most positive light, can refer to those texts written by so-called minority Americans that have reached the general dining table, or to the body of works that forms the corpus of a particular bicultural American literature. They are the texts most widely read and commented upon; those that, to borrow Jane Tompkins's term, are doing the "cultural work" for their time and their communities.

How is it that so many multicultural writers are emerging at this time? It is not that writers have attained a level of sophistication and maturation never reached before, for in my study of women writers of Chinese ancestry in the United States, I have discovered several highly sophisticated and accomplished writers of the past who were quickly forgotten and neglected. The answer lies in the matrix of political, social, economic, historical, and cultural forces today. The time is ripe, and the majority seems at this moment more and more ready to listen to the *other* and to its own formulations of the *other* as reflected in texts produced by these others. As Vietnamese American filmmaker/theorist Trinh T. Minh-ha has written in her poetic and provocative book, *Woman, Native, Other:*

> Third World dwells on diversity; so does First World. This is our strength and our misery. The West is painfully made to realize the existence of a Third

World in the First World, and vice versa. The Master is bound to recognize that His Culture is not as homogeneous, as monolithic as He believed it to be. He discovers, with much reluctance, He is just an other among others" (1989:98-99).

Four papers in this section of our present volume focus on texts that have emerged as part of the "classic canon" of Asian American literature: Marilyn Alquizola discusses the problematic ending of Bulosan's *America Is in the Heart;* David Leiwei Li analyzes Frank Chin's role in the struggle against the cultural colonialization of Chinese Americans and Chin's creation of a "counter-discourse" in his two plays; Wendy Ho examines the role that multivalent writing and talk-story play in the mother-daughter relationship in Kingston's *Woman Warrior;* and Shirley Lim places Joy Kogawa's *Obasan* into the "tradition of the thematics of the maternal in Asian American literature." David Mura's "Mirrors of the Self: Autobiography and the Japanese American Writer" traces the development of his selfhood as a Japanese American writer, seeking his reflection, his "myriad selves," in the stories his aunt told him and in the world literature he has read. Finally, two papers explore aspects of the 1989 Association for Asian American Studies (AAAS) conference theme "Comparative and Global Perspectives of the Asian Diaspora"; namely Woon Ping Chin's "Children of the Chinese Diaspora: A Comparison of Lee Kok Liang's *Flowers in the Sky* and Maxine Hong Kingston's *China Men,*" and Yong Soon Min's "Comparing the Contemporary Experiences of Asian American, South Korean, and Cuban Artists." Through cross-cultural, transnational, and intertextual comparisons, these papers seek new illuminations as they probe the questions: What sets us apart? What do we have in common? Yong Soon Min's is the only paper in the group to discuss Asian American artists, and though studies in this field are newer and fewer than in literature, clearly Asian American artists are growing in numbers and in significance. Using different media, artists are exploring the same terrain as the writers; for, as Yong Soon Min writes of one of her artists, their "works raise complex questions of identity in terms of the necessity to confront the differences as well as connections between the sociopolitical realities of here and there in relation to perceived notions of both here and there as well as the relationship between Asians as immigrants and exiles and Asian Americans who are more firmly rooted here."

Several vexing but interesting questions have fueled controversies in ethnic studies programs, and these questions underlay much of the heated debate at the 1989 AAAS convention over the work of the two most visible Asian American writers, Maxine Hong Kingston and David Henry Hwang:

1. Must the multicultural writer/artist be totally and exclusively answerable to his or her ethnic community, be the spokesperson of that community, tell the community's stories and tell them accurately? Or can she or he claim the

right to express an individual vision and personal concerns, and to modify the myths and legends of a group for his or her own artistic purposes? More often than not, a writer's "personal" concerns turn out to be the concerns of many, but this "many," this audience, may not necessarily be from the same ethnic community as the artist.

2. If Asian Americans write or paint about subjects other than their identity and our common cause – justice and equality – (Diana Chang and Kazuo Ishiguro, for example, people some of their novels with Caucasian characters alone) can they still be called Asian American writers or painters? In other words, how do we define an "Asian American" work – by the racial ancestry of its producer or by its subject matter?

3. Do we, as Asian Americans, claim exclusive rights to our "personal property": our history, our culture, our writers and artists, asserting that non-Asians cannot truly understand or interpret our material, our work? If we answer yes, are we not being racist? If we answer no, will we be relinquishing an advantage, assumed or real?

4. In the case that an Asian American writer/artist attracts a wide audience of non-Asian Americans, is this general acclaim *in itself* to be taken as evidence that the writer/artist has "sold out" and has become overly assimilated? Or should we all, as Asian Americans, be proud and happy that an Asian American perspective (even if we disagree with it in certain particulars) has found a wider audience, that we are not just talking among ourselves? Child psychologist Jean Piaget, in studying intellectual development, has observed that the infant "looks neither at what is too familiar, because he is in a way surfeited with it, nor at what is too new because this does not correspond to anything in his schemata." In other words, as I have written elsewhere, we learn by hooking small bits of moderately new knowledge onto old knowledge already in place in our heads. If something new is so radically different that it cannot be hooked onto what is already there, then it remains unattached or unlearned. Thus, those who may seem to be "accommodating" to the dominant sensibility are but the advance guard for other, perhaps more "authentic" "ethnic" sensibilities (I cannot use these terms without quotation marks because they are so slippery, emotion-laden, undefined, and perhaps undefinable).

5. Does an "ethnic" writer become more readily admitted into the general "canon" when she or he becomes less a writer with a cause (with content that is disturbing to the "majority"), and becomes more a writer with a style, a form that is intricate enough for scholars to sink their critical teeth into? From the majority perspective, the answer is probably yes, more style and less irritation is more welcome. However, our best "ethnic" writers today – and I think of Toni Morrison, Alice Walker, Maxine Hong Kingston – are doing both: clothing a serious and disturbing message in a medium so dazzling that

readers of all persuasions, except the most recalcitrant, cannot help being impressed and moved.

6. What happens to a writer whose very identity is defined by his/her marginality when this writer becomes "canonized" or "central" and is no longer on the periphery? Does she or he lose this identity?

I cannot claim to have the answers for all these questions. I merely pose them to stimulate further discussion at future conferences. The pessimist/realist in me believes that no matter how often literary canons are revised and no matter how many "minority" artists are shown in "majority" museums, only one small stratum of society is really affected. Thus, an efflorescence in cultural productivity and increased attention to it does not necessarily mean that Asian Americans have "arrived," for at the same time that we academics are rejoicing in the emergence of Asian American writers and artists, the community at large is experiencing an increase in violence against Asian Americans; that Maxine Hong Kingston's writing is widely admired did not preclude the murder of Vincent Chin. It is unlikely that American society itself will change to the extent that racial prejudice and injustice will be totally eradicated. We may have made ourselves places at the table and brought our dishes, but it may be that few people will partake of them or will at best only taste them politely. Thus, it is our affliction and our strength that we shall—if not always, then for a long time to come—have a cause and need to keep writing, painting, expressing.

References

Ishiguro, Kazuo. 1989. *The Remains of the Day*. New York: Knopf.
Ling, Amy. 1989. "I'm Here: An Asian American Woman's Response." *New Literary History* 19 (1):151-160.
Minh-ha, Trinh T. 1989. *Woman, Native, Other: Writing Postcoloniality and Feminism*. Bloomington: Indiana University Press.
[O. E. D.] 1971. *The Compact Edition of the Oxford English Dictionary*. New York: Oxford University Press.
Schweik, Susan. 1989. "A Needle with Mama's Voice: Mitsuye Yamada's *Camp Notes* and the American Canon of War Poetry." In *Arms and the Woman: War, Gender, and Literary Representation*, edited by Helen M. Cooper, Adrienne Auslander Munich, and Susan Merrill Squier. Chapel Hill: North Carolina University Press.
Sheehan, Teru Kanazawa. 1988. "Asian Americans Emerge." In *Without Ceremony, IKON #9*, Asian Women United.
Tompkins, Jane. 1985. *Sensational Designs: The Cultural Work of American Fiction 1790-1860*. New York: Oxford University Press.

Subversion or Affirmation:
The Text and Subtext of
America Is in the Heart

Marilyn Alquizola

This paper is based upon some assumptions articulated in a paper presented at the Association of Asian American Studies conference in March 1988. My previous paper (Alquizola 1989), entitled "The Fictive Narrator of *America Is in the Heart,*" had as its central assumptions, first, that Bulosan's narrator/protagonist was constructed out of the composite lives and experiences of Filipino compatriots in the United States. Second, that the idea that the protagonist is naive can be used as a narrative strategy, leading the reader to conclude that an undying belief in American ideals is dubious. By assuming that the narrator is naive, the reader can then draw the distinction between Bulosan, the analytical author, and Carlos, the bewildered narrator/protagonist. Bulosan, the author, is aware of glaring contradictions between American ideals and racist American reality; Carlos, the naive protagonist, expresses undying hope in an immigrant's American dream, the fulfillment of which is precluded by racism. Having made this important distinction, one can then arrive at a more subversive reading of the text, given that an assimilationist interpretation, strongly implied in the text's conclusion, is a problematic one, for reasons I will later articulate.

Written about Filipino American experiences in the 1930s, and published in 1946, *America Is in the Heart* is replete with racist violence against the Filipino. In this sense, the book historically represents factual aspects of its time, although it does so in a condensed and heavy-handed, dramatic fashion since its compositely constructed narrator bears the brunt of collective sufferings.

In this paper, I will highlight an analysis of the narrative's conclusion, which ostensibly affirms the American system seemingly to the point of urging acquiescence to colonial co-optation. The protagonist's concluding utterance has a dichotomous meaning that has potential for both a revolutionary and an assimilationist interpretation; however, it can be argued that were one to accept that Bulosan's protagonist is naive, the conclusion's surface inclination toward co-optation need not, of necessity, be taken prescriptively. I propose that reading *America Is in the Heart* as a subversive text is more tenable than reading it as a narrative which works toward the conclusion that assimilation in America is a viable and desirable goal. Applying an assimilationist interpretation would generate more problematic contradictions, both within the pages of the text and outside it, from its immediate sociohistorical context to its global implications.

The narrative's conclusion carries ironic meaning, for the America that the protagonist ostensibly affirms is a complex apparatus, dependent on a relationship that exploits Third World resources, both material and human. It can be argued that, in the final moment of the text, the protagonist is not affirming an exploitative system, but something more akin to Constitutional ideals. At this moment of utterance, however, he expresses a profound lack of cognizance that American freedoms and similar luxuries are afforded by a wealthy economy, which, in turn, is bought at the expense of the lives and labors of the Third World and Third World immigrants. For Carlos, this would specifically include the Filipinos in both the Philippines and the United States. This seems highly uncharacteristic of the protagonist, since, even in Part One of the text, Bulosan's narrative voice expresses class awareness and in some instances articulates class analysis. This apparent contradiction would remain problematic unless, of course, distinctions are drawn between the different narrative voices, or, at least, between the author and the narrator/protagonist.

Let us first take a look at the conclusion, which reads:

> I glanced out of the window again to look at the broad land I had dreamed so much about, only to discover with astonishment that the American earth was like a huge heart unfolding warmly to receive me. I felt it spreading through my being, warming me with its glowing reality. It came to me that no man – no one at all – could destroy my faith in America again. It was something that had grown out of my defeats and successes, something shaped by my struggles for a place in this vast land, digging my hands into the rich soil here and there, catching a freight to the north and to the south, seeking free meals in dingy gambling houses, reading a book that opened up worlds of heroic thoughts. It was something that grew out of the sacrifices and loneliness of my friends, of my brothers in America and my family in the Philippines – something that grew out of our desire to know America, and to become a part of her great tradition, and to contribute something toward her final fulfillment. I knew that no man could destroy my faith in America that had sprung from all our hopes and aspirations, *ever* (Bulosan [1946] 1973:327).

The revolutionary content in the ending pays credence to the fact that this land mythologized as "America" was built by Third World hands. When Carlos says that America was "something that grew out of the sacrifices and loneliness of my friends, of my brothers in America and my family in the Philippines," he expresses an awareness not only that Filipino American labor helped build this country, but also that colonial relations between the United States and the Philippines allowed the United States to prosper at the Filipinos' expense. The protagonist's implicit mandate that the Filipino immigrant worker should claim the right to America is, in fact, a revisionist response to historical precedents that excluded and marginalized the Asian immigrant. It also revises the definition of the American as exclusively an individual of European descent.

When Carlos explicitly states in the final passages that his "faith in America" was "something that grew out... of [the] desire to know America, and to become a part of her great tradition, and to contribute something toward her final fulfillment," he means to claim the status that was denied to the Filipino in manifest ways. The irony, however, is that the desire to contribute to such an exploitative system would only perpetuate the dynamics of colonial relations, unless one meant to change its very economic structure. In this case, what the protagonist means when he says "America" is ambiguous. On the one hand, Carlos' desire "to become a part of her great tradition" can be read as one that is generated from a colonial mentality that necessitates identification with the master. If one is to take literally his desire "to contribute something toward her final fulfillment," this would ironically imply acquiescence to a global form of Manifest Destiny. In other words, the economic and cultural domination that is the present reality in the Reagan and Bush America of the 1970s, the 1980s, and the 1990s, was steadily progressing since 1898, when the United States annexed the Philippines and other territories of the Third World. That the wealth of America would spill over onto its Third World satellites is a pipe dream, since, like the pyramid scam and social security, there definitively must be a loser in the end.

The logic of the narrative's conclusion is sound, in part. The immigrant worker should demand his due, since he participated in the building of this country, and especially because his wages were hardly commensurate with his labor. However, the logic of the second part of the conclusion does not hold, since the desire to contribute to a system that exploits one is self-defeating. A more radical alternative, of course, would be to subvert and transform it rather than to be co-opted by it, and the possibility remains that this is Bulosan's meaning; however, subscribing to this more radical interpretation certainly would preclude the current trend among many students of today, properly ideologized into accepting the old myth of the American dream, to interpret the text's conclusion as an affirmation of the American system. Naturally, this reading of the text itself reflects and parallels the desire to succeed via the professional or businessman's route, and involves ignoring glaring details in the global arena such as how and where microchips are manufactured, and at whose, or whose relatives', expense.

In the 1980s, if one were to look at some of the material success stories in the Filipino American community, one could mistakenly conclude that the Filipino in America has come a long way in achieving an American lifestyle that was not attainable by Carlos Bulosan simply because it was not permitted. In observing that Filipino American doctors and businessmen possess the material accoutrements of good living, such as property, a swimming pool, and a Mercedes-Benz or a BMW, one could indeed conclude that the Filipino in America has, at long last, arrived.

This judgment, characteristically assimilationist in nature, would ignore the complex economic apparatus that sustains middle-class American lifestyles. This is a contradiction that Bulosan makes apparent in Part One of his text, but which the protagonist apparently ignores in the text's conclusion. That this is basic knowledge to any socialist-oriented union organizer, such as Bulosan was, leads one to question the meaning and implications of the conclusion. The assumption that this verbal affirmation of the American dream was meant to be ironic and not literal would still lead one to ask, first of all, why this narrative strategy was employed.

Part of the answer, of course, entails marketing and readership concerns. In 1946, a major publishing house such as Harcourt, Brace and Company was able to publish a book that was such a scathing critique of the United States because, on the surface of things, it ultimately affirmed the American dream. Such an affirmation was especially timely at the end of the Second World War, when American morale was high. Other examples in mass media, such as Hollywood's production of numerous anti-Japanese films during the war, demonstrated that the sustenance of American morale was important. In 1946, the publishing apparatus would have had no stake in producing a text that ultimately conspired to subvert the American system.

It was the political alliance between the United States and the Philippines during World War II, combined with the threat of fascism, that enabled a man involved in socialist politics, such as Bulosan, to function as Filipino spokesperson for a democratic society against fascism. The political alliances during the war also placed socialists and communists on the same side as the so-called forces of democracy, an alliance that was short-lived given the advent of the McCarthy era of the 1950s and the Cold War. Not coincidentally, Bulosan's popularity also waned at this time.

In *Carlos Bulosan and his Poetry: A Biography and Anthology*, Susan Potter Evangelista describes Bulosan's fluctuating status as an Asian in the United States. Also mentioned in her description is the fact that Japanese Americans were incarcerated in concentration camps during this time, which emphasized the irony of being Asian in America. In other words, it did not matter that these Japanese Americans were born American. They were "guilty by reason of race"; thus they were not "American" enough to be saved from unfair imprisonment.

The national differences of Asian groups in America were either exaggerated or conflated, depending on the economic and political agenda of the American government. Being Asian subjected one to arbitrary treatment. The arbitrary treatment of Asians by the government attested to their secondary class status. At this time, for instance, Japanese Americans were incarcerated as if they bore some direct responsibility for Japan's part in the war. In this case, their ethnic and racial differences were exaggerated, and provided reasons for treating them as scapegoats for the tensions between Japan and the United States. The Filipino American, on the other hand, was patronized because the Filipinos were allies, and the Philippines was situated in a geographically strategic position. Evangelista says:

> But as the Depression lifted and the country headed toward war with Japan, the status of the Filipinos in the United States changed, if ever so slightly. Now they were the different Asians, the ones who might be expected to hold the line against the Japanese, as American allies. Not surprisingly, the war also marked the turning point in the acceptance by the American public of Carlos Bulosan as a writer. In the first year of the war, he published two thin volumes of poetry, *Letters from America* and *Chorus for America* [footnote omitted]. Later that year he was included in *Who's Who in America* (Evangelista 1985:14).

In *Asian American Literature: An Introduction to the Writings and Their Social Context,* Elaine Kim agrees conceptually with Evangelista's assessment of this phenomenon:

> Bulosan addressed his writing to an American audience in an attempt to win better treatment for his compatriots. *America Is in the Heart* is in many ways part of that inclusive and characteristic Asian American genre of autobiography or personal history dedicated to the task of promoting good will and understanding (Kim 1982:47).

Both Kim and Evangelista concur that the status of the Filipino, like that of other Asians, was manipulated to suit the political ideology of the time. It is significant that *America Is in the Heart* smacks of a "pinko" perspective that was regarded with suspicion during the Cold War and McCarthy era of the 1950s. It was not, of course, seen as problematic in the anti-fascist period of World War II. Bulosan's leanings toward socialism did not mean the same thing to the American readership of that era as they would to later generations.

In order to get a sense of the initial critical reception of *America Is in the Heart,* let us first look at some examples of the literary reviews that were published in the 1940s. Judging by the gauge of book reviews, the response to *America Is in the Heart* was quite positive. Some reviews reveal that the book was well-received, not so much on the basis of its craft, but because it was believed to have provided a clue to the Filipino sensibility. The book was read as affirming the idea that Filipinos were good, assimilable Asians after all, much in contrast to the wartime image of the Japanese. In a March 1946 review entitled "Loyalty in Spite of All," Bulosan's Philippines was said to have generated "a people whose capacity for work and whose ambition for their children bestow[ed] on them the heroic qualities of Pearl Buck's peasants." William S. Lynch thus summed up what he considered to be the real value of *America Is in the Heart*. Furthermore, Lynch perceived that the function of Carlos Bulosan was to serve as cultural translator or broker for the Filipino people. Implicit was the notion that Filipinos, like other working-class immigrants, should be, first and foremost, assimilable in order to facilitate co-optation of their lives and their labor.

> To the vast and still growing stack of tracts on intercultural relations "America Is in the Heart" is a valuable addition. As a treatise on a very special phase of the problem, a phase which had not had the literary treatment it deserves, it is particularly important. More than that, it is a promise from one who by his unusual background in American letters should bring to us something lacking today in our literature. There is unquestionably a new vigor in the Orient. We *need* Carlos Bulosan to *translate* it for us and to help us assimilate the attitudes and persons it sends to our shores [my emphasis] (Lynch 1946:78).

In the *United States Quarterly Book List* (1946:96), another reviewer reveals his belief that it was through contact with Anglo-Americans, whom he tellingly mislabeled as "native Americans," that Carlos was educated and made assimilable. This, of course, would imply a hegemonic co-optation. This reviewer's statement that "contacts with some of the native Americans interested in Filipinos, began an intellectual awakening which ultimately gave him a sense of his role in his group and in America," could be taken as an inadvertent implication that the dynamics which rendered the Filipino the *little brown brother* were necessary to the harmonious maintenance of the American status quo. Ironically, however, there is also inadvertent subversive content in the review itself. Since some of Bulosan's contacts were socialists and communists, the actual "sense of his role" could be taken as a mission to reveal the structural contradictions in American democracy. It is not surprising that the text, republished in the 1970s, was politically interpreted in light of a broader global perspective, and used in Asian American Studies classrooms as a critique of American society.

Even at the time of the first publication of *America Is in the Heart*, however, politically contradictory interpretations attested to the surplus of meaning and complexities in the text. A more perceptive review by Max Gissen appeared in the *New Republic* on March 25, 1946. Gissen, in a less patronizing voice, actually pays attention to the literary construction in the text. Furthermore, rather than liberalistically focusing on the niceties of assimilation as does Lynch, Gissen avoids whitewashing the American political reality:

> Like the others, Bulosan knew America first as a dream. The reality is one of the most sickening social truths confronting a minority in the United States. Bulosan didn't miss a step in the whole routine, from being shanghaied to an Alaskan fishery and cheated out of his poor wages to a beating by sadistic cops (Gissen 1946:421).

That Gissen's analysis emphasizes aspects very different from the previous reviews, pays credence to the fact that there is a surplus of meaning in Bulosan's work. Against the backdrop of the Vietnam War, in the 1970s the work was read as part of the general critique of foreign and domestic American policies. In the period directly following World War II, however, it was then socially produced and more easily interpreted as an affirmation of liberal American politics that saw assimilation as a progressive mode. Within the apparatus of social literary production, the subversive aspects naturally would be somewhat diminished if the U.S.-affirming aspects of the work are highlighted.

There is, no doubt, progressive political critique in *America Is in the Heart*. Bulosan certainly supplies his readers with ample and explicit examples of ideological (meaning unconstitutional) contradictions that occur within the boundaries of the United States. In Part Four of the narrative, Bulosan, using a cadre of unnamed Filipino characters, provides a list of situations that exemplify institutional racism in the country:

> "How come we Filipinos in California can't buy or lease real estate?" a man asked.
> "Why are we denied civil service jobs?" asked another.
> "Why can't we marry women of the Caucasian race? And why are we not allowed to marry in this state?"
> "Why can't we practice law?"
> "Why are we denied the right of becoming naturalized American citizens?"
> "Why are we discriminated against in relief agencies?"
> "Why are we denied better housing conditions?"
> "Why can't we stop the police from handling us like criminals?"
> "Why are we denied recreational facilities in public parks and other such places?"
> Ten important points—a broad generalization of our difficulties in California (Bulosan [1946] 1973:268-269).

Were one to restructure these interrogatives into declarative sentences, they would read like a syllabus for a Filipino American Studies history class. Bulosan, the author, well aware of the manifestations of institutional racism, explicitly lists examples through the mouths of these characters. That these problems continue to exist through the sequence of events in *America Is in the Heart* belies its concluding affirmation of America. It is, however, the global contradictions that stem from the United States imperialist apparatus that must be teased out of the subtext of the work.

The reception of the work as an assimilationist text is due partly to the surplus of meaning in the narrative; it contains a critique of both racism within American borders as well as colonialism outside its borders, in opposition to the affirmation of the American people themselves as vessels for American ideals. When the protagonist, in the end, finally interweaves his conclusion with a Walt Whitman-like sensibility that "sings the body electric," it is, at first, not clear whether he is celebrating American individualism or encouraging social agency. Certainly, taken by itself, the protagonist's tone in the conclusion seems more suggestive of romantic idealism. I propose that the reception of the work in 1946 as an assimilationist text is strongly influenced by the narrative's conclusion, which functions not only as a mechanism for closure, but as a logical, or rather, illogical, deduction. The question remains as to whether this judgment is authorial, spoken from an objective point of view, or ironic, spoken from the naive protagonist's point of view.

If the judgment is authorial, it could be construed that Bulosan himself is ambivalent concerning his position in colonial America given that he occupies a subject-position at the end of the novel that is different from that in most of the text. This arrived-at state of ambivalence may have been partly due to the way that the war had affected the Philippines, and the success that Bulosan must have felt, given his feat of publication. The alternative possibility is that the author wrote ironically and against the interests of his publishers and readership in the 1940s. If the meaning is ironic, then the author, who was possibly manipulated by the publishing apparatus to write an "American story," in turn manipulated the establishment by rendering his protagonist naive.

From the vantage point of 1990, we can see that the complexities of meaning in *America Is in the Heart*, along with historical changes, fluctuations in the socioeconomic context, and the restructuring of political alliances – which all affect personal politics – have allowed and still allow its readers to generate contradictory interpretations. This becomes apparent when one looks at the critical response that the text received after it was re-published in 1973 by the University of Washington Press. Unlike its reception directly after the war years, this more recent critical response and reader reception indicated that Bulosan's work was read as something other than a statement that concludes in the ultimate affirmation of the American system. Because of the historical period, and the fact that the university readership had a more politically radical point of view, critical interpretation focused on the text primarily as a subversion of the system. The general reception of *America Is in the Heart* after its second publication was one that subverted the pro-democratic, pro-American 1946 reception of the text. After publication in the

1970s, book sales were aimed at a university audience, particularly an ethnic studies university audience, which meant that the target market stood to the left of mainstream political sensibilities. This lies in contrast to a postwar American audience that was smug in its complacent sense of American democracy.

Antithetical to the notion that the United States is or can be a land of equal opportunity are a plethora of textual examples of racist America, which far outnumber examples in the affirmative mode. This ratio perhaps indicates what the author's true inclinations are. The narrator's ostensible faith in America is, however, the bottom line of the text, so to speak. Strategically, its placement tops off, encapsulates, and places the affirmation of Americanism as a benign veil that disguises the subversive nature of its content. That a Filipino immigrant could express an undying faith in American ideals ideologically suggests to its readers that the United States would be a nearly utopian environment if only racism were obliterated. This assumption conveniently ignores the exploitative functions extant in the maintenance of the American economy, and assumes that racism is not part of its structural mechanism.

It would seem that the affirmation of America is strategically placed in the conclusion in order to neutralize the numerous exemplifications of colonially-induced poverty and institutional racism, in the Philippines and the United States respectively. As a narrative strategy, it is teleologically effective, for it disguises and nullifies the subversive content of the book, ostensibly leaving the final impression that there is hope for America.

Pierre Macherey states in *A Theory of Literary Production* (1978:90), "To know the work, we must move outside it." My thesis is that within the narrative itself, Carlos's idealistic Americanism functions as a survival strategy for this protagonist, whether he is purely fictional, or whether he is partly Bulosan. This becomes a defense mechanism that, in part, aids one in precluding a terrible cynicism by keeping hope alive. For an idealistic immigrant who is stuck in America because of his impoverished condition, the survival mechanism of hoping against hope would save him from ultimate despair. That the Filipino immigrant protagonist would have to go to such psychological lengths in order to ameliorate the bleakness of his life in America only attests to the profound racism that forces one to lie to oneself. In this sense, Bulosan's strategic use of the naive narrator allows him to report and document the psychology of survival and adaptation utilized by many of his compatriots.

Politically, the conclusion is also effective as a strategy because it allows for its publication, i.e., its literary production. Had the reading been less hopeful and less affirming of America, it is logical to assume that it most likely would not have been published in its entirety in 1946 by a major publishing house such as Harcourt, Brace and Company.

In his book *Carlos Bulosan and the Imagination of the Class Struggle,* Epifanio San Juan, Jr. (1972:91) draws the conclusion that Bulosan was really "reassert[ing] his own notion of an 'America' that symbolizes an ideal classless society which informs the structure of *America Is in the Heart."* If this were indeed the case, then the American framework that the protagonist wishes to contribute to was an ideal that was much more characteristically Marxist than it was capitalist. Furthermore, this would still support the notion that the ending is ironic and subversive. Bulosan's apparent consciousness of class stratification in America allows critic Epifanio San Juan, Jr. to sustain a Marxist analysis of Bulosan's work.

That Bulosan's class analysis is interwoven throughout the narrative illustrates his desire to subvert America's positive image. Bulosan's strategy lies not just in the dialectical nature of his narrative style, which juxtaposes both positive and negative responses to America, but also in his dialogic interweaving of different narrative voices. In an authorial voice, Bulosan speaks from the standpoint of awareness of class structures, both in the Philippines and the United States, along with the interdependence between both countries. In the naive and bewildered voice of his protagonist, Bulosan attempts to create an empathy for the Filipino immigrant's situation in the United States. In "using every trick," he also plays on the paternalistic tendencies of his national hosts, be they publisher, editor, audience, or critic.

In spite of all this, authorial intent is an *ad hominem* consideration. Whether it was Bulosan's conscious intent to affirm or deny the American system is not as important as the textual product itself, and the dynamics between text, readership and political context, past and present. In terms of the text alone, one cannot deny that the narrative events in *America Is in the Heart* reflect the historical inequities that exist within the boundaries of the United States. In turn, the microcosm of Bulosan's Filipino community in *America Is in the Heart,* by implication, reflects the historical antecedents, starting from 1898, that made domestic oppression of the Filipino worker possible in the first place. It can be argued that the global relationships, which currently make emigration of the Filipino professional a desirable and sometimes necessary alternative to living and working in the Philippines, are an outcome of previous colonial history, even if they reflect more a neocolonial than a colonial situation. Although the particulars of these two separate historical moments are emphatically distinct, they share at a structural level the similar characteristic of dependency. Thus, even though the historical moments of emigration— the specifics of gender ratio, class background, motives for emigration, and configurations of racism—are different, parallels may still be teased out of the subtext of Bulosan's work, which would indicate that the text has a relevance beyond that of a period piece. Differing from the social context of the 1930s, the 1970s and 1980s provided a context that allowed relatively more privileges to the educated Filipino immigrant in the United States than was allowed to the Filipino immigrant worker in the past. In the 1990s, the ironic implication that the illusory freedom and relative wealth enjoyed by a middle-class Filipino American citizenry is somehow based on the unequal, inter-dependent relationship between the United States and Third World countries like the Philippines can inform the interpretive approach of the subversive reader. Bulosan's text provides a clue to this reader, since it demonstrates the connection between the Filipino American community and the dependency relationships of the United States and the Philippines; however, the configurations of dependency in the 1990s need to be subjected to careful analysis, since they are not invariable.

In summary, the rendering of the protagonist's hopeful utterance in the text's conclusion as naive, and therefore, ironic, helps make sense of the conclusion, and, in my view, provides a clue to the apparent contradictions in Bulosan's text. In the subtext of Bulosan's conclusion, his quest for social justice is implicit within a context that has the structure of exploitation already written into the equation. In the narrative of *America Is in the Heart*, Bulosan expresses the inequities in the political relationship between the United States and the Philippines both explicitly in his text, and implicitly in his subtext.

References

Alquizola, Marilyn. 1989. "The Fictive Narrator of *America Is in the Heart.*" In *Frontiers of Asian American Studies: Writing, Research, and Commentary*, edited by Gail Nomura et al., 211-217. Pullman: Washington State University Press.
Bulosan, Carlos. 1973. *America Is in the Heart, a Personal History.* Seattle: University of Washington Press. (Original edition 1946, by Harcourt, Brace and Company.)
Evangelista, Susan Potter. 1985. *Carlos Bulosan and His Poetry: A Biography and Anthology.* Seattle: University of Washington Press.
Gissen, Max. 1946. "The Darker Brothers." *New Republic* 114 (March 25):421.
Kim, Elaine H. 1982. *Asian American Literature: An Introduction to the Writings and Their Social Context.* Philadelphia: Temple University Press.
Lynch, William S. 1946. "Loyalty in Spite of All." *Saturday Review of Literature* 29 (7):78.
Macherey, Pierre. 1978. *A Theory of Literary Production.* Translated from the French by Geoffrey Wall. London: Routledge and Kegan Paul.
San Juan, Epifanio, Jr. 1972. *Carlos Bulosan and the Imagination of the Class Struggle.* Quezon City: University of the Philippines Press.
United States Quarterly Book List. 1946. 2 (June):96.

The Formation of Frank Chin and Formations of Chinese American Literature

David Leiwei Li

Frank Chin is an apparently fading figure on the Chinese American literary stage he has helped construct. Such an act of fading is typified by the institutional ignorance and the consequent under-read status of his works. The phenomenon is instructive: it exemplifies the tenacity of the hegemonic process in effacing the oppositional; it illustrates the need for the counter force to rethink its strategies; and it becomes the occasion for this piece of writing to fade in what seems to have been faded out.

Playwright, essayist, and short-fictionalist, Chin emerged in the late 1960s when the Third World strike at the University of California at Berkeley and the subsequent Asian American student movements resulted in the formation of two of its native intellectual groups, the political and the cultural. The former group of Chinese Americans identified themselves with the other minorities in the United States and was determined to wage war against their common enemy, the economic and political oppression of American imperialism, while the latter group undertook the task of correcting the racist stereotypes of colonialism and aimed at a reconstruction of Asian American images (Nee and Nee 1972:355-360). It is with the latter that Chin is closely associated; though he may not participate in the community project of anti-poverty and exploitation, his involvement in the founding of the Combined Asian Resources Project (CARP) and Asian American literary formations marks him as a writer and editor of conscious political resistance. His personal constitution interlocks and interacts with the recovery and the production of Chinese American literature in such a way that an evaluation of his role as a historic agent becomes indispensable.

Chin realizes that Chinese Americans have been made atrocious victims not only of legislative exclusion, resulting in drastic population reduction, but also of historic erasure, the consequence of which is the designation of their minor position or rather non-identity. Since denying minorities their historical involvement, their sufficiency as human subjects, and their right to participate in civil and political society has been the control mechanism of racist dominance, Chin's project is a war against such denial; in JanMohamed's phrase, "negating the negation as a form of affirmation" (JanMohamed 1987). Chin challenges the hegemonic deployment of the Chinese American, contends its oppressive signifying practices, and codifies a self identity. This paper will trace these stages of Chin's negative construction and ponder on their impact on Chinese American literary formations.

I

In his quest for the indigenous history of his ethnic community, Chin notes that the absence of the Chinese American from general American history books is a direct outcome of the 1882 exclusion law which was designed to "drive us out of the country, to kill us." The completion of the transcontinental railroad signaled the death of the use-value of the Chinese American even as "cheap labor":

> Out of our despair, we took to burning our letters from home, burning the pages of our diaries and journals as we wrote them, burning tickets, receipts, bills, burning everything with our names, everything written in our hand and throwing the ashes into the sea, in the hope, that, at least, that much of us would get home to China. America had taught us, finally that China was our home and inspired the invention of this little Chinese American ceremony (Chin 1972a:62).

The act of incineration is a gesture of desperation in the face of racial exclusion. Chin has us realize here that Chinese immigrants are deprived not only of their legitimate geographic belonging, but also of their temporal existence. In burning the records they themselves have kept, Chinese Americans are forced to denounce that part of their life which is anchored on American soil. The explicit genocidal attempt of the dominant coupled with such helpless suicidal compliance of the oppressed leads to the painful elimination of the linguistic trace, hence the social death of the ethnic group. The Chinese American becomes then an entity that can neither claim its predecessor with a positive historical identity nor expect a future in progeny.

The disastrous impact of this history is nowhere more pungently felt than in Chin's generation of writers, who take it as their duty to write about Chinese America when writing itself is considered to be exclusively white and especially non-Chinese American. Two forms of such attitudes co-inhabit the community.

The first is one of blind resistance by associating writing with white domination as an instrument of oppression that the oppressed does not share. The second is one of assimilation, "look[ing] upon writing as the proof," as some humanistic redeeming feature, that the Chinese American is "nearing white" (Nee and Nee 1972:394-395). Both reactions are programmed by cultural colonialism that intends to reinforce writing as white property and privilege, thereby effacing the minority subject position.

In his classroom experiments, Chin traces the responses in the original linguistic reification of his ethnic community: "The either-or thing is right in that scientific name we go by, 'Chinese,' hyphen, 'American.' " When asked to divide the self into such an arbitrary dichotomy, his students automatically assign all the adventurous, creative, and original qualities to their "American" part while attributing everything old fashioned, inhibiting, and dull to their "Chinese" part. Chin sees this as yet another instance of the dominant race instilling a schizophrenic uncertainty in the formation of the ethnic self. The question of division is an extension of the trite East-West construction that encourages the split self, and "what you break down, you break according to the lines of the stereotype," which aims to perpetuate the subjugation-submission power relation (Nee and Nee 1972:394-395). Chin aptly names this the reign of "racist love" and points out:

> The general function of any racial stereotype is to establish and preserve order between different elements of society, maintain the continuity and growth of western civilization, and enforce white supremacy with a minimum of effort, attention and expense. The ideal racial stereotype is a low maintenance engine of white supremacy whose efficiency increases with age, as it became "authenticated" and "historically verified" (Chin and Chan 1972:66).

The hegemonic process that underwrites the social notches of the minority group is mercilessly exposed. The naturalization of the social hierarchy, Chin cautions us, lies at the base of white control. But the success of the reign results in part from the manufactured consent of the Chinese American. "[T]his tyranny of culture by the whites," Chin observes, "has managed to produce a Chinese-American character that is without an ego, that has no self-respect, that has internalized almost fatal suicidal doses of self-contempt" (Nee and Nee 1972:385). He goes on to say,

> This self-contempt itself is nothing more than the subject's acceptance of white standards of objectivity, beauty, behavior, and achievement as morally absolute, and his acknowledgement of the fact that, because he is not white, he can never fully measure up to white standards.

It is, in short, "an expedient tactic of survival" (Chin and Chan 1972:67).

The desire to survive has exacted a costly toll. When the exclusion law of 1882 was finally rescinded in 1943 – due to the political exigency as well as expediency of America's and China's becoming allies in the war against Japan – Chinese American writing emerged not so much as an expression of its own sensibility but as a showcase model of the American dream. Among a handful of writers Chin disapproves of, the example of Jade Snow Wong stands out. *Fifth Chinese Daughter* was a tremendous commercial success and Wong was sent to Asia as a cultural emissary of American democracy. What is little known, however, is the fact that two-thirds of Wong's original manuscript was omitted from the published version (Kim 1982:60, 71). When Chin raised the question of what was left out, Wong replied, things "too personal." And she continued, "it takes maturity to be objective about one's self" (Chin et al. 1974). Wong's situation illustrates two major circumscriptions of minority writing. On the one hand, we witness overt censorship through the machinery of editors and publishers. On the other hand, we note an "automatic" acceptance of white standards of writing and the inherent ethnic deficiency in the attainment of white objectivity and beauty. The difficulty of getting by external gatekeepers, and particularly the unconscious assimilation of the "universality" of writing, cripple the normal growth of an ethnic literature. Cultural hegemony maintains itself not so much by imposing white writing upon the minority but by soliciting white writing from the objectified minority.

The material purged from Wong's manuscripts through ideological apparatuses is, one recalls, "personal." We witness here the greatest generic oxymoron ever: the ethnic writer can hardly print anything creative or "novel" because the validity of their feeling is not universal; neither can they publish their personal emotions because the autobiographical genre designed for their lot demands the omission of subjective valuations. In other words, the individual experiences of an ethnic entity will never be valorized unless they are approved by the dominant culture. It comes as no surprise that Wong's autobiography contains little more than an infantry of Chinatown restaurants and curiosity shops, a desirable representation of the Chinese American as a model minority devoid of subjectivity.

Placing minority writers in a passive, powerless mouth-piece position is a built-in function of white writing. During his days in Iowa, Frank Chin was often blamed for his failure to explore "the local color of Chinatown." "You know," remarked his instructor, "you're writing about the Chinese in a way that I don't think American people would be interested in," to which Chin retorted, "Because they were just like people, right?" Chin was stunned to learn not only that he "had a point of view" about his people, but that his "point of view wasn't white," for he depicted the individuality of the ethnic subject in ways that did not conform to mere "local color" (Nee and Nee 1972:379). Like the paradox of the ethnic autobiography Wong got into, the generic assignment for the minority writer to "cook up" regional flavor for the cosmopolitan cultural connoisseur seems to be a division of labor. Such division reproduces once again the marginal position of ethnic writers in the literary system: they are asked first to offer the beautiful and exotic facade of the periphery and then kept there because their writing is limited and not permanent.

Aside from generic constraints, Chinese American authors suffer from a lack of authority over the English they use; their language is either defaulted or rejected. The expectation that they employ standard white English enforces such a status of dependency that their autonomy as writers is at stake. Against this kind of aesthetic as well as ideological dictatorship, Chin and his fellow writers argue:

> The universality of the belief that correct English is the only language of American truth has made language an instrument of cultural imperialism. The minority experience does not yield itself to accurate or complete expression in the white man's language. Yet, the minority writer, specially the Asian-American writer, is made to feel morally obliged to write in a language produced by an alien and hostile sensibility. His task, in terms of language alone, is to legitimize his, and by implication his people's, orientation as white, to codify his experience in the form of prior symbols, clichés, linguistic mannerisms and a sense of humor that appeals to whites because it celebrates Asian American self-contempt. Or his task is the opposite—to legitimize the language, the style, and syntax of his people's experience (Chin et al. 1974:xxxvii).

The assertion of cultural and linguistic integrity is interestingly couched in terms of the writer's role within his or her community. His success is measured against his specific agency in the ethnic community. "What I value most," Chin says, "is what I am doing, trying to legitimize the Chinese-American sensibility. Call it my accident in time and space and all the talent, everything I have is good only for this... if Chinese-American sensibility isn't legitimized, then my writing is no good" (Nee and Nee 1972:386).

II

The legitimization of a Chinese American sensibility for Chin is necessarily a "noise of resistance" to the racist order; it entails a breaking of the imposed silence and stereotypes and a redefinition of the ethnic identity (Chin and Chan 1972:65). Chin's own literary production exemplifies his tenacious drive to combat the discursive modes of domination that encode the object position of the minority. In polemic or parody, two of his major literary strategies, Chin wages war against the hegemonic exercise of power in the form of the language. *The Chickencoop Chinaman*, Chin's first play, appropriately begins with an angry outburst from its protagonist, Tam:

My dear in the beginning there was the Word! Then there was me! And the Word was CHINAMAN. And there was me. I lipped the word as if it had little lips of its own. "Chinaman" said on a little kiss. I lived the Word! The Word is my heritage (Chin 1981:6).

Ontological alienation is a direct product of the kind of linguistic dispossession from which the Chinese Americans suffer. They have always been enunciated into an existence to which they do not belong. The biblical overtone of Tam's speech indicates at once a tradition of cultural hegemony inherent in Judeo-Christianity and its language, and a history of the oppressed who have to live the curse, as it were, despite their will: "Chinamen are made, not born... Out of junk-imports, lies, railroad scrap iron, dirty jokes, broken bottles, cigar smoke, Cosquilla Indian blood, wino spit, and lots of milk of amnesia" (Chin 1981:6). In the unfolding of Chin's textual space, Tam's volley of words has enacted an effective counter-memory that not only discloses the removal of Chinese American history and their subservient position, but in the very process of disclosure negates the discursive oppression and constitutes the ethnic self as subject. Tam has materialized as a multi-word magician who transforms the stereotype of the "tongue-tying" Chinese American into a defying figure of "backtalking, muscular, singing stomping full blooded language loaded with nothing but our truth" (Chin 1976:557). It is small wonder that Chin's dramatic characters have been accused of failing to "talk or dress or act like Orientals" (Chin 1975, 1989).

If polemic confrontation is for Chin one counterhegemonic formation, parodic dissemblance is the other. When Chickencoop Chinaman Tam meets his friend BlackJap Kenji, their greeting ritual soon turns into a parodic type of signification:

> KENJI (*as Helen Keller*): Moowahjeeffffurher roar rungs!
> TAM (*as Helen Keller*): Moowahjeeffffurher roar rungs?
> KENJI (*as Helen Keller*): Moowahjeeffffurher roar rungs.
> TAM and KENJI (*continuing*): My dear friends!...
> KENJI (*as Helen Keller*): Aheeeha op eeehoooh too ooh wahyou oooh.
> TAM (*as a Bible Belt preacher*): Yeah, talk to me, Helen! Hallelujah! I hear her talking to me.
> (TAM *jumps to his feet shuddering with fake religious fervor, KENJI supports with Hallelujahs and repetitions.*)
> TAM: Put your hands on the radio, children, feel the power of Helen Keller, children. Believe! And she, the Great White goddess, the mother of Charlie Chan, the Mumbler, the Squeaker, shall show you the way, children! Oh, yeah!
> KENJI: Hallelujah!
> TAM: Helen Keller overcame her handicaps without riot! She overcame her handicaps without looting! She overcame her handicaps without violence! And you Chinks and Japs can too. Oooh I feel the power, children. Feel so gooooood! I feeeeeel it! (Chin 1981:10-11)

Chin conglomerates Christian conversion with the cultural symbol of self-perfection, equates physical deficiency and ethnic experience, and juxtaposes passive endurance of oppression with the racist positioning of the Asian "model minority" so that the parodic conversation between two members of the ethnic communities constitutes both an epistemic violence of pervasive ideological persuasions and a merciless critique of its practices. By the same token, Chin engages a symbolic exchange between himself and his childhood hero, the indomitable "Lone Ranger," only to find the mythical figure of justice yet another white supremacist in disguise (Chin 1981:31-38). The parodic contestation of mythology has occasioned the stripping away of its power as the regime of truth.

The dismantling of the regime of truth involves a historicization of its pretentious claims. The happy and content Chinese American living in the colorful and joyful Chinatown is another ideological construct that Chin endeavors to demystify:

> The railroads created a detention camp and called it "Chinatown." The details of that creation have been conveniently forgotten or euphemized into a state of sweet confusion. The men who lived through the creation are dying out, unheard and ignored. When they die, no one will know it was not us that created a game preserve for Chinese and called it "Chinatown" (Chin 1972a:60).

Chin's geological scrutiny of origin calls our attention to the particular phenomenon of historical exclusion turned into a modern instance of the glamorous periphery. The work of racist love that barred the entry of Chinese women and prohibited Chinese American men from the practice of miscegenation so as to produce a dying bachelor society is now redesigning its instrument by presenting Chinatown not as an urban ghetto but an exclusive glass menagerie where the showcase minority dwell.

That Chinatown is a special hegemonic creation of the Chinese American sociogeographic space informs Chin's staging of *The Year of the Dragon*. The drama focuses not on Chinatown as an exotic setting but on the burden and dilemma it poses as an existential space for the Chinese American there. Fred Eng, the protagonist, is both a Chinatown tourist guide and a writer. This particular dual occupation plays out one of the most intensive dynamics of an ethnic other that Chin has provided. As a tourist guide, Fred accommodates the forces that determine his role while distancing himself through critical self-awareness from the circumstances that tend to dope him. He lives the fiction of white fantasy, posing as a blend of the best of East and West, and puts on a phony Chinese accent to sell that perennial pack of lies to an interested audience. Fred subsists, ironically, upon the museum mentality of the metropolis that marks the dependent economic structure of its periphery. To Ross, his white brother-in-law, a quintessential oriental monger, Fred ever so succinctly parodies the metropolitan designs of power: "Hell, Chinatown's your private preserve for an endangered species, and you're the park ranger" (Chin 1981:85). The sardonic remark underlies Fred's confinement within the very social relationships of Chinatown zoo, but his conscious faking of his role as tourist guide shows his fictionalizing potential to counter the supreme fiction of racism. However, his creative energy will find no outlet other than this, "cuz no one's gonna read the great Chinese American novel," but, if "I'll write a Mama Fu Fu Chinese cookbook," Fred says, "that'll drive people crazy ... It's gonna be the first Chinese cookbook to win the Pulitzer Prize" (Chin 1981:83). The will to write and to define a self identity has been circumscribed by the trivializing function always already designated.

Though the institutional suppression of Chinese American writing is not in the foreground of the play, Chin makes a more subtle analysis of how the hegemonic denial of ethnic writing can foster a slavish mentality among the ethnic community that itself automatically gives up writing. Pa, for instance, asks his son-in-law Ross, instead of Fred, his English major son, to edit his New Year speech; the distrust of his son's language reveals a typical inbred self-contempt that disclaims Chinese Americans' verbal culture. The conventional scenario of father and son dispute in the play opens another dimension in that Pa's demand of Fred's filial piety and rejection of his voice metaphorize the relationship between the colonizer and the colonized (Chin 1981:137). One recalls that the hegemonic exercise of control underdevelops the minority in such a way that the group in question is always considered child-like, desperately in need of parental guidance. Fred's rebellion can then be best construed as an act of resistance to the authoritarian father figure of the dominant. The scathing satire of this enforced tutelage in the play as well as in the modern mythology of Charlie Chan and his number one sons marks one of Chin's most persistent efforts at counterdiscourse (Chin 1989).

III

Chin's program of Chinese American literature has evolved with changing social and cultural contexts.[1] One notable shift of emphasis is manifest in his recent outlook on Chinese culture and its impact on the social and cultural formations of the Chinese American. In the 1970s when Chin and his group embarked on the journey to make their literary presence, the order of "racist love" relegated the Chinese American to either models of assimilation or absolute foreigners. The wish to forge an identity strictly on Chinese American terms necessitated Chin's adamant disassociation from both Anglo-American and Chinese cultures, the stereotypical illusion of a split personality or the mish-mesh blend of the "best" of East and West. Though this oppositional stance came as an imperative response to hegemony, its praxis of total negation was not immune to the ahistorical scripture it set out to subvert. That is, negation could be entrapped, made dependent on the hegemony either by merely opposing it or by abandoning the representations it so apparently tainted. In light of this, Chin's current celebration of Chinese culture signifies his conscious departure from the hegemonic norms of inscription to return to the ground of Chinese American historical specificity.

In his *Seattle Weekly* essay, "Our Life is War," Chin declares his continuous battle against white domination but cites Sun Tzu, an ancient Chinese military theorist, as saying "What is of supreme importance in war is to attack the enemy's strategy" (Chin 1983). The prominence given to Sun Tzu indeed informs us of Chin's strategic rethinking of his agenda, and his programmatic application of Chinese cultural traditions is everywhere visible. Such use for Chin, however, is not a nostalgic escape but an invigorating absorption that at once provides historic anchorage and directs present reality. Therefore, the Chinese tradition he invokes is a "heroic" one. *Three Kingdoms, The Water Margin,* and *Monkey's Journey to the West* are what "every Chinese kid has grown up reading and studying as a manual of personal ethics and strategy and tactics for a thousand years" and they are "available in English translation, comic books, coloring books, trading cards, figures, toys, puppets and operas in Chinatown right this instant" (Chin 1986). In short, they are part and parcel of the Chinese American living culture and their people's code of forming alliances and expressing loyalties. Chin reminds us that it is just these classic Chinese texts that have been models of organized resistance in Chinatown, the stronghold "against the Christian missionaries, wild eyed social Darwinists, racists and a hostile state" (Chin 1983:35).[2]

The reconstruction of Chinese tradition in the Chinese American grain is a double-edged sword that redefines Chinese culture and Western culture. Chin's claim is both Calibanic and Kwan Kung straight:

> You, dear reader of English, aren't used to a Chinaman act in "your" language...Forget it. Your Language is mine. I speak in the Chinaman "I" here, and write a Chinaman act. I don't mean to be impolite in my taking your language and dashing the moral universals you've built into it. But betrayal is in the heart of your English. You speak the "I" of "Revenge is mine sayth the Lord." Mine is the Chinaman "I." Whatever language a Chinaman speaks, it is always Chinaman, and the personal pronoun I, in any language, means "I am the law"...Chinese civilization is founded on history. Specifically the five classics, selected by Confucius the historian, are the basics of Chinese civilization...Religion as the foundation of civilization is a silly and offensive sissy notion in Chinese thought...Greek myth is the key to the white mind. The epic tradition of Homer and the Bible. All tragic. Tsk tsk tsk. Boo hoo and hilltop glory be. The perpetual power, the submissive individual...The rebellious individual smacked down by the state...If Prometheus were Chinese he would have stolen fire from the gods, burned their capital, after warning the citizens to evacuate the city, then cut off the heads of the gods who displeased him and stuck the heads on poles over their palace, then burned it down to the ground (Chin 1985:110-111).

Chin's maneuver is a complete revisioning of Chinese American culture; if his earlier refutation of the hegemonic stereotyping still bears the burden of the oppressor, his present assertion of the heroic tradition not only reverses the situation of "yellow writers... tell[ing] their yellow literary time by a white clock" but also poses a critique of Western tradition with a Chinese American measure.³ He now combines his disruption of Aristotelian unities, Christian universals and social Darwinian unidirectional progress narrative with his demand of the dominant to be literate in Asian American culture, breaking and relinking the semiotic chain.⁴

The renewed interest in cultural history has also resurfaced one perennial concern of Chin's, i.e., the definition and parameter of Chinese American literature. This obvious canonical debate hinges on three pivots: generic, representational, and institutional. First, the establishment of a heroic Chinese American tradition in which "the fighter writer uses literary forms as weapons of war," Chin argues, makes autobiography irrelevant in Chinese American writing since it is a literary style based on Christian confession "that celebrate[s] the process of conversion from an object of contempt to an object of acceptance"; "a Chinaman can't write an autobiography because it's not in our nature to hate ourselves." Those who do, however, are "converts," "spies, for white racist religion, out to Happy End us" (Chin 1985:112, 122, 124). Second, the popularity these writers of "Ornamental Orientalia" enjoy, in Chin's view, derives precisely from their "faking" of Chinese America (Chin 1985:111, 119-120, 123). Third, their success with white publishers is a natural "payoff" of their "selling out" (Chin 1985:122-123).

While dismissing autobiography, Chin promotes "raging satires, polemic and slapstick comedies" as viable Chinese American generic alternatives (Chin 1985:126). Doubtless, these literary devices have been proven effective in minority cultural independence; however, Chinese American literary strategies should not be limited to self-binding variables. The relentless necessity to negate is always a fine line to walk — its execution requires caution, for it runs the double jeopardy of being just a mirror-opposite of the writing whose tyranny it disputes and of writing into a corner territorialized for him or her. A Calibanic claim of language should therefore include a critical appropriation of generic possibilities. This critical recuperation embedded in the overall recovery of a heroic Chinese American tradition is promising in its confrontation with colonial discourse. The programmatic emergence of the tradition, we recall, arises from the specific need of our time. It results from Chin's adjusted project of cultural insertion and his invested hope in the changing Asian American diaspora.⁵ The nature of such a diaspora should dispel nativist illusions of recovering the source of tradition; the authenticity of experiencing the common cultural heritage lies exactly in the diversity of specific mediations through which the tradition is reproduced to enable change of current status. The will to change should be accompanied by an awareness not only of the mechanisms of institutional forgetting and distortion via publishing but also of the inability of such mechanisms to cover its holes. In a time when the availability of minority presses is still restricted, cultivating insurgency within the hegemonic structures, the publishing industry being one of them, could be an alternative mode of resistance. Capitalistic commercialism could, with strategic reworking, be turned into a form of minority distribution agency.

The questions of genre, tradition, and institution Chin raised above are particularly relevant to his envisioning of the role of the minority writer in relation to his writing and the community of which she or he is a self-appointed spokesperson. Underlying these is the urgent issue of responsibility, that the writer does not simply write but is obligated to write to mobilize social change. There is little question that Chin is everywhere motivated by this sense of moral integrity. However, in his fervent espousal of this moral sense, he is partially blind to the multiplicity of contemporary Chinese American reality and becomes equally susceptible to the temptation of what Sylvia Wynter calls a "dictatorship of the Minoriat" (1987:237). A deterritorialization of cultural domination must not be preceded by a reterritorialization within the marginalized group. What we need is an "axial reality," to use Radhakrishnan's concept, where "the trajectory of radical ethnicity can be seen in the convergence at the point where 'axis' replaces identity" to "enable the generous production of non-authoritarian and non-territorial realities/knowledges" (1987:218). Chinese American writers will have to form a collective subjectivity that at once embraces an inclusive solidarity and celebrates a heterogeneous production. Let us work for the day when the variety of Chinese American culture is sufficiently recognized on its own terms and the wealth of our literature becomes a cherished resource for a better world.

Notes

1. Important but not central to this essay is one of Chin's earlier definitions of Asian American sensibility as "the style of manhood" (Chin et al. 1974:xlviii). Though concurring with criticisms of this potentially phallocentric stance, I will argue that given the circumstances of the 1970s when Chin was staging his ethnic resistance, running such a risk could be understandable. A brief historicization will tell us the validity of his position. First, for almost a century, the Chinese American in the United States was predominantly male, yet the writing of this history was absent. Second, the male experience of Chinatown bachelor societies was largely ignored. While the female members of Chinese America were regarded as assimilable, hence often appropriated to play the acceptance sweepstakes, the males were either rejected or emasculated. The popular culture's image of effeminate Chinese American men was extremely damaging. The specificity of Chinese American "manhood" – even with its precarious essence and possibility of male domination – must be judged in terms of historical material conditions. For critiques of Chin's term, see Kim 1982:180-189 and Lau 1981:93-105.
2. For Chin's discussion of how Chinatown Tongs and Chung Wah Goon fight racism, see also his essays of 1985 and 1986.
3. Chin's phrase on time is from his "Letter to Y'Bird" (1977:42-45). That time is both race and culture specific is a theme of his short story, "Railroad Standard Time," in *The Chinaman Pacific and Frisco R. R. Co.* 1989:1-7.
4. Chin observes in "This is Not an Autobiography," "I am so fluent in your [white] culture...But you don't know our lullabies and heroic tales, the myth and drama that twangs and plucks our sense of individuality, our personal relations with the authorities and the state. You should know" (1985:118). His further critique of Western systems of thought is evident in his introduction to "The Big Aiiieeeee!" forthcoming from New American Library.
5. According to Him Mark Lai, immigrant Chinese comprised about sixty-four percent of the Chinese American population in 1980 (Lai 1988:xi-xiii). Chin regards his ideal audience as being "either immigrants fluent in American English and history" or "American born who were knowledgeable about the basic works of a universal Asian childhood" (Davis 1988:91).

References

Chin, Frank. 1972a. "Confessions of the Chinatown Cowboy." *Bulletin of Concerned Asian Scholars* 4 (3):58-70.

———. 1972b. "Don't Pen Us Up in Chinatown." *New York Times.* October 8, 1, 5.

———. 1975. "Confessions of a Number One Son." In *Speaking for Ourselves: American Ethnic Writing*, edited by Lillian Faderman and Barbara Bradshaw, 218-227. Glenview, Illinois: Scott.

———. 1976. "Backtalk." In *Counterpoint: Perspectives on Asian America*, edited by Emma Gee et al. Los Angeles: University of California Asian American Studies Center.

———. 1977. "Letter to Y'Bird." *Y'Bird Magazine* 1 (1):42-45.

———. 1981.*"The Chickencoop Chinaman"; and, "The Year of the Dragon": Two Plays.* Seattle: University of Washington Press.

———. 1983. *Seattle Weekly,* May 4, 28-32, 34-38.

———. 1985. "This is Not an Autobiography." *Genre* 18 (Summer):109-130.

———. 1986. "From the Chinaman Year of the Dragon to the Fake Year of the Dragon." *Quilt* 5:58-71.

———. 1989. "Sons of Chan." In *The Chinaman Pacific and Frisco R. R. Co,* 131-165. Minneapolis: Coffee House Press.

Chin, Frank, and Jeffrey Paul Chan. 1972. "Racist Love." In *Seeing through Shuck,* edited by Richard Kostelanetz. New York: Ballantine.

Chin, Frank, Jeffery Paul Chan, Lawson Fusao Inada, and Shawn Hsu Wong, eds. 1974. *Aiiieeeee! An Anthology of Asian-American Writers.* Washington, D.C.: Howard University Press.

Davis, Robert Murray. 1988. "Frank Chin: An Interview." *Amerasia Journal* 14 (2):81-95.

JanMohamed, Abdul R. 1987. "Negating the Negation as a Form of Affirmation in Minority Discourse: The Construction of Richard Wright as Subject." *Cultural Critique* 7:245-266.

Kim, Elaine. 1982. *Asian American Literature: An Introduction to the Writings and Their Social Context.* Philadelphia: Temple University Press.

Lai, Him Mark. 1988. "On Chinese Americans: State of the Art or Challenge of the Future." *Amerasia Journal* 14 (2):xi-xiii.

Lau, Joseph. 1981. "Albatross Exorcised: The Rime of Frank Chin." *Tamkang Review* 12 (1):93-105.

Nee, Victor G. de Bary, and Brett Nee. 1972. *Longtime Californ': A Documentary Study of an American Chinatown.* New York: Pantheon Books.

Radhakrishnan, R. 1987. "Ethnic Identity and Post-Structural Difference." *Cultural Critique* 6:199-220.

Wynter, Sylvia. 1987. "On Disenchanting Discourse: 'Minority' Literary Criticism and Beyond." *Cultural Critique* 7:207-244.

Mother/Daughter Writing and the Politics of Race and Sex in Maxine Hong Kingston's *The Woman Warrior*

Wendy Ho

In the autobiographical novel *The Woman Warrior,* by Maxine Hong Kingston, a young daughter attempts to bridge the gap among different and often conflicting cultures, generations, languages, and gender roles. She talks with a mother who tells her stories of the past and present; the stories are a complicated mixture of truths and lies by which she attempts to navigate her own life. The important factor is that mother and daughter talk-story, each struggling to reassess, translate, and articulate an authentic self-identity that is rooted in their needs for individuation/disengagement, mutual respect, and attachment to each other and their communities. In talking, they discover commonality and difference, weaknesses and strengths, anger and love.

In the book, the psychic bonding between mother and daughter through gender, socialization as women, and talk-story traditions is used to work through and express the new psychic landscape of the Chinese American daughter-writer in America. As her mother's daughter, she rejects, brutally critiques, and lovingly transforms her mother's life and stories. Through this personal struggle, she learns to speak and write a new language which is deeply rooted in the life and fictions of her mother, the champion talker in a Cantonese oral tradition. Talk-story becomes an important fluid, interactive mode of communication and discovery for the daughter as well as the mother. It becomes a way of ordering and fighting symbolic and real "ghosts," of learning ways to reclaim through language and image the cultural processes of achieving one's identity as a woman, writer, and individual in society. In the novel, the daughter learns to break her own suffocating silence in creative, subversive ways and thereby vindicates the ancestral women in her family/culture, reclaiming their names and their stories for herself and other women in America.

The mother, Brave Orchid, is a preserver of many different and often conflicting messages to her daughter. She speaks in a multiple- or double-voiced discourse often consisting of "dominant" and "muted" registers. The daughter also learns to speak, write, and live in multiple registers as a Chinese American woman writer. Showalter (1985:264) provides one illustration of the complexity of this model for some minority women: "A black American woman poet, for example, would have her literary identity formed by the dominant (white male) tradition, by a muted women's culture, and by a muted black culture. She would be affected by both sexual and racial politics in a combination unique to her case; at the same time...she shares an experience specific to her group." There is a similar entanglement for Asian American women. Both Brave Orchid and her daughter are affected by the similarities and differences in their social and material circumstances, interpretative systems, written and talkstory strategies, which have been influenced by China and America. The ways mother/daughter talk, bond with each other, and reach psychological maturity are based on issues of gender as well as on issues of class and race. It is a negotiation among complex choices of discourses involving a mother who hides and reveals truth; a Chinese mother and father who pass on Chinese culture in the mother's talk-story; and a New World culture. All have positive and negative impact on the life of a Chinese American daughter.

On one level, Brave Orchid as a traditional Chinese woman feels the need to preserve her family and Chinese traditions against the dominant culture of Western "ghosts" in America. She is the keeper of the secrets, stories, male descent lines, culture, rituals, food. Because of the importance of preserving ties with their own history, culture, and family, Brave Orchid attempts to pass to the daughter the puzzling remnants of Chinese culture, which are half-embedded in silence and contradiction, despite the often oppressive, inequitable circumstances for women within traditional Chinese family structure and society. Glenn (1986:192) provides a possible understanding of this type of behavior: "When individuals and their families confront economic deprivation, legal discrimination, and other threats to their survival...conflict over inequities within the family may be muted by the countervailing pressure on the family to unite against assaults from outside institutions...the family [becomes] a 'culture of resistance.' The locus of conflict...lies outside the household, as members engage in collective attempts to create and maintain family in opposition to forces that undermine family integrity."

Dual powerlessness as a woman and as a minority—the intersection of sex and race—burdens the relationship between Brave Orchid and her daughter. The personal relationship of mother or daughter and their families is intimately intertwined with the history of an immigrant race in America, a country which has a long, ugly history of discriminatory behavior against the Chinese and other minorities. The internal world of family is oppressive to women, but the external world is often perceived as the greater common enemy to the family collective, inhabited by non-Chinese "ghosts" who present a whole layer of problems/tensions in languages, cultural systems, and survival in America. These "ghosts" seem to threaten the physical, socioeconomic, and psychological well-being of Brave Orchid and her Chinese family. Kingston's memories are filled with her parents' fears of being sent back to China or being jinxed by white "ghosts"; with the silencing of Chinese women, and men, by the white patriarchy; and with the socioeconomic hardships of their shared life. To survive as a distinct ethnic group and family, minority women are often caught in a double bind between their own needs and concerns as women and those of their Chinese American communities in America.

Like her mother, the daughter negotiates the preservation and the subversion of aspects of traditional Chinese culture against the pressures of mainstream Western society. However, she is in a precarious position of her own: she is not Chinese enough for her mother, father, and ethnic community and not American-feminine enough to find a home among the white "ghosts." She therefore lives life on the edges of these communities, juggling complicated sign systems, languages, experiences. Her mother does not entrust the whole story of the family or their names or rituals to her. The intimate communications—the literal silences and talk-story—between mother and daughter are valorized and problematized in this book. She is half Chinese, half ghost-barbarian, taught and raised among the ghosts who might threaten her parents and their traditional way of life.

In her work of preservation, Brave Orchid is implicated in the culture or Law of the Father, the patriarchal ("official") stories and non-stories (silence) about fallen women and useless girl children in traditional Chinese society. The power of patriarchy is strong and demands filiality even from feisty survivalists who can talk-story like Brave Orchid, Fa Mu Lan, and Ts'ai Yen. For example, in the opening chapter the valuable work of preservation of family, culture, and society is linked physically and symbolically with women. The villagers fear that if women stepped out of the boundaries of their assigned roles as daughters, wives, and mothers, it would lead to the disruption or destruction of family, culture, language, and society. Women are valued according to their obedience, passivity, and maintenance of the traditional ways. And the Chinese mother and family attempt to instill in the young daughter (even in America) the virtues and habits that are considered ideally feminine in traditional Chinese culture (Bannan 1979:172). In such a societal framework, one can see how No Name Woman's private life as a woman—her desires, sexuality, dreams, needs—are silenced violently. As Cixous bluntly states: "Either the woman is passive; or she doesn't exist. What is left unthinkable, unthought of" (Marks and Courtivron 1981:92).

At home, Maxine is confronted by prejudices her parents brought from old China—the image of girls as useless maggots, stink pigs, or cow-birds, fit to be killed or sold. Her own mother's words and actions devalue her worth as a woman, crippling and silencing her. At school and work—the outside world—she is silenced not only by sexist but also racist stereotypes that haunt her childhood and womanhood. Maxine describes the pain of transforming her squeaking, quacking, ugly duckling voice. As a child, she speaks of years of silence and withdrawal, enjoying the silence and the world of her imagination, Chinese operas and crazy women, until she realized she had to talk in school to establish an "I" identity or be a non-person with no language to define herself. She is considered retarded by some of her teachers, handicapped and silenced in her second language English; her voice sounds "brittle." Later, she describes her voice as "a crippled animal running on broken legs," "a small person's voice that makes no impact" (Kingston [1975] 1977 [hereafter referred to as *TWW*]:196, 57). She says there were "splinters in [her] voice, bones rubbing jagged against one another" *(TWW*:196). She protests typing invitations for her boss in a "voice unreliable" *(TWW*:58). She accuses her mother of cutting her frenum, destroying her ability to speak, to acquire language. In her crippled voice, she struggles to explain to her mother "true things" about herself and to get rid of her throat pain; her mother, caught up in her own world of private frustrations and patriarchal stereotypes, fails to understand the crazy, lonely babbling of her awkward daughter. The daughter's throat pain is the struggle to articulate how she really thinks, feels, and acts—to make known the invisible and to come against her mother again and again though the power of language.

The daughter is warned by her mother not to tell anyone the secret about her father's sister, No Name Woman. This disobedient woman had "crossed boundaries not delineated in space" *(TWW*:9). For this reason, no words, name, or memory is allotted her. It was as if she had never been born. Thus, the daughter's learning of patriarchal relationships within the family and other cultural institutions coincides with her learning of the names and non-names and rules of naming and non-naming implicit in the system of language. To have no name is the punishment; to be remembered as a patriarchal caveat to other women is the punishment.

Brave Orchid has seen with her own eyes that the consequences of disobedience to this Law of the Father can literally mean isolation, exile, insanity, or death. There is the haunting terror for a communally-oriented individual of being "a bright dot in blackness, without home, without a companion, in eternal cold and silence" *(TWW*:16). The mother tells her daughter that "what happened to her [No Name Woman] could happen to you. Don't humiliate us. You wouldn't like to be forgotten as if you had never been born" *(TWW*:5). It could be a mixed warning that is based on fear, love, acquiescence to tradition, or even survival for herself and daughter.

The lesson is not totally lost on the daughter: "The work of preservation demands that the feelings playing about in one's guts not be turned into action. Just watch their passing like cherry blossoms" *(TWW*:9). The patriarchal tradition often determines that women inhabit silence—non-verbal, non-written—inhabit a confined boundary where internal/external, hardly visible reaction/action is deemed appropriate feminine behavior. She has more than enough models of "slaves" in her memory: No Name Woman, Moon Orchid, silent Chinese schoolgirls, crazy women. Even dragon-mother is reduced in her power in America. The "slave mentality" of women is just below the surface, waiting to make an appearance; even as an adult, the daughter feels that "China wraps double binds around [her] feet" *(TWW*:57). For example, Maxine wants to feel independent and yet she finds herself feeling envious, bitter, and unloved because she is not supported by a man. Despite the example of the fabulous woman warrior Fa Mu Lan, she learns that there is a Chinese word for the female "I" which means slave—*mui*. Women are powerless in this discourse; they are being defined, classified, and forced to articulate themselves in relationship to male perspectives—master/slave. The patriarchal structure of society and language appears to be set up to "break women with their own tongues!" *(TWW*:56)

Kingston is not out to valorize or privilege a seamless form of communication between mother and daughter; instead, I think she shows us the conflicting layers of this communication. Brave Orchid's voice, her talk-story, is not simply an unambiguous mirror for patriarchal Chinese discourse. There is, I think, indication of a muted subtext which seeps through the text, making for intricate knots, wrinkles, circles, and holes in her stories and injunctions. Mother speaks with a forked tongue. Her discourse is implicated in and hidden with other modes of discourse; thereby, her maternal subtext is very difficult to locate, evermore ambiguous, double-edged, and ambivalent, fraught with danger at best. On one hand, it would seem that she reinforces the laws of society by repeating the caveats of patriarchal society in talk-story. Yet despite the fact that Brave Orchid tells her daughter she will end up "a wife and a slave," the daughter distinctly remembers following her mother around the house chanting the song of the warrior woman *(TWW*:24). She learns that she fails if she becomes just a wife or a slave. Brave Orchid also tells the secret of No Name Aunt to her daughter, providing her with a small but tantalizing bit of information about her women ancestors. This ambiguous, ambivalent gift of a secret is raw material through which, in her own written, talk-story text, the daughter imaginatively resurrects this rebellious dead aunt after years of silent fear and neglect.

In opening her book with this story, the daughter makes visible the secret that her mother, father, and the Chinese village have kept hidden. She demonstrates and asserts her affinity for this ostracized aunt by exploring possible reconstructed versions of the truth where there had been only silence or one absolute patriarchal version of the story. Kingston restores the aunt through musings on her imagined lives, feelings, and motivations. She provides herself and her readers the dynamic opportunity of choice between the interstices of patriarchal privilege. It is a subversive form of ancestor worship which would not have the approval of the father; and it takes its form not with paper boats, clothes, or money to honor the dead—those decorative and ephemeral things burned—but with the enduring power and memory of the written word (the power of authorship) which had been predominantly the preserve of males in Chinese society. It is a double transgression of patriarchy: No Name Aunt was erased from family memory by the taking away of her name and place in society and by the family's silence about her very existence. In this way, Maxine breaks the complicitous, vicious cycle of silence with her mother and the Chinese community against this outcast woman.

But consequences of the neglect and resurrection of her aunt after so many long years, as well as her rebellion against the fathers, haunt Kingston. To resurrect the restless dead—the spite suicide, the wild woman—into living memory as well as to speak so boldly in a patriarchal society is a serious act with many possible consequences for Kingston: "The Chinese are always very frightened of the drowned one, whose weeping ghost, wet hair hanging and skin bloated, waits silently by the water to pull down a substitute" *(TWW*:19).

The other voice is Brave Orchid's private (coded/indirect) language as a woman and the example of her own life as a doctor, which is "secret and apart from them" *(TWW*:14). She lives two years without servitude, acquiring a job, a room of her own, and new women friends. These women called Brave Orchid back from the spirit world by shouting out (non-vertical/hierarchical) directions for her spirit to follow: "They called out their own names, women's pretty names, haphazard names, horizontal names of one generation" *(TWW*:89). It is akin to what Showalter (1985:259-266) means when she talks about the muted culture of women, "the boundaries of whose culture and reality overlap, but are not wholly contained by, the dominant (male) group." It is Brave Orchid's own marginalized/repressed woman space, seeping indirectly through the cracks and fissures of the malestream as well as mainstream Western and Eastern thought about definitions/roles for women. For it is the same mother who suffers not only sexism in two cultures but also racism in her adopted country. She suffers racism in America where she is reduced to work in a laundry and in tomato fields. The woman warrior, the mythical dragon-mother, who ghostbusted, who made herself strong in China, is reduced to fending off, rather unsuccessfully, the mundane "ghosts" (such as shopkeepers, mail carriers, police, winos) that occupy her ordinary life in America. Mother, as well as daughter, develop multiple voices to encode or signify in language as a way of surviving in a racist, sexist world; similarly, they must develop the capabilities to decipher and pass on this intricate encoded language.

Thus a remaining source of power for this displaced woman warrior is her magical stories about transformation, heroic swordswomen, and female doctors; these signify or suggest a woman's freedom and potential. The mother exercises her daughter's mind beyond daily limits: "I learned to make my mind large, as the universe is large, so that there is room for paradoxes... The dragon lives in the sky, ocean, marshes, and mountains; and the mountains are also its cranium... it breathes fire and water; and sometimes the dragon is one, sometimes many" *(TWW*:35). It is no surprise that mother and daughter in this magic real world are dragons born fierce and powerful in the Year of the Dragon. It is the mother who sings her "out of nightmares and horror movies" and makes her feel safe and loved. The daughter feels the presence of great power in her mother's talking-story *(TWW*:24).

Chinese heroic motifs are preserved through oral or talk-story traditions: talk-story, however, is transformed in Kingston's work into a history from a personal and communal standpoint. She participates in and directs the history of her people, a position she inherits from her mother. The daughter attempts to speak with the communal voice of assorted legendary and real-life characters: the voices of ancient heroines, the Fa Mu Lans and Ts'ai Yens; the ceremonial voice of the family scop rehearsing and reclaiming biographies of worthies and genealogies from the collective family memory; the shamanic voice that chants magical incantations and women's names to keep away ghosts, demons, and nightmares; as well as the more impersonal voice of history.

In this book, heroism is constantly being redefined in myths/fantasies and real life experiences. For on one level, the talk-stories of mother/daughter are about inner psychological, imaginative quests or adventures which are often invisible or closed to readers, to outsiders. And yet the borders they challenge—cultural, social, and psychological—and their specific discoveries should be of central importance not only to the writer herself but also to us. Mother/daughter engage in painful struggles with languages, cultures, inherited oral/literary traditions, and with each other to find more adequate ways of telling about women's experiences, fighting their way out of silence, out of traditionally sanctioned roles and stereotypes, to project more authentic images of how they feel, think, and act.

As a Chinese American woman, the daughter-writer is carving out new territory in alien lands (literally and figuratively) which would marginalize her, her family, and heritage. With time, she realizes her own power as a storyteller; she is not simply a storehouse for her mother's stories, life, and secrets. Neither is she simply an extension or double for her mother. In working out her identity, there is as much active collaboration/bonding as there is brutal resistance/disengagement between mother and daughter.

In terms of mother/daughter collaboration/bonding in process, Kingston says, "Here is a story my mother told me, not when I was young, but recently, when I told her I also talk story. The beginning is hers, the ending, mine" *(TWW*:240). The ego boundaries between mother and daughter are not clearly defined even in adulthood, but there is a sense of separation, of a new voice branching out from mother. For the Chinese American daughter's fictions insistently seem to challenge and/or reject the authority of patriarchy/imperialism as well as mother, paying attention to what has been traditionally seen/unseen as marginal. She questions the stereotyped images and fictions of her mother, their split cultures as well as the language of their value judgments. The daughter, as her mother before, and each in her own challenge and degree, attempts to disrupt and subvert the discourses which confine their potential. Both their stories and voices generate an interactive and multiple sense of their similarities and differences as mothers/daughters, of their possible complicity in traditional/dominant power configurations and strategies of appeasement, and of their subversive signifying strategies for survival. Brave Orchid jampacks, pries, crams, funnels her daughter with continual harping, advice, and stories. She will marry off or sell this useless, squeaky, duck-voiced, bad girl. In contrast, the young daughter is later associated with Ts'ai Yen's singing voice.

The need and search for self-expression—to break the silence of oppression and victimization in terms of sexism and racism within the dominant Western culture and the sexism in her own Chinese culture—becomes a way to hold on to sanity and to find identity. As the protagonist says in *The Woman Warrior* to another silent Chinese girl, "If you don't talk, you can't have a personality...talk, please talk" *(TWW*:210) or "I thought talking and not talking made the difference between sanity and insanity. Insane people were the ones who couldn't explain themselves" *(TWW*:216). Yet, what to say?

In the search for a personal voice and self, the daughter's awkward first steps are mirrored in her voice, the self-conscious, awkward voice of an immigrant daughter attempting to assess—to make sense of no sense—her mother's contradictory statements: her truths and lies. The frustrations between daughter and mother are very evident. There is a point in the story that the daughter wishes to escape the "hating range" of home and her mother's stories which appear to have no "logic." These Chinese stories scramble her up. She tells her mother, "You lie with stories. You won't tell me a story and then say, 'This is a true story,' or, 'This is just a story.' I can't tell the difference. I don't even know what your real names are. I can't tell what's real and what you make up" *(TWW*:235). There is no unified, centered tradition in her communities in America that allows her as a Chinese American woman to speak easily and forthrightly in her own person. The self is often fragmented, split and invisible to the self and is defined indirectly by a conflicting web of interpersonal relations and roles. It is more a constant struggle to break from the community of "we"; whether with mother, family, or society, to reach an understanding of oneself as an individual "I" in community.

Maxine is caught then with her weak voice in this hyphenated position between cultures/languages, parents: Paula Gunn Allen notes that people caught between two cultures are often "inarticulate, almost paralyzed in their inability to direct their energies toward resolving what seems to them insoluble conflicts" (Cheung 1988:163). She has definite handicaps. She is excluded from mainstream culture and from centers of power in her own racial community. She is faced with social prohibitions and language barriers that silence her authentic experiences, and she is confused by her own mother's mixed messages in patriarchy. As a child in school, Maxine paints layers of black paint over pictures of houses and flowers and suns. And when her confused parents take them home, she "spreads them out (so black and full of possibilities) and pretended the curtains were swinging open, flying up, one after another, sunlight underneath, mighty operas" *(TWW*:192). There is indeed a rich life even under what appears to be black/lack — absence.

Writing becomes a heroic form of verbal expression for this silent, but imaginative, young girl: it is a way to defend herself with words — potential is discovered in the process of learning to articulate herself — to write talk-story. It becomes a courageous act that leads to transformation and discovery. Through the book, she is training, disciplining herself to control the voice and pen before she can be a writer. At first, she appropriates patriarchal rhetoric and codes of behavior; she fights as a woman in the guise of a male warrior, with bloodthirsty warring and lopping off of heads. To become a boy is an early rebellion against her mother and her mother's harping on the uselessness of girls. It is a way of denying her connection with what is devalued in her society. Fa Mu Lan wears armor while pregnant, which makes her look like a "powerful, big man" *(TWW*:47). She gives up her child to fight in the wars as a "slim young man" *(TWW*:48). Upon her return home, she impresses her son not so much as a mother but as a war general *(TWW*:53). In this male disguise, she learns to articulate and redress her rage and grievances; at the same time, she wins the love and respect of her family and community as a warrior. For a time, she leads the life of the privileged male sex — the apple of her mother's, father's, country's eye. And then she returns to filial servitude as a daughter, wife, and mother.

Alas, the nightly legends, movies, and dreams of the fabulous swordswomen do not change Maxine into a precious boy. Even heroines and mothers, it seems, return to lives as filial daughters, wives, and mothers. The daughter discovers that there are no easy ways to resolve contradictions or to be all things to all people and to herself. Life in fantasy movies or myths/legends is hard to translate into real-life experiences. The slave mentality attacks even the brave with the fear of isolation, loneliness, and danger. To take a sword to her lousy boss is a comic, pathetic scenario. There are no supporting casts of eighty pole fighters, self-sacrificing bunnies, or psychic kung-fu training for the kind of social and cultural wilderness a Chinese American woman must negotiate in America. Not even straight A's at Berkeley or working for change in her daily life can make her a loved boy, or American-pretty, or the fabulous swordswoman of old. Mother's stories are not easily translatable in a daughter's life.

In her anger and frustration, Kingston gradually discovers one good similarity: the Chinese idiom for revenge literally means to "report a crime"; to report—witness and record—the injustices suffered by her Chinese women ancestors and to herself as a Chinese American woman. It is the *language* of contradiction and the *language* of sexism and racism—painful, ugly words which maim and kill—that she as a warrior attempts to purge, to decapitate with violent vengeance: "Girls are maggots in the rice" or "It is more profitable to raise geese than daughters!" *(TWW*:222, 51). If there is a group of women she could identify with in this episode, it would be those amazon swordswomen who "did not wear men's clothes," but "rode as women in black and red dresses. They bought up girl babies so that many poor families welcomed their visitations. When slave girls and daughters-in-law ran away, people would say they joined these witch amazons. They killed men and boys" *(TWW*:53).

The image of wilderness, inherited from her own mother's stories and life, is reclaimed and adapted by the daughter with her "witch amazons." She uses it to describe the "wilderness" of her Chinese American experiences as a woman in the territories of patriarchal language, descriptions of the world, and definitions of personal experience. She even tests her growing voice by undermining her mother's voice and stories. It is an adventurous journey of survival, testing, and knowledge as a Chinese woman in America. Maxine's perception of the wilderness begins to shift to the unexplored space beyond the patriarchal prison house—the symbol of the wild territory to be appropriated and transformed into a rich and imaginative female space that displaces male power.

This awareness of such potential female space for the private self problematizes and enriches the daughter's sense of identity: instead of the self ever being fully solid, unified, or defined, it becomes a more shifting, fluid, decentralized notion of selfhood without hard, finite boundaries. Wilderness can provide the perfect image of the wild-zone, the "the mother country of liberated desire and female authenticity," which Showalter (1985:263) calls the repressed area of women's culture that can never be fully known. (It may even bear connections to Kristeva's semiotic space.) There is in this female space the potential for a new feminist mythology centered on matriarchal principles at once biological and ecological in contrast to much of patriarchal history

(Showalter 1985:263). Such writing may signal the potential of the feminine voice as an alternative source of power and exorcism of the past; the image of wilderness provides textual space for such revisionary play. The young girl is learning to traverse this wilderness territory—at home, in America, in barbarian lands, in writing, in self—as a woman not disguised as a male warrior.

As the novel progresses, Maxine processes different models such as No Name Woman, Moon Orchid, mother Brave Orchid, woman warrior Fa Mu Lan, and finally Ts'ai Yen, the poet. She takes back their stories and experiences with her imaginative power as a Chinese American woman writer. Cheung (1988:169) notes that, "In reshaping her ancestral past to fit her American present, moreover, Kingston is asserting an identity that is neither Chinese nor white American, but distinctively Chinese American. Above all, her departures from the Chinese legends shift the focus from physical prowess to verbal injuries and textual power." In this endeavor, she fights the invisible hurts—the prejudices, the sexism and racism against her and her community. She fights the suffocating aspects not only of mainstream ideals of beauty/behavior (American-feminine) but also of her mother's traditional views of female children: that she is a bad girl because she refuses to cook, cracks dishes. She is rebellious, silent, surly, clumsy, ugly—wanting to be a boy—not to marry. She expands the fight not only as a woman but as a Chinese American woman against racism in America: "The swordswoman and I are not so dissimilar... What we have in common are the words at our backs. The reporting is the vengeance—not the beheading, not the gutting, but the words. And I have so many words—'chink' words and 'gook' words too—that they do not fit on my skin" *(TWW*:63).

From Chinese mothers and female relatives, the daughter brings to her writing coded, talk-story language such as secrets, dreams, myths, folk wisdom, legends, incantations, paradoxes, singing/chanting, gossip, jokes, crazy talk, and parables. The descent lines of this daughter-writer are located in matriarchal bonding, with slave women and with heroic, rebellious, trail-blazing women who step outside the circle of the known and approved status quo of patriarchal society. In terms of form, Kingston's realistic fiction registers the surface details of her daily life; yet, on another level, the conventions of realism are frequently disrupted by shifts into magical, visionary moments, fantasy, and myth, often reappropriated from her mother's talk-story tradition, which may be truer to her new sense of reality and self beyond patriarchal discourse.

In such ways, her writing becomes split-level/multiple discourses where alternative ways of seeing are contained within the same fictional structure. This is reflected not only in her retelling and rewriting of myths, but also in her use of mixed genres, such as autobiography, poetry, legend, ghost story, dream vision, and oral tradition. This style disrupts the story line of rigid, structured classifications or of traditional power. It opens to question and executes disarrangements and defamiliarization, which demand new perspectives and solutions to questions of power, gender, socioeconomic, and cultural order. The emphasis is on process and revision so that absolute truth is only provisional and writing is not transparent but something to be decoded and reconstructed through the reader's or listener's collaborative efforts. In other words, the text is not finalized meaning or a mere recording of actual life or interpretation, but the self-talking story, an enactment of the continual dynamic struggle to construct and deconstruct meanings.

As much as her mother puts her down, Maxine as an adult finally comes to terms with her Chinese heritage and her mother. Stifled and frustrated, she leaves home and mother in order to see the world differently. She needs breathing space outside of her Chinese world. She explores the other parts of America "where the 'I' is a capital and 'you' is lower case" *(TWW*:193). It is no wonder that Maxine is fascinated by the potential in the language of the New World: the American "I" is straight, assertive and capitalized; it is not written in small, crooked strokes as in Chinese. The symbolic language of the barbarians—the "ghost" fathers—suggests a new language in which to talk about self in a new way, other than as a slave. What she learns is that there is also a logical world: "I learned to think that mysteries are for explanation. I enjoy the simplicity. Concrete pours out of my mouth to cover the forests with freeways and sidewalks . . . shine floodlights into dark corners: no ghosts" *(TWW*:237). Hannah Arendt has noted that intellectual freedom or a new sense of reality can exist only in the context of psychic space, while psychic space can be created only between distinct and contrasting points of view. In this space between viewpoints, the daughter continues to "sort out what's just my childhood, just my imagination, just my family, just the village, just movies, just living" *(TWW*:239). She can return to the ambiguous, ambivalent facts and fictions of her life and her mother's for raw material and find creative inspiration without losing her developing sense of a separate self in her split communities in America.

From a qualified distance, she can begin to see her mother as an intelligent, energetic, feisty, and courageous woman who transmits complex messages in difficult social and historical circumstances; not simply as a repressive, egotistical, insensitive tyrant who is quite capable of victimizing and destroying other women (sister Moon Orchid, her daughter Maxine, servant girls) in the name of bully love. Brave Orchid is a very powerful role model and hero to her daughter, who acknowledges her affiliation: "I am practically the first daughter of a first daughter" *(TWW*:127). Brave Orchid, after all, was a ghostbuster in her own time, a doctor, a survivor, and fellow dragon. Kingston had blamed her mother for cutting her frenum to stop her from talking, but the mother says, "I cut it to make you talk more, not less, you dummy. You're still stupid. You can't listen right" *(TWW*:235). Her mother has untied her tongue in order for her to "speak languages that are completely different from one another" (TWW:190). She senses the point of the duplicity: "The emigrants confuse the gods by diverting their curses, misleading them with crooked streets and false names. They must try to confuse their offspring as well, who, I suppose, threaten them in similar ways—always trying to get things straight, always trying to name the unspeakable. The Chinese I know hide their names; sojourners take new names when their lives change, and they guard their real names with silence" *(TWW*:6). Duplicity is again evident when the daughter accuses her mother of calling her ugly all the time. Her mother protests that she did not actually call her daughter ugly: "That's what we're supposed to say. That's what Chinese say. We like to say the opposite" *(TWW*:237). Duplicity is a way of life that protects the powerless, that ensures survival when one feels threatened or has something to hide from the powerful — whether we are speaking of jealous ghosts or a racist/sexist community or country.

In this autobiographical novel, Kingston has begun to counter the earlier destructive, limited male warrior guise with the woman warrior. There is discovery and reclamation of psychic territory and of connections for the daughter-writer between the Old and the New World; between the individual and her mixed communities; between mother and daughter. She challenges social and symbolic codes which delineate the position of women in society as an absent presence. Her corrective is a collective female vision of talk-story, of open-ended, multiple roads to truth and meaning, of transforming art. Her challenge is the voice of the Chinese woman singing of her sadness and anger in a barbarian land: hers is a voice that continually orders and reshapes meaning through art. This is one way out of psychic paralysis, silence, separation, or death. The daughter-writer has begun to achieve a confidence and power in her own distinctive Chinese American voice; as she says, Ts'ai Yen's songs from the savage lands translated well in Chinese and in barbarian terms. As she frees her own voice, she also frees the oppressed women who have haunted and still haunt her. She is, after all, the one escaping to tell. Like mother and No Name Aunt, the daughter-writer pieces "together new directions," following them "instead of the old footprints" *(TWW*:89). From the position "not to tell" to "tell," she is a hopeful voice singing in the desert.

References

Bannan, Helen. 1979. "Warrior Women: Immigrant Mothers in the Works of Their Daughters." *Women's Studies* 6:165-177.
Cheung, King-Kok. 1988. " 'Don't Tell': Imposed Silences in *The Color Purple* and *The Woman Warrior*." *Proceedings of the Modern Language Association* 103:162-174.
Chodorow, Nancy. 1978. *The Reproduction of Mothering: Psychoanalysis and the Sociology of Gender.* Berkeley: University of California Press.
Dasenbrook, Reed Way. 1987. "Intelligibility and Meaningfulness in Multicultural Literature in English." *Proceedings of the Modern Language Association* 102:10-19.
Gates, Henry Louis, Jr. 1984. "The Blackness of Blackness: a Critique of the Sign and the Signifying Monkey." In *Black Literature and Literary Theory*, edited by Henry Louis Gates, Jr., 285-321. New York: Methuen.
Gilligan, Carol. 1982. *In a Different Voice: Psychological Theory and Women's Development.* Cambridge: Harvard University Press.
Glenn, Evelyn Nakano. 1986. *Issei, Nisei, War Bride: Three Generations of Japanese American Women in Domestic Service.* Philadelphia: Temple University Press.
Jelinek, Estelle C. 1980. "Introduction: Women's Autobiography and the Male Tradition." In *Women's Autobiography: Essays in Criticism*, edited by Estelle C. Jelinek, 1-20. Bloomington: Indiana University Press.
Juhasz, Suzanne. 1980. "Towards a Theory of Form in Feminist Autobiography: Kate Millett's *Flying* and *Sita;* Maxine Hong Kingston's *The Woman Warrior.*" In *Women's Autobiography: Essays in Criticism*, edited by Estelle C. Jelinek, 221-237. Bloomington: Indiana University Press.
_____. 1985. "Maxine Hong Kingston: Narrative Technique and Female Identity." In *Contemporary American Women Writers: Narrative Strategies*, edited by Catherine Rainwater and William J. Scheick, 173-189. Lexington: University of Kentucky Press.
Kazuko, Ono. 1989. *Chinese Women in a Century of Revolution: 1850-1959.* Edited by Joshua Fogel. Stanford: Stanford University Press.
Kingston, Maxine Hong. 1977. *The Woman Warrior: Memoirs of a Girlhood among Ghosts.* New York: Vintage. (Originally published 1975.)
Marks, Elaine, and Isabelle de Courtivron, eds. 1981. *New French Feminisms: An Anthology.* New York: Schocken Books.
Rich, Adrienne. 1986. *Of Woman Born.* Tenth edition. New York: Norton and Company.
Rowbotham, Sheila. 1973. *Woman's Consciousness, Man's World.* London: Penguin.
Showalter, Elaine. 1985. "Feminist Criticism in the Wilderness." In *Feminist Criticism: Essays on Women, Literature, Theory*, edited by Elaine Showalter, 243- 270. New York: Pantheon.
Snow, Helen Foster. 1967. *Women in Modern China.* Paris: Mouton and Company.
Takaki, Ronald. 1989. *Strangers from a Different Shore: A History of Asian Americans.* Boston: Little, Brown and Company.
Wolf, Margery, and Roxane Witke, eds. 1975. *Women in Chinese Society.* Stanford: Stanford University Press.
Wong, Diane Yen-Mei, et al., eds. 1989. *Making Waves: An Anthology of Writings by and about Asian American Women.* Boston: Beacon Press.

Asian American Daughters Rewriting Asian Maternal Texts

Shirley Geok-lin Lim

Seldom in the body of Asian American writing does the thematic of daughter-mother bonding appear as central, problematic, and rewarding as in Joy Kogawa's 1981 novel, *Obasan*. What may surprise uninformed readers is the deep and broad tradition of the thematics of the maternal in Asian American literature, a tradition which Kogawa's novel appeals to and plays against. The maternal figure has inevitably been problematized as possessive, passive, powerless, or over-powerful. Merle Woo's (1981:140-141) "Letter to Ma," for example, interrogates an ambivalent and rejecting daughter/mother relationship:

> I was depressed over Christmas, and when New Year's rolled around, do you know what one of my resolves was? Not to come and see you as much anymore. I had to ask myself why I get so down when I'm with you, my mother, who has focused so much of her life on me, who has endured so much; one who I am proud of and respect so deeply for simply surviving.

The daughter's answer is to speak through the positive heritage to the legacy of racism and sexism engendered by her mother's generation:

> You gave me, physically, what you never had, but there was a spiritual, emotional legacy you passed down which was reinforced by society: self-contempt because of our race, our sex, our sexuality. For deeply engrained in me, Ma, there has been that strong, compulsive force to sink into self-contempt, passivity, and despair.

On the other hand, Cathy Song's poem, "Blue and White Lines After O'Keefe," valorizes a harmonizing and protective mother in whose maternal tradition the woman artist practices her art:

> Yet, I am here, Mother.
> I have come to rest at your feet,
> to be near the familiar scent of talc,
> the ticking of the china clock,
> another heartbeat.
> It has taken me all these years
> to realize that this is what I must do
> to recognize my life.
> When I stretch a canvas
> to paint the clouds,
> it is your spine that declares itself
> arching,
> your arms stemming out like tender shoots
> to hang sheets in the sky (Song 1983:48).

In Asian-American fiction, these conflicting features of the maternal are more often ridden and riddled by compelling specificities of gender and race. John Okada's (1957) *No-No Boy*, for example, presents a protagonist (Ichiro) whose psychological, political wounding and paralysis are caused by the internalized unresolvable war between a Japanese mother who has raised him in the United States as a Japanese, and American society which is patriarchal and hegemonically racist. In this double bind, Ichiro symbolizes the twice-crippled victim whose only power lies in his ability to be twice negative, to say no to a Japanese matriarchy and no to a white patriarchy. In contrast, Monica Sone's (1953) autobiography, *Nisei Daughter*, demonstrates that other alternative, to negate the matriarchy associated with the defeated racial Other and to accept the patriarchy, including the white male politicians in Washington who had legislated the internment of 111,000 Japanese-Americans. For the victim to survive in a racist society, she can attempt to obliterate the differences that have aroused racial hostility in order to disappear into the mainstream. In the process described in Sone's book, assimilation is simply another name for ethnocide. The Issei, first-generation Japanese, have their racial possessions destroyed; any object faintly related to their mother culture is taken away; the American authorities confiscate and burn their Japanese-language books, even the Japanese translation of the Bible! The daughter who emerges from the camp where her Issei parents are still incarcerated has also had her pride in her racial origin, her Japanese mother, destroyed, and she takes on a Caucasian surrogate mother associated with happier memories.

Kogawa's novel, *Obasan*, presents us with yet another alternative: neither the paralytic hatred of double negation nor the suppression and destruction of the Japanese matriarchy, both of which inscribe the Japanese maternal figure in order to erase it, but instead the re-inscription of racial origin through a recuperation of a lost maternal figure. Aptly, neither Okada's novel nor Sone's autobiography are self-reflexively writerly texts. *No-No Boy* is written in the style of social realism, and in some ways anticipates the protest literature of the 1960s. Sone's autobiography is more *bios* than *autos*. While its subject matter is made urgent by historical events (the internment, the Pacific War, the course of legislative and social race discriminations), the subjectivity of the subject remains in shadow.[1] Georges Gusdorf (1980:30) defines the autobiographical genre as emerging from "the mythic framework of traditional teachings" in the presence of "the perilous domain of history." But the narrator in *Nisei Daughter,* despite her own testimony to racist terrors and oppressions, accepts uncritically the myth of assimilation. Her text, therefore, remains faithful to an ideological construct of the coherent, autonomous, and assimilated American self, and resists any representation of ambiguity which would subvert this ordering construct of the American subject.

Moving away from the restrictions of such autobiography, however, Kogawa's novel, *Obasan,* written almost three decades later, insists on the interrelations between the subject of the "I" and the language through which that subject is expressed, and bases the thematics of recuperation of a lost mother in the thematics of the recuperative powers of language itself. In *Obasan,* the writing project is inseparable from the reconstruction of the maternal. The figure of the daughter is also the figure of the writer figuring out her self; the images of writer, narrator, speaker, and protagonist collapse into a series of intimately related "I"s, all creating, as Gunn (1982) has said of the autobiographical genre, a trompe-l'oeil effect of depth. *Obasan,* therefore, is both and more than a work of social realism. Using elements from her own life story as well as letters, diaries, and historical documents, Kogawa chose to write a fiction which impersonates the discourse of autobiography, while at the same time she has masked the genre of autobiography through the liberating effects of poetic language. The integration of the thematics of the maternal with the text's structure is modernistic and totalizing. The subject of the novel can only be produced in the language of the novel, giving to the work an integrity of depth which distinguishes it from the earlier books.

As I have written of the the recovery of the lost mother elsewhere, I would simply summarize it here. The novel presents the riddle of Naomi's childhood, when her first-generation Japanese-Canadian mother leaves her five-year-old daughter, her older son Stephen and her husband in September 1941, to return to Japan to visit her aging mother. To the young Naomi, "I hardly dare to think, let alone ask, why she has to leave. Questions are meaningless. What matters to my five-year-old mind is not the reason she is required to leave, but the stillness of waiting for her to return" (Kogawa 1981 [hereafter referred to as *OBA*]:66). But the mother never returns. Only thirty-one years later, when Naomi is thirty-six, unmarried, never having had a satisfying emotional relationship, an age when it would seem unlikely she would ever be a mother herself, does she learn the answer to the riddle of her mother's disappearance. (Naomi's emotional mystification, which is central to her adult development, is contrasted subtly with her brother's response. Where Naomi remains trapped in the miasma of maternal deprivation and unsuccored by her two surrogate mother/aunts, Stephen escapes from the defeated family to fame as a pianist and love with an outsider. Stephen, as a male child, is able to remove himself physically and psychically from the absent mother's clasp.)

Prevented by the outbreak of the Pacific War from returning to Canada, the mother was in Nagasaki at the time the atom bomb was dropped and, hideously disfigured, died a few years later. Her years as a victim of the nuclear holocaust and her death were kept from Naomi and her brother by the mother's injunction to the family for silence: "Do not tell Stephen and Naomi," you say. "I am praying that they may never know" (OBA:241). This Japanese mother's story is in itself a powerful tale, displaying that "perilous domain of history," in Gusdorf's apt term. The re-creation of the lost mother culminates the narration of the daughter's story, which is also the story of the writer who has to overcome silence in order to create her text and her identity.

The novel begins with a prologue which encapsulates the dialogic struggle between silence and speech:

> There is a silence that cannot speak. There is a silence that will not speak. Beneath the grass the speaking dreams and beneath the dreams is a sensate sea. The speech that frees comes forth from that amniotic deep. To attend its voice, I can hear it say, is to embrace its absence. But I fail the task. The word is stone.

This brief passage presents at least three types of silence: the silence that is powerless to break itself, which is the silence of the Japanese aunt, Aya, uncle Isamu's childless picture-bride who raises the children after their mother's disappearance and their separation from their father during the internment. Then there is willful silence, one which has the power of speech but denies it, the silence of refusal, seen in the mother's injunction against "telling the children." But there is also the silence of "that amniotic deep," of "speaking dreams" from which comes "the speech that frees." Kogawa exploits the resonances of the biblical passage, "Ye shall know the truth and the truth shall make you free" (John 38:8) to conflate truth with "speaking dreams." The freeing speech comes from underground, from the subconscious, associated with the period of unity between child and mother, the fetal sleep of the child in the mother's womb. In the prologue it is never clear whether the speaker is the author, the narrator, or the protagonist Naomi. The prologue serves as the writer's opening statement of her hardship, the quest for "the hidden voice," "the freeing word," and the admission of failure before the quest begins recalls the convention of the modest disclaimer, characteristic of introductions in Japanese literature. The truth sought here is both the answer to the mother's disappearance and the truth of the political fate of Japanese-Canadians dispersed from and forbidden to return to their original West Coast homes and exiled to the wintry hardships of the Canadian wilderness.

The novel's thirty-nine chapters possess a coherent and complex timeframe, giving to the fiction the deepening effect of immediacy, temporality, and chronological sequencing that is the peculiar property of diaries. Many chapters, for example, begin with dates. Chapter One tells us "9:05 p.m. August 9, 1972." The exact dating in the opening chapter prepares us for the importance of time in the narration. Early in the chapter we learn that Naomi had moved to Granton with her uncle in 1951 (*OBA*:1); then that her uncle first brought her to the coulee in 1954, in August, two months after aunt Emily's initial visit to Granton (*OBA*:2). Of course, once we have figured out this opening riddle (the coulee is a symbol of a memorial to Naomi's mother), we turn to the account of Emily's visit to Granton, picked up later on page 213 ("a puzzling incident one night during [Emily's] first visit to us in 1954") and piece together the riddle: that Emily's visit was occasioned by news of her sister's death, and that the mysterious conversation between the adults which the high school teenager overhears has to do with their decision not to inform the children of her fate. "Kodomo no tame" – "For the sake of the children" – continues to be the injunction against speech even as aunt Emily protests, "But they are not children. They should be told" (*OBA*:219).

In the opening chapter, Naomi is thirty-six; she flashes back to the first visit to the coulee at Granton when she was eighteen. The second chapter similarly begins with a date: "September 13, 1972," when news reaches her as she is teaching in Cecil, Alberta, that her uncle has died of a heart attack. Many chapters carefully track the passing hours of her return to Granton to attend her uncle's funeral. This careful chronicle of events forms the data for the evolving historical and psychological mystery and the materials for their resolution. Significantly too, it creates a representation of what Gunn calls "the depth-dimension of temporality" (*OBA*:21) of the autobiographical genre.[2]

But like a Chinese puzzle there are other narratives within the major temporal mode that narrates the adult Naomi's grieving for her uncle. Obasan finally gives Naomi the letters and documents that aunt Emily had sent her. The reader reads these texts through Naomi's interpretation of them; the texts themselves are carefully chronologized and belong to several different genres, each offering a different discourse on the same subject. "There are several packages here – an old scrapbook full of newspaper clippings, a brown manilla envelope, one grey cardboard folder, a three-ring-binder-size hardcover book full of aunt Emily's handwriting" (*OBA*:31). The parcel contains aunt Emily's diary, unmailed letters to her sister, Naomi's mother, conference papers on the Japanese Canadian internment, and various memoranda and correspondence. The chapter flashes back to another occasion five months ago on Emily's last visit to Granton when she gives Naomi a pile of papers to read, including her own autobiographical manuscript and uncle Isamu's official correspondence with Canadian authorities during the internment period.

The narrator/writer incorporates these texts in various ways in her own narrative, quoting selections to comment on them. This particular technique succeeds in creating a fiction of sociological documentation; for Naomi's response as reader to these sociological texts, her interpretation of them, is as vital to our own reading as these texts themselves. And Naomi is ambivalent. She is not an already ideologically committed reader. Kogawa interposes Naomi between one text and her reader to create an intertextual dimension which enriches our own responses to the sociological content. Unlike that "repressive sociologizing" which Kristeva (1984) has condemned as keeping apart literary practice and political horizon, Kogawa, through her fiction of sociological content, expands the political horizons in her novel.[3] The novel coopts the political consciousness extant, intended, and pervasive in official papers, memoranda, newspaper clippings, and conference papers, as well as in personal letters, diaries, journals, and autobiographies, genres which approach close to the historic moment. In *Obasan,* therefore, time is experienced, as Gunn (1982:14) says of the autobiographical mode, "more like the thickness of a palimpsest . . . like a parchment on which layers of writing have been superimposed."

The novel's theme, however, is profoundly mythopoeic; Naomi's search for her lost mother echoes in a sharp-edged ironic reversal of the ancient myth of Demeter and Persephone.[4] While it is the daughter who survives here, her life is one of barren mystification until she can resurrect for herself the fate of that young mother with whom the child had had her single experience of love. This *mythos* of loss, quest, and eventual recovery is so grounded in the historically created chronology that the speaking subject of the daughter becomes also the speaking voice of a generation. *Obasan* is, after all, not an autobiography, even while it exploits the narrative nuances of the autobiographical mode. If it is a *bildungsroman,* it is not one in the sense of an education of an individual; indeed, it is an entire ethnic group that is being schooled into the political horrors of a recent past, a past that shamed Japanese-Canadians and that an oppressive Canadian government would prefer silenced and buried. The lost mother is thus a trope for the lost racial memory: her exile in Japan during the war, her disfiguration in the Nagasaki holocaust, and the attempt to extinguish her memory through a corresponding conspiracy between Japanese cultural suppression of unacceptable fact and white Canadian oppression of the unacceptable alien. The daughter as writer who struggles with various genres of documenting these horrors, and who finally gives personal voice to her emotions of devastation and grief, is therefore not simply an individual subject but a powerful witness whose task of writing is to reclaim voice as a tool against the silence of the dead, against ethnocide.

In the choice of the name "Naomi" for the abandoned daughter, the text presents yet another set of ironic paradigms. In the Book of Ruth, Naomi is that nurturing surrogate mother to whom Ruth is bonded, who leads her daughter-in-law into exile and later into fruition. *Obasan* again reverses the mother/daughter paradigm; here Naomi is the daughter who must rescue the mother from her exile in Nagasaki, and in the process of "saving" the mother's memory finally comes to "author" herself, to authorship herself.

Obasan is a text of intersubjective memories, each imbued with racial identity, and all centered on forms of mother/daughter bonding. There is a passive memory, muted, unvoiced, but enduring, most strongly associated with Obasan, the childless Japanese aunt, whose sufferings appear futile and unregenerative. There is active memory, associated with Emily, the Canadian aunt, who records, documents, and indicts the injustices suffered by Japanese-Canadians during the internment and after. Aunt Emily is also childless; in her own logocentric manner, she also has failed the young Naomi. Then there is poetic memory springing from the amniotic deeps. Speaking in a different voice, the voice of image and feeling, it encompasses the two negative mirrorings of aunts Aya and Emily and exceeds them. Reconstructing the maternal figure, the speaking subject is firstly an interrogative voice. It questions both the Eastern mode of silence and the Western mode of public speech; it questions memory and language; and above all it represents an inquisition of history, specifically the recent history of nuclear destruction and Western racism.

With the discovery/recovery of the "Young Mother of Nagasaki," it becomes finally an affirmative voice. In the poetic voice, the speaking subject celebrates the most personal of human bonds; and it is this child-mother bond which then functions as the trope for the public bond of self and race. The presence of this poetic language in the novel re-orders the other genres of writing (and memory) and gives to the expression of racial memory the power of the semiotic. As Kristeva uses the term, we see the *semiotic* working in *Obasan* in the way that "repressed consciousness"—all that is left out of Obasan's silence and Emily's documents—erupts and disturbs the narrative.[5] The *semiotic* is what the narrator appeals to in her reference to "speaking silence"—silence which bears eloquent testimony and speech which re-creates the experience of such silence. The novel encompasses and moves through the stages of muteness or aphasia (Obasan's character); logocentric documentation (Emily's character); and a speaking subject (the narrator's poetic voice). The fiction therefore enacts the movement of the daughter's marginal discourse into a central position, placing the subjectivities of an aunt Aya and aunt Emily into question. The power of its message is also the power of its language which shows this daughter's subjectivity *in process*.[6]

The novel begins by interrogating an absence (of speech and mother), creates the presence of such absences, and finally reclaims the maternal figure in its conclusion when Naomi condemns and forgives the mother's complicity in her own erasure:

> Silent Mother, you do not speak or write. You do not reach through the night to enter morning, but remain in the voicelessness... Martyr Mother, you pilot your powerful voicelessness over the ocean and across the mountain, straight as a missile to our hut on the edge of a sugar-beet field. You wish to protect us with lies, but the camouflage does not hide your cries... Young Mother at Nagasaki, am I not also there? (*OBA*:242)

The adult narrator is able to mourn both for the mother and the young girl who is destroyed when the bond between mother and child is severed. In reconstructing the mother's story, unriddling the riddle of loss, the adult is finally able to move beyond the mute suffering of childhood: "I am thinking that for a child there is no presence without flesh. But perhaps it is because I am no longer a child I can know your presence though you are not here" (*OBA*:243). The mystery of Japanese memory for the Japanese-Canadian corresponds to that of relationship between a martyred silent mother and fearful silent child; only to an adult, in memory, can the racial mother's presence be admitted.

In *The Woman Warrior*, Kingston (1975) rewrites the Asian maternal figure by rewriting a Cantonese mother's talk-stories. She answers the question "Who am I?" by tracing her matrilineal heritage. In *Obasan*, however, in the presence of an erased maternal figure, the text does not seek to answer the question, "Who am I?" but instead attempts to answer the question, "What are the different ways of being?" In tracing "being," as constituted both in silence and in language, it is concerned with how non-language or language maintains or breaks down psycho-social repressions. *The Woman Warrior* provides us with an autobiographical herstory; *Obasan* gives us a poetic language which, by insisting on fusing the personal with the historical horizons, collapses the boundaries between autobiography and fiction and admits itself into the domain of the political.

Notes

1. The Canadian counterpart to the United States Executive Order 9066, Order in Council P.C. 1486, was issued on February 24, 1942. Because they were more concentrated on the West Coast than Japanese Americans, this order affected more than ninety-five percent of the Japanese Canadians. More than half of the evacuated people were sent to Interior Housing Centres, located in six old mining towns in the interior of British Columbia; 3,600 British Columbians were also sent to work in the beet fields of Alberta and Manitoba. An "official policy of dispersal" discouraging Japanese Canadians from returning to their West Coast homes, and including a program of deportation, repatriation, and expulsion, was not ended until April 1, 1949, in contrast to the United States "where, under pressure of impending Supreme Court decisions, restrictions on the return of the Japanese to the West Coast were removed at the end of 1944" (Daniels 1981:191).
2. According to Gunn, "Autobiography is a mode of fictional and historical narrative that delves into time in order to take up the problem of depth... The

autobiographical act of bringing life to language involves a temporal gathering of what Hannah Arendt calls 'the absent tenses,' the 'no-more' of the past and the 'not-yet' of the future, into the fullness of the present... *To speak one's life is, rather, to take up occupancy within the mobile setting of time as depth"* (1982:42-43).
3. According to Kristeva, "The text is a practice that could be compared to political revolution: the one brings about in the subject what the other introduces into society. The history and political experience of the twentieth century have demonstrated that one cannot be transformed without the other... Hence, the questions we will ask about literary practice will be aimed at the political horizon from which this practice is inseparable, despite the efforts of aestheticizing esotericism and repressive sociologizing or formalistic dogmatics to keep them apart" (1984:17).
4. The narrator/daughter's quest for the lost mother echoes the theme struck by *The Lost Tradition: Mothers and Daughters in Literature*. In their foreword, editors Davidson and Broner underline "a mourning for the mother-daughter relationship in contemporary fiction" and emphasize how "By searching in unusual literature—in the private or hidden literatures of diary, tale, myth, song, and autobiography— women have been restoring the blurred image of our mothers. There has been an embracing of the maternal past" (1980:xii)
5. Kristeva, *Revolution in Poetic Language*. As she points out, her "positing of the semiotic is obviously inseparable from a theory of the subject that takes into account the Freudian positing of the unconscious. We view the subject in language as decentering the transcendental ego, cutting through it, and opening it up to a dialectic in which its syntactic and categorical understanding is merely the liminary moment of the process" (1984:30). She clarifies her concept of the semiotic further: "Although originally a precondition of the symbolic, the semiotic functions within signifying practices as the result of a transgression of the symbolic... As a precondition of the symbolic, semiotic functioning is a fairly rudimentary combinatorial system, which will become more complex only after the break in the symbolic. It is, however, already put in place by a biological setup and is always already social and therefore historical" (1984:68). For Kristeva, the writing subject includes not only the consciousness of the author but her unconsciousness. The subject of writing, therefore, includes the non-conscious, the domain that, while not subject to repression, is also not within the reach of consciousness either (see Roudiez 1984:8.)
6. Kristeva distinguishes between the subject as enunciated and the subject in process. The subject in process, she elaborates, "moves through the linguistic network and uses it to indicate... that the linguistic network does not represent something real posited in advance and forever detached from instinctual process, but rather that it experiments with or practices the objective process by submerging in it and emerging from it through the drives. This subject of expenditure is not a fixed point—a "subject of enunciation"—but instead acts *through* the text's organization (structure and completion) where the *chora* of the process is represented" (1984:126).

References

Daniels, Roger. 1981. *Concentration Camps: North American Japanese in the United States and Canada during World War II*. Malabar, Florida: Robert E. Krieger.

Davidson, Cathy N., and E. M. Broner, eds. 1980. *The Lost Tradition: Mothers and Daughters in Literature*. New York: Ungar.

Gunn, Janet Varner. 1982. *Autobiography: Towards a Poetics of Experience*. Philadelphia: University of Pennsylvania Press.

Gusdorf, Georges. 1980. "Conditions and Limits of Autobiography." In *Autobiography: Essays Theoretical and Critical,* edited by James Olney. Princeton: Princeton University Press.
Kingston, Maxine Hong. 1975. *The Woman Warrior: Memoirs of a Girlhood among Ghosts.* New York: Knopf.
Kogawa, Joy. 1981. *Obasan.* Boston: Godine.
Kristeva, Julia. 1984. *Revolution in Poetic Language.* Translated by Margaret Waller. New York: Columbia University Press
Okada, John. 1957. *No-No Boy.* Rutland, Vermont: Charles E. Tuttle.
Roudiez, Leon. 1984. Introduction to *Revolution in Poetic Language,* by Julia Kristeva. New York: Columbia University Press.
Sone, Monica. 1953. *Nisei Daughter.* Boston: Little.
Song, Cathy. 1983. *Picture Bride.* New Haven: Yale University Press.
Woo, Merle. 1981. "Letter to Ma." In *A Bridge Called My Back: Writings by Radical Women of Color,* edited by Cherrie Moraga and Gloria Anzaldua. Watertown, Massachusetts: Persephone Press.

Mirrors of the Self: Autobiography and the Japanese American Writer

David Mura

Perhaps even more than for most writers, the autobiography of a minority writer centers on the struggle to be a writer, to claim access to the language. Given the exclusionary nature of the traditional canons and the erasures of official histories, a young minority writer soon finds, as I did, that many of the necessary mirrors for his or her experience are somehow missing. I became a writer, in part, because I felt that it was absolutely necessary for me to find those missing mirrors, even if I needed to create them myself. Otherwise, I would never know where I came from, who my family was and is, or who I am. Early on in that search, certain sources outside of literature possessed a necessity it is impossible to underestimate.

Let me begin then with a scene that took place several times during my college years and early twenties: I am sitting in the dining room of my Nisei aunt, whose small house in Stamford looks out on Long Island Sound and is wedged in between the larger mansions of rich businessmen and executives. The foundation of my aunt's house was once a playhouse for the children of the mansion next door, and, even though the house had long since been added to both by previous owners as well as my aunt and her Japanese roommate, the house retained for me, all through my youth, an air of childhood fantasy. After I first read *The Great Gatsby*, I sometimes imagined my aunt's house as the carriage house in which Nick Carroway resides, just next to the mansion of the fabled, mysterious Mr. Gatsby.

But it was more than my aunt's house which entranced me. There was the way my aunt and her roommate, who was an artist and an illustrator of children's books, lived. Theirs was a life informed by New York City, where my aunt worked as a manager for a Japanese restaurant, a life filled with talk of Broadway shows, ballet, and the opera. When she was younger, my aunt had worked for a Broadway producer, had met Kathryn Hepburn, had watched Eugene O'Neill direct *The Ice Man Cometh*. She had gone to parties in the Village where writers like Frank O'Hara and e. e. cummings had appeared.

Beyond the heady East Coast atmosphere of her life, my aunt's house contained various objects of culture, from classical records to Japanese pottery, from children's books to various Japanese foods. She was the only person in my family with books like Robert Lowell's *Lord Weary's Castle* and W. C. Williams' *Paterson* in her bookcase. And because, as the eldest in her family, she spoke the best Japanese, and because her roommate was Japanese, my aunt's house was the one place where I heard Japanese spoken with any frequency.

So: In this archetypical scene I am setting, it is just after dinner, I am sitting with my aunt Ruth and Baye and Susie, the woman who was to become my wife. I am asking my aunt Ruth about her and my father's childhood, about my grandfather, my grandmother. I am asking because my father never talks of the past, nor does my mother. At home, when I have tried to bring up the subject of the camps, my father has simply said, "I had fun in the camps. Back in L. A., after school, I had to work in my father's nursery. In the camps I could go out and play baseball." My mother simply replies that she does not remember, she was too young, it was not all that important. Only my aunt will talk about the camps, about the past, about her parents. On visit after visit, I listen to story after story. Sometimes they are humorous, such as the time she was on a pass from camp and was walking through the town of Jerome, Arkansas, and some ladies on a porch, drinking mint julips, called out to her, "Dear, are you Anna May Wong? You look like Anna May Wong." Or there was the night my grandmother, suspecting that my grandfather was cheating on her, woke him up with a knife blade pressed to his throat. At other times, the stories are mysterious, filled with the psychic powers of my grandmother, how she foresaw my grandfather's car accident, begged him not to go out, sent my father to the temple to pray and light candles; later, long after dark, after hours of anxious waiting, she looked up to see my grandfather at the front door, a great white bandage blooming around his head: "Don't ever tell me your dreams again," he muttered. There was also the night in camp when my grandmother dreamed of firebombs falling on her sister's house, the house in flames, and woke up sobbing: six months later, a letter arrived, confirming her dream. Still other stories invoked generational differences, such as the time my aunt came up to my grandfather and asked him to sign the loyalty oaths; she believed the Nisei needed to prove they were good Americans, she wanted to believe she could be a part of the country. My grandfather looked at her and said, "When they let me out of here, then I'll sign up," and walked away.

As told by my aunt, these stories took on in my mind a legendary quality. Japanese are not necessarily known for their oral story telling traditions, and, though my aunt was an adequate story teller, I do not think it was the way she told these stories that mattered to me. No, I loved them because they were a clear link to the past that my parents had not provided; just as importantly, the stories had a certain romantic cast to them, seemed to involve picaresque happenings; the stories pictured my grandfather as a certified character, a somewhat lazy and fun-loving man, who liked to gamble, smoke cigars, and play the Japanese *biwa*, who wrote *haiku* until a stroke kept him from holding a brush (he began to cry then, went upstairs, and stayed in his room for a week); I saw my grandmother, on the other hand, as a seer, a ghostlike creature with an eye for the future and the other world.

My aunt's stories provided me with mirrors I could not find in the world of literature, neither in the American and English tradition I studied in college and graduate school, nor in the few works of Japanese literature I had begun to read, nor the even fewer works by Japanese Americans. At the time, in my early twenties, I was still possessed by an overwhelming sense of the importance and majesty of the mainstream literary tradition and with a concomitant sense that minority literature was an interesting, exotic sidelight, a ghetto of local color and nothing more. And because of these attitudes I did not understand the complexities behind my aunt's stories, nor the way in which I used the stories to hide from my own situation. It was easier to romanticize the Issei than to look at the complexities of my own life. And yet, my Issei grandparents and their stories kept showing up in my poems, despite my early devotion to such poets as James Dickey, Robert Bly, and Richard Wilbur, poets whose life experiences were nothing like mine. It was as if, despite my decision to work toward a graduate degree in English literature, something in my unconscious was pulling me toward my Japanese past, toward Asia, toward a cultural identity I wanted to do without.

I have gone over much of my struggle with the mainstream English literary tradition in other writings (Mura 1987, 1988), so I do not want to say too much about that here. Growing up outside an Asian-American community in a Jewish suburb of Chicago, I was perhaps more enamored of the mainstream tradition than other Asian American writers; certainly, my parents' dedication to fitting into the white middle class, their desire to not call attention to our Japanese background, influenced the way I thought about literature; so did the images of Asians in American culture, the stereotypes of houseboys, Jap soldiers, and camera-toting tourists, Charlie Chan and Mr. Moto.

In certain ways, my position was similar to that of the scholarship boys from the colonies who come to England; such boys are envious and eager for the heart of the Empire and yet uncertain of themselves, of their experience.

Subsequently, they often learn to identify themselves with British upper-class ways and to look down on their own native countries and culture. They see their past and their family's past as a source of shame, something to be shed, to be put behind them. Unfortunately, in their interactions with their classmates, in the books and other objects of culture they encounter, they are constantly reminded of their status as an outsider. A fierce anger grows inside them, and, depending upon their character, they may be thoroughly discouraged in their desire to fit in and quit with a mass of bitter resentments. Or they may use that anger as a fuel in their drive to belong, to shed the past, and accumulate another set of bitter resentments. At some point, if they are lucky, they may begin to see the impossibility of shedding their backgrounds, to see that the hope of belonging to the white, upper-class culture of England is not only chimeric but is also a source of their bitterness. They realize they must go back home, certainly psychically and perhaps even physically, if they are going to know and accept who they are. And if they are very lucky, they will see that this return does not entail the denial of their experiences in England, of their attempts to belong: for those experiences and those attempts are now part of their past, are what has formed them, what has made them into a hybrid creature.

There are a number of authors whose lives parallel this paradigm I have set up and who have examined its workings: Salman Rushdie's *The Satanic Verses* is one such examination; another is V. S. Naipaul's *The Enigma of Arrival;* the poetry of Derek Walcott and Aime Cesaire comprise two other versions; the brilliant psychologist of racism and revolution, Frantz Fanon, and his works *The Wretched of the Earth* and *Black Skin, White Masks,* represent still another.

Recently, I came across an autobiography which seems to me one of the first Japanese American versions of this tradition—Gene Oishi's *In Search of Hiroshi* (1988). Superficially, the outlines of Gene Oishi's life seem to fit the standard American success story associated with the Nisei. Like the 110,000 other Japanese Americans living on the West Coast in 1941, Oishi and his family were deemed a threat to national security and were interned in relocation camps. And, like most of the Issei, Oishi's parents never recovered economically from the internment; although his father had been a prosperous farmer and a community leader, both of Oishi's parents could find work only as field laborers after the war. In contrast, their children, including Gene, flourished and ostensibly overcame the experience of the camps. After a stint in the army and a brief stab at law school, Gene Oishi received a journalism degree from the University of California at Los Angeles, became a successful reporter at the *Baltimore Sun* and then the press secretary for the governor of Maryland; in the process he wrote many articles for national publications. Presently, he is the director of publications of the Maryland State Teachers Association.

Thankfully, despite Oishi's apparent upward mobility, his autobiography, *In Search of Hiroshi*, does not give us a simple-minded paean to hard work and the American way, nor does it provide the brightly polished ameliorative myth of Bill Hosokawa's *Nisei; the Quiet Americans* (1969), a book where the psychic damage of the internment is elided over in favor of a list of Nisei who have reached positions of relative prominence. Early on, Oishi, who was eight at the time of Pearl Harbor, demonstrates how the war and the camps created problematic contradictions in his sense of identity; and despite his desire to resolve those contradictions, he senses that perhaps they cannot be reconciled, that any reconciliation would be a denial of the complexity of the past. In a particularly telling incident at the Gila relocation camp, he describes the reaction of the young Nisei to a war film, depicting American bombers destroying a Japanese ship: "Young people in the crowd began to giggle, and as the ship sank they cheered and applauded... surrounded by my friends who were shouting, whistling, and clapping their hands, I cheered and applauded too. *It seemed as if I were doing a bad thing, but it felt good nevertheless.* The parents in the crowd were appalled. Their own children were turning against Japan, and if they turned against Japan, they were turning against them" (Oishi 1988:12; italics mine). Oishi associates his cheering with a teenage Nisei who, for no seeming reason, hurled a rock at the window of one of the barracks and injured a little girl: "he [the boy] just wanted to do something bad... just as I had wanted to do something bad when I applauded the sinking of a Japanese battleship" (Oishi 1988 [hereafter *ISH*]:52).

If Oishi does not explicate the connection between the internment and this desire to be bad, he at least recognizes they somehow do connect. His younger self's reaction seems to follow naturally from the dictates of the internment situation: each Japanese American was imprisoned not for any particular act, but simply by the fact of their race. An equation was set up then between being Japanese and being bad. In addition, if you are imprisoned and have committed no crime, you may understandably attempt to find ways to relieve your feelings of helplessness and confusion. One way is to commit a crime; then, at least, your own actions have determined your fate.

For most Nisei, with their strong sense of propriety, of obedience and diligence—traits derived from Japanese culture—such a reaction was not possible. Oishi's own achievements might seem to indicate that he was also able to shake his confusion of identity. Yet, as Oishi's autobiography progresses beyond the war, he reveals more and more the difficulties of his assimilation. In high school, when a Caucasian girl announces in civics class that she likes a boy of another race, Oishi wonders "why a nice girl like Lenore would be fooling around with a boy of another race. Eventually, I began to wonder whether I was the one Lenore liked and was tortured by the thought...My parents would have been devastated if they thought I liked a *hakujin* girl, and

I had no doubt that Lenore's parents would have been equally distressed if she had a Japanese boyfriend" (*ISH*:91). Although an honor student and seemingly accepted by his teachers and fellow students, Oishi feels that he is different from white Americans; at the same time, he chooses not to associate with other Japanese. Yet, as he reaches adulthood, incidents of racial slights or insults remind him of his inability to separate his identity from his race. Perhaps the culminating incident occurs when Oishi is covering Spiro Agnew's vice-presidential campaign. Seeing Oishi asleep in the back of the press plane, Agnew asks, "What's the matter with the fat jap?" (*ISH*:155) As word of Agnew's remark spreads, Oishi soon finds himself embroiled in a small national controversy.

Throughout the book, scattered facets of Oishi's life reveal him to be seemingly atypical of many Nisei, more wayward in his experiences. In his late teens, Oishi becomes a jazz musician and arranger and begins to associate with other jazz musicians, including a talented young black trombone player named Oscar. Oscar introduces Oishi to marijuana, which ultimately disappoints Oishi, because it fails to release him into some mystical realm of oblivion and forgetfulness. A bit later, the suicide of his white music teacher becomes the trigger for Oishi's own aborted suicide attempt. As a military serviceman stationed in France, Oishi eventually becomes fluent in French, travels through Europe, plays and hangs out in black jazz clubs, and has a brief relationship with a black waitress. He then lives for a year in Japan with relatives and eventually has a relationship there with a young widow. Later, during his stint as press secretary for Maryland's governor, Oishi enters a period of confusion where he separates from his Swiss wife and has a few affairs. Throughout all these experiences there are points, such as his half-hearted suicide attempt or his separation from his wife, when his sense of self seems to crack: the strain of fitting in, of trying not to call attention to himself as a Japanese, of pushing back the past, become too much: "I told my friend that I felt as if I were a jigsaw puzzle that I had carefully and painstakingly put together over the years, and now was falling apart and I no longer knew who or what I was" (*ISH*:171).

One obvious question is whether Oishi's difficulties with identity and assimilation are shared by others of his generation or are simply aspects of his own particular personality and psychology. Many Nisei, as well as many white Americans, may prefer the latter explanation, but Oishi implies that despite certain outward peculiarities, his own experiences reflect that of other Nisei; to back up this assertion, he provides quotations from interviews with various Japanese Americans. (The interviews are from an article Oishi wrote for *The New York Times Magazine;* originally, the article was slated for *National Geographic*, but was eventually refused in part because it did not uphold the myth of the "model minority" Japanese-Americans). One Nisei woman remarks that "for years she remembered the internment as a 'fun' experience and it was only in psychoanalysis that her true feelings came pouring forth. In working as a therapist with other Nisei...she discovered that they, too, had repressed much of their feeling surrounding the experience. Repression, she said, was our means of protecting ourselves from the frightening realization that our government was acting against us" (*ISH:*179).

In a perceptive insight, Oishi points out that the stereotypes of "the model minority image, '*The Quiet American*,' the smiling, hard-working, reliable professional Mr. Nice Guy" are all a part of this repression: "I thought of how *hakujin* upon meeting me would often ask whether I knew a certain Japanese American acquaintance of theirs. 'You happen to know George...?' a man would say. 'A real nice guy...'" (*ISH:*179) Oishi contrasts this typical Nisei nice guy with one young Sansei's experience in Japan; not surprisingly, this Sansei found that the "Japanese of Japan have the whole range of human behavior through which they express themselves," and are both quiet and shy, loud and aggressive, polite and rude. To the Nisei, the camps gave the message: such freedom is not allowed. Compared to the often hard-drinking, fun-loving, and idiosyncratic Issei, the Nisei were more uncertain of their cultural identity and became "comparatively quiet, meek, and bland" (*ISH:*178-179).

Ironically, although I found much of interest in this book, I felt the qualities Oishi ascribes to the Nisei are somehow related to the book's weaknesses. Having been a jazz musician, having become fluent in Japanese, French, and German, having traveled in both Asia and Europe, having covered a presidential campaign and worked as a governor's press secretary, having had relationships with a number of women of different races and cultures, Oishi and his story should have imprinted themselves on the page with more energy and verve than is present in his autobiography. Often, he tells us what happened to him without bothering to recreate the incidents dramatically, without sufficiently providing the details and atmosphere that would let us enter into his experience, and without highlighting the inherent conflicts of his story (one wonders: is the lack of dramatic detail another form of repression?). Perhaps, if Oishi were a better stylist or more resolutely introspective or if he had brought to his task greater intellectual resources, the lack of dramatic tension and precision would not be so telling a fault.

My feelings then about Oishi's book are divided. In many ways, he has given us an honest and thoughtful account of his life; for Japanese Americans in particular, he has provided us some tools to begin taking apart the myth of the "model minority" and to see the past and ourselves in all their contradictory complexity. And yet, as a Japanese American writer, I am troubled by the lack of literary sophistication in Oishi's work, and I am reminded of some remarks by Daniel Okimoto in his *American in Disguise:*

> it appears unlikely that literary figures of comparable stature to those minorities like the Jews and the Blacks will emerge to articulate the *Nisei* soul. Japanese-

Americans will be forced to borrow the voices of James Michener, Jerome Charyn, and other sympathetic novelists to distill their own experience. Even if a *Nisei* of Bernard Malamud's or James Baldwin's talent did appear, he would no doubt have little to say that John O'Hara hasn't already said (Okimoto 1971:149-150).

There is an obvious self-hatred in these remarks and a denial of the uniqueness of the Nisei experience, but beyond this, there is Okimoto's choice of Michener and Charyn as literary models, a choice which reflects a middlebrow taste and perhaps is further evidence of Okimoto's feelings of inferiority.

This brings up an intriguing dilemma. In certain ways, I feel Okimoto's tastes reflect something in the Japanese American sensibility, which is, for the most part, fervently middle-class and middlebrow in its aesthetics. This sensibility in part stems from the desire of many Nisei to fit into mainstream American culture, to "outwhite the whites"; this desire may be similar to that of other second-generation Americans, but it has been greatly exacerbated and distorted by the experience of the camps. The prevalence of this middlebrow American sensibility also explains the cultural gap that many Sansei feel: since they have not grown up with extensive experience with Japanese culture, as was the case with the Nisei because of their Issei parents, the Sansei would seem to have no choice but to continue the direction their parents took, to continue mainstreaming. The high incidence among the Sansei of marriage to non-Japanese is part of this trend, as is their general unfamiliarity with the Japanese language.

Unfortunately, for a Japanese American writer, middlebrow culture and its literary models are simply inadequate for conveying the Japanese American experience. This point becomes even clearer when I compare Oishi's autobiography to some of the autobiographical works that I admire—Czeslaw Milosz's *Native Realm*, Marguerite Duras's *The Lover* or *The War*, Levi-Strauss's *Tristes Tropiques*, Maxine Hong Kingston's *The Woman Warrior*—or to the work of some of the "scholarship boys" I mentioned earlier—Naipaul, Rushdie, Fanon, Walcott—or to the work of certain theorists and critics who have informed my thinking—Adorno, Benjamin, Barthes, Foucault. In making this list, I am struck by how uncomfortable I feel with placing Oishi's work alongside these writers. It is not just that the comparison feels unfair, that I am asking from Oishi something he never intended to deliver, that I am perhaps arbitrarily singling him out. No, it is the sense that to refer to these other writers feels like a betrayal of Japanese American experience, of the middle-class and middlebrow consciousness I grew up with. What could be a more inappropriate mirror for my experience than a writer like Milosz, whose works invoke centuries of European culture, or Duras, whose works are associated with the French New Novel? And has not Maxine Hong Kingston been taken to task by writers such as Frank Chin for distorting

Chinese culture and Chinese American experience? And is not Naipaul famous for his scorn of the Third World? Of course, blacks in this country have realized that Fanon's psychoanalysis of colonialism and revolutions speaks cogently to their condition; and very early on, Walcott in the poem "A Far Cry from Africa" showed himself to be aware of some of the strains I am examining: "Where shall I turn, divided to the vein?" he writes, "I who have cursed / The drunken officer of British rule, how choose / Between this Africa and the English tongue I love? / Betray them both, or give back what they give?/ How can I face such slaughter and be cool? / How can I turn from Africa and live?" (Walcott 1986:17-18) But how can Marxist theorists like Adorno or Benjamin, with their abstract dialectic, or those diadems of French abstraction and intellectualism, Barthes and Foucault, have anything to say about the Japanese American experience? Certainly, Charyn and Michener are a lot closer to us than they.

A few years ago, in an article in *The San Francisco Poetry Flash,* the poet and critic Yuri Kageyama (1985) argued that Japanese American poetry, which is for the most part Sansei poetry, often seems to be caught in a welter of politically correct stereotypes: all the poets have their obligatory barbed wire relocation poem, their obligatory Issei grandparent poem. Within the confines of this implied aesthetic, to write without reference to race or culture, to write, for instance, a non-ethnic love poem, or to write with any degree of literary sophistication, would be deemed "banana" writing, a servile bow to the dominant culture.

In many ways, I agreed with Kageyama's article, particularly in the need for greater literary sophistication among Japanese American writers, for a more free-wheeling, *bricoleur* approach to culture, one where the writer grabs whatever he or she needs from a wide range of sources. And it might seem at first glance that I am arguing that the issue of race or of our minority culture need not be of utmost priority to the Japanese American writer.

But such an argument is exactly the opposite of how I feel.

What I am arguing is that the models of white middle-class America, the model for Oishi's prose-writing and autobiography, the models that Okimoto holds up, or even the aesthetics of mainstream contemporary American literature, can uncover only the briefest, surface aspects of Japanese American experience; there are depths and complications to that experience that require more sophisticated literary tools. If we cannot find those tools within Japanese American or Asian American literature, that may be unfortunate, but, on the other hand, those tools will never be there unless Japanese American and Asian American writers begin creating them. At the same time, I need to be aware that my position stems in part from being of a different generation than Oishi or Okimoto, of growing up under very different historical circumstances: I write about their generation without a direct experience of the camps, at a further remove from Japanese culture; at the same time, my relationship to the dominant culture is filtered through what might be called a post-modernist sensibility, through a period where divisions between cultures—whether by class, country, or historical period—seem to be breaking down.

In his essay on Marvell, T. S. Eliot argues that the poet ought to possess sophistication, a characteristic which he says involves a certain degree of learning, but whose essence is something deeper: an awareness that experiences and emotions other than one's own are possible and have occurred. Eliot was speaking mainly of how writers must step beyond the limited vision of their culture or historical moment; but an awareness of the exigencies of class and race are no less necessary. Obviously, sophistication increases the more multifaceted one's cultural background is. In one sense, such sophistication is always present in minority experience, since, as many have pointed out, the members of a minority must know both their culture and the dominant culture.

Unfortunately, for minorities in America this heightened awareness is often cut off in several ways. One such barrier is the argument that a knowledge or use of the dominant culture constitutes a betrayal of the minority culture, a selling out; such an argument mistakes ignorance for liberation and, at the same time, ignores the complexity of minority experience. Another hindrance that American minorities face lies in the fact that they often share the general myopia of American culture. Part of this myopia manifests itself in a concentration on local experience without reference to cultures and events beyond the American border; part involves a profound lack of a historical sense, a lack fostered not only by the basic dream of America—to shed the past and start anew—but by our status as worldwide purveyors of media culture, a culture that thrives on instant obsolescence and memory spans briefer than a sound bite. This myopia also contains a political component: the sense that the distant happenings in the Third World have no economic or political relationship to our lives. This political myopia then dovetails with an American anti-intellectual bent and helps form one of the great gaps in American writing: the ignorance of the theories of Marx and of the tradition which he fostered. In contrast, even the most fervent anti-communist writers from Europe, such as Kundera or Milosz, possess a firm grounding in dialectic. Perhaps this is one reason why American writing often seems disturbingly adolescent and facile: our anti-intellectualism represents simply another rejection of history.

How then is the Japanese American or Asian American writer to overcome the limits and prejudices of American culture? This has been a question I have struggled with in all of my writing. At present I am working on an autobiographical work about a year I recently spent in Japan. At first, I thought that the book was going to be mainly a travelogue about Japan, but, gradually, it more and more began to focus on my life and what it means to be a Japanese American. It has not been an easy book to write, and I find I keep uncovering complexity after complexity, question after question.

Perhaps the most problematic of these questions has concerned sexuality, a theme which Oishi alludes to in his autobiography, but never examines in any great detail. In order to examine the relationship between writing and literary sources, I want to give three examples here of how very disparate authors have helped me both to understand my sense of sexuality in greater depth and to form a language with which to convey it. I will start first with Frantz Fanon's *Black Skin, White Masks,* perhaps because Fanon's intellectual framework enabled me to approach this problem on a feeling level, on the level of experience and memory. In the chapter titled, "The Man of Color and the White Woman," Fanon opens his examination of interracial sexuality directly, almost brutally:

> Out of the blackest part of my soul, across the zebra striping of my mind, surges this desire to be suddenly white.
> I wish to be acknowledged not as black but as white.
> Now—and this is a form of recognition that Hegel had not envisaged—who but a white woman can do this for me? By loving me she proves that I am worthy of white love. I am loved like a white man.
> I am a white man.
> Her love takes me onto the noble road that leads to total realization...
> I marry white culture, white beauty, white whiteness (Fanon 1967:63).

Of course, any sexual interaction between two human beings cannot be reduced to the bare bones of these harsh sentences; on the other hand, I would argue that the thinking Fanon expresses here invariably invades any relation between a man of color and a white woman in America. Although Gene Oishi skims the surface of these thoughts in his autobiography, the picture he paints of his sexual relations observes taboos that Fanon broaches. For one thing, Fanon's examination of sexuality leads to a linking between sexuality and race and politics, a volatile and dangerous mixture:

> The sexual myth—the quest for white flesh—perpetuated by alienated psyches, must no longer be allowed to impede active understanding.
> In no way should my color be regarded as a flaw. From the moment the Negro accepts the separation imposed by the European he has no further respite, and "is it not understandable that thenceforward he will try to elevate himself to the white man's level? To elevate himself in the range of colors to which he attributes a kind of hierarchy"?
> We shall see that another solution is possible. It implies a restructuring of the world (Fanon 1967:81-82).

Fanon believes that one can mistake the nature of a mental and spiritual sickness by looking at it only through the lens of a personal history; one must also employ the lens of one's social group and the surrounding society. The inferiority that a colored man feels in white society affects his sexual identity, and so his sexual identity cannot be separated from his status as a minority. On one level, with great effort, with a large supply of spiritual energy, he can partially erase those feelings of inferiority and thus change his individual sexual identity. But on another level his sickness is caused by a sick society: for the cause to be erased, society must change.

As a young writer, when I looked within Japanese American literature I found that sexuality had somehow been avoided, that the tales and poems of the camps rarely move into the realm of the body and sexuality. And I began to sense that the deepest wounds in the Japanese American psyche, the deepest levels of repression may have taken place within that realm. In Japanese literature, such as Kawabata and Mishima, or in the movies of Nagasa Oshima, I could see a sense of sexuality that seemed quite different from the repression of sexuality I sensed in Japanese American literature and in my surrounding family. Similarly, when I lived for a year in Japan, I felt that there existed among the Japanese a much wider range of sexuality than whatever I had associated with Japanese Americans, and I began to wonder why this was so.

In my particular case, it seemed strange to me that it was not the almost Greek sense of sexuality of *The Sound of the Waves* that I responded to, but the darker, more confusing *frisson* of Mishima's autobiographical novel, *Confessions of a Mask*. The protagonist of the novel is homosexual, and the novel is, in some ways, his discovery and acceptance of that fact. But this was not my source of identification. What I identified with was the sense of sexuality as a source of shame, of some hidden self; for Mishima's protagonist, sex is a place where certain energies of debasement and delight are released and where one's worst fears about oneself are somehow confirmed. Here is the protagonist talking about his discovering his "toy":

> Then I took it into my head to try listening more dispassionately to the toy's wishes. When I did so, I found that soon it already possessed its own definite and unmistakable tastes, or what might be called its own mechanism. The nature of its tastes had become bound up, not only with my childhood memories, but, one after another, with such things as the naked bodies of young men seen on a summer's seashore, the swimming teams seen at Meiji Pool, the swarthy young man a cousin of mine married...
> The toy likewise raised its head toward death and pools of blood and muscular flesh. Gory dueling scenes on the frontpieces of adventure-story magazines...photographs of hard-muscled sumo wrestlers, of the third rank and not yet grown too fat (Mishima 1958:34-35).

None of these desires reflected the specifics of my own, and yet the protagonist's sense of the forbidden nature of his desires, his sense that his desires were evil—that I recognized. And nowhere did I feel this identification more than in the scene where the protagonist discovers in his father's study pictures of St. Sebastian; very quickly he becomes aroused and has his first sexual experience:

> That day, the instant I looked upon the picture, my entire being trembled with some pagan joy. My blood soared up; my loins swelled as though in wrath. The monstrous part of me that was on the part of bursting awaited my use of it with unprecedented ardor, upbraiding me for my ignorance, panting indignantly. My hands, completely unconsciously, began a motion they had never been taught. I felt a secret, radiant something rise swift-footed to the attack from inside me. Suddenly it burst forth, bringing with it a blinding intoxication (Mishima 1958:40).

I still do not understand all the reasons behind my responses to Mishima, but I do know that this scene in *Confessions of a Mask* parallels my own discovery of sexuality with the white goddess foldout of a Playboy magazine, a magazine that I found hidden in my parents' closet. There seems to me a certain irony in all this: for many Japanese Americans, the experience of the camps, their own sense of shame about being a racial minority, still remains in the closet; perhaps we should not be surprised then that their sexuality remains there too. It seems sad but fitting that to find the language to express my sense of sexuality I had to go back to Japanese literature, to a figure who represents both the more unbridled quality of Japanese sexuality and at the same time a profound sense of the forbidden and shameful. Understandably, one may wonder what the shame of a Japanese homosexual has to do with the experience of Japanese Americans. The similarity, I think, lies in the fact that both have faced condemnation and ostracism not for what they have done, but for who they are; that is, both have been judged guilty on a level of being rather than action. The result is that a deep suspicion of worthlessness may begin to corrode the very center of the self.

The final place I have gone for language to explore my own sexuality is the work of Marguerite Duras, particularly her novel *The Lover*, an autobiographical work which chronicles the affair of a young French girl in Vietnam with a young Chinese businessman. In Duras's novel, the dialectic of sexuality is filtered not only through the neuroses of her family, but also through the power games of colonialism and race. In part the novel was useful to me for the way it captures a certain view of Asian men as seen through Western eyes:

> The skin is sumptuously soft. The body. The body is thin, lacking in strength, in muscle, he may have been ill, may be convalescent, he's hairless, nothing masculine about him but his sex, he's weak, probably a helpless prey to insult, vulnerable. She doesn't look him in the face. Doesn't look at him at all. She touches him. Touches the softness of his sex, his skin, caresses his goldenness, the strange novelty. He moans, weeps. In dreadful love.
> And, weeping, he makes love (Duras 1985:38).

Duras's ability to reveal a darkness within sexuality, her ability to reveal sexual weakness and self-abandonment, is quite unsettling and is nothing like the surface reality of Japanese American life, at least as seen so far in most Japanese American literature. And yet, I recognize the Chinese lover's sense of desperation here, his enthrallment with white beauty; I have felt it myself. Reading Duras, I discovered a language which contained a depth and resonance, a sense of the dark, anarchic forces of sexuality, that I needed to express in my own experience.

It is an old but useful truism that one writes not only to tell what one knows, but to discover what one does not know. As a Japanese American writer, I must not only remember the particulars of my own life or my aunt's stories of our family; I also must work to understand the questions within those experiences, to uncover the layers of mystery and confusion and delight. And in this process I have found that I have had to go beyond the mainstream tradition of American or English literature to those of Europe and beyond to the tradition of Japanese literature, from Zeami to Kenzaburo Oe to the post-structuralist analysis of that tradition by Roland Barthes. I have found that to understand the camps I have had to look at them not just through the eyes of the Issei or Nisei or the whites of that era or the eyes of the Sansei, but also through the lenses provided by Kafka, Foucault, Fanon, and Marx. And in writing about the camps, I have found that I could rest not just with middlebrow writers like Michener, nor only with Asian American literature, but with novelists like Woolf, Marquez, Kundera, Coetzee, and Faulkner.

It is chimeric to believe that we can render experience without understanding it, as if experience could somehow be separated from its meaning, as if there existed some neutral, transparent language which would give us the thing itself. If I have learned anything in my progress as a writer, it is that all languages carry with them their own distortions, carry a reflection that is not quite the self. My hope then is that with enough mirrors I might be able to convey, to identify with, to understand, not just the young Japanese American man, from the suburbs of Chicago, listening intently to his aunt's tales, but the myriad selves he came to contain, from his Issei grandparents and Nisei parents to the global culture he now finds himself a part of.

References

Duras, Marguerite. 1985. *The Lover.* New York: Pantheon Books.
Fanon, Frantz. 1967. *Black Skin, White Masks.* New York: Grove Press.
Hosokawa, Bill. 1969. *Nisei; the Quiet Americans.* New York: William Morrow.
Kageyama, Yuri. 1985. "Thoughts on Our 'Yellow Light'." *The San Francisco Poetry Flash,* December.
Mishima, Yukio. 1958. *Confessions of a Mask.* New York: New Directions.
Mura David. 1987. "A Short Intellectual Biography of a Japanese American Writer, or How I Learned Not to Write Like James Michener or John O'Hara." *Kyoto Review,* Spring.
―――――. 1988. "Strangers in the Village." *Graywolf Annual V: Multi-Cultural Literacy.* Graywolf Press.
Oishi, Gene. 1988. *In Search of Hiroshi.* Tokyo: Charles E. Tuttle.
Okimoto, Daniel. 1971. *American in Disguise.* New York: Walker/Weatherhill.
Walcott, Derek. 1986. *Collected Poems, 1948-1984.* New York: Noonday Press.

Children of the Chinese Diaspora: A Comparison of Lee Kok Liang's *Flowers in the Sky* and Maxine Hong Kingston's *China Men*

Woon Ping Chin

A black friend from Philadelphia who visited China last year tells the story of how he had a hard time getting across to the Chinese the fact that he was American, until he came up with idea of calling himself an Overseas African. With the use of that term, it seemed, the Chinese instantly understood.

My own experience in China, during the year I lived and taught in Shanghai as a Fulbright Lecturer (1983-1984), would seem to corroborate this story. Though the people I encountered in various provinces, at least at first, had difficulty conceptualizing my Malaysian origins and my subsequent American citizenship, they seemed to be able to place me as soon as I said that I was a *hua qiao,* or an Overseas Chinese. Everywhere in the cities, separate institutions and privileges—from special rates and places in hotels, restaurants, and shops to special permits for visiting places otherwise closed to foreigners—indicated a ready niche for and acceptance of the group I apparently represented. And, once my Chinese ancestry was known, I was often told, in warm, receptive tones, that I was "one of them."

According to the historian Wang Gungwu (1981:123-127), the term *hua qiao* did not gain currency until the 1880s and did not accrue its strong political and emotional overtones until after 1903, particularly with the dissemination of "The Song of the Revolution," and the propagation of Chinese nationalism by Sun Yat-sen, leading to the Nationalist Revolution of 1911.[1] During the Cultural Revolution, returned Overseas Chinese faced a great deal of resentment, however, and it was not until after 1978, with the announcement of the National Conference on Overseas Chinese Affairs, that the mainland Chinese government "revived the rhetoric not only of calling various kinds of Chinese abroad 'Overseas Chinese' but also declared that 'they constitute part of the Chinese nation.' "[2] Whether for purposes of raising funds for Sun Yat-sen's anti-Manchu campaign, or for the current communist government's modernization program, implicit in its use seems to be not only the notion of a common Chinese history, even destiny—no matter how far one has wandered and no matter what nationality one has adopted—but that those who left can be re-sinicized again. In terms of the Association of Asian American Studies 1989 conference theme—the Diaspora—it raises questions of identity and identification, with attendant implications of a shared "source," heritage, or ethos, and the effects—historical, cultural, political—of dispersal. As a double exile born of Chinese parentage in Malaysia and a naturalized citizen of the United States, these implications carry some freight for my own sense of roots, place, and commitment.

I have chosen the two texts, Lee Kok Liang's *Flowers in the Sky* and Maxine Hong Kingston's *China Men*, for the purposes of comparing two treatments of the Chinese immigrant experience by *hua qiao* descendants in Malaysia and the United States, respectively. I would especially like to examine the extent to which local conditions have shaped theme, characterization, and narrative strategy and to examine each author's identification with China and with his or her own country. Without, I hope, falling into the danger of propagating a notion of "race" as a term for an essence, and avoiding, as much as possible, giving grounds for what Anthony Appiah warns as "the inscription of new and bizarre stereotypes" (cited in Gates 1985:13), I would like to see what continuities there might be between the two authors' works and to consider whether these continuities, if they exist, could be discussed at all as being recognizably "Chinese" or products of a Chinese diaspora.

Whereas the immigration of Chinese to Southeast Asia long preceded that to North America (going as far back as the fourth century and certainly significant by the Ming dynasty), it was during the nineteenth century that both regions saw a large influx; in part due to the growing demand for Chinese labor and in part because of economic and political conditions in China. It is important to recognize both the role of European imperialism in China and the latter's extremely weak position in world politics to understand the prejudice and ill treatment directed toward these laborers and immigrants, particularly in the United States toward the later part of the nineteenth century. In Malaysia (or what was then known as Malaya), the Chinese enjoyed some measure of privilege and economic advancement after the establishment of the British Straits Settlement in the 1830s, and their numbers swelled so that between 1891 and 1901, for example, while the Chinese population in the United States had dropped significantly, 299,739 came to Malaya (amounting to an increase of 83.4 percent) (Bedlington 1978:36). In recent years, however, we can see a significant contrast between the status of Chinese descendants in the two countries. In the United States, since the end of the

Exclusion Act in 1943 and in the wake of the civil rights movement of the 1960s, citizens of Chinese descent, comprising less than one percent of the total population, have enjoyed greater political and economic parity. Malaysians of Chinese origin, on the other hand, comprising thirty-four percent of the total population, have suffered what they perceive to be serious setbacks in their political and economic rights after independence in 1957, after the rise of Malay nationalism, and especially after the race riots of May 13, 1969.[3] Although both countries can be described as being multicultural, in Malaysia, the linguistic, economic, and political interactions of the country's racial percentages (nearly fifty percent Malay, thirty-four percent Chinese, eleven percent Indian, and the remainder a mixture of others) create a potentially volatile situation. Unlike mainly monolingual, white-anglo-saxon-protestant-dominated America, Malaysia's is a highly sensitive system of what has been called "balanced" or "consensual pluralism." In both countries, however, issues of racism and assimilation remain.

Against such a background, the two authors, Lee and Kingston, can each be seen as representing a generation of Chinese descendants come of age, so to speak, and an emergent literary group writing in the English language — a relatively besieged minority in Malaysia, in the face of pressures to publish in the national language, Malay; and in the United States a resurgent, larger movement of Asian Americans currently enjoying what amounts to an artistic renaissance.

Lee Kok Liang, a fifth-generation Chinese Malaysian of Hokkien or Fujianese ancestry, was born in 1927 in Alor Star in the state of Kedah, Malaysia. Educated in English in primary schools in Sungai Petani and at the Penang Free School, he joined a Chinese-medium school during the Japanese occupation and returned after the end of the war to the Free School. Lee then transferred to the Chung Ling High School, and eventually studied law in Melbourne and at the Inns of Court, London.[4] This background, though seemingly fragmented, gave him the advantage of an education in both the Chinese vernacular and in English; it also gave him an international perspective. As a reviewer suggests, his local and overseas experience gave him the outsider's detachment while retaining the "insider's understanding" of the community ("Speaking for the Mute" 1985:50). He currently practices law in Penang and writes in his spare time.

In *Flowers in the Sky*, published in 1981 and set in the 1950s, Lee has chosen to recreate fictionally the Chinese immigrant experience through the eyes of one of his two protagonists, a Buddhist monk named Reverend Hung who, "unlike Fa Hsien who travelled to collect the scriptures... travelled to collect devotees" (Lee 1981 [hereafter referred to as *FS*]:9). That Lee has chosen to deal with religion, a subject considered taboo in Malaysia, suggests Lee's fascination not only "with a complex cultural issue, namely, a comparison of different religious value systems in terms of what they have to offer modern man" (Harrex 1982:40), but also with an aspect of Chinese immigrants hitherto ignored in the literature of the region, that is, their spiritualism.

Hung's response to the new country of Nanyang is a painful process of accommodation to an alien environment, accentuated by the contrast between his own Mahayana Buddhist ideals of asceticism and the attainment of emptiness, and the icon-loving simplicity of the natives. In a letter back to his abbot in China, he reports:

> Some of them having some learning, read through the books of San Kuo (The Three Kingdoms) and were keen to have Kuan Kong, the God of War, on the main altar with the World-honored one. Resistance against them seemed to displease the powerful merchants and your humble one's temple stands on a piece of land over which these merchants have control. The laws of this country are strange. And so today your humble one started the prayers to bless the figures of Kuan Kong. The people here like sounds: chants, ringing of bells, cymbals and drums impress them. Silence they ignore like a falling leaf (*FS*:109-110).

Hung's self-distancing from the locals, amounting to what might be considered his objectification of the latter, is an insistence on the spiritual gap between self and other as well as Lee's way, perhaps, of suggesting degrees of difference in naturalization between the new immigrant and the old. It is a measure too of the real spiritual and moral journey Hung must make to come to terms with the new land. This act of distancing is echoed in more stark terms by Hung's sister Pek Sim, who joins him to help manage his affairs and who is responsible for turning the temple into a prosperous enterprise. Pek Sim's original response, for instance, is that her brother "should not have accepted the mission to the Nanyang where the people were so crude" (*FS*:119). Like Hung, Pek Sim must eventually come to terms with these alien people. For Hung, the process of naturalization is a slow surrender of once-mastered senses to the extreme onslaught of the country's climate:

> In the afternoons, as the heat seeped through the plank walls of his small room, he continued to sit. He tried to calm his mind and when he thought he was on the point of success, a line of sweat trickling from his armpit suddenly disturbed his concentration and at once he felt the intense pressure of the heat in the small room and his breathing became hoarse. This usually happened an hour after he had begun to sit. He had fought against the distraction. But on some days he was tired and instead of fighting against it, he lay down on the plank platform, not moving, staring up at the thatched roof of the temple, studying the wooden poles and brown undersides where the sunlight pin-pointed among the apertures. Closing his eyes as the tears came out, he wished he could go back. In this strange country, everything had become grotesque (*FS*:117-118).

More dramatically, Hung's very morals are threatened by his growing attraction to a local mute girl, Ah Lan, whom his sister has adopted:

The figures had merged and somehow or other Ah Lan was standing at the doorway, looking at him. In the great distance between them, she seemed so large and she raised her arm, resting her white hand on the doorpost. He willed her to go away. He was on the point of succeeding when the call of the muezzin pierced his consciousness and he felt the great heat inside him... And he forgot what he was sitting for. He forgot (*FS*:147).

Flowers in the Sky, says Australian critic Syd Harrex (1982:40), "charts the process of corruption that accompanies transplantation of old cultural traditions in a new environment." Certainly, physical corruption is embodied in the person of Ah Looi, a woman dying of stomach cancer in the hospital where Hung is admitted for a hernia operation. Pek Sim, visiting her brother, describes Ah Looi as "a dark Chinese of this hot land," while Mr. K., a surgeon and the other protagonist of the novel, observes her as being "corroded by the disarray of her cells" (*FS*:99). Ah Looi's futility and terror is vividly captured in a recurrent nightmare:

> she dreamt of a large hand descending from a gaping hole in the ceiling reaching down to drag her up and how she fought against it and woke up in a sweat. She sometimes wished she had allowed the hand to pull her up and then she could know what happened next and not be so puzzled over it. She was not afraid so much of the hand but of the huge dark hole in the ceiling. She prayed, but she did not know what she prayed for, at times, she prayed at Chinese temples, Indian temples, wayside shrines, during festivals and on the birthdays of the gods. She was not afraid to go. But the dark hole frightened her a lot (*FS*:98-99).

Ah Looi's dream is an undiscriminating and desperate religious faith, typical to some extent of the syncretism of her fellow countrypeople. The hand in her dream—disembodied, impersonal, and merciless—symbolizes not only the inscrutable power of death but more pervasively, the inarticulate and inarticulable fears of many Chinese. Harrex's reading of the theme as that of corruption of old cultural traditions, however, imputes to Lee an essentialist position unsupported by the rest of the text. Indeed, it ignores or de-emphasizes the political undertones and constraining mechanisms within the work. In an analysis of Lee's first work, *Mutes in the Sun*, however, Harrex was more responsive to these political undertones, especially as conveyed in the metaphor of muteness:

> in the contemporary political climate of Malaysia, in which Malay nationalism and Chinese self-assertion are rival forces, the Chinese tend to air their grievances in hushed and muted tones. Therefore the image of the mute—a creature silenced by nature, fear, communal pressure, or political authority—is potent with political implications (Harrex 1981:143).

Muteness and malaise are thus central tropes in Lee's fiction. John Kwan-Terry (1984:49) notes, for instance, that Lee's stories are "about marginal men, imprisoned in their circumstances, it may or may not be of their own making, inarticulate for the most part, struggling for release or dimly conscious, even unaware of their desire for release." In Lee's fictional world, says Kwan-Terry (1984:153), political reality does not enter as an explicit subject but "as anxiety, as an acute awareness of individual powerlessness."

It is significant to note that the two protagonists in *Flowers in the Sky*, Hung and Mr. K., the Indian surgeon who immigrated from Ceylon, are both healers. That Hung should himself need medical healing and self-punishment (the reader learns that he inflicts burns on his chest in an attempt to exorcise his passion for Ah Lan—an ironic parody of the ritual branding of his scalp during his initiation to monkhood) is surely a commentary on his own imbalance and isolation. Mr. K.'s skepticism, materialism, and sensuality, however, hardly seem to be the answer. In the end, it is the two women, Pek Sim (whose name White Heart after all suggests real purity) and Ah Lan, who hold some promise of hope. It is their spontaneous, gentle, and pragmatic administrations that help Ah Looi come to terms with her sickness and impending death. They comfort her with Buddhist chantings and with their friendship, concretized by a jade bracelet ordered from China by Pek Sim as a gift for Ah Lan and which the latter slips over the dying woman's thin arm. Ah Looi, we are told, is last seen "happily" fingering the jade bracelet.

China, thus, as symbolized by the jade bracelet, is the repository of comfort and familiarity, and of custom, ritual, and authority, as symbolized by the figure of the Abbot of the In Liang Sun Monastery where Hung received his training. Hung's novitiate there, however, is treated with ambiguity, since he has been told by his Master that he has a tendency to "cling," and his incomplete victory over his senses is vividly portrayed in his fascination for a large white carp living in the monastery pond. The old country, in other words, is not necessarily perfect and one carries to the new land one's own flaws.

Even as Hung writes back (in the letter quoted earlier) to send money and request advice from his Abbot, he is negotiating a pragmatic compromise with his superior, evident in the request for permission to allow the local merchants to put up the statue of Guan Goong. Rather than being a corruption, Hung's concession to the local populace must be seen as a necessary compromise for survival. The turning point for Hung's naturalization is when "after a year or so," Pek Sim—who plays a crucial role here—buys a piece of land with the generous contributions from Hung's congregation and builds a residence for her brother, a replica or transplantation of the old country:

> a tall and large residence with a curling roof and dragons, at the back of it she built what she thought would look like the quarters of her brother's former Master, with a pool and some imported gold carps in it . . . Pek Sim knew that he had felt very pleased and she knew it would now be easy to dissuade him from thinking of going back home (*FS:*127-128).

By the novel's end, Hung is pictured leaving the hospital (comically called the Marvellous Cure Center) recovered from his surgery, and chauffeured in a Mercedes. Mr. K. sees him depart and notes that the car's license plate shows the figures 666 – Book of Revelation, Chapter 13, the sign of the Devil. "What Mr. K. did not know," the narrator tells us, "was that 666 sounded like, 'Joy, Joy, Joy' in Cantonese. And the monk was very proud of the numbers and had used considerable influence upon the Registrar Inspector of Motor Vehicles to get them" (*FS*:157).

Such mutual misreadings of cultural indices by each ethnic group are part of the tangle of misunderstandings that arises when a statue of Ganesh is mysteriously washed up on the seafront property of Mr. and Mrs. K. – an event that forms much of the subplot of the novel and which I regrettably do not have time to discuss. Indeed, these misreadings are a strong motif in the novel. For instance, when Inspector Gopal joins in prayer the crowd of devotees who have come to worship the statue, his colleague Inspector Hashim (the only Malay character in the novel) misinterprets his gesture as "breaking the line" and sends riot policemen to rescue him.

Lee's narrative technique, a form of social realism varied by lapses into inner monologue and stream of consciousness, is full of indirections, ellipses, and innuendoes – a necessary discretionary method, perhaps, of skirting sensitive issues forbidden for discussion by the Internal Security Act. Thus, the only hint of the pervasive presence of the dominant power structure is in the call of the muezzin that drifts above the meditation of the Reverend Hung. These clashes of languages and icons, then, are Lee's way of indicating the extremely precarious position of the ethnic Chinese in Malaysia, which, for all its traps and flaws, is still home to them.

Maxine Hong Kingston, a second-generation Chinese American born in 1940, raised in the Chinatown of Stockton, California, and later educated at the University of California, Berkeley, sees herself very much as an American. As she stated at a recent address at Haverford College, she has been influenced by and has gained from the civil rights movement, giving her work an aggressive, feminist cast and undisguised liberalism. Her reconstruction of the Chinese immigrant experience in *China Men* is an attempt to celebrate and write into American history the contributions of the Chinese laborers – railroad builders, cane cutters, farmers, cooks, and laundrymen – who built the country. As she states,

> What I am doing in this new book is claiming America. . . . That seems to be the common strain that runs through all the characters. In story after story Chinese American people are claiming America, which goes all the way from one character saying that a Chinese explorer found this place before Lief Ericson did to another one buying a house here. Buying that house is a way of saying that America – and not China – is his country (cited in Kim 1982:209).

This positivist, heroic strain that runs throughout the book is tempered, however, by a central chapter titled "The Laws," which reproduces in documentary fashion a list of the discriminatory statutes and laws enacted by state and federal governments against the Chinese, from the Burlingame Treaty of 1868 and the Nationality Act of 1870 to immigration quotas and censuses in 1980 when, Kingston wryly tells us, "the ethnic Chinese population of the United States has doubled" (1980:150-158). This chapter, in fact, informs the entire book and functions as a centripetal force in a work of otherwise fragmented, experimental nature.

Comparing Kingston's treatment of the theme of oppression and discrimination with Lee's, we see in *China Men* much less guardedness and ambivalence. Muteness, enforced by the "white demons," is also a theme (as it was in *The Woman Warrior)*, but with the enemy ("white demons") clearly identified, Kingston is able to describe a simple victory led by her great grandfather Bak Goong. Using the talk-story of the king who shouts into a hole, Bak Goong encourages his coworkers to vent their hitherto unvoiced emotions:

> The next day the men plowed, working purposefully, but dug a circle instead of straight furrows. They dug a wide hole. They threw down their tools and flopped on the ground with their faces over the edge of the hole and their legs like wheel spokes.
> "Hello down there in China!" they shouted. "Hello, Mother."
> "Hello, my heart and my liver" (Kingston 1980 [hereafter, *CM*]:115).

This highly improbable account is of course an imaginative attempt to resolve and concretize what otherwise would remain an intolerable mystery, that is, the absence of Chinese people from the chronicles of American history. Kingston's narrative technique can be described as an exploratory one that probes and mines nearly every facet of Chinese folklore and collective memory—from ancient legend, ghost tale, myth, and historical fact to contemporary yarn—by way of defining her own identity and that of her ethnic tribe. That *China Men* opens with an allegory derived from Li Ju-chen's *Jing Hua Yuan* or *Flowers in the Mirror* is highly significant:

> The women who sat on him turned to direct their attention to his feet. They bent his toes so far backward that his arched foot cracked. The old ladies squeezed each foot and broke many tiny bones along the sides. They gathered his toes, toes over and under one another like a knot of ginger root. Tang Ao wept with pain (*CM*:2).

The critic Hsin-sheng Kao, writing on Li Ju-chen, says of the theme of Tang Ao's travels,

> voyage in and of itself is a liberating experience from which one can never return home again nor revert to one's old self... To begin with, we may naturally cite the theme of departure, the first step toward change. Change here is two-fold in meaning: on the physical level, it indicates a moving from one

place to another, and on the spiritual level, it indicates a transformation from one state to another. Joseph Campbell terms this the "call to adventure" which summons the quest hero "from within the pale of his society to a zone unknown" (Kao 1981:55).

Change, then, or adaptation and transformation, seems to be the dominant theme and imperative in Kingston's *China Men*. Whereas the figure of Guan Goong in Lee's *Flowers in the Sky* is viewed problematically (at least by the protagonist), a concession to the baser mentalities of the natives, its appearance in *China Men* is an occasion for celebration. When Ah Goong visits the theater in Sacramento (known to the Chinese as Second City), he is "refreshed and inspired" to see the popular folk hero on stage:

> Ah Goong's heart leapt to recognize hero and horse in the wilds of America... Guan Goong, the God of War, also God of War and Literature, had come to America—Guan Goong, Grandfather Guan, our own ancestor of writers and fighters, of actors and gamblers, and avenging executioners who mete out justice. Our own kin. Not a distant ancestor but Grandfather (*CM*:147-148).

As opposed to Lee's passive and recessive protagonist, Hung, who must shun the physical world, Kingston's book is peopled with men of action—pirates, miners, railroad workers, soldiers, and warriors—each one, as she has said, a "celebration of physical labor."[5] In contrast to Lee's depiction of Hung's celibacy, Kingston deals with the problematic issue of the enforced bachelorhood of Chinese American men by having her hero, Ah Goong (exultantly and shamelessly, it should be noted) masturbate into the air while at work:

> Suddenly he stood up tall and squirted out into space. "I am fucking the world," he said. The world's vagina was big, big as the sky, big as a valley. He grew a habit: whenever he was lowered in the basket, his blood rushed to his penis, and he fucked the world (*CM*:130).

While this episode might strike some as being farfetched and perhaps misleading, distorting the very real privations suffered by Chinese men, it is indicative of Kingston's Americanness as a writer. In Kingston's world, problems are surmountable through individual will, and protest is a viable option, as instanced in the railroad strike of June 25, 1867, described in the chapter "The Grandfather of the Sierra Nevada Mountains." Indeed, Kwan-Terry (1984:167) would categorize Kingston as belonging to that community "whose members possess 'North American' intellectual equipment that accords profound respect to the centrality of the individual," whereas the fiction of Lee, by his account, is "not concerned with the individual; it is, very much so, not for itself but as a source of statements originating and resulting in some significant understanding on a communal and national scale."

In conclusion, then, I would say that while common historical and ancestral experiences may have rendered to our two authors similar icons, themes, and even idioms of speech, the literary works they have produced are strikingly different in their characterizations, values, and worldviews. It would thus be more accurate to call these authors not "Children of the Chinese Diaspora"—as I have done perhaps overarchingly—but children of their own native countries, Lee of Malaysia, and Kingston of North America.

Notes

1. In another essay in the same volume, "The Question of the 'Overseas Chinese,'" Wang (1981:249-260) points out that the term *hua-ch'iao* is now less widely used in Southeast Asia, and that those of Chinese descent tend to refer to themselves as *hua-jen* (Chinese person) or *hua-i* (descendant of Chinese) (Wang 1981:249-260).
2. Wang Gungwu, "China and the Region in Relation to Chinese Minorities" (Wang 1981:274-279). Stanley Bedlington (1978:59) also points out that when Chiang Kai-shek imposed a firm Kuomintang government in China, "Sun Yat-sen's 'Three Principles of Government' were adopted as the official state credo. The first of Sun's three tenets...reaffirmed the principle that all Chinese, no matter where they might be were of one race and one nation."
3. After the 1969 race riots in Kuala Lumpur, the Malaysian government implemented a "New Economic Policy" (NEP) granting special economic rights to Malays. Restructurings such as a target of thirty percent equity capital in all businesses for Malays by 1990, and lowered proportions of non-Malays admitted to tertiary educational institutions, have given rise to fears and resentment among the non-Malays (Coppel, Mabbett, and Mabbett 1982:7; Esman 1975:405).
4. Lee Kok Liang, viva voce, at a meeting with students at Universiti Sains Malaysia, Penang, in March 1984.
5. Maxine Hong Kingston, viva voce, at a Haverford College Collection Address, March 20, 1989, Haverford, Pennsylvania.

References

Bedlington, Stanley. 1978. *Malaysia and Singapore: The Building of New States.* Ithaca: Cornell University Press.
Coppel, Charles A., Hugh Mabbett, and Ping-ching Mabbett. 1982. *The Chinese in Indonesia, the Philippines and Malaysia.* London: Minority Rights Group Report.
Esman, Martin. 1975. "Communal Conflict in Southeast Asia." In *Ethnicity: Theory and Experience,* edited by Nathan Glazer and Daniel P. Moynihan. Cambridge University Press.
Gates, Henry Louis, Jr. 1985. *"Race," Writing and Difference.* Chicago: University of Chicago Press.
Harrex, Syd. 1981. "Mutes and Mutilations in the Fiction of Lee Kok Liang." In *Only Connect: Literary Perspectives East and West,* edited by Guy Amirthanayagam and Syd Harrex. Adelaide: Center for Research in the New Literatures in English.
———. 1982. "Scalpel, Scar, Icon: Lee Kok Liang's *Flowers in the Sky.*" In *The Writer's Sense of the Contemporary,* edited by Bruce Bennett, Ee Tiang Hong, and Ron Shepherd. Nedlands: University of Western Australia Press.
Kao, Hsin Sheng C. 1981. *Li Ju-chen.* Boston: Twagne.
Kim, Elaine. 1982. *Asian American Literature: An Introduction to the Writings and Their Social Context.* Philadelphia: Temple University Press.
Kingston, Maxine Hong. 1980. *China Men.* New York: Random House.
Kwan-Terry, John. 1984. "Narrative and the Structure of Experience: The Fiction of Lee Kok Liang." In *Tropic Crucible: Self and Theory in Language and Literature,* edited by Ranjit Chatterjee and Colin Nicholson. Singapore: Singapore University Press.
Lee Kok Liang. 1981. *Flowers in the Sky.* Singapore: Heinemann.
"Speaking for the Mute." 1985. *Asiaweek,* February 1, 50.
Wang Gungwu. 1981. "A Note on the Origins of Hua Ch'iao." In *Community and Nation: Essays on Southeast Asia and the Chinese.* Singapore: Heinemann.

Comparing the Contemporary Experiences of Asian American, South Korean, and Cuban Artists

Yong Soon Min

We live in the era of the Coca Colony. Dynasty, Dallas, Rambo, McDonald's, Madonna, and Michael Jackson all head the list as our foremost cultural ambassadors to the world. Their fame and popularity in many countries supplant that of native pop products and stars. In the more rarefied heights of High Culture, it is hard to imagine a contemporary artist anywhere in the world unfamiliar with the likes of Jackson Pollock, Andy Warhol, and Frank Stella. How many of us have been jolted by the all too familiar sights and sounds lifted from United States media and transplanted to some remote reaches of this planet making us feel as if we have never left home even if we had rather go native? It is difficult to escape from the all-pervasiveness of the "Voice of America" sort of cultural dominance, the handmaiden of multinational capitalism.

How Western cultural hegemony impacts non-Western cultures both here among Asian Americans and beyond our shores is the focus of this presentation. I have singled out Cuba and south Korea[1] to be the foreign components of this examination. This selection for a comparative study must seem quite arbitrary or farfetched considering the many factors that set them apart. And yet, these enormous differences do not undermine critical historical connections; and upon closer scrutiny, an unexpected confluence of issues and concerns can be discerned in the contemporary art fields of both countries. Furthermore, the questions and issues raised by the experiences of Cuban and south Korean contemporary artists are essentially identical to those discussed widely here. A cross-cultural analysis of these two dynamic art centers offers significant perspectives relevant to a greater understanding of the relationship of Asian American artists and other artists of color (a term I prefer to "minorities") to the mainstream here in the United States.

My specific focus is Cuban and south Korean contemporary art since 1980, as this recent period offers the most fertile field for our comparative observations. For both Cuba and south Korea, the 1980s have signaled a revitalization, a renaissance by some assessments, of a contemporary art scene which by Western standards is exceptionally sophisticated and developed relative to other Third World countries. In both contexts, a younger generation of artists has emerged whose works reflect a significant departure from the status quo of the previous generation. This new artistic "wave" in Cuba represents a liberalization from the stagnant and reductivist orientation of revolutionary culture which prevailed during the 1970s. The Korean counterpart is identified under the rubric "Min Joong" art, which can be translated roughly as "people's" art. Min Joong proponents consider this new spirit broadly as a new multidisciplinary cultural movement. Highly politicized, the Min Joong cultural movement is engaged in efforts to invent and promote a new cultural identity.

Various factors within each country contribute to this high level of artistic development, but what is most notably held in common are the following: (a) the relatively high literacy rate within the general public, (b) advanced fine arts training at the university level, (c) significant institutional support, i.e., Cuba's Artists and Writers Union (UNEAC), and, in south Korea, numerous official and unofficial artist collectives and organizations, (d) a number of fine arts museums which offer contemporary art exhibitions as well as lively gallery scenes, and (e) solid bases of publications and forums for critical and theoretical discussion and assessment. In both countries, these conditions and institutions serve to foster the development and growth of a substantial number of professional artists. Both countries also have in common mainstream art establishments which are equally influenced by developments in Western contemporary art. Other signs of artistic vitality are, in Cuba's case, the ambitious hosting of the 1989 Third Havana Biennial—regarded as an impressively comprehensive showcase for contemporary art from the Third World. In south Korea, commercial viability of contemporary art is evidenced in its bullish art market: a handful of contemporary blue-chip Korean artists are garnering prices for their art on par with United States market prices.

Those who adhere to stereotypical assumptions about what art from a socialist country, in contrast to that from a rapidly industrialized capitalist country, should look like, would understandably wonder whether the Cuban and Korean artists had exchanged roles. Ironically, Cuban artists are faulted by many Western observers for not being socialist enough, even though it is precisely for their sociopolitical system that the Cubans have been outcast from the Western world. From just the appearance of the work, the currently touted Cuban avant-garde art, which has been receiving increased Western recognition and which also has official government sanction and support, has no easily recognizable political form and could easily blend in with much of the modern art found in New York's Soho galleries. In comparison, some of the current Min Joong works convey with emotional directness various forms of social-commentary and descriptive and symbolic realism. But even these Korean works still avoid the generic style of "socialist realism" (which still has currency in north Korea). While most of the younger Cuban artists have abandoned the more populist formats such as mural art or poster art (the stellar achievement of Cuban art in the 1960s), these and other more populist strategies aimed at getting the work out of the galleries and into the streets are a strong component of Min Joong cultural activity. Unlike the Cuban situation, it must be understood that this Min Joong cultural movement is linked, directly or indirectly, to a growing sociopolitical opposition movement in south Korea which is pressing for the withdrawal of U.S. troops as a concrete step toward reunification of north and south Korea, and greater self reliance and democracy in government. In a political climate in which opposition to the government's staunch anti-communist ideology and its quest for "modernization" is deemed subversive, draconian measures have been imposed to censure and suppress the more militant manifestations of this movement.

An instance of the earliest government crackdown on the Min Joong movement came in 1980 at its founding exhibition entitled "Reality and Utterance." Although this exhibition, held at a government sponsored gallery, was shut down by the authorities right after its opening, the artists gained much initial public and critical attention. Some of these artists began to identify themselves as part of an organized art movement. Later, in 1985, the government intervened in another exhibition ("Power") by confiscating works and detaining some of the exhibiting artists. A 1977 National Security Law has convicted artists whose works display anti-United States or reunification of north and south Korea sentiment or themes. This law was most recently imposed against artists this summer during a massive crackdown on dissidents suspected of having any connections to the historic unauthorized visit by a south Korean student to north Korea to attend an international solidarity youth festival. Most of the artists arrested were affiliated with The Kwang Ju Visual Arts Research Institute, a populist oriented artists collective in the southern city of Kwang Ju. One of the several violations they were charged with was sending to north Korea a reproduction of a collaboratively created monumental mural depicting the history of Korea. Many of the overtly political Min Joong artists were effectively blacklisted from mainstream commercial galleries, purveyors for the most part of the more commercially viable and academically accepted range of Western-influenced contemporary art.

Coincidentally, in 1981, a year after the aforementioned pioneering "Reality and Utterance" show in Korea, a Cuban exhibition entitled "Volume One," showcasing works by recent art school graduates, marked a watershed moment of public recognition for a new generation of artists. This show drew an audience numbering an incredible 9,000 in the first ten days and generated intense debate. What was evident in that exhibition and in others which followed was the absence of any unifying theme. A great pluralistic syncretism became predominant in which Western influences of conceptualism and neofiguration and postmodernist eclecticism were experimented with and reassimilated with playful irony and confidence. For the generation of Cuban artists educated within the revolution, there was an unexpected prevalence of individualism. Cuban artists have never expressed a wish to break radically with the Western history of art. There is a move to expand rather than contradict this history. As one prominent Cuban art historian notes, "the most effective Cuban practice in relation to 'international currents' has been, in my opinion, critical and independent assimilation, except for the mercantile and alienating mechanism typical of the distribution channels operating in the capitalist world" (Mosquera 1985:45).

Beneath this veneer of internationalism and openness to Western influences lies a strong dialectical presence of nationalistic concerns and localized idioms. Some of the most interesting recent works synthesize an international aesthetic formal vocabulary with elements of, or allusions to, popular culture and kitsch as well as the diverse indigenous Indian, African, and Spanish cultural heritage. (Part Chinese and part mulatto, Wilfredo Lam was a pre-revolutionary painter proudly cited by Cubans as an exemplary embodiment of the racially pluralistic Cuban society. Lam is the most internationally recognized artist of his generation who later supported the revolution and in return received its full sanction.) There is a particularly strong African "presence" in Cuban culture that is also abundantly manifested in contemporary visual arts. A more personal and introspective exploration of and a "digging at" the "roots" of the rich cultural and social history of Cuba is one of the noticeable shifts in sensibilities in the current work in comparison to the works from the earlier decades since the revolution. The current liberalized official cultural policy reinforced by Fidel Castro's recent pronouncement amending his earlier infamous 1961 dictum "Within the revolution, everything; outside the revolution, nothing" to include the exploration of both form and content within the revolution has tolerated works which contain pointed social critique.[2]

Many in this new generation of artists are keenly sensitive to the criticism that their desired participation in an international dialogue may place them in a neocolonized dependent position; likewise, they are equally mindful of the pitfalls of a defensive and isolationist form of cultural nationalism. This dilemma is clearly expressed by Armando Hart, Cuba's Minister of Culture and an influential voice for cultural "openness": "The world marches toward a deeper connection of the many countries and cultures. Such interrelationships pose serious identity problems for each of our cultures. But it shall not be through isolation and chauvinism that we will maintain our own identity. We are obligated to live in an interrelationship with the rest of the world; we cannot flee this dilemma" (Mosquera 1985:45).

One way that this dilemma is brought back home to our doorstep, so to speak, is perhaps found in this frequently cited quotation of Vietnamese filmmaker/composer/writer Trinh T. Minh-ha who lives and works in the United States: "there is a Third World in every First World and vice versa." In this sense, Asian Americans, along with other people of color, constitute the Third World within the First World.[3] As such, Asian American artists encounter and struggle with the same Third World issues — the Western cultural hegemony, for example, that marginalizes artists of color here by virtue of their racial difference and "otherness." Like works from other non-Western sources, works by U.S. artists of color often suffer from the same patronizing "token" acceptance or are critically dismissed as derivative, provincial, too specifically political, or lacking "universality," which in reality is synonymous with Eurocentrism.

The spectre of Eurocentrism, underying almost all attempts to examine or evaluate cultural production of non-Western sources, raises issues central to the crisis currently experienced in several interrelated disciplines dealing with cultural studies (e.g., art history/criticism, literature, anthropology, and ethnology). In all these fields, there are voices expressing the urgently-felt sense that a fundamental reassessment and departure from Western European and North American hegemonic and monocentric cultural perspectives is long overdue. Global socioeconomic and political shifts and the growing emergence and assertions of Third World liberation and independence movements, alongside the struggle for socioeconomic and cultural parity waged by people of color on the homefront, have pushed the more progressive sectors within Western institutions to question their basic assumptions and privileges in relation to the rest of the world. Nevertheless, the forces operating to assert North American and Western interests in the world are a powerful everyday reality for all of us to confront.

A survey of contemporary Asian American art of this past decade would probably parallel that of the general mainstream art in its seemingly diffuse diversity and pluralistic tendencies. It must be clarified from the outset of this discussion of Asian American art that, as with the Cuban and Min Joong art, my focus is directed to the visual arts — painting, sculpture, and mixed media, or performance and installations, works in experimental modes that involve interdisciplinary approaches and defy conventional categorizations. The more conventionally narrative art forms such as literature, drama, film, video, and documentary photography have already achieved much greater exposure and recognition within and beyond the Asian American community largely due to the efforts of institutions such as Asian Cinevision and National Asian American Telecommunications Association, which have faithfully charted the development and growth of Asian American contributions in some of these areas. And in literature, scholarly works such as Elaine Kim's *Asian American Literature: An Introduction to the Writings and Their Social Context* (1982) provide an in-depth overview and assessment of a significant perspective toward understanding the wealth of Asian American literary works. In the visual arts, however, a deplorable dearth of published documentation or scholarship, which is one of the consequences of institutional underdevelopment, leads me to rely mostly on my own observations of the field from the vantage point of an active participant. Due to limited available resources, the focus is further restricted to the New York scene, which does at least render a fair representation of the state of affairs to the extent that, along with Los Angeles, San Francisco, and Seattle, it is one of the largest centers of Asian American cultural activity.

Despite the aforementioned difficulties in assessing the Asian American visual arts, a brief overview of one cultural organization offers some insight into a significant transitional point in the recent history of Asian American contemporary art. The closing of Basement Workshop Incorporated in 1986, after over a decade of service and contributions, signaled a significant passage in the coming-of-age of Asian American arts. Located in the heart of New York's Chinatown, it was, during its tenure, the pioneering and catalytic Asian American multidisciplinary cultural center. According to its founding member and executive director Fay Chiang, it emphasized "the needs and voices of the American-born Chinese and Japanese artists and writers." With strong roots in the Chinese and Japanese progressive community, it provided in its heyday a nurturing, family-like support system for creative explorations of Asian American identity.

In hindsight, it appears that the end of Basement coincided with various other signs of change apparent in both the demographic and sociopolitical makeup of Asian American communities and among Asian American artists. Newer Asian immigrant communities, particularly the burgeoning Korean community, began to assert their presence in all facets of city life. Recent waves of Chinese immigrants injected new monies and politics, and established satellite Chinatowns. Japan's economic ascendency began to manifest itself as a cultural contender in the mainstream. With the dispersal of diverse Asian communities outside Manhattan, New York's Chinatown became more of a symbolic center, no longer the concentrated focus of all Asian American activities. These changes are reflected in the diverse mix of recent-immigrant (less than ten years here), older-immigrant, and American-born Asian artists.

Many of the recently immigrated artists received full or partial professional arts training in their country of origin. In either case, these artists are generally well versed in contemporary art history.

In the current environment of increased multicultural awareness, this new composition of Asian American artists occupies a strategic position in relation to the mainstream and the Third World. I would venture to guess that the cutting edge of Asian American art is moving away from the cultural provincialism of an introspective Asian American sensibility, associated with the Basement generation, to something necessarily more expansive. The growing impact of the recent influx of immigrants with stronger, less mitigated ties to their respective homelands, the volatile sociopolitical developments in the past decade in these Eastern homelands, and a greater exposure to contemporary art of Asia such as Min Joong art or the sophisticated mixed media works of Filipino artists such as Santiago Bose, is reflected in a newly evolving and expanded sense of identity, one that is informed by multiple perspectives and realities.

For example, in an insightful review of her recent Soho exhibition of mixed media paintings and installations, the artist Hung Liu, who immigrated from the People's Republic of China five years ago, is quoted as saying that one of her images comments "on the true condition of liberty in China as seen through the voyeuristic lens of the Western media." Her works raise complex questions of identity in terms of the necessity to confront the differences as well as connections between the sociopolitical realities of here and there in relation to perceived notions of both here and there, as well as the relationship between Asians as immigrants and exiles and Asian Americans who are more firmly rooted here. Trinh T. Minh-ha's unconventional films such as *Reassemblages,* which in film critic Daryl Chin's words is "an ethnographic film about Senegal made by a Vietnamese woman living in the United States, with a narration in English," reveal an identity fully sensitized to its own hyphenated or juxtaposed nature and capable of developing deep, unpatronizing affinities to other non-Western cultures and people. This sort of cultural osmosis has an unsettling effect in its ability to explore and examine this and other cultures from both a multifaceted perspective and as an outsider/insider looking both in and out. It furthermore has the potential to be subversively powerful and powerfully subversive.

The following comparative observations of Asian American art with its Min Joong and Cuban counterparts focus on the issues of empowerment and identity as they relate to these three different contexts. A significant point of convergence for the Korean Min Joong artist and the Asian American artist is that in their respective contexts, both are minority voices striving for empowerment within a capitalistic society. Inasmuch as empowerment in both contexts involves a change in the status quo, Min Joong artists adhere to an underlying political agenda while Asian American artists consider empowerment in more pragmatic terms, challenging the cultural mainstream to give a fairer share of the "pie." Therefore, Min Joong artists' efforts to critique their sociopolitical system parallel some of ours, but also differ from and surpass ours in terms of the depth of their commitment to collective cultural practices, militancy, and impact on the sociopolitical environment. Numerous associations large and small have been organized by Min Joong artists to promote collective support and strength as there are few outside sources of support. For some sectors of the movement, this kind of collective cultural production represents a means to challenge the commodification tendency and personal-profit motivation of individualism.

Another model for socially engaged cultural practice lies in the close working alliances formed by some of these artists with other sectors of society such as farmers, blue-collar workers, and students, who are also striving for the same sociopolitical empowerment. Community-based Asian American arts and cultural organizations function in a similar manner, but with deeper ties to the fuller dimension of community life. A number of organizations showcase and provide support services for individual Asian American art—the Amauan Workshop for Filipino artists, Asian American Arts Center, Korean American Women Artists and Writers Association, and the Asian American Arts Alliance, to name a few which come to mind—but by and large a great majority of artists function without any organizational affiliation, and maintain at best an ad hoc relationship with organizations and with their respective communities. There is also a lesser sense of urgency and less at stake for the artist and organizations within the Asian American context as compared to the Korean because of the Min Joong movement's ties with a national political struggle.

As we approach the new decade, the interrelated issues of empowerment and crossing-over vis-à-vis the mainstream still remain unresolved in the careers of most Asian American artists who have struggled in this field for a decade or more. These artists are up against cultural institutions which continue to be incredibly resistant to change, and commercial and private support systems that prove to be ultimate bastions of privilege and exclusiveness. The chosen few who successfully cross over often encounter barriers to further success in the form of the "glass ceiling" syndrome, which seems to affect Asians disproportionately in almost all fields. There is a limit to the height of success Asians can reach regardless of how good they are or how hard they try. Their work may be bleached of any tell-tale signs of ethnicity but the fact that they are the "eternal alien" makes all the difference. Luis Francia, a Filipino poet and critic, declared recently, in a review of Chinese American performing artist Ping Chong, that "the peculiar logic of the crossover, of cultural hyphenation—where the hyphen sways like a frayed rope bridge over a roaring chasm—dictates a one-way movement, from the 'particular' to the 'universal'." Or, as Chong puts it, "How white do I have to be?" With further "peculiar logic," one of the worn-out stereotypes attributed to Asian Americans, that of the "model minority," subtly and not so subtly works against them in terms of their creative image. As one byproduct of this stereotype, Asians are perceived as technical and scientific whizzes lacking that certain "verve," "passion," "fire," and "spontaneity" when it comes to creative and expressive endeavors. Our artistic forebears such as Utamaro are recognized and emulated for their creative distinction and mastery, but in the contemporary arts we are perceived to be derivative; we are perceived to lack the Zeitgeist.

Another area of common concern and focus for Asian American and Min Joong artists is the question of how history is constructed and by whom. Like most other non-Western people, Asian American and Min Joong artists insist on telling their own history in an effort to be the masters of their own past and destiny and to set the record straight. This stems from a shared sense that much of their history has been distorted, when not suppressed, to serve the interests of various foreign powers or its own ruling class. In contrast to the split between the political and the poetic inherent in the Western cultural canon, much current literature and artwork by both Asian American and Min Joong artists asserts the interrelatedness and interdependence of the political and the poetic. Historical analysis is a prerequisite in almost all art-historical and critical discourse relating to the Min Joong movement. In the catalogue for a recent Manhattan exhibition of Min Joong art, foremost Korean critic Wankyung Sung (1988:9) expresses skepticism about North Americans' response to the artwork, particularly in light of America's ignorance of Korean history and of Korea's problematic encounters with the United States. This strong nationalistic sentiment and rhetoric is tempered by the recognition that, "it is dangerous for Koreans to dismiss Western culture altogether."

Concern about the American reading public's ignorance of Chinese American history led Maxine Hong Kingston to digress in the middle of her novel and deliberately list historical facts year by year, starting with the Gold Rush. "The reviews of my first book made it clear that people didn't know the history – or that they thought I didn't. While I was writing *China Men*, I just couldn't take that tension any more" (Kim 1982:xvii). There is a growing consciousness that in order to ensure that our distinct voices are heard in the groundswell of a multicultural chorus, we must stand our ground and assert the value of our own personal and collective experience. The proliferation in the past two decades of autobiographical works, predominantly by second-generation artists, contributes to Asian Americans' "community of memory," as Ronald Takaki calls it, our self-determined collective effort to keep our history alive. In a related effort, a few Asian American arts organizations, and individuals such as artist Margo Machida, have responded to the invisibility of Asian American contemporary artists in most mainstream documentation and scholarship by initiating their own archives. In "Directions for Scholarship in Contemporary Asian American Art," her presentation to the sixth national conference of the Association for Asian American Studies, Machida stressed that "our stance must remain pro-active... Nonwhite artists, in having to create their own institutions, develop audiences, and document art and exhibitions have had to be almost completely self-dependent... it is our responsibility to not only insure that our artists' work does not disappear but that we take an activist stance as exponents for the co-equality of contemporary Asian American visual art within American culture."

A closer look at the Cuban artistic new wave reveals a similar social nexus in their view of art. In spite of the fact that these artists are seeking more eclectic and individualistic directions which question many of the strongly held notions about what revolutionary culture should be and look like, they still uphold an underlying consciousness that art is fundamentally linked to their society and is meant for their society. One of the artists expressed it this way: "The artist always has a social function. As mythmaker, the artist has always created the personality of each culture. I am interested in the social repercussions of my work. But not in a simple, schematic way as in the case of the pamphleteer. I want to make people conscious of things, make them think. I'm not interested in elitism; rather, the artist should cultivate the minds of the people, enrich their cultural development. This does not mean giving them goods, entertaining them or making them happy... I do not believe in art as a palliative" (Fusco and Knafo 1966:42). An art-for-art's-sake attitude, which prevails in mainstream context here, is virtually nonexistent in the Cuban context. Rather, there is an underlying assumption that art should be for the common good. "The common good is not defined; what is defined, implicitly, is the notion that the artist has an organic responsibility to think out for himself or herself, what connections with the common good are possible, interesting and individually satisfying. There is, in other words, a palpable moral dimension to the intellectual life of the Cuban artist, a dimension that arrests the attention of an outsider stumbling upon this discourse" (Camnitzer 1988).

This presentation highlights only a few of the many interesting relationships which can be drawn from observations of these three groups of contemporary artists in their complex relationships to the dominant Western cultural influence. Clearly, artists and the arts alone cannot substantially decenter or counter the unidirectional flow of information from the centralized Western mainstream. But I hope that this discussion challenges to a degree the monopolistic flow of information by looking and listening elsewhere and in our own communities of color. Great potential for meaningful and empowering dialogue exists when we begin to talk and listen to each other – our multitude of diverse non-Western voices. Imagine that over the relentless drone of "Voice of America" muzak could be heard a lively discussion by Korean Min Joong, Cuban, and Asian American artists who have never before had the opportunity to meet all together. Other voices, Native American, Namibian, Brazilian, and Palestinian, to name just a few, join the conversation. Can you hear them?

Notes

1. When used to designate the country, "south" and "north" is not capitalized throughout this article out of respect for the Koreans who oppose the imposed division of their country.
2. On my recent visit to Cuba to attend the Third Havana Biennial this past November, I was informed of the emergence of a distinct younger generation of artists: students, mostly in their mid-twenties, of the artists I had been involved with in this study (who are themselves only three to seven years older). Reacting critically against the increasing avant-garde internationalism of their predecessors, these younger artists are producing works which focus more on the situation at home and are more explicit in their sociopolitical content. I was also informed that some of their works directly critical of Castro have encountered official censorship. There is speculation that the balance of power between the liberal/moderates and the hard-liners in the Ministry of Culture has shifted in the past year, reflecting the overall government's guarded if not entirely negative response to *perestroika*.
3. It is interesting to note here that a group of Asian Americans, including myself, who attended this year's Havana Biennial, made a presentation about Asian American art as part of a program concerning art of the Third World in the First World. Along with a group of black and Asian artists living in England who have organized themselves as "Black Artists from England," we proposed that the art of immigrants from the Third World living in non-Third World countries be considered part of an expanded and more inclusive showcase of Third World contemporary art.

References

Camnitzer, Luis. 1988. "Between Nationalism and Internationalism." In *Signs of Transition: 80's Art from Cuba*. New York: Center for Cuban Studies, and the Museum of Contemporary Hispanic Art.
Fusco, Coco, and Robert Knafo. 1966. "Interviews with Cuban Artists." *Social Text* 15:41-53.
Kim, Elaine. 1982. *Asian American Literature: An Introduction to the Writings and Their Social Context*. Philadelphia: Temple University Press.
Mosquera, Gerardo. 1985. "The Conflict of Being Updated." In *New Art from Cuba*. Old Westbury: Visual Arts Program, State University of New York.
Sung, Wankyung. 1988. "Two Cultures, Two Horizons." In *Min Joong Art*. New York: Artists Space.

Notes on Contributors

Marilyn Alquizola teaches Asian American Studies at San Francisco State University and is in the doctoral program of the Department of Ethnic Studies, University of California, Berkeley.

Edward T. Chang teaches at California State University Polytechnic, Pomona.

Woon Ping Chin is a writer.

Peggy Choy is program coordinator at the Center for Southeast Asian Studies and teaches Asian performance in the School of Music at the University of Wisconsin-Madison.

Stephen S. Fugita is an Associate Professor of Psychology and Ethnic Studies at Santa Clara University, California.

Lee S. Hayakawa is an undergraduate student at Santa Clara University, California.

Jeremy Hein is an assistant professor in the Department of Sociology at the University of Wisconsin-Eau Claire.

Wendy Ho is a lecturer in the English and Women's Studies departments at the University of Wisconsin-Whitewater.

Evelyn Hu-DeHart is director of the Center for Studies of Ethnicity and Race in America (CSERA) at the University of Colorado, Boulder.

Shirley Hune is associate provost and professor of social foundations of education at Hunter College of the City University of New York.

Tomoji Ishi is with the Japan Pacific Resource Network.

Hyung-chan Kim is a professor in the Department of Educational Administration and Foundations at Western Washington University, Bellingham.

Yvonne M. Lau is Assistant Dean of Students at Loyola University, Chicago.

David Leiwei Li is an assistant professor in the English department at the University of Southern California.

Shirley Geok-lin Lim teaches at the University of California, Santa Barbara, and is a poet and short-story writer.

Amy Ling is a visiting professor of Asian American literature at Harvard University.

Xin Liu is a graduate student in the Department of American Studies at the University of Hawaii.

Sucheta Mazumdar is assistant professor of history at the State University of New York (SUNY), Albany.

Yong Soon Min is an artist and a recipient of a 1989-1990 National Endowment of the Arts Visual Artists Fellowship.

David Mura is a writer.

Wendy L. Ng is an assistant professor in the Asian American Studies program at San Jose State University.

Gary Y. Okihiro is associate professor of history at Cornell University.

Kyeyoung Park is a visiting assistant professor of anthropology at the University of California, Los Angeles.

Renqiu Yu is an assistant professor of history at the University of New York (SUNY), Purchase.

Judy Yung teaches at the University of California, Santa Cruz.